SECOND TO NONE

BE2

SECOND TO NONE

The History of No.II (AC) Squadron Royal Air Force – 1912-1992

HANS ONDERWATER

Published by
Airlife
England
with the support of Rolls-Royce plc

DEDICATION

In its entire history No.II (Army Co-operation) Squadron bravely and loyally served Sovereign and country whenever and wherever they were asked to do so.

At times the Squadron suffered severe losses. The battle honours on the Squadron standard show the battlefields where members of 'Shiny Two' fought and died.

WESTERN FRONT 1914-1918
YPRES 1914
NEUVE CHAPELLE
SOMME 1916
FRANCE AND THE LOW COUNTRIES
DUNKIRK
NORMANDY
ARNHEM

This book is dedicated to the Officers, Non-commissioned Officers and Other Ranks who faithfully and bravely served in times of war and peace between 1912 and 1992 and who will continue to serve in the years ahead.

PER ARDUA AD ASTRA
HEREWARD

No.II (AC) Squadron
Standard at Courteenhall
Church.

First published in the UK in 1992
by Airlife Publishing Ltd.

British Library Cataloguing in Publication Data

A catalogue record for this book is
available from the British Library

ISBN 1 85310 351 9

Printed in England by Livesey Ltd., Shrewsbury.

Airlife Publishing Ltd.

101 Longden Road, Shrewsbury SY3 9EB.

CONTENTS

FOREWORD

COURTEENHALL,
NORTHAMPTON.
NN7 2QG
ROADE (0604) 862-204

Marshal of the Royal Air Force, Lord Trenchard, was an old friend of my father's. He asked him if he would give permission for No. II Squadron to be named "Hereward". He readily agreed and suggested that they also use our ancient family crest, the Wake Knot, as shown above.

"Hereward" is a Saxon name denoting "Leader of an Army". No name could be more appropriate for an Army Co-operation Squadron.

My father, who died in 1963, took a lively interest in the Squadron. I too am proud of this association with the Squadron that is "Second to None".

In 1975 I paid a happy and rewarding visit to the Squadron at Laarbruch and, in October 1984, how delighted we all were when the Squadron's link with the family was further strengthened, the Squadron's old Standard being laid to rest with an inspiring and impressive service in Courteenhall Church beside the family home of the Wakes.

For centuries our island has kept its freedom and independence by having command of the sea. The Gulf War has further brought home to us that Navies and Armies can only survive with command of the air - complete air supremacy as demonstrated by the R.A.F. and "Shiny Two" in particular.

Hereward Wake

Major Sir Hereward Wake, Bart., M.C., D.L.

INTRODUCTION

AIR MARSHAL SIR ANDREW WILSON KCB AFC RAF

As the present Commander-in-Chief of Royal Air Force Germany and a former Commanding Officer of II(AC) Squadron, it gives me the greatest pleasure to have been invited to write a foreword to the history of this famous squadron written by Hans Onderwater.

As the number implies, No II(AC) Squadron is one of the oldest squadrons in the Royal Air Force. I say one because there has been considerable debate over the years about which squadron was the first to fly fixed wing aircraft for, when the Royal Flying Corps was formed on 13 April 1912, No 1 Squadron operated balloons. However, No II(AC) and 3 Squadrons were the first to fly aircraft from Farnborough a month later (although No 3 Squadron was actually formed at Larkhill). The argument about which unit actually got airborne first was happily resolved by a Squadron Leader Eric Bush, an Octogenarian who attended a squadron reunion in 1976. He had been an airman on the squadron the day it formed in 1912 and recalled quite clearly that the first flight by both Nos II(AC) and 3 Squadrons was made by the two Squadron Commanders who deliberately took off in line abreast to avoid just such a controversy!

In the intervening 80 years the Squadron has fought with distinction in 2 World Wars and most recently in the 1991 Gulf Conflict. Its history is rich in every sense and in this book Hans Onderwater has sought to bring those years to life with many fascinating insights and anecdotes often provided by former members of the squadron.

I commend this book to you and, on behalf of the Royal Air Force and all who have served with 'Shiny Two', I thank Hans Onderwater for putting the Squadron's unique history on the record.

Sandy Wilson

PREFACE

In 1986 I had the privilege of being invited to RAF Laarbruch in Germany to meet the Officer Commanding No.II (AC) Squadron, Wing Commander (now Group Captain) Jock Stirrup AFC and his officers, NCOs and Other Ranks. In those days I was writing the biography of a remarkable officer and gentleman, Air Commodore Andrew James Wray Geddes, CBE, DSO, Legion of Merit (US), RAF, Retd. As Air Commodore (Plans), 2nd Tactical Air Force, Andrew Geddes had been instrumental in the negotiations prior to the food drops over Western Holland in April and May 1945. To the Dutch this combined air supply operation by Bomber Command and the 8th USAAF is well known as 'Operation Manna/Chowhound'. It saved the lives of millions of starving people in that part of my country which was still under German control after the Allied armies had pushed into the Reich. No less than 5,500 sorties were flown in only eight days, supplying the Dutch with desperately needed food.

In April 1985 our government had decided that these food drops were to be remembered by inviting former 'Flying Grocers' to the Netherlands and entertaining them for a week. Being the Secretary of the Food and Freedom Foundation as well as the author of a book about 'Operation Manna/Chowhound' I had been in touch with hundreds of aircrew members, Dutch civilians and German soldiers who saw Manna rain from heaven and never forgot it. Finding Andrew Geddes in Seaford, East Sussex was the greatest pleasure of my life as a researcher and an author. He was a man with a razor-sharp memory, full of amazing stories and entirely dedicated to the RAF in general and his 'old' Squadron in particular. He had been Officer Commanding No.II (Army Co-operation) Squadron at the outbreak of the Second World War. Under his command 'Shiny Two' as he preferred to call it, had crossed to France as it had done in 1914 and settled at Abbeville aerodrome. During the War Geddes had served in many positions until he retired in the mid-fifties. Before he came to the Netherlands as our guest of honour during the Manna/Chowhound Reunion, he virtually ordered me to write the history of 'Shiny Two'.

It was an honour and a pleasure to be part of the Squadron for six years. Succeeding Commanding Officers granted me total support. Every individual member of the Squadron made himself available for my questions. Past members, some of them having served as far back as 1915 sent me photographs, letters, log books and diaries. Little by little I felt that something unique was in the making.

This book is the result of a Squadron Spirit beyond understanding for those who did not experience it. At reunions 'Old' and 'New' Boys are one of a kind, the men of 'Shiny Two'. I cannot thank them enough. Unfortunately this is not the place to mention all my contributors. I hope to thank them sufficiently in the Acknowledgement at the end of this book. However, I would feel very unhappy if I did not mention some of them here and now.

I sincerely thank Group Captain Jock Stirrup, Group Captain Phil Sturley, Group Captain Alan Threadgould and Wing Commander Barry Holding, four Commanding Officers who made me feel a Squadron member. I am very grateful to Sir Hereward and Lady Wake, who received me with great kindness at Courteenhall. Sir Hereward is extremely proud of the long relationship between the Wake House and No.II (AC) Squadron. Having been an Army Liaison Officer at HQ Middle East he fully appreciates the importance of a close link between both forces.

Members of No.II (AC) Squadron served the RAF in many important places. To mention a few: Air Chief Marshal Sir W. Sholto Douglas, a First World War member; Air Chief Marshal Sir Alasdair Steedman; Air Marshal Sir R.B. Jordan; Air Marshal Sir Kenneth Porter; Air Vice Marshal J.P. 'Flossy' Moss; Air Marshal Sir John Thomson; Air Commodore Lousada; Air Commodore

Geddes and Air Commodore Towler are just a few of 'Shiny Two'.

Present names of course are the Com-TWO-ATAF and CinC RAF Germany Air Marshal Sir 'Sandy' Wilson, who flew no less than four tours with the Squadron, the last as one of the most successful COs, and his SASO Air Commodore 'Tiger' Tim Thorn, who superbly flew the Hunter and masterly commanded the Squadron during the early Jaguar-years. He and his wife Rosemary offered me their hospitality and were a mountain of encouragement.

This book would not have been published if it had not been for the support of one of the oldest connections between the Royal Air Force and the aircraft it has used, Rolls-Royce. The generous financial aid they gave both the publisher and myself shows their interest in the production of this book.

Last but not least I must express my gratitude to Flight Lieutenant Tim Robinson. Tim, a Tornado navigator and Squadron History Officer, is to be thanked for his invaluable services. At times I sent him chapters which he virtually re-wrote to turn my prose into the Queen's English. He was an inexhaustible editor, an unsurpassed translator of the untranslatable and a patient friend and helper. When war took him to Saudi-Arabia his task was taken over by Flight Lieutenant Kim Dawson, the second woman serving with 'Shiny Two'. She too was 'Second to None', helping with the correct translation of this book.

I would make a grave error if I forgot to thank the people most important to me, my wife Marjoan, my daughter Gerdy and my son Mark-Johan, who sacrificed so many holidays when I closed the door and drove to Laarbruch or flew abroad to research this book. Without their support and consideration this book would never have been written.

Hans Onderwater
13 May 1992

CHAPTER 1
SECOND YET FIRST

Montrose, 1913. Two of the first officers serving with No.II Squadron, Commanding Officer Major Burke (r) and B-Flight Commander Captain Longcroft.

When it comes to inventions it always seems that the military are somewhat slow in appreciating the advantages of the new. This is probably one of the reasons why many new things come to us through the hands and minds of civilians and are only later perfected by the Soldier. It was so with the aeroplane; four years after the Wright brothers had flown at Kitty Hawk, the British government decided that its soldiers were also to fly. In the early months of 1911 the Aeroplane Company of the Air Battalion was established as part of the Royal Engineers. On 13 April 1912 a Royal Warrant declared the formation of the Royal Flying Corps. With the formation of the RFC, No.1 (Airship) Company and No.II (Aeroplane) Company became Nos.1 and 3 Squadrons respectively. On the same day, 13 May 1912, the first 'real' Squadron was formed as No.II Squadron at Farnborough. A relatively short period of Army flying had started five years earlier. The army had acquired its first airship in 1907, built at the Balloon Factory, Farnborough, it was called *Nulli Secundus*. At first the airship had an eighty horsepower Antoinette engine which was soon found to be too weak to drive the two metal-bladed propellers. A stronger engine was installed in 1908.

In 1911, the Navy also decided to make use of the airship. The *Mayfly* was constructed as Naval Airship No.1, with two 200 horsepower Wolseley engines. Unfortunately, it broke its back in September that year. The largest Naval airship, HMAS No.3, *Astra Torres* was fitted with a Hotchkiss machine gun, making it a battleship.

In 1913 a class of young pupils of Pelham House School were invited to visit Farnborough and see the Navy's latest airship, HMAS *Parseval*. One of the pupils was the son of its commanding officer, Commander Masterman RN. The highlight of the day was when Masterman invited his son and a second pupil into the gondola to join the crew for a short flight over Farnborough. That very moment the second boy decided that he was to become an aviator one day. His name was Andrew Geddes. In 1939 he commanded No.II (AC) Squadron when it crossed the Channel to fly to Abbeville in France at the outbreak of the Second World War.

BE No. 228 of No.II Squadron preparing for take-off

There has been constant difference of opinion as to which squadron was the first to fly aircraft. No.3 Squadron proudly carries the motto: 'Tertius primus erit'. i.e. 'the Third will be the first'. However, there is strong evidence that neither No.II (AC) Squadron nor No.3 can claim seniority. History indicates that on 13 May 1912 No.II (AC) Squadron was formed independently as an aeroplane Squadron at Farnborough while No.3 Squadron was re-named and formed at Larkhill from a detachment of No.II Aeroplane Company, Royal Engineers on the same date. However, when looking at the allocated aircraft serial numbers, an interesting conclusion can be drawn. The first 200 numbers were given to the Navy. No.201, a BE-prototype, was in service with No.II (AC) Squadron, and the first aircraft for No.3 Squadron was a Bleriot X with serial number 219. It would appear that, as far as aircraft allocations are concerned, No.II (AC) Squadron is the senior fixed-wing squadron in the RFC. A second claim for seniority could be made on the basis that No.II (AC) Squadron was the first squadron to occupy a specially designed airfield — Montrose in Scotland. This is besides having been formed at Farnborough, the birthplace of British aviation, rather than at Larkhill as No.3 Squadron was. The problem was solved, in 1976 by Squadron Leader Eric Bush. He recalled clearly that when the first aircraft of Nos.II and 3 Squadrons ascended from Farnborough, the respective Commanding Officers deliberately took off in line abreast, lifting off at the same time, to avoid just such a controversy.

No.II (AC) Squadron's first Commanding Officer was Major G.J. Burke. After serving in the Boer War, he was commissioned into the Royal Irish Regiment and in 1909 he was promoted to Captain. Burke was tremendously interested in flying and, being determined to learn to fly an aeroplane, he went to France. Burke believed that the new machines could be of great use to the armed forces, and wrote two papers on military aviation. 'The First Aeroplanes of Today and Their Use in War' dealt with the tactical use of flying machines to the advantage of army commanders. In his second paper 'The Airship as an Aid to the Solution of Existing Strategical Problems' he wrote of the use of large airships as 'flying warships' able to hit the enemy behind their lines and thus force them to deploy frontline troops and valuable equipment. It was not a coincidence that Burke was posted to the Balloon School in May 1911. He became part of the newly formed Air Battalion, and flew the BE prototype of the Royal Aeroplane Company. Burke was not a good pilot and he was famous for his rough landings, often severely damaging his aircraft. However, he was a respected leader, an advocate of military aviation and a very brave man.

The history of the construction of the BE prototype is an interesting tale. Of course there was no money available to build a truly British factory-designed aeroplane. However there was money available for 'repair and overhaul' of the aeroplanes already in service with the Army. The first BE was created by very drastically 'repairing

No.II Squadron officers, 1913. Standing left to right: Lts. Harvey-Kelly, Empson, Corballis, Noel, Rodwell and Barry-Martin. Seated left to right: Capts. Todd and Dawes, Major Burke (CO) and Lts. Waldron and Dawes.

Lt. Dawes' BE2a No. 267 after its successful forced landing with engine trouble near Gedney on 21 October 1913. In those days aircraft could be identified by the large number on the tail.

and overhauling' a Voisin Pusher with a sixty horsepower Wolseley engine. This aeroplane had been presented to the Army by the immensely rich Duke of Westminster, a great supporter of aviation. One day the Voisin was sent to the Aeroplane Factory for repairs after a rather hard landing. When it emerged, like the Phoenix, from the process of reconstruction, only the engine remained to testify to the aircraft's previous incarnation. Some time later this engine was also removed and replaced by a sixty horsepower Renault engine. The aeroplane was called the BE. In March 1912, the BE was handed over to the Air Battalion and subsequently assigned to Burke. It had a long and adventurous career and was often flown over Farnborough for the testing of experimental devices. While serving with No.II Squadron it was crashed beyond hope of repair. It had been crashed and damaged more often during its three years of service than probably any other aircraft in the history of aviation. . .

In January of 1913 No.II (AC) Squadron left Farnborough. It was the first Squadron to occupy an entirely new and specially chosen airfield, at Montrose in Scotland. The Squadron moved by rail, road and air, and a complicated expedition followed before everyone arrived safely at the new airfield. Five officers were detailed to fly the aircraft north. It would be the longest flight ever made by an entire unit. The pilots were Captains J.H.W. Becke and C. Longcroft in BE machines and Captains Herbert and Dawes and Lieutenant Waldron in Squadron Farmans.

The pilots had to take a lot of risks to reach their new airfield. The first stage of this epic flight was from Farnborough to Towcester. Three of the pilots landed at Reading while the others returned to Farnborough, the fog making it impossible to continue the flight. A fresh start was made on Monday when Captain Becke reached Towcester from Farnborough, after making a stop at Blakesley for petrol. Lieutenant Waldron, who started from Farnborough, came down at Port Meadow, Oxford, and Captain Dawes reached Banbury. Lieutenant Herbert started from Reading and landed at Moreton-in-the-Marsh. In each case a landing had to be made for petrol. Captain Longcroft, who had started from Reading also, made a forced landing at the village of Littlemore near Oxford. As there was no accommodation available for him he had to spend the night in Longmore Lunatic Asylum. Some said it was exactly the right place for a young officer who willingly risked his life and a promising career by taking to the air. On the 19th Longcroft and Herbert also reached Banbury, while Captain Dawes landed about two miles short of Towcester on account of engine trouble. Lieutenant Waldron also had engine trouble and landed at Bicester. On 20 February, Becke, Longcroft and Herbert went on to Kelham, near Newark, while Lieutenant Waldron progressed as far as Towcester, where Captain Dawes was engaged in repairing his machine. The next day Lieutenant Waldron went on to Newark and, after a brief stop to replenish his petrol tank, continued his journey to York. He was closely followed by Lieutenant Herbert and Captain Longcroft, while on the arrival of Captain Dawes at Newark later in the day Captain Becke also started for York. When nearing Doncaster, however, Becke had serious trouble with his engine, forcing him to land. During a landing at Newark Captain Dawes had slightly damaged the chassis of his machine and had to stay there for repairs. The pilots who finally arrived at the racecourse of Knavesmire, not far from York, had to spend part of the morning signing autographs for young boys who had invaded the racecourse to see the latest invention of mankind, but on Saturday 22 February, a foggy and hazy day, three pilots flew to Newcastle. Only two of the three found the landing ground at Gosforth Park that evening, and they had to make several approaches before landing safely. Captain Longcroft went fifteen miles north of the city, and then had to land to get his bearings, while Lieutenant Herbert had to descend twice. Lieutenant Waldron landed with the idea of discovering his whereabouts at Benwell to the west of Newcastle, but a problem with the elevation gear prevented him finishing the three or four miles to Gosforth Park. Captain Dawes in the meantime had started from Newark, but had to land after covering eight miles. A second descent was necessary three miles further on, and he finally landed twenty miles south of York. On Monday Captain Becke, having had a new engine fitted to his machine, flew from York to Newcastle and arrived about twenty minutes after Captain Dawes, who had to descend once to find his way. Captain Becke found the fog even more troublesome, and had to descend no less than four times before reaching Gosforth Park. Tuesday saw Captains Longcroft, Dawes and Becke, and Lieutenant Herbert completing the fifth stage, from Newcastle to Edinburgh, the landing in each case being effected near Retford Barracks. Lieutenant Waldron started on this stage but was forced to land due to engine trouble at Stamford Bridge, about twenty-eight miles south of Berwick. After adjustments to the engine, he took off again during the afternoon and reached Berwick without further incident.

Flying these distances had been a very dangerous and difficult job indeed. Navigation consisted of a map and a piece of paper with the names of well-known public houses and easily visible landmarks. These directions would have been very useful for travellers on foot or horseback. For pilots, however, they were of little use. Since the engines were not at all reliable the pilots had to be very careful in choosing their route, especially since the forests and hills they would cross would be very dangerous in the event of a forced landing. On Wednesday Lieutenant Waldron got away early and flew straight to Montrose, the first Squadron pilot to arrive there. After an interval Captains Becke, Dawes and Longcroft arrived and were duly received by the Provost and Corporation, with Lieutenant Herbert completing the journey in the afternoon. The evening of 25 February saw the four machines assembled at Edinburgh, while a fifth, Lieutenant Waldron's Farman, was at Berwick. The next day they took off again for the last leg of the flight. When the airmen arrived at Montrose they had been on the way for no less than nine days. On the 27th and 28th all the officers of the Squadron were out in their machines, exploring the country around Montrose.

Understandably, the reception of No.II (AC) Squadron was the event of the year at Montrose and the country around it. Everyone who was anyone came to see the aeroplanes and the men who flew them. The Squadron continued a strenuous programme of navigation and reconnaissance. Many NCOs and Warrant Officers received flying instruction during the eighteen months in Scotland. Some thirty miles south of Montrose, across the Firth of Tay near Saint Andrews a stretch of level sand about three miles long had been spotted. It looked like a perfect place for practice landings and take-offs. At times however, great problems were encountered with the ever-present locals, whose irresponsible wandering caused a major hazard to the pilots and aircraft. At the same time the more skilled pilots undertook long cross-country sorties. All deliveries of aircraft to Montrose were done by air from the Royal Aeroplane Company of Farnborough. Inspecting officers and other important visitors to the camp were usually met at Edinburgh in the morning. They were then flown to Montrose to spend the day and flown back again in time to catch the night mail train to the south. By allowing people a passenger flight in one of the Squadron's aeroplanes, it was hoped that they would understand the importance of aircraft and support the RFC in the places where they had influence. At the same time, record breaking flights ensured that military flying caught the interest of the general public. On 13 August 1913 Captain Longcroft with Colonel Sykes, the Officer Commanding the RFC, as his passenger flew BE number 218 from Farnborough to Montrose. Their only landing was at Alnmouth and they covered 540 miles, staying airborne for no less than seven hours and forty minutes, thanks to a specially fitted petrol tank between the pilot and his passenger. Later in the year, Longcroft flew solo from Montrose to Portsmouth, and then on to Farnborough, doing the whole journey non-stop in seven hours and twenty minutes. Lieutenant Waldron managed to take his aircraft to a height of 16,000 feet, making him the holder of Britain's altitude record.

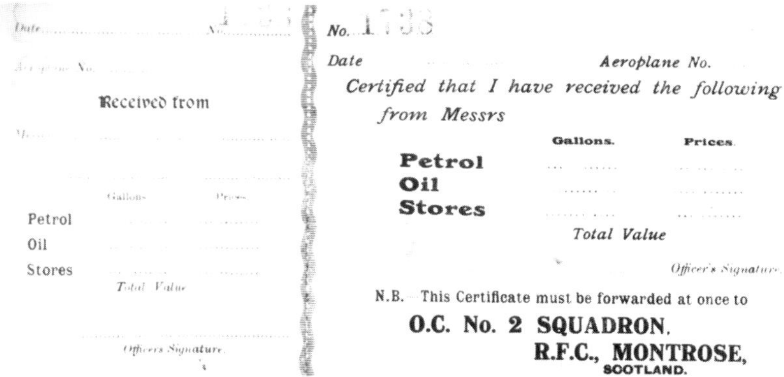
Date

Received from

Gallons Prices

Petrol

Oil

Stores

Total Value

Officers Signature

No.

Date Aeroplane No.

Certified that I have received the following from Messrs

	Gallons.	Prices.
Petrol		
Oil		
Stores		

Total Value

Officer's Signature.

N.B. This Certificate must be forwarded at once to

O.C. No. 2 SQUADRON, R.F.C., MONTROSE, SCOTLAND.

This small certificate allowed pilots to obtain petrol, oil or stores for their aircraft if necessary.

In September 1913, No.II Squadron participated in the Irish Command Manoeuvres. Both the out and inbound journeys, which included the crossing of the Irish Sea about 500 miles by air — were a severe test for men and machines. The local inhabitants were deeply concerned about the fate of the aviators. The people of Limerick crowded into the local churches to pray for the safety of the airmen. Despite the goodwill and great enthusiasm of the pilots and their ground crew which arose from these flights, the exercise was of minimal military value. The manoeuvre area was bad for aviation, as landing places were very sparse and often at totally the wrong place. Moreover, the two opposing armies were separated by too small a distance for aeroplanes to be of tactical use to either of the two commanders, although some of the braver field officers took to the air, to see the deployment of their troops. For the first time, the importance of camouflage was understood. The principal battle, however, took place in a mountain defile where the aircraft were virtually unable to fly in anything but straight lines. Commanders used the aircraft as carriages or carrier pigeons, the pilots were treated as if they were the Generals' drivers. Feelings in the Squadron were somewhat bitter as it had been a missed opportunity for both the army and the RFC. Yet each of the machines flew an average of about 2,000 miles. That is to say, 1,000 miles in reconnaissance and about the same distance in transits to and fro. During the entire exercise there were no cases of engine failure and no-one landed in 'hostile' territory. An account of the Squadron's work during the manoeuvres showed that of the eighteen machines in constant use only three were wrecked, due to human error. This feat says much for the great efficiency of the ground crew.

In spite of all the hard work a lot could happen during a sortie. More than once sudden malfunctions would force a pilot to have a quick look around for a place to make an even quicker landing. Accidents could also easily happen during the long delivery flights from Farnborough to Montrose. However, it is likely that forced landings were not always made because of a serious emergency. A report about such a forced landing may illustrate the tremendous freedom pilots had when they were in the air. On 21 October 1913 Lieutenant Dawes was on his way to Scotland in a brand new BE2a with the serial number 267. In the afternoon he landed at Tydd Saint Mary airfield for a night stop and refuelling. The next morning Dawes took off but was forced to return due to engine trouble and landed at Long Sutton. After taking off for a second time the aircraft was forced down to land once again, this time the problems were caused by a faulty magneto. Dawes now landed near Gedney Station. As the official report stated 'by coincidence the pilot lived in the same area'. As he was the first pilot from this area and as his aircraft was the first ever to land there it was soon surrounded by several thousand people wishing to see the aeroplane. While repairs were carried out on the Vickers-built BE2a a local photographer took a picture of the people gathered around this latest example of human ingenuity. No.267 was surrounded by boys and adults alike, all eager to see what had happened as closely as possible. Lieutenant Dawes in the meantime took the opportunity to visit his parents, have a good meal and a bath. We do not know what Major Burke said when Dawes arrived at Montrose, reported his troubles and the coincidental location of his emergency landing. We do know, however, that when War broke out Dawes bravely served in No.II Squadron, distinguishing himself by shooting down a German plane in full view of the French front line in September 1914 — for which he was awarded the Legion d'Honneur.

During the Irish manoeuvres the pilots had flown under the most arduous weather conditions. Sometimes the wind was faster than their aircraft. More than once the Squadron organised so-called 'Tortoise Races'. The winner of the race being the pilot whose machine had been blown back over a given course at the highest speed. . .

There was tremendous public interest in flying. Whenever an aeroplane landed, enormous crowds gathered in amazement to witness the aviator's daring exploits. A good example of the way the press reported on such occasions can be read in an article printed in the *Northern Daily Mail* of West Hartlepool when No.II (AC) Squadron landed at Seaton Carew in May 1914:

> **ARMY AIRMEN'S FLIGHT**
> **Montrose Squadron lands at Seaton Carew**
> **Fascinating Spectacle**
> Probably once previously, on the occasion of the visit of Lord Wolsely nine years ago, has there been at Seaton Carew a scene approaching that which was presented today. By common consent the day became to all intents and purposes a general holiday in the Hartlepools and people thronged to Seaton Carew in hundreds of thousands to get a glimpse at close quarters of that latest and most striking of human inventions, the aeroplane.
>
> The visit of the members of No.II Squadron of the Royal Flying Corps, who are making their way by short stages from Montrose to Salisbury Plain, has been the chief topic of conversation locally for weeks past. But even the most optimistic could scarcely have hoped that the visit would be made under such splendid weather conditions as has actually been the case. The weather was, in fact, ideal; and more superb descents than were made by the ten machines, which arrived in such quick succession between 11 o'clock and 11.45, could scarcely be imagined. It was low tide, and the fine stretch of sand at Seaton Carew more than justified its selection as a landing place, every descent being made without any apparent difficulty and certainly without the slightest hitch. As a guide to the airmen a cross had been outlined in white sheeting on the beach and all the landings were made at a point almost immediately opposite the Marine Hotel; the machines, after alighting, running along on the hard sand for a few hundred yards or so, and then being lined up well above the high water mark.
>
> Whilst every one of the descents formed a truly fascinating spectacle — (the planes of each machine as it swept round in the air in one or more noble curves tilting until the spectators, hundreds of feet below, could

see the glint of sunlight on the upper surface) — the landing of the machine which arrived last but one was especially remarkable. This aero-plane was flying at unusual height of about 6,000 feet. In a series of graceful spirals the machine quickly descended and was soon brought into a position alongside the others, amidst the gratified plaudits of the huge crowd.

As already indicated, the aeroplanes arrived in quick succession, the longest interval between any two arrivals being not greater than five or six minutes. In some cases, indeed, one aeroplane was in the course of being parked as the one immediately following alighted.

The officers piloting the aeroplanes, in the order of arrival, were as follows:

Captain C.W.P. Dawes
Captain F.F. Waldron
Lieutenant N.D. Harvey-Kelly
Lieutenant R.B. Martyn
Captain G.E. Todd
Lieutenant E.R.L.Corballis
Lieutenant J. Empson
Lieutenant R.M. Rodwell
Lieutenant L. Dawes and
Major C.J. Burke

All had a warm welcome as they arrived, the crowd applauding heartily. In several instances the pilot was accompanied by a mechanic.

The first machine to arrive left Blythe, Northumberland, at 10.30 hours, thus making the journey of 40 miles in 30 minutes, about the average time occupied in the flight by the other aircraft. The average height at which the machines were piloted was about 3,000 feet. Captain Dawes, in a brief conversation with one of our representatives, emphasised the fact that the present journey from Montrose to Salisbury Plain is essentially in the nature of a transport test, rather than a flight test; hence the short stages in which the journey is being made. The aeroplanes themselves could of course complete the journey in two of three days at the most; but some of the heavier mechanical road transport wagons, which form part of the equipment of the Squadron, are only able to proceed at 8 to 10 miles an hour, the machines weighing as much as four tons apiece.

The transport consists of three flight-repairing lorries fitted with lathes, drilling machines and spare engine parts.; a plane lorry carrying spare wings; 21 transport wagons carrying the men with their equipment etc.; 6 light tenders which cover the route of flight in case of breakdown; and 9 motor cycles. The big travelling workshop is sent on by train.

The transport section, composed of 115 men with the vehicles indicated above and the heavier wagons, left Blythe at 5 a.m. reaching West Hartlepool a little after 9 a.m. The light tenders did not leave until after the aeroplanes. The whole of the transport vehicles were parked in the Armoury Field, the men being accommodated in the Armoury itself.

Our representative gathered, in his conversation with Captain Dawes, that the choice of Seaton Carew as one of the stopping places in the present test was a consequence of the report he was able to make with regard to Seaton beach as a suitable landing place for aircraft.

"Is there any possibility". asked our representative, "of a flying depot being established here?" "It is quite possible", replied Captain Dawes, "Seaton Carew might become a permanent landing ground". It is on the main route between Montrose and Farnborough and it is well away from the fog-bank of the Tyne.

When the aeroplanes had all been lined up, the cordon thrown around them was being besieged by eager spectators to see at close quarters the details of the machines.

Throughout the descents, despite the huge crowd, admirable order was maintained by a large staff of police, the local force having been augmented. The Chief Constable for the County of Durham, Mr. W.G. Morant, was present and the local contingent was under the command of Superintendent McDonald.

The cinema man was on the scene, a representative of the Royal Electric Theatre taking photographs of the descent.

Messrs. Hugh Rae, Ltd., of Thornton Street, West Hartlepool, supplied the necessary oils for the aeroplanes.'

The arrival of No.II (AC) Squadron had been the most important event of the year in Seaton Carew. However, it was not until the fifties that this film, made by a local cinematographer called Reynolds was found. Immediately after discovery it was presented to the Squadron, then based at RAF Jever in West Germany.

In June 1914 the so-called Concentration Camp of the entire Royal Flying Corps was held at Netheravon and No.II (AC) Squadron flew down from Scotland. On the journey from West Hartlepool to York the aircraft ran into a thick bank of fog. Three aircraft were wrecked and a further one damaged in a forced landing, one of these accidents causing the deaths of Lieutenant Empson and his passenger Air Mechanic Cudmore. When the fog cleared Major Burke concentrated the Squadron at York and, after a weekend's halt, proceeded south again, arriving at Netheravon on 30 June. The camp lasted the whole month of June. Mornings were devoted to flying trials and experiments; afternoons to lectures and discussions. Major Burke's contribution to the lectures was 'Notes on Aviation'. Tactical exercises, reconnaissance, photography, balloon handling and co-operation with all the other arms were practised. Rivalry between squadrons was intense, but records seem to prove that No.II Squadron had the more skilled pilots.

Two well-known officers of No.II Squadron photographed at Rathbone, Limerick in early 1914. Seated in the BE2a is Captain Charles Longcroft, first winner of the Britannia Challenge Trophy after flying non-stop Montrose-Southampton-Farnborough and Montrose-Rathbone-Limerick. Standing in front of him is Lieutenant Waldron, holder of the British altitude record of 16,000 feet.

Lt. Harvey-Kelly was the first RFC pilot to land on French soil when he touched down near Amiens with BE2a No. 347.

CHAPTER 2
BATTLE AFTER BIRTH

Then came war.

At Sarajevo Gabriel Princip shot Archduke Franz Ferdinand and his wife, beginning the First World War. On 3 August 1914 No.II Squadron received orders to move to Dover where the RFC assembled for the crossing to France. On 12 August at 0625 hours the first Squadron aircraft took off. Piloted by Lieutenant Harvey-Kelly BE2a No.347 arrived at Amiens, being the first British aeroplane to land on the Continent to fight a war later. The same day the other pilots followed. The Squadron stayed at Amiens for only three days. During the next six weeks it moved to no less than thirteen different airfields. Major Burke was still in command, his three Flight Commanders were Captain Dawes of the Royal Berkshires, Captain Waldron of the 19th Hussars and Captain Todd of the Welsh Regiment. Major Longcroft was second-in-command. On 20 August the first reconnaissance flight was carried out. Longcroft with Captain Bourke as his observer flew over Nivelles, Halle, Enghien and Solignies while another crew, Captain Todd with Lieutenant Corballis reconnoitred Nivelles, Louvain, Wavres and Quatre Bras. Longcroft and Bourke spotted seven German aircraft, but being on their own they could do nothing else but report what they had seen. On 22 August Lieutenant Noel and Sergeant-Major Jillings took off for a recce flight. Little did Jillings know, that this was his day to lay claim to fame in the history of the Squadron. While flying over Odignies the crew came under heavy rifle and machine gun fire from the ground. This happened again when they flew over Ghislinghien. Still unscathed they continued the sortie, but over Maffle the inevitable happened. The aeroplane was hit, as was the Sergeant-Major who took a bullet deep in his buttocks. Noel turned for home with his observer bleeding very badly. Jillings became the first member of the RFC to be wounded in battle while flying in an aeroplane. The same day, Major Longcroft and Captain Dawes were on a recce flight accompanied by Lieutenant Dawes and Major Burke. Over Maubeuge they spotted a German Scout. It was an Albatros which hastily retreated, when bounced by the BEs. On the 23rd, however, the Squadron was forced to retreat when it became clear that the Germans were about to overrun Mauberge, the Squadron's base. In spite of this the pilots continued flying reconnaissance sorties to provide details of enemy movements to the BEF commanders. During one of these sorties, on the 25th, three Squadron aircraft were on a patrol. A German Rumpler Taube flying near Merville below them was chased by one aircraft with Lieutenants Harvey-Kelly and Mansfield on board. When confronted with three British aircraft the German obviously panicked and landed in a field. What happened was typical for the early days of the War. Harvey-Kelly landed next to the Taube, both crew members jumped out and chased the German pilot on foot. The German disappeared into a forest which the two Britons did not dare enter. They set fire to the Taube, jumped back into their aircraft and took off, covered by the two aircraft still circling overhead. In the meantime British troops captured the German. It was the first aerial success for the RFC.

The weather in France could be absolutely atrocious. During a severe storm, in the second week of September 1914, so many RFC aircraft were blown away and severely damaged that only ten machines remained operational. Another problem was the technical state of some aircraft after having been in action for a long time. It could be quite hazardous to fly such machines, as Lieutenants Dawes and Freeman were to find out while on a reconnaissance flight over the Saint Quentin area. Somewhere south of Anizy-le-Chateau between Sauvisons and Laon their aircraft suddenly began to rock and vibrate. It seemed as if the tail would break off at any moment. Dawes descended at once and made a perfect forced landing. Unfortunately the field in which they came to a standstill was a long way behind German lines. Taking off again would be impossible, as the undercarriage had been damaged beyond repair. At the same time large German columns were moving over a road not far from the two crewmen. Taking only some biscuits and a couple of tubes with bully extract, the officers left the aeroplane and headed for a nearby forest to hide for the rest of the day.

Apparently the Germans had seen them going down, for a group of German cavalrymen appeared and started a search for the crew. After 1½ hours the Germans gave up and left. Dawes and Freeman remained hidden until the evening, Then started walking towards the Aisne River some eight miles away. During the night they safely crossed roads and bypassed German pickets who were making so much noise that they could be spotted long before they noticed the two fugitives. At 0300 hours, Dawes and Freeman finally reached the banks of the Aisne, where they lay down for a few hours' sleep. At 0600 hours they were rudely awakened by shell explosions not far from them. In the dark, they had chosen the worst possible spot to cross the river: the site of a German battery. The Germans were shelling the British who were responding by sending over their own shells. German cavalry patrolled between the guns and the two had to be extremely careful to avoid capture at this stage of their evasion. Unnoticed by the enemy they managed to swim across the river and reach the British side. They found an abandoned house where they dried their clothes and ate a little. They they walked to the British battery and gave the battery commander some useful information about his opponent. Men of the 3rd Cavalry Brigade supplied them with a meal and a supply column took them further back into friendly territory. When they reported back to Major Burke they had been missing for almost three days. Rather than congratulating them on their successful return from enemy territory however, Burke rebuked them in no uncertain terms. He said that they knew perfectly well than under no circumstances were pilots to team up. They had disobeyed his strict order that valuable pilots should stay with their observers. They should be grateful for not being court martialled.

On 30 May 1915 this photograph of 'The Dump' near Béthune was taken. From here the Germans stopped the Allied advance during the Battle of Loos.

At the end of September 1914 Major Longcroft was posted home for instructional duties. In France it seemed as if the front had stabilised a bit. For the first time air and ground crew expected a lull and some badly needed rest. However, everything turned out differently. Allied High Command planned a big offensive and No.II Squadron had to fly many recce sorties before the first Battle of Ypres took place. On 19 October a barrage started the offensive. The Squadron in support of First Corps flew continuously. On 24 November it moved to Merville while one Flight stayed at Saint Omer. Merville was to become the Squadron's home for seven months. Following the reorganisation of the RFC in the field and the formation of Wings, Major Burke was promoted to Lieutenant-Colonel and left the Squadron. His new command was 2nd Wing, comprising Nos.5 and 6 Squadrons. Major Dawes who had been with the Squadron from its formation, now assumed command. It was November 1914, Nos.II and 3 Squadrons forming the 1st Wing working for the First Army. It was obvious that better means of communication with the ground were necessary. The aircraft were equipped with Verey pistols and occasionally with signalling lamps. At the same time a Flight of No.4 Squadron equipped with W/T and known as the 'Wireless Section, RFC' did efficient work. It opened an avenue of development in wireless co-operation between air and ground forces and vice versa. It was during the Battle of the Aisne that wireless was used for the first time to direct artillery fire and met with great success. The demands for W/T-equipped aircraft became more and more insistent. Great strain was put on the ground staff to equip the aircraft as quickly as possible. The Battle of Neuve Chapelle was the next test the Squadron was put through. This battle was unique in that it was the first time that cameras were used to record the German defences. Nos.II and 3 Squadrons used cameras designed by Lieutenants Moore-Brabazon and Campbell in co-operation with the Thornton-Pickard Manufacturing Company. The squadron covered an area varying between 700 and 1500 yards in depth, in front of the British positions. The cameras were hand held and the observer had to lean over the side of the aircraft to take his pictures. One of the first photographers over the enemy trenches was a young No.II Squadron officer by the name of W.Sholto Douglas. He was appointed photographer for the simple reason that he had owned a camera since he was a boy.

He came up with a different technique: first he cut a rectangular hole in the bottom of the aircraft. His technique was to put the camera through the hole and take a picture when the area to be photographed nearly filled the aperture. Though it was not an easy procedure the results were excellent and the photographer was somewhat protected from the freezing wind which made over-the-side photography such an unpleasant task. It was difficult to move in the confined space available, especially as the bulky flying kit hampered movement, Sholto Douglas remembered when he went on a sortie with Harvey-Kelly. Since he was a rather heavy man and as the load of the equipment for photography was considerable they decided to take off without the carbine and ammunition they usually took with them. Gaining height was essential. In spite of these modifications the aircraft climbed slowly and it took a long time before they were cruising at the ordered altitude. While they were flying and taking pictures of the trenches in the Neuve Chapelle area they spotted a German scout aircraft dong the same job a few hundred yards below their BE2. It seemed as if the German was carrying no arms either. Both aircraft circled for a while looking at one another. Then the German waved and disappeared. Nevertheless, it was the last time Sholto Douglas and Harvey-Kelly flew without armament.

Lieutenant Colonel Trenchard, who had been posted to France to command No.1 Wing, was a great supporter of aerial photography. His biographer records that it was part of Trenchard's practice to 'whip up emulation by setting the camera enthusiasts at odds with each other', especially between Sholto Douglas of No.II and Dardley of No.3 Squadron. Sholto Douglas wrote that, 'whenever Trenchard visited our Squadron, he would pull out of his pocket a bunch of Dardley's photographs which he would show to me with encominiums, apparently believing that he was inciting me to better my efforts. But as Dardley and I discovered in talking with each other that Trenchard used to do the same things the other way around on his visits to No.3 Squadron, showing Dardly my best efforts, we soon agreed that the old boy was wasting his time'. However, the continuous work of Nos.II and 3 Squadrons enabled the Allies to build up a mosaic of the whole German trench system in front of the First Army back to a depth of 700-1500 yards. All features of interest were transferred on to a 1:8000 map to give Haig a clear idea of the terrain he had to cover during his proposed spring offensive at Neuve Chapelle. Some 1,500 copies of this map were distributed to commanders before the attack and, 'for the first time in its history, the British Army went into action with a picture of the hidden intricacies of the enemy defences.' The lesson was repeated again at Loos and Aubers Ridge; to Trenchard, the RFC and No.II Squadron it was all very encouraging.

On 8 March 1915, Major Dawes left the Squadron. He was succeeded by Major T.I. Webb-Bowen. At this time new opportunities had been discovered for the RFC: the tactical bombing of enemy railways and road communications. On 26 April, four aircraft of No.II (AC) Squadron were detailed to bomb enemy junctions. One of the pilots to take off was Lieutenant Williams B. Rhodes-Moorhouse. He had been briefed to attack the railway junction at Courtrai. Rhodes-Moorhouse had been a keen flyer for many years. Long before he joined the RFC he and a friend named James Radley had built their own aeroplane, the Radley-Moorhouse monoplane. He had travelled to the United States where he participated in all kinds of record breaking and racing meetings. While in California he had flown through the archway of Golden Gate bridge in San Francisco. Back in England in 1912 he had crossed the Channel with his wife Linda and a newspaper reporter called Ledeboer as passengers — the first passenger flight between England and France. He carried a Royal Aero Club certificate, number 147, making him a very experienced aviator. On 20 March 1915 Rhodes-Moorhouse had been posted to No.II (AC) Squadron and joined it at Merville aerodrome. One of his first encounters with war took place when he flew recce sorties during the first Battle of Ypres. It was one of the first times that the Germans used mustard gas and Rhodes-Moorhouse was shocked and disgusted. On 24 April the Germans broke through the Allied lines. They began to bring up their reserves to replace the terrible losses they had suffered during the battle. Allied intelligence behind the German lines in Ghent reported that this town was one of the major rallying points for German troops and equipment on the way to the front. At 1550 hours Rhodes-Moorhouse took off from Merville, he carried no observer since the single one hundred-pounder he carried was almost too much for his aircraft. When he reached his target he went down to 300 feet to ensure an accurate attack. Then he released his bomb. Immediately he plunged into a barrage of rifle and machine gun fire. One burst tore open his thigh and holed the plane. It would have been possible for him to land immediately and await capture. However, although becoming a prisoner meant proper treatment of the terrible wound he had, Rhodes-Moorhouse decided that he had to try to return to Merville. He turned his aircraft around and went down to 100 feet to increase his airspeed. Again he ran the gauntlet and was hit again. One bullet tore open his abdomen and another hit him in the hand. Loosing blood and fighting to remain conscious he flew for another half hour before landing at Merville. When his aircraft came to a standstill Rhodes-Moorhouse was virtually unconscious and covered with blood.

On 27 April 1915 2Lt. W.B. Rhodes-Moorhouse died after carrying out a very dangerous sortie against the Germans. In recognition of his brave actions he was the first airman to be awarded the Victoria Cross.

This remarkable photograph was taken on 11 November 1915 during the Battle of Loos. It shows Lt. Keith Murray in BE2c No.1729 at 5,000 feet during a reconnaissance over the battlefield. The picture was taken by Murray's observer Lt. Gilbert.

Ground crew and fellow officers ran to his aircraft. One of them was a fitter named P.E. Butcher. In his book *'Skill and Devotion'* he described Rhodes-Moorhouse's last return. After being lifted out of the aeroplane Rhodes-Moorhouse insisted on making a full report about his sortie, then he was taken to the Casualty Clearing Station at Merville.

> 'We were not altogether surprised to learn of his death shortly after, as his fitter counted ninety-five holes in his BE-machine.'

On 27 April 1915 William B. Rhodes-Moorhouse died with his Flight Commander Blake and Padre Chavasse at his bedside. His last request was to be buried in England. This request was granted and Moorhouse was interred in the grounds of the family estate at Parnham House. On 22 May 1915 the *London Gazette* reported that a posthumous Victoria Cross had been awarded to him. This No.II (AC) Squadron pilot was the first officer to receive the highest honour for heroism in the air. Ironically enough his son, Flying Officer Willy Rhodes-Moorhouse, also lost his life in battle, as a pilot with No.601 Squadron during the Second World War. He had already received the DFC for his bravery during the Battle of Britain. He was laid to rest next to his father.

When the Battle of Aubers began on 9 May 1915, No.16 Squadron joined with No.II (AC) at Merville aerodrome. The strength of the Squadron was three BE2a, four BE2b and five BE2c aircraft. This battle was the beginning of the so called 'Contact Patrol'. The reason for these patrols was that the commanders on the ground had great difficulty in finding out the exact location of their troops during the battle. The ever-present barrages cut communications so often that it became virtually impossible to establish contact until the battle came to a lull. As an experiment, forward troops were now issued with strips of white material to be laid out in front of them. Aircraft seeing this were to contact the ground via W/T and supply the commanders with the necessary information to allow them to update their troop positions.

At first this system was used by infantry only, but soon other troops also used it. By mid-1916 it was a well-established and frequently used system. No.II (AC) Squadron often reported how far forward the troops were. In June 1915 Major Webb-Bowden was posted to Home Establishment. An old veteran of the Squadron, Captain Becke, now a major, assumed command. On 30 June there came an end to the long peregrination of the Squadron when it settled at Hesdigneul aerodrome. It was to stay there until June 1918. Becke served with No.6 Squadron before rejoining No.II. His first duty was to lead the Squadron during the Battle of Loos. During the battle he had to come to the rescue of his old Squadron when its airfield at Poperinghen was shelled by a German armoured train. Aircraft of 'Shiny Two' attacked the train and it withdrew. One of the most frightening experiences for the pilots of No.II (AC) Squadron were encounters with Fokker E.III monoplanes. These aircraft had caused a revolution in air warfare and for months the Germans controlled the sky. The Fokker E.III was the first fighter with a synchronised machine gun, firing through the propeller blades without hitting them. It appeared at a time when the Allied aircraft were badly armed. The single-seater was much faster than its Allied counterparts. Its appearance caused panic and, until a suitable Allied fighter entered service, all scouts had to be escorted by at least three other aircraft. In spite of this lethal danger the Squadron could do little else but continue its recce flights. By now, the rather mixed bag of BE2s were replaced by brand-new BE2cs. Two Flights were detailed to fly counter-battery sorties while one Flight flew continuous trench bombardments. It became crystal clear that fighter escort was necessary to enable the Squadron to carry out its duties. Fighter production, however, seemed to be extremely slow. The BE12, a single-seat version of the BE2, was the first attempt to counter the Fokkers. Unfortunately the aircraft was so stable that it proved useless as a fighter. It was not until the arrival of the Sopwith Pup that the Fokker could be attacked successfully.

Until then the Allied losses in aircraft and personnel mounted so fast that a decline of morale was expected.

On 11 October 1915, Lieutenants Medlicott and Russell shot down a German two-seater near Vermelles. Sadly, their luck was to run out fairly soon after this. A month after his victory Medlicott himself was shot down while on a photographic recce with Lieutenant Arthur Whitten-Brown.

Both were taken prisoner by the Germans and disappeared into a POW camp in Germany. Medlicott would not accept this and tried to escape several times but was captured on each occasion. The Germans obviously got fed up with his persistent attempts at escape and during his last attempt, a sentry opened fire and killed him. Whitten-Brown survived the war and returned to England after the Germans signed the Armistice. He became famous when, in June 1919, he made the first crossing of the Atlantic in a Vickers Vimy bomber. Together with Captain John Alcock he flew a 1,900-mile route from Saint Johns in Newfoundland to Cliften in Northern Ireland. Another member of No.II Squadron had earned his place in the history of flying.

While at Hesdigneul, the Squadron was honoured by a visit from HM King George V who was making an inspection tour. It would would be one of the most memorable contacts between the Monarch and the Squadron. P.E. Butcher remembered:

> 'Three cheers for His Majesty', the CO's voice rang out at the end of the King's speech. At the first roar I noticed that almost imperceptible backwards movement of the rear hooves of the royal mount, which always marks a frightened horse. Then, before any of us realised what was happening, the animal reared up, the immaculate white picket rope flashing between the pawing front legs, before it crashed to the ground on top of the King, and rolled over him. I was one of the NCOs who helped to push the horse off and carry His Majesty to his car. Everyone was sworn to secrecy lest the Germans got the news of the accident, and the Squadron was detailed to patrol over the hospital at Aire throughout the time that the Royal patient lay there.'

On 3 November 1915, Major Becke left the Squadron. He was to take command of 1st Corps Wing RFC. His successor was Major C.F. de S. Murphy who was to command the Squadron for only a few months. During his command, another reorganisation of the RFC took place. Army and Corps commanders increasingly requested aircraft to be employed in their respective areas. As the war progressed not only had the Army and RFC expanded, but the workload of the Squadron grew as well. It developed in two main directions. First there was the Army cooperation, close reconnaissance and aerial photography for Corps Headquarters. Secondly there were the patrols, the long-range recce sorties and photographic work for Army headquarters. Besides which, every now and then the aircraft were detailed to carry out bombing operations over and behind the enemy lines. This necessitated the formation of far more squadrons than the four original. Very soon each Wing began to control considerably more squadrons. It also became clear that it would be necessary to place some kind of an intermediate between the RFC and the GHQ. The outcome was the formation of Air Brigades in 1916. Each Air Brigade consisted of two Wings with a different 'employer'. There was a Corps-Wing and an Army-Wing. All requests from Corps or Army would be passed to the Wings through the Brigade commander, a Brigadier-General. This Brigade also had a Kite and Balloon section, aircraft workshops etc. No.II (AC) Squadron with Nos.3, 10 and 16 Squadrons comprised the first wing, which was designated First (Corps) Wing. Nos.18 and 27 Squadrons formed Tenth (Army) Wing.

The Squadron's second VC was awarded to Lt. Alan McLeod, a Canadian pilot. While his observer Lt. Hammond engaged the Fokker triplanes with this machine gun, McLeod, standing on the wing of the burning FK8 piloted the aircraft down to a forced landing. Hammond was subsequently awarded a bar to his Military Cross.

On 9 April 1916 Major Murphy left the Squadron and Major R.A. Cooper DSO took over command. Visitors would often come to the front to see what a modern war was like. One of these visitors, the Duke of Connaught, came to see the important work the Squadron did. Major Gould, at that time commanding C-Flight told *Flight* magazine in the 9 June 1949 edition how a 'shoot' was put on as a special demonstration for the Duke. The targets, some German batteries among ruined houses, had been agreed upon by Major Gould and the artillery commander, while No.25 Squadron would provide fighter cover. On the appointed day Major Gould and his observer were flying at a height of about 3,000 feet. The Duke was late arriving so the signal 'K', meaning 'Battery receiving signals but guns not ready to fire' was sent up. When the Duke duly arrived with a cavalcade of four cars, he got out and walked to the battery with several staff officers. Gould felt a little squeamish about four big staff cars, with high black roofs, being in such a conspicious position. If the Germans spotted them there would be serious trouble as they were only 2,500 yards from the front line. Gould wheeled around over the battery just as the 'L' ground signal ('Ready to engage target') appeared. The pilot turned towards the target, sending down the 'AAA' ('Stand by'), then flew until he was positioned well over the four doomed houses. Looking back towards the battery he sent down the signal 'GGG', meaning 'Open Fire'. Then there was a colossal flash. Gould counted eight seconds and then was a tremendous explosion about 100 yards beyond the German positions. Orbiting over the battery Gould expected the Germans to return fire but nothing happened. He sent the signal 'G5' which was the clock code to the battery meaning '100 yards long'. He turned towards the target sending the 'AAA', flew until he had a good view and then sent 'GGG', whilst looking at the English battery. To Gould's consternation there was no flashing of the guns. Wondering what was happening Gould made a low pass over the British guns, his observer frantically pointing at the ground. The square signal was out, meaning 'wait'. Then Major Gould saw the Duke and his staff walk over to their cars and drive away. 'I learnt afterwards that the Duke, being an old gunner, had gone right down into the gun-pit to see the first shot fired and then moved off to some vantage-point to watch the shoot generally. How he could have stood the shock of the report from a sixty-pounder at his age — he was not far off seventy — passes my comprehension', said Gould in 1949. After a short pause came the 'L' again and away they went, backwards and forwards, giving the 'Standby', 'Fire', and then the correction by the clock-code system. The shooting was marvellous, with an 'OK' at the third shot, brick dust and clouds of smoke rising into the air. Eventually 'Archie', as the German battery was nicknamed, joined in, and it was only by quick manoeuvring that Gould managed to get away with nothing more serous than a few jagged holes through the wings and fuselage. Then Gould made straight for the British battery to give the Royal Salute according to instructions. Down they went in a steep dive, flattening out over the Battery Commander's HQ House — on which Gould left his aerial, having forgotten to wind it in. He pulled the stick back and jammed open the throttle so as to zoom up, clear of the many chimney stacks around the coal fields in that district, but to his horror the engine choked and the revs died. He shoved the nose down putting the aircraft into a dive, and prepared to land in among the ruined houses. Just before flattening out the engine spluttered and came on full power. Chimney stacks rushed passed Gould and his observer from all directions and they had to violently bank and twist to avoid a collision before eventually emerging at the far end of the town. There was a strange pallor to the observer's face as he looked out from his front seat. At moments like these, being the observer sitting in the front with no control over the aircraft was no fun at all.

'Babe' McLeod recovering from his wounds after the encounter with German scouts which earned him the Victoria Cross.

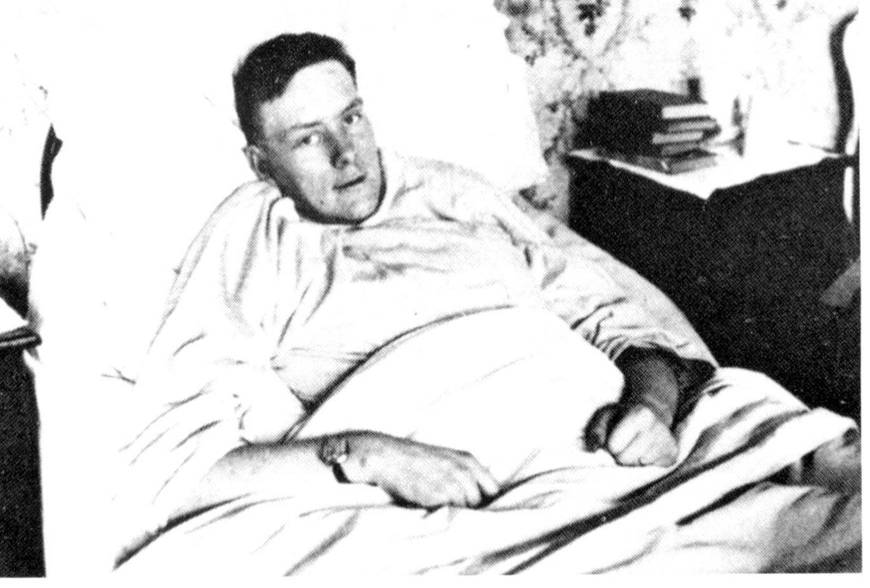

During the same month decisions were made to ensure that no more aircraft were shot at by friendly troops. Therefore No.II (AC) Squadron received orders to paint a black triangle on both sides of the fuselage aft of the roundels. Similar triangles were to be painted on the top and bottom of the fuselage. Later in the year, when all aircraft were doped green or khaki, the triangles were changed to white ones.

In July the Battle of the Somme began. The Squadron had ten BE2c and eight BE2d aircraft available for action. The battle started with the bombing of Douai railway station by a mixed force of aircraft, made up of BE2bs of No.26 and all the aircraft of No.II (AC) Squadron. During the following days the Squadron flew continuous attacks against Busigny, Don and Le Cateau. The Squadron was temporarily split into two units; one staying at Hesdigneul while the other went to Fienviller. In the early morning these aircraft would fly to their landing grounds, and return to Hesdigneul in the evening. The detachment was commanded by Captain P. Huskinson. Later in the year the squadron establishment was increased from eighteen to twenty-one aircraft. For pilots and observers continuous flying was extremely tiring. As an eyewitness said 'one could see the anguish slowly mounting in their eyes, until the night would come when upon entering the mess they would see one or two chairs being turned up to show that once again comrades had failed to return and might be lying somewhere out on the battlefield'.

Back home in England, war seemed to be chivalrous and rather exciting. The press did not help. Some quotations from a 1916 newspaper gives an indication of how the public at home was being informed about the air war in France:

> *'Tales of the RFC; Finding Targets for the Artillery.* **Hawks of the Air; Daring in attack. from: H. Perry Robinson.**
>
> Our flying men continue to dominate the air in a way which, as we know, is very discouraging to the German troops and must be intensely humiliating to German aviators.
>
> Lieutenant . . . encountered a formation of 12 Rolands. He dived in amongst them, firing one drum. The formation was broken up. Lieutenant . . . then got under the nearest machine and fired one drum at 15 yards into the pilot's seat, causing the machine to plunge to earth. Shortly afterwards some more hostile aeroplanes came up in formation. Lieutenant . . . attacked one, which went down and landed in a gap between two woods. Several other machines were engaged with indecisive results, and, having expended all his ammunition Lieutenant . . . returned.'

Reality however, was entirely different. The Fokkers, Albatrosses and Halberstadts were definitely no easy prey. The German pilots were skilled, brave and determined. The RFC had to fight hard to carry out the necessary reconnaissance and other sorties. For the Arras offensive of April 1917 the Squadron engaged in artillery spotting and on the opening days of the battle flew a total of over eighty hours. 'Bloody April' 1917 had seen the devastation of the RFC. The Squadron too had suffered terribly and it was obvious that a new aircraft was necessary to equal the balance. On 14 April Lieutenant Wilson and his observer were killed. On 5 May Lieutenant John Coupland lost his life and his body was never found. Today his name can be read on the Arras Memorial. On 16 August 1917 Major Snow DSO, MC, assumed command. Throughout the year the Squadron was hard pressed to hold its own; encounters with enemy fighters, which usually outnumbered the Squadron's aircraft were a daily occurence. After the Arras offensive of April 1917 the Squadron markings had been changed from triangles to white zig-zags on the sides of the fuselage to identify the aircraft to sometimes trigger-happy 'friendly' troops. Towards the end of the month of May the Squadron received new aeroplanes — the Armstrong Whitworth FK8s — designed by a Dutchman named Koolhoven. The FK8 had a 160 horse-powered Beardsmore six cylinder liquid-cooled in line engine. Its maximum speed was about 100 mph and it could climb to 13,000 feet and stay there for three hours. It was a magnificent aircraft carrying a crew of two, two machine guns and a bomb load of 150 pounds. At the same time another lethal aircraft was being developed for the Germans, the Fokker Triplane. Its designer was a Dutchman too, Anthony Fokker. . .

By the end of July all BE2s had been withdrawn and replaced by the 'Big Acks', yet the Squadron still suffered losses. On 25 August a pair of No.II (AC) Squadron's aircraft were attacked by four enemy fighters over Pont-a-Vendin. One German aircraft was shot down, and the FK8s escaped unscathed. In addition to its everyday tasks the Squadron began night bombing operations. During the night of 30/31 October no less than thirth-nine twenty-pounders were dropped on Henin, Lietard and Billy Montigny. The following morning the Squadron attacked enemy objectives near Wingles and Pont-a-Vendin, dropping three 112 pounders and finishing their attack by firing no less than 1,200 rounds into enemy communication trenches.

Then came the final year of the War, in which a second VC was awarded to a Squadron member, Alan Arnett McLeod. He was a Canadian whose grandparents had left Scotland to search for a better future in the Colonies. Alan was born on 20 April 1899. At the age of fourteen he bluffed his way into the Fort Garry Horse, a local territorial volunteer force. Once his real age was discovered, he was sent home to his parents with the message never to do something so silly again. In April 1917 he was accepted by the RFC for pilot training. After two postings in England he was finally sent to France and joined No.II (AC) Squadron on 29 November 1917. He was allocated to B-Flight as a pilot on the FK8. A very tall man although he was called Babe for his boyish appearance, he was a very skilled pilot. However, every time he returned from a sortie he loved to dive to ground level to strafe German troops, trenches, gun sites or whatever appeared in his sights. On 19 December 1917, while flying FK8 number B5782 with Lieutenant Comber as his observer, Babe McLeod single-handed attacked a formation of eight yellow and green striped Albatros fighters. The Germans were completely surprised by the audacity of the young Canadian and scattered in all directions. Comber managed to shoot down the nearest Albatros before McLeod disengaged and ran for home. On 14 January 1918 McLeod and his observer Lieutenant Key were detailed to attack a German observation balloon at Beauvin, south of Lille. It was an extremely dangerous sortie as the balloons were normally well-protected by Ack-Ack and German fighters circling above. It was a hit-and-run job for a fast fighter, not for a two-seater with a maximum speed of barely 100 mph,

Major Snow, DSO, MC, Officer Commanding No.II Squadron from August 1917-August 1918.

but McLeod never questioned his orders. When he arrived over his target and dived down to attack, three Albatros fighters also dived down determined to shoot the lone 'Big Ack' to pieces. McLeod succeeded in destroying the balloon but had to bank sharply right to avoid the burning debris. One Albatros tried to get under the tail of the FK8 but Lieutenant Key shattered its upper wing centre-section and the Albatros disintegrated. Fighting off the other two, McLeod and Key returned to Hesdigneul. Subsequently both were mentioned in dispatches. Two days later, in foul weather conditions, McLeod took off with Lieutenant Hammond. During their sortie they reconnoitred a group of soldiers manning a German AA-gun near La Bassee. McLeod dived down and while flying at fifty feet strafed the emplacement. Then Hammond fired another volley into the group and dropped two twenty-pounders. After this McLeod was granted a fortnight's leave in England.

While he enjoyed his rest, the Germans were making preparations on a scale never seen before for the spring offensive to break the horrific deadlock of trench warfare and push the Allies back to the Channel once and for all. Behind the German lines massive stockpiles of equipment were made. German reserves arrived in a steady stream, both by day and night. Allied reconnaissance took place every day. On 21 March the German offensive was set in motion and after widespread initial success, they pushed the Allied troops back. No.II Squadron was one of the units hastily ordered into the Amiens battle area to stop the German advance at Baupaume. Reinforcements for local German air force units were also moved in. One of these were the four 'Staffeln' forming Manfred von Richthofen's famous Flying Circus. The Red Baron occupied Lechelle airfield, directly opposite No.II (AC) Squadron. On 27 March, seven FK8s took off from Hesdigneul to bomb and strafe infantry in the Bray-sur-Somme area. It was a very misty day and each aircraft was soon on its own, desperately trying to find out where the enemy was. It was not long before the pilots realised they were completely lost. McLeod and Hammond flying B5773 crawled through the clouds for two hours, before landing at Asvesnes-le-Comte, where No.43 Squadron was based. During his landing McLeod severely damaged the aircraft's tail skid. At 1300 hours, after the aircraft had been repaired and refuelled, they took off again. The weather had not changed at all. When McLeod was about to abandon the sortie he suddenly spotted a German balloon not far from him. The FK8 dived towards the enemy, but before the balloon came into firing range a Fokker Triplane came into view. McLeod changed his mind and decided to attack the Fokker first. After a successful attack the Triplane fell into an uncontrolled spin and crashed on the outskirts of the village of Albert. However, a formation of eight Fokker Triplanes had witnessed McLeod's victory, and dived for the Big Ack. The Fokkers belonged to Jagdstaffel 10 of the Flying Circus. As the first Triplane attacked, Lieutenant Hammond answered with a long burst and the German fell in flames. While the other Fokkers attacked, one of the Germans, Leutnant Hans Kirchstein, decided to try and attack the FK8 from below. The Big Ack was raked from nose to rudder inflicting two serious wounds on Hammond. A simultaneous attack by a second Fokker from the beam resulted in a third wound for Hammond while McLeod was hit in the leg. In spite of agonizing pains Hammond levelled his gunsights at the nearest German, his bullets hit its petrol tank and the Fokker exploded in mid-air. Kirchstein again banked steeply towards the FK8 but this time his bullets ruptured the petrol tank. The Big Ack erupted in flames. The fury of the fire burnt away the fragile flooring between McLeod and Hammond, and destroyed McLeod's cockpit floor, his knee-length flying boots and the lower skirt of his leather coat were also burnt away. The instrument board and control column started smouldering. Having no other support Hammond was forced to climb on top of the fuselage, desperately clinging to the gun mounting to prevent himself from falling. McLeod was also forced to climb out of the cockpit. He stood on the port lower wing root, holding the smouldering column with one hand and yet managing to bring the FK8 into a side-slip to keep the flames from burning Hammond alive. A Fokker pilot followed the FK8, probably anxious to witness the crash which seemed inevitable. He paid the price for his curiosity when Hammond succeeded in giving him a final burst with his machine gun as the German closed in. A short while later infantry saw the FK8 crash violently into no-man's-land. McLeod, badly burned, bleeding and in shock managed to pull his observer from the aircraft before the bombs it was still carrying exploded. With Hammond on his back, he crawled towards the Allied lines. While doing this he was again wounded, this time by shrapnel. Exhausted, he reached an outpost occupied by South Africans, where he collapsed. As a German barrage made it impossible to move them, both had to stay there for five more hours, until it was possible to carry them to a dressing station. A long road of convalescence followed. First they stayed at Etaples Hospital. Then they were sent to Boulogne and Dover to be admitted into the Prince of Wales' Hospital in London. For weeks McLeod's life hung in the balance, while Hammond lost a leg. On 1 May 1918 the *London Gazette* announced that a Victoria Cross had been awarded to Babe McLeod. On 4 September he walked on crutches into

Buckingham Palace, accompanied by his father who had sailed from Canada to be with his son. Immediately after the King had presented him with the VC McLeod returned to Canada. His observer was awarded a bar to his MC. Invalided out of the RFC Hammond also sailed to Canada. Sadly McLeod did not live long enough to enjoy his medal. In November 1918 when an epidemic of virulent influenza swept through Canada the young man died. At nineteen years of age he had been the youngest recipient of an aerial VC and the second youngest serviceman ever to receive this great honour.

While the German offensive continued in March 1918, No.II (AC) Squadron carried out artillery and photo reconnaissance sorties. During one of these sorties, on 27 March, Lieutenant Purnell Barford was killed. Only nineteen years old he was denied a known grave. In addition, day and night bombing plus low level strafing attacks were made. On 1 April great changes took place within the flying elements of the British forces. The Royal Flying Corps and Royal Naval Air Services were joined together into a separate force, the Royal Air Force. An Air Ministry was created and Lord Rothermere appointed Secretary of State and President of the Air Council. There was no doubt whatsoever who was to become the first Chief of Air Staff. Major-General Sir Hugh Trenchard, KCB, DSO, would be the only possible candidate. To satisfy the Navy, Rear-Admiral Mark Kerr, CB, RN was appointed his deputy. There were other changes as well: Majors became Squadron Leaders, Colonels were to be called Group Captains, and the green army uniforms and navy blues made way for Air Force blue. The colour of the uniforms of the new force was coincidental really. After the Russian Revolution a large shipment of cloth for the Czar's Imperial Guard remained in store in England. Rather than waste this material, the cloth was chosen for the RAF uniforms. The new RAF had little time to celebrate its birth and neither did the Squadron. On 2 April 1918 it co-operated with 3rd Brigade in a successful daylight attack against German positions. Five aircraft bombed enemy battalion headquarters and fired 1,100 rounds into the trenches. Losses also continued. On 4 April Sergeant Pilot S.J. Mitchell AFM crashed after a violent encounter with German fighters. He was buried at La Chauduire cemetery.

On 9 June 1918 the Squadron left Hesdigneul and moved to Floringham aerodrome in Belgium. On 22 August Major P.G. Ross-Hume took over the Squadron with the war almost over. On 20 October a new aerodrome was occupied, Mazingharbe, which was abandoned again after a few days for Genech, from where the last operational sorties were flown. It was very clear that Germany would not be able to fight on much

Above: A beautiful photograph of a No.II Squadron FK8 over Hesdigneul, flying in the direction of Béthune. The observer Lt. Riding is visible in the rear cockpit.

Below: Hesdigneul aerodrome from the air.

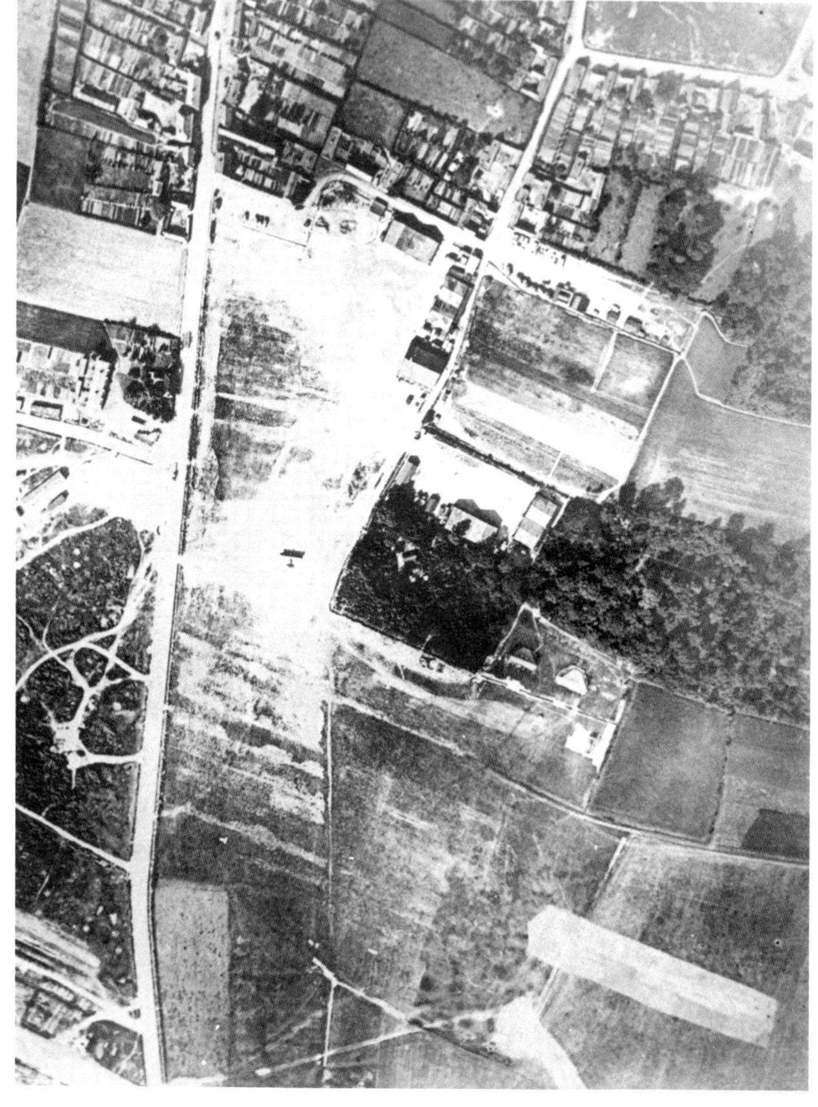

longer. A temporary success after the Armistice with the new Soviet leadership on 3 March 1918 could not help the Germans to win a final victory. On 27 October the Austrians gave up and soon after this the Turkish government also surrendered. The German Hochseeflotte rebelled at Wilhelmshafen, soon followed by other troops. On 8 November a German delegation arrived at Compiègne to discuss the terms for an Armistice on the Western Front. The next day, after the German government proclaimed itself a republic, the Emperor fled to the Netherlands where he became a lumberjack, cutting wood at the castle to which the Dutch confined him until he died in 1941. On 11 November the Armistice was signed and the Great War was over. Though the work of Army co-operation was vital, the Squadron did not have any spectacular scoreboard of kills to show for over four years unremitting labour and courage. Its casualty figures, however, were a vivid testimony; they included twenty killed or dead of wounds, nineteen missing, fifty-one wounded, twelve prisoners of war, three accidentally killed and fourteen accidentally injured. Two of its members had earned Victoria Crosses for exceptional bravery.

The Squadron stayed at Genech until February 1919 when it flew to Bicester where it was reduced to a cadre only. In September the same year it departed for Weston-on-the-Green under the command of Squadron Leader Moore, the first CO with an Air Force rank. Summing up No.II (AC) Squadron's war experiences, it cannot be overemphasised how bravely it performed a very dangerous and demanding duty. Many pilots and observers as well as ground crew paid with their lives.

On 20 January 1920 No.II (AC) Squadron RAF was temporarily disbanded at Weston-on-the-Green.

The Officers' Mess at Hesdigneul.

CHAPTER 3
THE INTER-WAR LULL

Only eleven days after being disbanded, No.II Squadron was re-formed on 1 February 1920 at Oranmore in Ireland. The little town was situated near Galway Bay in the west of the country. The Squadron was made part of 11 (Irish) Group with one Flight at Fermoy, County Cork, and one at Castlebar, County Mayo. The Bristols were in wartime camouflage with white fuselage serials and three broad stripes around the rear fuselage. Two red stripes flanked one in the Flight colour — white for A Flight, yellow for B and blue for C. It was in those days that the Squadron proudly added '(AC)' to its name and it has kept this addition since.

A lot had changed since the War had ended. On 1 April 1918, after the 'new' RAF had been formed, there were no less than 188 Squadrons and fifteen Flights, made up of over 290,000 officers, NCOs and men and over 22,500 aircraft. Now that peace had returned, the RAF was reduced to only thirty-three Squadrons. However, the independent air force under the inspired leadership of Trenchard and strongly supported by the combined Secretary for War and Air, Winston Churchill MP, was to become the most modern branch of His Majesty's Armed Forces. Trenchard had devised a plan full of purposeful farsightedness. There was to be a Cadet College for Officers at Cranwell, a short-service commission scheme, an Air Force Staff College, and above all an apprenticeship scheme, where young men could undergo a course of three years' training in technical skills at the RAF School of Technical Training at Halton. Trenchard ended his proposals with an unforgettable remark: 'I have laid the foundations for a castle; if nobody builds anything bigger than a cottage on them it will at least be a very good cottage'. No.II (AC) Squadron fully intended to be part of that castle. With their Bristol Fighters, designed in 1916 by Captain Barnwell and powered by a Rolls-Royce Falcon engine, they supported the troops fighting the riots in Ireland.

The first Annual Dinner took place at the Trocadero restaurant on 20 November 1920. the woman shown on this illustration is Mademoiselle Berthe, who ran the Officers' Mess at Hesdigneul.

We can only assume that Squadron Leader Moore took the Squadron to Ireland and handed over command to Squadron Leader Stent on 20 May 1920. This CO commanded the Squadron for a mere three months before being succeeded by S/L Butler on 16 August 1920, the reasons for this short period in command are unknown. The Squadron HQ moved to Fermoy and was accommodated at the local race course. For operational purposes it was placed at the disposal of the Commander of the Forces in Southern Ireland, Lieutenant-General Sir P. Strickland. He had his HQ at Cork and was responsible for law and order south of the line Waterford-Galway. Due to many cuts in the defence budget the Squadron's operational efficiency was very poor. Their aircraft were nearly obsolete and there was a constant change of personnel due to the continuing General Demobilisation. There was a terrible lack of spares and mechanical transport. After a written complaint a Staff Officer from the Air Ministry visited the Squadron with the result that it was re-equipped and brought up to War Establishment efficiency. From that moment on No.II Squadron consisted of three Flights of six Bristol Fighters each, six aircraft in immediate reserve on the station, and six in general reserve stored at Group Headquarters. A supplementary vote-in-aid was passed to build accommodation for personnel and equipment. No.II (AC) Squadron's activities during the Irish Rebellion were limited to non-offensive operations as no guns or bombs were carried. The Squadron carried out recce flights and conveyed mail, stores and personnel between the various military and police detachments in the Southern Region. To facilitate this, emergency landing grounds were constructed all over the Region. In many cases, these were just a couple of fields surrounded by banks and stone walls, with a hole knocked in one wall to give the aircraft a long enough run for take-off and landing. It is needless to say that considerable care was required by whoever had to land there. For tactical purposes the area was divided into three zones with one Flight operating for each Zone-Commander. An officer from each Flight was attached to each commander's staff for liaison duties.

The main incident, as far as flying was concerned, occurred when an aircraft flying from Oranmore to Fermoy had to make a forced landing in the Galtie mountains after it had been shot at by rebels. The pilot, Flying Officer Mackay, stayed behind with the aircraft while the observer, having won the toss, set off in an attempt to reach friendly forces. Mackay was soon captured by the rebels. He stood a very good chance of being shot, as all captured British officers and policemen were held as hostages for those rebels who had been arrested by the police or the Army. When these rebels were tried by military courts, sentenced to death and executed, a British prisoner was shot in retaliation by the rebels. In fact, all British officers and policemen who were captured were killed by the rebels with the exception of Flying Officer Mackay. He was constantly moved around the countryside by his captors to prevent him from being found and liberated by British patrols. Finally the rebels released him carrying a long propaganda letter for the British Commander-in-Chief.

The camp at Fermoy was surrounded by barbed wire entanglements, interspersed with Mills bombs and Verey Lights on trip wires. There were two block houses and a tower with machine guns and search lights to cover the camp and the aerodrome in case of a rebel attack. The local British Army unit provided a standing aerodrome guard of one officer and fifteen other ranks. Two of Colonel Richardson's trained war dogs (Airedales) accompanied the guards during their rounds at night. In the event of a determined night attack by rebels, reinforcements could be summoned from Fermoy Barracks by rocket signal. In addition, officers and airmen of the Squadron received firearms training. As personal arms were not at that time a general issue to airmen, rifles, bayonets and webbing were purchased from the Army Ordnance Department. On several occasions the local rebels made abortive night attacks on the camp, mainly to test the defences, and sniping at night was a frequent occurrence. The Squadron was inspected by the Commander of the 'Force, Southern Ireland' as well as by the Commander-in-Chief, Forces in Ireland General McCreedy, both of whom praised No.II Squadron's work. With the settlement of the Irish troubles the Squadron returned to England in February 1922 and was based at Digby. They were now part of the 'Inland Area'. Shortly after the Squadron arrived the AOC Inland Area visited them. Sir John Salmond commented very favourably on the state of the Squadron's aircraft. In May 1922 Squadron Leader Butler handed over command to Squadron Leader Smythies, who was sadly killed shortly afterwards. A new commander, Squadron Leader Forbes took his place from 15 May 1922. The Squadron stayed for only four months at Digby, on 31 May it was sent back to Ireland and was stationed at Aldergrove in the north of the country. Little is known about this period of the Squadron's history. We do know that two Flights of the Squadron returned to Farnborough in September 1922 while one Flight stayed in Ireland until February 1923. At the end of the year the entire Squadron went to Andover, again as part of Inland Area Command. One of the pilots serving at that time was Pilot Officer (now Air Marshal Sir) R.B. Jordan, who vividly remembers some of the events during the Twenties:

> 'I joined No.II (AC) Squadron in December 1922 as it was about to return to England after the Irish troubles. Part of the Squadron went to Farnborough. As the troops had had a very hard time it was decided that they were to be taken for the day to Brighton Carnival. I was one of the officers in charge of one of the coaches. We all had a marvellous time and I had a photograph taken of F/O Pratt and myself in a rather ridiculous position: I was photographed as a baby in a small bath while 'Mother' Pratt gave me a good wash. In April 1924 the Squadron was posted to Manston. There had been no Squadron at Manston since the 1914-18 War and we attracted a lot of attention from the public. The Ramsgate Road went right through the aerodrome and quite large crowds used to assemble there. One afternoon we thought we would give them a show, so I went up with a dummy stuffed with rags in a Sidcot flying suit and flying helmet in the back seat. While doing my aerobatics I dropped it out at the top of a loop. The dummy fell down to the aerodrome and hit the ground in a cloud of dust. An ambulance dashed out and picked the dummy up on a stretcher. The body was then put into the ambulance which drove to the front of our hangars. Inside the ambulance the dummy was quickly hidden and someone else took its place on the stretcher. When the ambulance stopped the

bearers carried the stretcher with the man out. He was covered with blood and all thought he would not live much longer. Then the chap got off the stretcher and limped into the hangar. The crowd gave him tremendous cheers and applause. All believed that the pilots of No.II (AC) Squadron were a very tough lot. . .'

Jordan left the Squadron in 1926 and was posted to a Squadron in India. During his time with No.II he had seen Squadron Leader Saul take over command from Squadron Leader Forbes in April 1925. Saul stayed with the Squadron for about two years. In early 1927 he left and Squadron Leader Sowery DFC, AFC, took over. It was under his command that the Squadron went to the farthest outpost of its entire history: the vast Chinese Republic, troubled by revolution and fighting War Lords. For many years, foreign powers had occupied small parts of China. After the Boxers had attacked the International Zone of Peking in 1903 life for the Europeans was tense. In April 1927 the situation around the International Settlement at Shanghai became very dangerous. It was feared that Chinese Nationalists would soon attack the whites. China had been in chaos for a long time. Generals fought each other and horrible massacres took place. When they were not engaged in internal disputes they harrassed the 'White Devils' in every possible way. The British government decided that a show of strength was needed. On 8 April 1927 the Squadron received orders to 'proceed to China', and they were to sail from Southampton in two weeks. Immediately the Squadron was brought to War Establishment and packing began. The following day five aircraft were flown from Manston to Farnborough and then on to Ascot to be crated. The pilots of these aircraft were F/L McBain and P/Os Mumford-Mathews, Wilson, MacEvoy and Stokes. Mathews stayed behind to supervise the crating while the others returned to Manston in a No.9 Squadron Virginia. The Squadron Operations Book gives a detailed record of the days prior to the Squadron's departure to the Far East. On 10 April F/L McBain, F/O Hadden and P/Os F.G.S. and E.L. Wilson took the remainder of the Squadron aircraft to Farnborough. Then orders came that on 20 April at 0420 hours the Squadron was to embark on H.M.T. *Neuralia.* The following days were spent packing. Everyone must have been extremely busy, for apparently even the Squadron diarist hardly had time to make any other notes than:

10 April 1927. Packing all day.
11 April 1927. Packing all day.
12 April 1927. Packing all day.
13 April 1927. Packing all day.

The same day Wing Commander Primrose, Director of Equipment, Air Ministry visited the Squadron. Four Crossley tenders and three trailers arrived to take the Flight stores to Birkenhead. Transport and stores were to be loaded on to SS *Sarpedon* on 23 April. The ammunition was to be transported separately on the *City of Poona.* Flight Lieutenant Lock went to the Air Ministry to collect maps of China. On 14 April, while packing continued, every Squadron member was equipped with tropical kit. Two days later a convoy of four lorries, four tenders and three trailers left for Birkenhead accompanied by F/O Alderson and P/O Stokes. On 20 April at 0215 hours the Squadron began to march to Birchinton where they were to board the train for Southampton. Two hours later the train left. On arrival at Southampton there was a last inspection at 1030 hours, Air Vice-Marshal Longcroft, who had been with the Squadron during its first years, accompanied by the AOC No.22 Group, Air Commodore Pitcher, saw the Squadron off. Then began a long voyage which took the Squadron first to Malta, where it arrived on 27 April. Three days later the *Neuralia* arrived at Port Said. The entire Squadron was allowed to leave the ship and made a march through the town. On 12 May the *Neuralia* docked at Colombo where another march was made, as happened again in Singapore. On 21 May, after having been at sea for almost a month, the Squadron finally reached Hong Kong. After four days rest the Squadron embarked on another vessel, the P&O liner *Karmala.*While in Hong Kong the Squadron estabishment grew as new officers joined. The last part of the journey to Shanghai took four more days, but on 30 May at 0730 hours

The longest journey ever made by the Squadron was to Shanghai during the unrest in 1927. The racecourse there was used as an airfield while the troops were based in nearby hotels.

the *Karmala* finally arrived at her destination. The men disembarked and set up a base at the Shanghai Racecourse, with billets in the New World Cafe in the Bubbling Well Road. F/Os Parker, Walker, Grenfel, Gilbert and P/O Younge were attached to No.II (AC) Squadron. During the following night four Bristol Fighters arrived ashore still in their crates, and were assembled during the early morning of the following day. In the meantime Wing Commander Barratt travelled to Tientsin to see if it was suitable for the establishment of an airfield.

Officers, NCOs and Other Ranks gathered around the CO S/L 'Daddy' Probyn, 1929.

On 7 June the total strength of the Squadron was thirty-three officers and 205 other ranks. The first casualty the Squadron suffered in China was AC2 Taylor, who had be be admitted to No.12 Field Ambulance on the 7th. The aircraft were soon ready to be tested. The commander of B-Flight, F/O Moreton tested J6735, J7651 and J7652 while the CO test flew J7665. An Officers' Mess was established at the Race Club. Personnel of all three Flights took up billets at a shop opposite the Star Garage. Chinese 'sweepers' were employed for sanitary duties at a monthly pay of thirteen Chinese dollars. On 17 June the first sortie was flown, F/Os Moreton and Hadden with their respective air gunners LAC Wilkins and AC Adams taking the first vertical photographs of the Shanghai Detachment. Principally, all flying was done at 12,000 feet taking vertical photographs to map the area of operations. The trips were usually around two hours long and during that time, up to 117 plates might be exposed. A few weather tests, using borrowed instruments from the Siciwei Observatory were carried out and it was on one of these flights that one of the Bristols was coaxed after one hour fifteen minutes to no less than 14,900 feet. Wing Commander Barratt made another recce for landing grounds using hired civilian transport early in August. The same month brought the Squadron the first bit of excitement. During July they had daily flown photographic sorties and some message dropping exercises with ground troops, such as Hungtao with the Coldstream Guards on the 21st, but in August the first serious encounter with the Nationalists took place. On 15 August F/O Hadden with AC Adams made a reconnaissance trip in Bristol J7652. Unfortunately they had to make a forced landing on the Kiangwan race course, where the Nationalists had established one of their camps. The Chinese commander saw the possibility of a good business deal brought about by the unintentional visit of the British airmen and he promptly confiscated the aeroplane. Warned by the pilot, a crash party was sent out to bring the Bristol back to Shanghai. When they arrived the Chinese met them with great cordiality and entertained them for days. After a little pressure the Chinese commander allowed the party to retrieve the engine and the fuselage of the aircraft. However, to make sure that he was paid a substantial reward for the safe-keeping of the aeroplane, the commander decided to keep the wings. Of course the crash party was in no position to argue or negotiate so they left with what they could get. Wing Commander Barratt, F/L Hollinghurst DFC, F/L Moreton and the MTO F/O Hill stayed with the Chinese. Finally they got sick and tired of the Chinese trying to stall negotiations and left. A message was sent to the Chinese that the wings were to be handed back before 1100 hours on 17 August. The Chinese commander replied that he needed more time to think it over. Four Bristols were then refuelled, bombed-up and prepared for action. Again the Chinese were told that the wings had to be returned immediately but not later than 1300 hours. At exactly 1300 hours the Headquarters North China Command ordered the cutting of the railway lines 300 yards north of Jessfield Station at 1600 hours. Now the Chinese commander understood that the British were not prepared to pay for what was rightfully theirs. Shortly after 1600 hours he reported that the wings were ready to be returned. Fortunately it had not been necessary to use force to make the point that the RAF would not yield to blackmail. Once the wings were back in the hands of the Squadron the Chinese were told that they could repair their railway lines again. . .

The vast distances in China made W/T an absolute necessity. F/L W.F. Dole, then a wireless mechanic, has given an interesting insight into the communications arrangements of those days. Each aircraft carried two W/T sets. One was operated by the pilot, and consisted of only a transmitter, which was used for conducting artillery shoots. The set had a range of about ten miles and was driven by a wind generator on the lower wing struts. The second set was operated by the wireless mechanic in the back seat, it had both a transmitter and a receiver and its range was about 100 miles. This set was also driven by a wind generator which was pushed out into the slipstream when the set was used.

No.II (AC) Squadron scored another 'first' when they built a short wave radio set in Shanghai which was operated on a wavelength of about 50 metres. With this self-built piece of equipment the Squadron was able to communicate with the Air Ministry in London directly from the race course. It was the first time that direct communication over such a large distance had been made. The set was later officially adopted by the RAF as 'Set A'.

After the incident with the wings the Squadron flew only a few more photographic reconnaissance sorties before No.441 (FR) Flight, using the Fairey 3D from HMS Hermes, took over the race course on 6 September 1927. A substantial number of airmen were then posted across to the Fleet Air Arm while the rest of the Squadron prepared for the home voyage. On 13 September No.II (AC) Squadron's detachment embarked on SS *Devanha* at Holt's Warf in Shanghai. The detachment included W/C Baratt and consisted of twenty-one officers. The vessel left Shanghai on 14 September at 0500 hours. After two days the ship arrived in Hong Kong, leaving there on the 17th. The return voyage went to Singapore, Penang, Colombo and Aden where the ship arrived on 5 October at 1730 hours. Six hours later the voyage was continued via Port Sudan, Port Said and Marseille. The *Devanha* finally arrived in London on 25 October. The Squadron disembarked and took the train to Victoria station. At 2130 hours on the same day they returned home to RAF Manston. Two days later a second detachment arrived in London with SS *Novara*. On 1 November 1927 RAF Manston looked as if No.II (AC) Squadron had never been away.

With the return from Shanghai the Squadron settled down to a routine that was to see little change until September 1939. Being an Army Co-operation Squadron it was part of No.22 (AC) Group. Although the Group was a part of the RAF, the Army was responsible for the operational duties of the Army Co-op Squadrons. Some said that the Army Co-op Squadrons were the Army's final attempt to have an air force of its own, which might have been the case. During the inter-war years there was nearly always a Flight of an Army Co-op Squadron flying recce sorties for the Artillery regiments at Larkhill, in which No.II (AC) Squadron often participated. Each autumn the whole Squadron took part in the annual Army manoeuvres, often operating from an Advanced Landing Ground called Friday Wood, Further activities took place during annual visits to the Armament Practice Camps (APCs). In 1928 it took place at Sutton Bridge, after that at the North Coat Fitties. The 1929 detachment was the last one to use the Bristol Fighter and S/L Probyn DSO, who had taken over the Squadron from S/L Sowery in 1928, controlled the Squadron formation of nine aircraft en route to the APC from a tenth aeroplane using W/T. At the end of November 1929 a dual-control Armstrong Whitworth Atlas was collected from Old Sarum to start conversion of the pilots onto the new aircraft. The first service Atlas arrived in early December 1929. It was the very first RAF type specially designed for Army Co-operation duties. The Atlas was powered by an Armstrong Siddeley Jaguar engine. It carried a .303 machine gun for the pilot and a Lewis gun for the observer. Under each wing it could carry a maximum of four twenty-pounders. Although the Atlas was a fairly new aircraft the Squadron's APC results for 1930 were excellent. F/O Atcherly was the best shot in No.22 Group with an average of 74.8%; on one shoot he got no less than 198 hits out of 200 rounds fired. F/Os Bennett and Mole, were 1st and 2nd in the Group competition having a direct hit with nil and three yards error respectively for their bombs. In the High Level Bombing

LAC Field had a mere thirty-five yards error while AC Rice got 53.3 yards. B-Flight won the bombing competition with an average error of only eleven yards for seven aircraft. Squadron officers attended courses at the Camberley Staff College and aircraft were sent to the Squadron for evaluation trials. In August 1930 the entire Squadron proceeded to Friday Wood for a divisional co-operation exercise with 4th Division. The division was concentrated around Framlingham, Suffolk, and during Brigade manoeuvres Squadron aircraft flew from dawn till dusk. On 29 September 1930 S/L S.E. Toomer DFC took command of the Squadron from S/L Probyn who was posted to Hawkinge to command No.25 (F) Squadron. One of the officers serving with the Squadron during those days was P/O (now Group Captain) Richard McMurtie. He was a Squadron pilot between January 1931 and September 1932. He remembers:

'I completed my initial training in December 1930 after a year's course. My flying instructor was a P/O Frank Whittle, who was to claim fame in later years as the father of British jet propulsion. The three of us who passed out top of the course were given choice of our future postings. We all asked to be sent to Manston. We were Silwyn-Roberts, Frank Wintringham and myself. We reported at No.II (AC) Squadron in January 1931. Silwyn-Roberts was nicknamed "Pythagoras" or Pye for his academic achievements. We joined B-Flight while Wintringham went to C-Flight. Our Flight Commander was "Cap" Love.

One day during take off, my engine lost power at fifty feet. I crashed for the first and only time in my entire career in the RAF. I was not injured but taken to hospital suffering from shock. However, our Flight Commander was reprimanded for having failed to carry out an urgent modification to the fuel supply system, specifically to the off-on cock which had been found to cut off the fuel due to vibration. Poor "Cap" Love was replaced by F/L Frank Farrington, a very pleasant World War One pilot who came from the School of Army Co-opertion at Old Sarum. "Pye" and I flew formation with Farrington almost daily. Flights in those days seldom exceeded an hour's duration, so there were a lot of take-offs and landings. However, night flying sorties were always done alone. All future pilots in Army Co-op Squadrons were to qualify for night flying at Old Sarum which meant three months or so away from the Squadron. Farrington was such an excellent instructor that we passed the test without having ever been to Old Sarum. . .

'Our CO was S/L Sydney Toomer, a man who lacked any sense of humor. He suffered from an injured eye, said to have been the results of an apple being hurled at him at a guest night. His wife Topsy liked to entertain the young single officers, but as soon as I left the happy state by getting married, in November 1931, I was earmarked for posting from the Squadron, and eventually went to the Fleet Air Arm. Our Squadron Adjutant was F/O Mole, who wrote a book about those days called *Happy Landings*. We often flew photographic sorties, taking obliques and verticals of archaeological remains, which were very revealing. We also did front camera gun attacks on other aircraft which was great fun. Another typical Army Co-op job was to pick up messages with a hook lowered below the fuselage, called the Stilwell-hook, Stilwell being the Flight Commander of C-Flight.

'At Manston was a man hardly anyone knew except as the Station Commander's batman. His name was Shaw and he loved motorbikes. One morning Shaw was very late returning to Manston. The Station Warrant Officer, who was feared by all, including the young officers, gave Shaw a ticking-off and asked him: "Where have we been last night AC Shaw?" The airman answered that he had been to dinner with the Archbishop of Canterbury and the great George Bernard Shaw himself. The SWO almost had a fit at having to listen to such utter nonsense. It was not until then that it became widely known that AC Shaw was none other than Lawrence of Arabia. . .

'Also based at Manston was No.600 'City of London' Squadron of the Auxiliary Air Force, and the School of Technical Training. Our hangars, however, were known as the "War Flight" and we had to march with the troops across the entire airfield every morning after station parade, in breeches and puttees, hard white collars and shirts. Manston had no runways nor did it have a proper tarmac apron. They tried putting down some kind of heavy oil on the grass edge near the hangars and rolling it in, to form some kind of hard standing. During my time at Manston only one accident happened.'

The accident referred to by Richard McMurtie took place on 27 March 1931. F/O Wintringham and his observer/air gunner AC1 Ellard took off in Atlas J9952 for a local sortie. The weather was clear but with frequent fog patches until about midday, by which time all the fog had cleared. The aircraft of Wintringham and Ellard failed to return. A report was received in the early afternoon that a piece of propeller had been washed up near Herne Bay. It turned out to be a part of J9952. Witnesses said that they had heard an aircraft around 1020 hours and both air and sea search parties set out to try and locate the aeroplane and the crew. The aeroplane was discovered one mile out and taken into Sheerness. Both crew members were dead.

Between 10 April and 1 May 1931 the annual APC took place. The entire Squadron consisting of HQ, A-, B- and C-Flights took part. The Squadron's results were absolutely marvellous; all previous records for AC Squadrons were broken both in air gunnery and bombing. The Operation Record Book proudly mentions the results:

Squadron front gun average: 59.8%

Highest individual front gun average: F/O Silwyn-Roberts with 85.8%

Highest individual Lewis gun average: AC1 Whitehead with 65.0%

Total Squadron gunnery average: 45.0%

With these results the Squadron was the winner of the No.22 Group Air Gunners' Cup which was presented by Air Commodore MacEwen when he visited the Squadron on 3 June. In July the squadron badge was officially approved. It looked much like the existing unofficial one with the difference that the large Roman 'II' made room for the Wake knot and was placed right and left of the roundel. In September 1931 the AOC Inland Area approved the Squadron tie and permission was given to carry the World War One insignia, the black equilateral triangle on the sides of the aircraft. It was not uncommon for foreign pilots to be attached to the Squadron to learn Army Co-operation methods. The first foreign pilots mentioned in the Ops. Record Book were two Iraqis, Lieutenants Yasin and Naji. From then on many foreign pilots have flown with the Squadron up until the present day.

The 1932 Armament Practice Camp was another Squadron victory. F/O Silwyn-Roberts won the Front Gunners Cup for a second time. His result was an amazing 95.75 percent. AC1 Whitehead too repeated his success. In fact the entire Squadron did well and took the Group Air Gunners' Cup back to Manston once again.

The Squadron had influential friends. One of them was Sir Philip Sassoon, the Under-Secretary of State for Air, who visited the Squadron on 8 September 1932. Two months later, on 14 November the Air Member for Personnel, Sir Edward Ellington KCB,CMG,CBE, paid a visit. On 13 January 1933 S/L Fullard assumed command from S/L Toomer. Shortly afterwards the Atlas aircraft were replaced by Hawker Audax biplanes. Only eleven months after taking over S/L Fullard left. The new CO was S/L Green who, incidentally, celebrated his new command by turning the Squadron's only dual control Audax on its back on landing. The aircraft had wheel brakes and Green landed with the brakes on. . . It was a lesson not likely to be forgotten. On 30 June 1934 the Squadron sent six aircraft to take part in the annual RAF Display at Hendon. Three aircraft of B-Flight commanded by F/O

While stationed at Manston the Squadron flew Hawker Audax biplanes. On this 1933 photograph we see, standing from left to right F/O R. Richmond, F/O F. Dixon-Wright P/O M.K. Porter (who retired from the RAF as an Air Marshal), F/O K.N. Smith, F/O C.G. Stowell, F/O L. Olivier, P/O R.G. Stone, F/O Legbone and F/O W.R. Farley, who was the pilot carrying out the first Black Lysander sortie into Occupied France. Seated from left to right are F/O J. Younghusband, F/O L. Cundell, F/L C. Moloney, F/L J. Blackford, S/L P.F. Fullard DSO, MC, AFC (Commanding Officer), F/L T.G. Bird, F/L A.V. Hammond, F/O I.N. Roome and F/O J.J. Murphy.

Murphy and three of C-Flight commanded by F/L Blackford, flew in an immaculate formation performing a message pick-up and a message drop. The APC results that year were, as usual, phenomenal. Murphy wrote in his logbook:

> 'The Squadron was placed as follows, securing an easy best aggregate among the other squadrons:
>
> Pilot's ground target 1st
> Pilot's quarter attack 1st
> Pilot's astern attack.......... 1st
> Air gunner's ground target.......... 1st
> Air gunner's towed 2nd
> Individual diving bombing.......... 4th
> Flight diving bombing.......... 1st
> High altitude bombing .... 3rd'

The Annual Dinner on 10 December 1934 was at the Victoria Hotel in London. Guest of Honour was Air Vice-Marshal Sir Thomas Webb-Bowen, a First World War Squadron pilot.

CHAPTER 4
CLOUDS OVER THE HORIZON

In January 1933, when Germany elected Hitler as the new Chancellor, it seemed as if no-one apart from a few pessimists had any idea of the tremendous changes that were to take place in the years ahead. Yet, a little over a year later, in July 1934, the British government decided that the Royal Air Force was to expand to over forty squadrons in the next five years. Both the Commons and the House of Lords believed this to be ridiculous and that there would never be another war. Had not the new Chancellor, Herr Hitler, spoken of peace? Besides, he was far too busy solving Germany's internal problems. Yet it was known in England that from February 1934 the German economy began preparing for a major war. The last signs of democracy disappeared when on 27 February the Reichstag went up in flames. In June Hitler had his rivals in the SA killed. For the next eight years disarmament negotiations were fruitless; many countries were busy expanding their air forces and thought that Britain should do the same. After long debates the House of Commons came to the conclusion that the RAF should expand to forty-one squadrons. At the same time many young Germans were being trained to become Lufthansa pilots. Every one of them knew that very few would ever fly a commercial airliner as Hitler was building a new and modern air force. In fact he had set himself a clear goal: now that Germany had left the League of Nations it was free to create a military power that would be able to avenge the defeat of 1918. In August the German armed forces had to swear an oath of loyalty to the Führer. Hitler was preparing for war.

In October 1934 a realistic mobilisation exercise took place in Great Britain. Orders to mobilise came on 6 October at 1200 hours. The next morning Flights and Sections began loading up vehicles with all kinds of equipment and at 1830 hours the first reservists arrived at Manston. The following day at 1715 hours the Squadron MT convoy left Manston for Biggin Hill while the aircraft flew to Sealand the next morning. The road convoy drove on to Castle Bromwich and three days after mobilising the entire Squadron had departed from Manston. Who would have believed that less than five years later the Squadron would leave Hawkinge at the same speed but under much more serious circumstances?

In the thirties the Squadron establishment was sixteen aircraft. Each Flight had four, and four more were in the Squadron reserve looked after by the Workshop. The Workshops, although part of the Squadron and presided over by a Warrant Officer-Engineer, were really a miniature maintenance unit. Minor and major inspections were done by the Flights. Overhauls on time-expired engines, major airframe repairs and modifications were all done by the Workshops.

On 1 July 1935 the Squadron participated in the Royal Review at Mildenhall. Three weeks later a new CO came. His name was Desoer, his nickname was Dizzy. . . On 1 January 1936 the Squadron's Nominal Roll showed the following names:

Commanding Officer: S/L N.L. Desoer.
A-Flight: F/L T.F. Maloney (Flt.Cdr.), F/O A.A.N. Malan and P/Os C.L. Dann, C.F. Sassly, G.P. Flew and R.K. Jeffries.
B-Flight: F/L F.A.R. Mangles (Flt.Cdr.), F/Os A.J.W. Geddes and P.W. Stansfeld, P/Os P.W Ashton, D.H. Hatfield and B.G. Carroll
C-Flight: F/L A.V. Hammond (Flt.Cdr.), F/Os F.A. Paynter and R.C.M. Ferrers, P/Os J.W. Deacon and R.P. Widdowsen.
Adjutant and Signals Officer F/L Watson
Stores: P/O Salmon; Accounts: F/O Stewell;
ALOs Lts. F. Festing and S.E.N. Everett.
Warrant Officers: W.S.A Steward and C.F. Hayward.

In February 1936, on the formation of the Air Defence of Great Britain, No.22 (AC) Group and its squadrons left Inland Area and became part of Fighter Command. During the same year, a very unfortunate accident took place involving a Squadron aircraft. It was Empire Air Day at Hawkinge on 23 May. Many spectators had arrived at the aerodrome to see immaculate formation flying and dazzling aerobatics by single aircraft. Three aeroplanes of No.II (AC) Squadron were detailed to attack a cardboard fortress which had been built in the centre of the airfield. For the viewers' excitement the fortress had been sprayed with petrol and covered with tar to ensure a spectacular view once the attacking aircraft had disappeared. A three-ship formation led by F/O Geddes flew over Folkestone in line astern and swept down for the kill. After leaving the enemy stronghold burning and smoking two of the three Audax biplanes climbed steeply away from the target. Contrary to the

Follygate, also known as Okehampton Landing Ground, was the most dangerous of all ALGs. It was situated on the crest of a hill, the top being marked by the white circle. Follygate did not allow pilots to make mistakes while coming in for a landing (1936).

Friday Wood was the other ALG where the Squadron spent a couple of weeks each year. These pictures were taken on 30 July 1936 from 500 and 2,000 feet respectively. The bell tents are visible as are the cook house and the Officers' Mess. Friday Wood farm is in the right upper corner of both photographs.

briefing one aeroplane remained at low level and seemed to want to add to the suspense by leaving the target as near to the ground as possible. Sadly, the pilot P/O Ashton did not appear to notice the HT cables about two miles west of the aerodrome. With a flash the Audax hit the wires and exploded, killing Ashton and his air gunner LAC Simpson. It was a sad ending to a beautiful day.

Two of the best known places among pre-war members of the Squadron were Follygate and Friday Wood. Follygate was situated in Devon and it was probably the most isolated, small and difficult of all Advanced Landing Grounds the Squadron ever used. It was located on the crest of a very steep hill about one mile north of the town of Okehampton which is part of Dartmoor and 144 metres above sea level. There still is a steep climb along the A386 road from Okehampton to Heatherleight leading to a minute grass strip, surrounded by stone walls. Follygate however had exceptional rainfall and was often hidden for days in fog. It was one of the strangest landing grounds to be used regularly in bad weather. The field was bounded by walls six feet high and was one of the very few places in the country where the 2/6d Rambling Fine was not in force. Usually every landing on an airfield was done as a practice forced landing, use of the engine was not allowed below 1,000 feet. If someone was caught using the engine they would be fined half-a-crown to be paid immediately after landing. At Follygate, however, an entirely different type of approach was necessary. One had to do a normal engine-off approach to the top of the rear wall at the start of the selected strip. The strip then appeared to rise 50-100 feet, ending in a blind crest with a narrow gap on the wall. At this point there was usually a good deal of turbulence, particularly if the pilot was lucky enough to land with the wind blowing in the direction of the strip, which did not happen very often. Just before reaching the lower wall the pilot applied full throttle and pulled the nose right up to get the right angle of attack to the slope. Then the wheels would hit the turf while the aeroplane still had an airspeed considerably higher than normally used for landings. It was therefore necessary to ensure the aircraft stopped by the time it reached the top of the hill. If this was not possible, as soon as one reached the crest it was a matter of quickly applying fully throttle again to get airborne as fast as possible to try another landing. It was more like landing on an aircraft carrier, wondering if the hook was going to catch the wire, than landing on an airfield. The pilots were certainly very careful on approach into Follygate.

From the airfield the Squadron could watch the artillery firing their volleys. Okehampton

Camp Artillery Range started one mile south of the town and extended over most of Dartmoor. The highest point on the Moors was Yes Tor, some 600 metres above sea level. Flying here could be quite tricky, especially as the aircraft engines were notoriously unreliable and could fail at a moment's notice. Flying being somewhat different from the present day a pilot would make a quick decision and land at the nearest suitable spot. David Allfree, an air gunner who frequently flew with F/O Geddes had vivid memories of sorties ending this way:

> 'We were sent out to look for the artillery which had concealed their guns in amongst trees and hedgerows. The reflections from their accroutrements always seemed to give them away. Geddes, who was a seconded Artillery officer always looked for polished brass. He would say to me: "They are so keen on their brass. It always betrays them. Let's go for brass, Allfree". Once he had spotted them their position was sent by Morse code or we would drop a message container near "our" troops. On one occasion Geddes' engine suddenly cut. He force-landed on the side of a hillock surrounded by trees. After the mechanics had been informed they arrived and sorted out the problem. Once the aircraft was ready Geddes decided that he would save them the trouble of dismantling the aircraft and loading in onto a trailer. He wanted to take off but I was not at all happy with this. Geddes told the airmen to sit on the tail and warned the others not to pull the chocks away until he gave the signal to do so, then he applied full throttle and gave the signal. The chocks were pulled away and the airmen on the tail slid off. Within fifty yards the Audax was airborne. In the Mess Geddes was the talk of the town that night. Some said he was a bloody fool, others silently hoped to be able to fly as brilliantly as he did. Anyway, I must have been a participant in the shortest take-off ever by an Audax . . .

Apart from observing the Army during exercises, artillery spotting was a routine occupation. Yet it was not without its dangers as it entailed ultra-low flying near the volleys of exploding shells. The Audax aircraft lost many aerial weights when the aerials touched the ground. The static, when there was any nimbus cloud about, was terrific and often after the air gunner had finished winding out the aerial and applying its brake, the pilot had to tell him not to touch the contact plunger on the aerial wire because of the warning electric flashes whenever he put his hand near it. It was not safe to touch again until one was flying clear of cloud and its static charge. The pilots used a Morse key for reporting artillery observations in those days and it was not unusual for the pilots to get an electric shock while using the Morse key. Once he managed to get his hand off the key it would make a crackling blue flash about five inches long which was not very pleasant while flying at 500 feet over the rocky moor.

Although there was little entertainment at Follygate, many pilots have happy memories of the Devonshire couple that lived in a nearby cottage. For a fixed price they provided the officers of the Squadron with three good meals a day served in their own cottage parlour. Many former members still remember the scrumptious breakfasts of porridge and Devonshire cream.

P/O (now Group Captain) R. Keith Jeffries arrived at Hawkinge in January 1936, having spent two years at the RAF College, Cranwell. He remembers what a demanding job it was to fly an Army Co-op aircraft. The pilot had to do everything as well as flying and navigating the aircraft. For instance, on a reconnaissance sortie, he had to search out enemy activity on the ground, locate its position on the map, write out a report and transmit it to base in Morse code. 'Possibly one of the hardest tasks was photographic reconnaissance', he remembers. 'A mosaic or photographic map involved flying the aircraft in a dead straight line, without varying height or speed and pressing the camera operating button every few seconds. Then one had to repeat this several times on parallel courses at precise distances from each other.'

Three squadron pilots during the good old pre-war days. From left to right: R.A.G. Petrie, D.B. Hatfield and A.J.W. Geddes.

All these various duties and skills meant that a highly intensive training system was essential if pilots were to be proficient in all of them. Initially it was left to individual Flight Commanders to evolve their own training programmes within the framework of the annual winter APC which was for a month of aerial gunnery and bombing practice. This often involved operating the aircraft from open land, not a prepared airfield, such as Salisbury Plain or the Downs on the South Coast, with the entire Squadron under canvas. Eventually the Squadron Commander decided that all three Flights were to adopt the training programme Andrew Geddes had carried out with B-Flight. In due course Group introduced it for all Army Co-op Squadrons under its control.

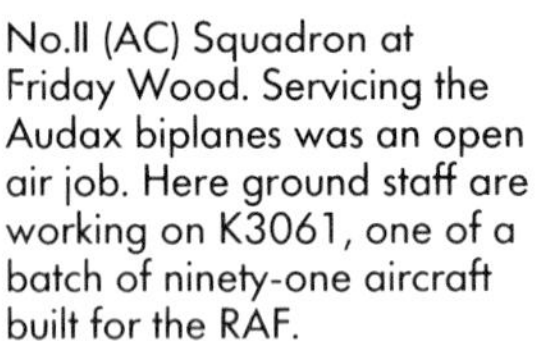

No.II (AC) Squadron at Friday Wood. Servicing the Audax biplanes was an open air job. Here ground staff are working on K3061, one of a batch of ninety-one aircraft built for the RAF.

Hawkinge was a delightful station to live on. The Officers' Mess was a well-appointed, large and modern building. The officers were waited upon hand and foot by staff who served them their drinks in the ante-room, beer in silver tankards and attended them at formal dinner each evening. Apart from weekends, when lounge suits were allowed, in the mess everyone was required to wear mess dress or dinner jackets each evening, involving the usual struggle with starched shirts, winged collars, recalcitrant studs and cuff links; all for the purpose of sitting down to a lengthy meal lacking any real gastronomic merit . . . During the day pilots would wear smart white flying overalls emblazoned with the Squadron crest. It was official policy that about fifty per cent of the Army Co-operation squadron pilots should be Army officers. Not every RAF officer liked the idea. Mike Pedley recalls his feelings when he arrived at Hawkinge in June 1936 as a newly-fledged Pilot Officer:

'I was dismayed, on arrival, to find at least half the officers wearing various regimental uniforms. I had just been painstakingly indoctrinated in the traditions of the Royal Air Force and my loyalty was exclusively to that service. I later came to understand the philosophy giving rise to the joint-service manning of Army co-operation units but I never appreciated the need for it, or its desirability. Each of our armed forces had its particular characteristics and set of values. When Army officers attained positions of authority in their Squadrons in my opinion they were wont to place undue stress on matters of "ceremonial" and to have such inflexible attitudes to discipline as to tend to stifle the initiative and "press-on" spirit inherent in their Royal Air Force subordinates.'

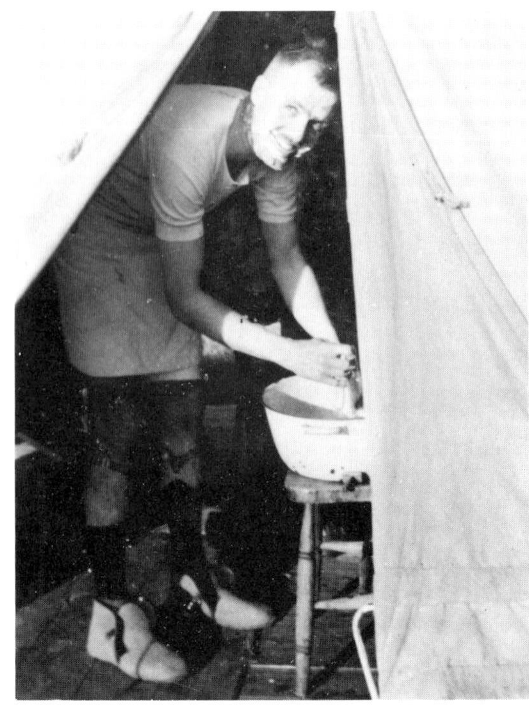

Right: At Friday Wood the Squadron lived under rather primitive conditions. Yet it was considered the most pleasant of all ALGs. Often wives and girlfriends visited. Many dogs would join their masters at Friday Wood.

In 1937 the Squadron's Nominal Roll was as follows:
Squadron Commander: S/L Desoer.
A-Flight: Flight Commander F/L A.A.N. Malan (Royal Tank Corps). Pilots: F/O A.C.G. Wimbush (Royal Tank Corps), P/O R.K. Jeffries (RAF), P/O M.G.F. Pedley (RAF) and P/O C.B.E. Burt-Andrews (RAF).
B-Flight: Flight Commander F/L A.J.W. Geddes (Royal Artillery). Pilots: F/O P.W. Stansfeld (Royal Tank Corps), F/O D.B. Hatfield (RAF), P/O B.G. Carroll (RAF), P/O J.G. Fowle (RAF) and P/O J. Butterworth (RAF).
C-Flight: Flight Commander F/L F.A. Paynter (RAF). Pilots: F/O R.C.M. Ferrers (Cameron Highlanders), F/O Deacon (Dorsets), P/O G.P. Flew (RAF), P/O P.J. Edinger (RAF) and P/O M.G.F. Petrie (RAF).
Adjutant: F/L C.L. Dann; Signals Officer: F/L A.C. Watson; Equipments Officer: P/O R.J. Folley; Accounts Officer: F/O C.G. Sharp. The ALOs were Captains Festing and Everett.

Before No.II Squadron said goodbye to the faithful Audax a last great event took place. Long-distance flights had been very popular since Italo Balbo had crossed the Atlantic with a formation of twenty-five Savoia Marchetti 55X floatplanes from Orbetello in Italy to New York and back to Rome in 1933. F/L Geddes decided that something similar, though on a much smaller scale, could be done by No.II Squadron. He therefore prepared and asked permission for a long-distance flight around Britain by four Squadron Audax biplanes. Strangely enough nothing has been recorded about this flight in the Squadron Operations Record Book. Yet it must have been an expedition demanding a lot of preparation, maintenance, navigation and flying. The initial idea was to fly from Hawkinge to Catterick and then on to Leuchars, Inverness, John O'Groats, Abbotsinch, West Freugh, Aldergrove, Sealand, Filton, Land's End, Old Sarum and back to Hawkinge. While flying this route, oblique photographs were to be taken of three of the aircraft over principal points to show that the four had actually been there. Secondly the enterprise would show the usefulness of long-range reconnaissance. A whole string of support bases covered the route. Overnight maintenance was organised and fuel depots were established. Compasses were swung to ensure they were accurate and many maps were studied. The four pilots flew repeatedly during good and bad weather, both by day and night.

On the morning of 19 April 1937, the four aircraft took off from Hawkinge. If all went well they would touch down at their station again in three days. The first leg from Hawkinge

Three officers of the Squadron, their cars, a lady friend and a dog. Left to right are Peter Stansfeld, Andrew Geddes and Basil Carroll. Carroll was to earn a George Cross in 1940 for flying an autogiro behind the German lines, landing and destroying a large petrol and equipment store abandoned by the BEF before the German troops were able to use any of it.

to Catterick went very smoothly. Then, unfortunately the weather deteriorated. It turned out to be impossible to fly from Leuchars to John O'Groats. Therefore Geddes decided the formation was to head for Nova and Iona and then to proceed to Abbotsinch near Glasgow. The Met Office at Leuchars, however, forecast a depression coming from the northwest, which could mean the group would run into fuel problems having to fly dead against the air stream. While they flew over Inverness the barometer dropped rapidly. Geddes turned down into the Great Glen, past Fort Augustus and Loch Arking to head for Fort William. As the clouds thickened they took photographs of Ben Nevis. Before they reached Oban the front caught up with them. Flying just under the cloud base they continued to Loch Linnie, Connell Bridge, Loch Ehoe, Pass of Brander, Gladich, Glen Aray and Inverary. There the four made a sharp turn to Dundarve Point. When they entered Hells Glen they saw the clouds covering the mountain tops. After landing at Abbotsinch it was found that the Audaxes had only enough fuel for ten more minutes flying.

Between November 1935 and September 1939 No.II (AC) Squadron was stationed at RAF Hawkinge.

The remainder of the Balbo was a piece of cake. Beautiful pictures were taken and all the sites were passed over as planned. Nothing could stop the four aircraft from a glorious return at Hawkinge. However, while approaching Hawkinge from the west Geddes unwound his trailing aerial to contact base and ask for a final weather report. At Hawkinge the weather was appalling. The famous Hoodoo had arrived and entirely covered the aerodrome. The worst thing that could happen to the eight crew members was to have to land at any other airfield than their own. Geddes knew that everyone at Hawkinge was waiting for them. The aircraft circled for half an hour until one of the pilots saw some thin cloud. The aircraft descended, lit their Holt flares and made a glorious though rather speedy landing. The Squadron's honour had been saved. Later in the year, in June, the Squadron made headlines quite differently. Both Hawkinge Squadrons, Nos.II and 25 were involved in an exercise in formation flying. Each squadron had nine aircraft in the air. No.25 Squadron, flying line abreast headed out to the sea while No.II Squadron flew inland in a similar formation. So far so good, but what eighteen pilots didn't know was that both formations

Groundcrew servicing Hawker Audax biplanes at Friday Wood. All work was done in the open air. It speaks for the professionalism of the technical staff that aircraft were never unserviceable while on detachment at Friday Wood.

were at the same altitude on exactly opposite courses . . . Now eighteen aircraft were approaching each other at about 800 feet, less than half a mile apart, no-one realising that southern England was about to see the greatest mid-air collision in the history of British aviation. Then the first pilots spotted what looked like little spots on their windscreens. In seconds these spots changed into real aeroplanes, it seemed as if a giant hand suddenly scattered two immaculate formations. Audaxes and Furies were all over the sky, their pilots with adrenalin furiously pumping. By some miracle they all got away with it and all the aircraft landed safely. As far as former members can recollect it was the first time in the history of Hawkinge that a Station Commander allowed the Mess bar to be opened for drinks at mid-day. Rumours have it that no more alcohol was available by 1400 hours . . .

Each year No.II (AC) Squadron sent a composite Flight to Friday Wood near Colchester for co-operation with Army units such as 11th Infantry Brigade. Friday Wood consisted of a small landing ground at Friday Wood Farm, Berechurch, about two miles south of the town. It was a very quiet spot in the middle of beautiful countryside. The field itself was a square grass landing area which was about 600 yards from east to west and a little over 300 yards from north to south. However, the Squadron was faced with a typical No.II Squadron problem. Around the field were high elms, making it virtually impossible to use more than half of the field when coming in to land and causing considerable problems when attempting a normal airfield take-off. Since this problem was too big even for the Squadron it was decided that a gap was to be cut in the row of elms: if the Squadron did not interfere with nature, nature would seriously interfere with the Squadron. Although Friday Wood was only a flight-sized detachment, life was quite pleasant. There was a full camp quota of tentage with a mobile generator, water lorries, a petrol-cooking tender and a W/T station tender. Squadron officers were automatically honorary members of the Colchester garrison Officers' Club. Even the Squadron pets, a number of goldfish, would accompany the Flight to its destination. Like all self-respecting mascots the fish were to make the trip to Friday Wood by air. All went well up until the moment when the Audax was climbing over London. Suddenly the air gunner warned the pilot not to climb any higher. 'The fish are blowing up like balloons, Sir'. The pilot immediately descended to a safer altitude and the goldfish arrived at Friday Wood shaken but still alive.

Many people on their way to Mersea Island would come and invite members of the Squadron to their own social events. Needless to say, the young, dashing and single pilots were most welcome with the girls. They were happy days. Life in the RAF was rather akin to being a member of an exclusive club. Petrol was five pence a gallon and, as a former Squadron pilot remembers, like all pilots, No.II Squadron officers 'were popular with aspiring young actresses and they were assured of a full month's leave in summer and winter. After the last exercise the Squadron would go off en masse skiing in Switzerland.' Friday Wood was popular too since Mersea Island was only four miles south of the Landing Ground, and since it was a very nice spot for yachting, the Squadron enjoyed many trips on the North Sea. The two Squadron ALOs Captains Freddie Festing and George Everett kept their yachts at Mersea Island and all ranks took full advantage of the Squadron's 'private fleet'. Festing's yacht was called *Green Jacket* as her owner was a very proud member of the Rifle Brigade. George Everett had sailed his yacht *Tai Mo San* all the way from Singapore to England. Both ships were ten-tonners, Fastnet race types and beautifully kept. Every individual member of the Squadron was quite willing to work hard to keep both yachts in top shape. In winter Festing and Everett sailed their boats back to Folkestone where they spent the winter.

During the big army manoeuvres of 1937 an Experimental Communications Squadron was incorporated into No.II (AC) Squadron. A gaggle of light aircraft were sent to Friday Wood for a month's practice trials. Andrew Geddes, then commanding B-Flight was made 'OC E.C. Squadron'. All aircraft had civilian markings and were of all shapes and types. Geddes had the Vega Gull prototype G-AEYC made by Percival at Luton and used it as a communications aircraft: It landed in fields more often than on actual aerodromes, yet he never pranged it. It was a highly polished light blue monoplane, the Squadron kept it with its wings folded in its very own marquee with just the tail sticking out. As a result of the trials the Vega Gull was put into service as the Percival Proctor. It became famous in the hands of Jean Batten, who flew a Gull from England to Australia in October 1937. Geddes' flying career was nearly brought to an early conclusion while flying the Gull. When flying it solo it was better to have a healthy load of ballast, like a large bag of sand in the locker behind the rear seats. One day Geddes flew from Friday Wood to Hawkinge to see S/L Desoer for lunch and discuss some Squadron matters. He got into the Gull, took off and happily flew southwest. While he was airborne, however, one of the Flight Sergeants rang up the Squadron stores at Hawkinge for a consignment of stores. These included a number of heavy tins of paint. He told the people at the stores that the Flight Commander was on his way to Hawkinge. Since

During the famous No.II Squadron Balbo many photographs were taken from one of the aircraft. Here three Audaxes fly over Glengarry, Scotland, in close vic formation.

he was coming back before nightfall he might as well bring everything with him to Friday Wood. While Geddes was having his meeting friendly hands loaded the Gull, pushing the somewhat awkward sandbag to the far back end of the locker. Then they closed the little hatch. After finishing his interview with Desoer, Geddes returned to the Gull without checking the locker behind him. On take-off he found the Gull a bit tail-heavy. However, since it was a nice day he enjoyed the beautiful panorama of the Thames and the countryside around it. When arriving over Friday Wood Geddes wanted to show off a bit and put the Gull into a spin to lose altitude. He found immediately that the centre of gravity was much too far aft. The Gull went into a flat spin, actually the first one ever made in such an aircraft. It took Geddes all the way down to recover and at one moment he could predict almost exactly where he was going to crash. Once on the ground the reason for the Gull's extraordinary behaviour was soon found. Geddes always checked the locker of his aircraft after that day . . .

Flying trials were a popular occupation among the pilots. No less than fourteen different aircraft appeared at Friday Wood. The Squadron flew the Cierva Autogiro, Monospar, Vega Gull, Tiger Moth, Puss Moth, Moth Minor, Klemm Swallow, 6, Tipsy, Miles Whitney Straight, Hawker Tomtit, Avro Tutor, Miles Falcon and Magister. It was a most enjoyable, very interesting and extremely competitive time. Serviceability was no problem. If any aircraft developed a problem the pilot just picked up the phone and called the manufacturer. Anything wrong would be put right in no time at all especially if the pilot mentioned loosely that he might have to file an official report. Aircraft factories were bending over backwards to keep the Squadron happy and a lot of smiling civilians could be seen at Friday Wood.

For some of the RAF officers, Army language could be difficult to understand. One day during the 1937 manoeuvres a young F/O ran into problems when he was faced with an Army request. While the Flight Commander was out in his Vega Gull he had put the young officer in charge of daily life at Friday Wood. One of his responsibilities was the incoming and outgoing telephone calls. One of the first incoming calls came from the General in charge of the Exercise Directing Staff. He called from Exercise Control at Bedford and said with a very country voice: 'I say, old chap, are you the commander of those little aeroplanes?' Before the young subaltern could answer that he had merely been put in charge for the day, the general continued: 'Well,

Above: 'David', the famous Squadron mascot with P/O Keith Jeffries in the air gunner's cockpit of a Hawker Audax, 1936.

Squadron officers in front of an Audax at RAF Hawkinge, November 1936. Standing left to right: P/O R.F. Folley, F/O B.G. Carroll, F/O D.B. Hatfield, P/O G.P. Flew, Captain F. Festing (ALO), Lt. G. Everett (GLO) F/O R.K. Jeffries, F/O P Edinger and P/O J.G. Towle. Seated left to right: F/O C. Dann, F/O F.A. Paynter, F/O A.J.W. Geddes, F/O R.C.M. Ferrers, S/L Desoer (OC), F/L A.C. Watson, F/O P.W. Stansfeld and F/O J.W. Deacon. Dogs were prominent pets in No.II (AC) Squadron as the photograph shows.

that is very nice. Now listen, I hear you have this G2 laying about at your airfield. This is the place where all the action is and I wonder if you could oblige? Of course you can. Marvellous. I want your G2 over here at once. Make it snappy, won't you. Thanks ever so much, old chap', and hung up. The poor Flying Officer, having no idea whatsoever what a G2 might be, turned to the only source of wisdom available in moments of near disaster, the Flight Sergeant. In those days the best solution to almost any problem was: 'When in doubt, go and see Flight'. The Flight Sergeant, when asked, had no idea what the general wanted either. In his work he never dealt with General Staff Officers Grade Two. Of course it was impossible for him to admit to this young officer that even Flight was puzzled. He did some serious thinking and then said to the F/O: You remember the Flight Commander leaving in the Gull this morning, Sir? His own aircraft is still here and the G2 is still in it. The general must need the G2 gun camera and wants you to have it taken out of the Commander's aircraft.' Grateful for the solution of his problems the F/O ordered the Flight Commander's gun camera to be removed at once. The camera was carefully packed and crated. Half an hour later a staff car rushed to Exercise Control with the crate accompanied by a Pilot Officer. One can imagine the General's amazement when an hour and a half after his phone call a young RAF officer entered the room, threw a very smart salute and put a wrapped box on the table, saying: 'Here is No.II Squadron's G2, Sir. It would be appreciated if the Flight Commander could have it back today as it takes a while to put it back in again, Sir . . .'

Once a year some RAF stations were invaded by dashing young men in RAF uniforms, clearly very wealthy, driving beautiful fast cars and treating life as a big joke. Their arrival was watched with great worry by senior Flight Sergeants and Station Warrant Officers. The Auxiliary Air Force had arrived for its annual Summer Camp. Each year RAF Lympne would receive No.601 'County of London' Squadron, AAF. At nearby Hawkinge many regulars prepared for the annual 'exchange of views'. Rivalry between the RAF and AAF was intense. Some said the difference between them was that the RAF officer was an officer who behaved like a gentleman, while the AAF officer was a gentleman who behaved like an officer. Clashes between them would virtually destroy Messes and often ended in near disasters, but all in good spirit, old chap. Many pre-war members of No.II (AC) Squadron remember the brawls and in particular one incident which caused rather unpleasant circumstances with top brass. One day No.601 Squadron decided that it was necessary to fly their Hawker Demons to Hawkinge and carry out a bombing attack on the

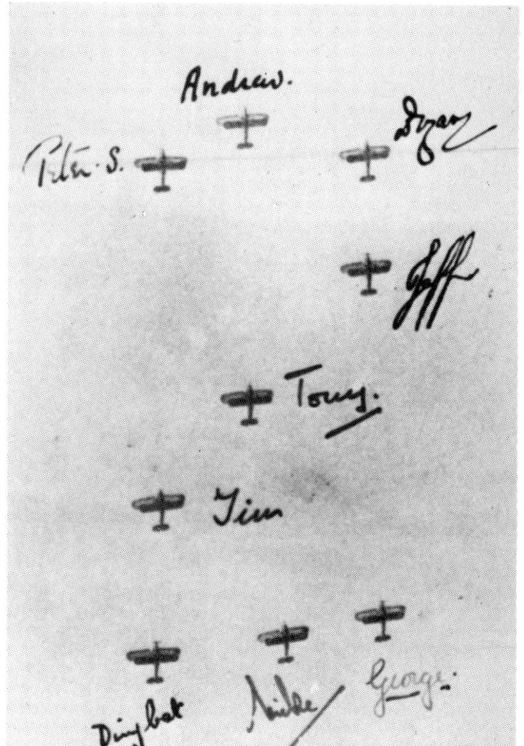

The first known photograph of Squadron aircraft while flying their famous 'II'. This picture was taken on the occasion of the 25th anniversary of 'Shiny Two'. The participating pilots are Peter Stansfeld, Andrew Geddes, Bryan Hatfield, Keith Jeffries, Tony Malan, Tim Wimbush, Peter 'Dingbat' Edinger, Mike Pedley and George Flew. The 25th Anniversary coincided with Empire Air Day. In 1987, at the 75th Anniversary the same formation was flown by Jaguars of the Squadron.

Hawkinge Officers' Mess with bags full of chalk and soot and many, many rolls of toilet paper. 'Group' was not pleased at all and a stern warning came that under no, repeat no circumstances were Service aircraft to be used for such purposes. No.601 Squadron clearly understood the meaning and returned the next day for a second attack, this time flying a gaggle of private aircraft. Unfortunately the wind was not on the Auxiliaries side and all 'bombs' landed at Hawkinge cemetery, colouring it with a mixture of black, white and pink. The Church was not amused and soon afterwards a joint force of regulars and auxiliaries could be seen scrubbing head stones and collecting the remains of a glorious flying display.

In February 1937 rumours spread that the Audax was soon to be replaced by a new aircraft. On 1 November 1937 the new Hawker Hectors arrived. Instead of the sleek Kestrel engine it had a Napier Dagger, an unusual looking 24-cylinder air-cooled engine with its cylinders arranged in a 'cross-H' section. The swept-back wing gave way to a straight one. The Hector was faster than the Audax, by just seventeen miles per hour. The service ceiling was 24,000 feet. It carried a Vickers forward gun and a Lewis gun aft. Below the wings was room for two eleven-pound bombs or two containers. It was the last Army Co-operation biplane.

On 10 December 1937 No.II (AC) Squadron celebrated its 25th Anniversary with a Squadron Jubilee Dinner at the Hotel Victoria in London. It was the last official function before S/L Desoer

After the Audax the Squadron flew twenty-four-cylinder Hawker Hectors. In this photograph taken in 1937 F/L Andrew Geddes and his air gunner LAC Bengres have returned from a sortie. On the tail the six-pointed star with the Squadron crest can be seen. Underneath the lower wing is a supply container.

Squadron Leader Opie, OC No.II (AC) Squadron from 21 January 1938 until 29 April 1939.

left upon his promotion to Wing Commander. He was succeeded by S/L W.A. 'Bill' Opie. One of the young pilots joining in early 1938 was P/O (now Group Captain OBE) Brian Walford. He came straight from the School of Army Co-operation in the Spring of that year. He was the proud owner of a 1927 Austin Seven and it was in this vehicle that he arrived outside the Hawkinge Officers' Mess. Walford remembers:

> 'Making my way through the swing doors of the entrance to sign in, I saw that there was a party in progress in the Ladies Room. The door of this room was open and through it an officer emerged. He had cropped hair, a clipped moustache and smoked a pipe as one would expect of a Regular. He was a Gunner. He introduced himself as Andrew Geddes and made me welcome, ushering me into the party with introductions all around. He asked how I had got to Hawkinge and I said that my Austin was outside. He wished me a pleasant evening and then disappeared. A short time later he returned to the party and said that some idiot had parked his car inside the Mess hall. We all peered through the door and to my horror I saw my little Austin occupying the centre of the reception area. Geddes thought it was a terrific joke. I did not . . .'

The arrival of the Hector was a boost for the Squadron's morale. At the same time, No.25 Squadron had to hand in their Hawker Fury MkIIs and received old Demons in return. Suddenly No.II Squadron was faster than the fighter pilots. From that moment on all made sure that regular encounters between both Squadrons took place over Kent. The big joke was to form up on the Demons, smile at its pilots, then give full throttle and leave with a very kind but extremely demoralising wave of the hand. For a while it was great to be an Army Co-op pilot.

As mentioned earlier Sir Philip Sassoon, the Under-Secretary of State for Air, was a great friend of No.II (AC) Squadron. Andrew Geddes and Tim Wimbush, and a No.25 Squadron pilot Max Upton often flew Sir Philip's private Percival Q6, G-AFFD, a luxury twin-engine executive plane. Sassoon lived at nearby Port Lympne and had an airfield near his house. He frequently entertained officers, often sending his Q6 over to collect them. Once when the Squadron was on detachment in Northern Ireland, Sassoon lent them the Q6 to enable the men to go home for weekends. Once a year Sir Philip organised a dinner for the officers of No.II (AC) Squadron at his Park Lane house. Anyone who stayed overnight experienced the incredible when in the morning at breakfast, in bed of course, they would not only be presented with the major British papers but with any newspaper of their choice, British or foreign.

While at Friday Wood the Squadron was informed that the Hector was to be replaced by a new, specially designed Army Co-operation aircraft. It was the Westland-built Lysander. Peter Stansfield had the honour of collecting the very first MkI from the factory at Yeovil. W/C George, Hawkinge's Station Commander, laid on a special reception for Peter and duly presented him with a large six-pointed star 'For Valour' on a long red ribbon. Andrew Geddes flew in the second 'Lizzie'. He could not resist doing a bit of aerobatics before touching down. Throwing the Lysander into a loop and making a slow roll Geddes noticed a slight fall-off in flying performance. Once on the ground it was found that a hinge had snapped on the brake-slots. All Lizzies were modified at the factory to prevent such an event happening again. As for the time being the Hectors remained with the Squadron, in September 1938 it had the incredible number of thirty-two aircraft at its disposal . . .

The Lysander was a two-seat high-wing monoplane. It had a metal structure and was fabric covered. The aircraft had a 890 horsepower Bristol Mercury XII radial engine. For the first time both pilot and air gunner had a closed cockpit which was quite an improvement after having flown in an open 'office' for all those years. With a maximum speed of 219 mph the Lysander was faster than the Hector. It could cover a distance of 600 miles and go as high as 26,000 feet. Two fixed .303 guns pointed forward while the air gunner had a .303 machine gun in his cockpit. Underneath the two small stub wings on the landing gear six tiny bombs could be carried. For the first time the Squadron had a camouflaged aircraft. This had been ordered for all aircraft after tensions on the Continent seemed to make war inevitable. Britain was not at all prepared. All ranks were recalled from leave and no-one was allowed to leave Hawkinge without a pass. Buildings were being camouflaged and thousands of sandbags were stored in the Clerk of Works' building. In spite of all these tensions the Squadron celebrated with great pomp and circumstance the wedding of one of their ALOs, Captain Freddie Festing. Being somewhat older than most of the officers Freddie was quite content with his posting with the Squadron. Little could he know that during the Second World War he would become famous when as a general he single-handedly charged a Japanese machine gun post and killed the occupants. After the war Freddie Festing as a Field Marshal would become the Chief of the Imperial General Staff.

During the Munich crisis of September 1938 all Squadron Lysanders received type B roundels and medium grey code letters KO were adopted. The aircraft were camouflaged dark green and dark brown with silver undersides. In spite of the German march into the Sudetenland it seemed that the international situation had become more peaceful. On 15 October 1938 there was a Reunion Dinner at the Saint Stephen's Tavern, Westminster Bridge, London. On 4 November several ex-members were invited to attend a Guest Night in the Officers' Mess while on the 13th no less than forty Old Boys who had served with 'Shiny Two' during the Great War spent the day with the Squadron at Hawkinge. Some of them were taken up in the sky again. One of them being Captain Whitten-Brown who had been a German POW and who had crossed the Atlantic with Alcock in 1919.

George Flew flying a Hector over Southern England.

Keith Jeffries demonstrating the pick-up hook at Hawkinge on 13 May 1938.

Before the War, Squadron officers continued to wear the parent regiment uniforms. On this photograph of November 1937 the officers sit in front of a Hector. Standing left to right: P/Os J.G. Towle, P.F. Edinger, M.G.F Pedley, F/Os J.D. Green, R.K. Jeffries, P/Os R.A.G. Petrie, T.D. Calnan and F.G.C. Gilbert. Seated left to right: Lt. A.C.G. Wimbush, F/O D.B. Hatfield, Lt. P.W. Stansfeld, Capt. A.A.N. Malan, S/L N.L. Desoer (CO), F/L M.K.D. Porter, Lt. J.K.M. Drysdale, P/O G.P. Flew and Lt. I.C.B. Worthington-Wilmer.

On 1 January 1939 the Nominal Roll read:
Officer Commanding: S/L W.A. Opie.
A-Flight: Flight Commander F/L H.W. Starr (RAF). Pilots: F/O E.J.M. Lang (Sherwood Foresters), P/O J.K. Rogers (RAF) and P/O I.L.M. Hallam (RAF).
B-Flight: Flight Commander F/L A.F. Anderson (Royal Warwickshire Regiment). Pilots: F/L I.C.B. Worthington-Wilmer (Royal Tank Corps), F/O R.A.G. Petrie (RAF), P/O G.B. Walford (RAF).
C-Flight: Flight Commander F/L P.W. Stansfeld (Royal Tank Corps). Pilots: F/L J.K.M. Drysdale (Royal Scots), F/O F.M. Benito (Prince of Wales Volunteers), F/O P.F. Edinger (RAF), P/O C.F.M. Chapman (RAF).
Adjutant: F/O J.D. Green (RAF); Signals Officer: F/L M.K.D. Porter (RAF); Equipment Officer: P/O R.G.J. White (RAF); Accountants Officer: F/O T.P.F. Trudgian (RAF); ALO: Major H.M. Whitcombe (Royal Engineers); Warrant Officers: D.W. Hamilton and S.G. Lucas (both RAF).

In April 1939 the Squadron carried out Fighter Affiliation exercises with No.64 Squadron at Church Fenton. At about the same time the news came that a new CO would take the Squadron from S/L Opie. On 1 May 1939 Andrew Geddes who had temporarily left the Squadron for a tour of duty with the Royal Artillery, assumed command. His arrival coincided with a visit of aviation journalists who had been invited to see the Lysander perform. There was a reason for this visit. Three days earlier, on 28 April disaster struck when at about 1500 hours a Squadron Lysander took off to give an air display for a group of visiting Army soldiers. On board were F/O R.A.G. Petrie and his air gunner AC2 Stacey. Part of the demonstration consisted of a very slow flypast at the end of a series of fast low passes. The Lizzie was literally hanging on its flaps and slots and all were very impressed. About 100 feet in front of the spectators Petrie made a 180 degree turn. In doing so he stalled the aircraft. It plummeted to the ground and burst into flames. Geddes sprinted to the wreckage to try and save the crew, but the flames beat him back and both men perished. The same day Geddes took off and carried out the same manoeuvres as Petrie, but at a higher altitude. He too went into a stall but was saved by his altitude and was able to recover the aircraft. After this test however, clear restrictions were imposed upon operations at low altitude with slow speed.

On 10 May 1939 the magazine *Aeroplane* wrote an extensive article about the capacities of the Lysander with the title 'A Spartan Demonstration'. Yet no mention was made of Petrie's accident when the article appeared.

> 'The Air Ministry and Westland Aircraft Ltd. combined on May 1 to stage a demonstration of the Westland Lysander II two-seat Army Co-operation monoplane (905hp Bristol Perseus XII) with No. II (AC) Squadron as the demonstration medium. There was legendary justification for hoping that May 1 might be seasonably fine, but the historical reverse happened, and what is known as the "Hawkinge Hoodoo" sat very damply and coldly on the afternoon's programme. The result was a display of fortitude by pilots and spectators alike worthy of the great Spartan after whom the machines have been named. No.II Squadron started receiving its Lysanders last autumn but was not fully equipped until some months later. It now

Soon the Squadron received a new aircraft, the camouflaged Westland Lysander. Peter Stansfeld flew in the first aircraft. Peter was an officer in the Royal Tank Corps and was seconded to the Squadron twice. The second time he was its Commanding Officer from February 1942 to June 1943.

has its full complement of Lysander IIs, which differ from the Mark I model mainly in the use of the 905hp. Perseus XII sleeve-valve engine in place of the 890hp. Mercury XII poppet-valve motor. These two motors are not inter-changeable, as the Perseus mounting has been modified to allow essential motor-driven accessories, such as the electric generator, air compressor and vacuum pump, to be driven from a gearbox attached to the airframe. This gearbox remains in place when the motor is removed, thus making complete motor replacement easier.

'For the demonstration a short flying programme of eleven events had been drawn up by No.II Squadron, but low rain-clouds sitting on the hills made advisable the washing out of three of these events. The programme began with the take-off of formations of five and three Lysanders respectively, the intention being that while the five were giving demonstrations of various formations the three should lurk in the background waiting to follow with a display of high and low level dive bombing. The low level bombing was done in line astern and the simulated smoke puffs, obedient to the hidden hand, duly appeared in the wrong places at the wrong time in the true Hendon style. Six machines then landed singly and five were loaded with supply containers. While the loading was in progress, the remaining two machines flew past at the extremes of the Lysander's 4 to 1 speed range. One flew very much tail down with automatic slots and flaps in full play, and maintaining a steady 55 mph under full control. The other careered past with everything shut except the throttle, and doing its 230mph with characteristic ease and a lot of grace. The supply-laden machines then took off and dropped their parachute containers in the middle of the aerodrome. The next event was obviously introduced to stir the emotions of the hard-bitten press and to infuse a little hilarity into what, to the non-technically minded had been a smooth running and therefore featureless programme. A sacrificial Flying Officer (Geddes remembered it was P/O Edinger, JGO) opened his parachute in the slipstream of a stationary Lysander's Perseus and the sight of the victim being helplessly dragged across the ground on his back in the wake of a fully opened Irving chute was meat for the photographers, but most were caught

Several aircraft were tested for communication duties. The Squadron was asked to carry out these tests. One of the most popular communication aircraft was the Vega Gull which later became the Percival Proctor. Fourteen Vega Gulls were built for the RAF. Andrew Geddes, then a Flight Commander, was the lucky pilot to fly the Vega Gull in No.II Squadron.

Q6 Petrel G-AFFD was the private aircraft of Sir Philip Sassoon. Beautifully painted dark and light blue it was very comfortable, a real VIP aircraft. As Sir Philip was a great friend of the Squadron he allowed pilots to use the Q6 during leave from exercises. Andrew Geddes was often asked to act as Sir Philip's private pilot. The Q6 had two 205 horsepower de Havilland Gipsy Six II engines. At the outbreak of the Second World War the aircraft was impressed by the Air Ministry and served as a communication aircraft for high-ranking RAF officers.

unaware. So the victim was offered up again and the indignity was, we hope, duly recorded for posterity in the photographic archives of Fleet Street.

'Finally a single machine flown by S/L A.J.W. Geddes (Major, Royal Artillery) demonstrated the take-off and landing qualities of the Lysander. He made a series of impeccable departures and arrivals and amply showed off those qualities so desirable in a machine which may often be called upon to operate from small fields. The chilly visitors then divided into parties and were shown the various ground activities of No.II Squadron and ultimately delivered to the Mess for a welcome tea. The demonstration was nicely planned to show the many outstanding qualities of the Lysander when flown by Service pilots, a method as convincing if not so spectacular as if one machine was shown by the firm's pilot. The programme is substantially that which will be staged by the Squadron at Hawkinge on Empire Day. Each event, with the exception of the parachute-episode, covers a definite phase of the Squadron work and is done with all ancillary services, including ground-signals and two-way radio.

'One interesting sidelight of a visit to a modern Army Co-operation squadron is the picturesque diversity of uniform presented by the seconded Army officers, who in No.II Squadron form approximately 30% of the flying personnel and include the Squadron Leader. Army officers continue to wear the uniform of the Corps or unit while seconded to the RAF with the addition of RAF-wings, a practice which is reminiscent of the old RFC. In these days of shadowing and general elimination of spit and polish such a touch of colour is refreshing, even if it is not prophetic . . .

In the meantime life at Hawkinge continued. One after the other experienced pilots left to return to their Army units. Peter Stansfeld returned to the Royal Tank Corps, to come back a few years later as Officer Commanding the Squadron. New pilots arrived, P/Os Maccaw, Gordon Scotter, Shearman, Grant-Govan, fresh from training. On 20 May, Empire Air Day was a tremendous success. Soon after that the entire Squadron left for the yearly jobs at Okehampton and Friday Wood. Around them the world was heading towards disaster: Mussolini had taken Abyssinia, Hitler had annexed Austria and Czechoslovakia. In spite of conferences and signatures war was on its way.

On 23 August 1939 at 2230 hours Squadron Leader Andrew Geddes opened an envelope with a telegram which had been handed to him by a despatch rider. No.II (AC) Squadron received orders to prepare for battle . . .

A-Flight, No.II (AC) Squadron, 24 August 1938, flying over Lyminge Village a little north of Folkestone and Hawkinge. The pilots are Dale Green, Stansfeld and Hallam.

CHAPTER 5
TO THE TEST ONCE AGAIN

The invasion of Poland came as a tremendous shock. The Squadron, however, like all military units had already received orders to mobilise on 23 August. Work began to double the size of dug-outs. Guards were issued with ammunition and arrangements were made to send home the personal belongings and luggage of all Squadron personnel. The church parade that day was attended by virtually everyone. All knew that hard times were ahead.

On 3 September, after a message had been received at the Squadron that 'WAR HAS BROKEN OUT WITH GERMANY ONLY — 1115', troops were ordered to wear steel helmets, respirators and anti-gas clothing in the alert positions. The Squadron was on one hour's readiness. So began a war for which everyone had studied and trained without really knowing what it would be like. Reservists began to arrive at Folkestone Railway Station with requests for transport up Caesar's Camp Hill to Hawkinge aerodrome above the town. Like all practised organisations official jargon was widely used to make things more easily and accurately understood. One can imagine that at times this caused major problems for new arrivals who had recently left a civilian occupation and had hardly had any time to familiarise themselves with this 'new language'. It was, therefore, obvious that problems would arise. Imagine the reaction of the new Squadron Orderly Officer, one of the reservists, when he received a message from No.22 (Army Co-op) Group at Farnborough saying that twenty-five 'unclothed' reservists would arrive by night train having been posted to No.II (AC) Squadron. The Squadron was to supply them with transportation to the aerodrome. The keen officer went through great pains to get twenty-five blankets put into the Crossley lorry to spare the blushes of the naked reservists, not realising that this expression in forces language defined the new arrivals as wearing civilian clothes rather than uniforms.

At the outbreak of the war the Squadron was at full strength, consisting of three Flights. According to the Nominal Roll the officers were: Commanding Officer S/L A.J.W. Geddes (Royal Artillery).

A-Flight: Flight Commander F/L P. Edinger (RAF). Pilots: Lt. E.M.J. Laing (Sherwood Foresters), P/O I.L.M. Hallam (RAF), P/O J.K. Rogers (RAF) and P/O F.M.G. Scotter (RAF)

Lysander L4705 flying over the Leas near Folkestone. It was standard procedure to fly with the rear cockpit open, even if the gunner was seated behind the pilot. During an operational sortie the air gunner sat with his back to the pilot scanning the half circle backwards. L4705 was Grant-Govan's aircraft. He always flew it with his air gunner Cpl. Tomkins. This particular aircraft went with the Squadron to Abbeville in 1939. However, before it saw action it was flown back to Brize Norton to be replaced with a Mark II.

B-Flight: Flight Commander Lt. A.F. Anderson (Royal Warwickshire Regt). Pilots: Lt. I. Worthington-Wilmer (Royal Tank Corps), F/O D.C. Maccaw (RAF), P/O M. Henderson (RAF) and P/O W. Shearman (RAF).
C-Flight: Flight Commander Lt. J.K.M. Drysdale (Royal Scots). Pilots: Lt. F.M. Benito, P/O A.F. Doidge (RAF), P/O C.F.M. Chapman (RAF) and P/O G. Grant-Govan (RAF).
Adjutant F/O G.B. Walford (RAF); Signals Officer: F/L D. Saward; Medical Officer: F/O H.S Samuel; Equipment Officer: P/O S.R.W. Amor (RAF).

Suddenly, however, RAF Hawkinge was declared a Recruit Training Pool. No-one understood the reasons why, it meant that a perfectly organised battle station was turned into a beehive of people coming and going. Consequently, No.25 Squadron and its Blenheims left for North Weald. With recruits pouring in the station had changed its appearance entirely. The bulk of the reservists entered No.II (AC) Squadron. They were mature characters and mostly much older than the men already serving in 'Shiny Two'. After a few days the Squadron consisted of a War Establishment of 386 people of all ranks, commanded by a Squadron Leader. It had eighteen Lysanders and 454 vehicles. Nearly all the MT drivers were former Green Line coach drivers with tremendous experience and skill.

The first weeks of the war were very hectic. All Flights underwent rifle training and first aid lectures commenced. Many officers visited the station to lecture on a variety of subjects. As a precaution against a possible German air raid, black-out was ordered. Since no-one was allowed to leave the station except in exceptional circumstances F/L Dudley Saward was put in charge of entertainments. Everybody from the CO down to the youngest airman had to undergo a lot of necessary inoculations. AC1 Richards was appointed as Squadron Postman. Four men of each Flight were detailed for contamination duties and each Flight had a permanent Gas Orderly. On 14 September a whole day's Kit Inspection took place. All felt that something was brewing up. In the meantime the pilots and air gunners were practising artillery reconnaissance in co-operation with 22nd Field Regiment RA. Rumours were rife in the huts and hangars. Some said the Squadron was to go overseas. Others said from reliable sources that a move of the entire Squadron to the eastern border of France was being contemplated. A few believed that they were to patrol the border between Ireland and Ulster, just in case the Irish government should chose the 'wrong' side in the war. One reason for all these rumours was the amount of inoculations. The injections began to pall the men. Some, knowing that another shot was at hand hid themselves or pretended to be too busy to come, others insisted they had had that one twice already. Therefore F/O Samuel spread a rumour about one particular inoculation. He 'leaked' that this one was very special; anyone who had received it would be quite safe to drink from any ditch, pond, river, brook or fountain. The injection contained a new and highly secret drug which would enable aircrew to evade and survive immune to almost every known disease including the plague while running from the enemy. Suddenly the entire Squadron turned up and interest grew miraculously. All agreed that the recipient of this injection would be invulnerable if not immortal.

Lysander L4687 with running engine. Barney Benito sits in the cockpit. He left the Squadron in 1937 and later became the owner of a public house, the Crown Inn, at Everleigh in Wiltshire. In 1939 he re-joined as a Flying Officer and accompanied the Squadron to France. He flew in C-Flight under Jimmy Drysdale. This photograph was taken at Hawkinge before they left for France. The Message Pick Up hook underneath the fuselage is clearly visible. The mud spats have been removed since mud often clogged the wheels after a few landings in muddy fields. Note also the inter-connected flaps and slots for very slow landings, flying or take-offs. With a wind of 50 mph it was perfectly simple to fly backwards with full enginepower and fine pitch. It was quite funny to do this when civilians were watching. Some of them would swear that RAF had finally built the perfect aeroplane, flying forwards and backwards.

Coming in low. L4700 buzzing RAF Hawkinge. In the background are the houses of the Station Commander W/C Bobby George, the Squadron Commander S/L Andrew Geddes and the OC No.25 Squadron S/L Hallings-Pott. L4700 was a Mark I, one of a total of 144 aircraft built. The empty bomb racks on the wing stubs are clearly visible.

Within hours Samuel was out of supplies and the entire Squadron's morale went sky high. Weeks later, when the Squadron ground party was on its way to Abbeville, airmen who had received 'Samuel's Miracle Drug' showed off their privileged status by refusing to drink from the water tenders. Instead they ostentatiously filled their mugs from ditches beside the roads, village ponds and horse troughs. The dirtier the water the better they liked it. If possible they emptied their mugs with as many onlookers present as possible. Samuel grew increasingly worried, especially when the news of No.II (AC) Squadron's medical miracle reached top brass. Air Marshal Brook-Popham when writing an evaluation of the Flanders campaign had a detailed investigation carried out and found conclusively that the 'aircrew injection' was quite useless, although for some reason not a single Squadron member suffered ill effects from their drinking habits.

Great problems were caused by the volume of cypher traffic coming in. Since war had been declared staff at Group Headquarters seemed to have gone cypher-mad, seemingly unable to communicate in anything else except cypher — an old-fashioned method which could only be dealt with by officers. The Squadron also had to relay the incoming and outgoing cypher for the Training Pool as well as for No.25 Squadron at North Weald. It was a hell of a job dealing with the spate of signals. It got so bad that Andrew Geddes decided to swear in officers' wives to help with the avalanche. One of these ladies was a Scandinavian national by birth, and as such she was a 'neutral'. Once the Air Ministry found out what had happened, long after the Squadron had departed to France, Geddes received a severe reprimand in writing for 'allowing aliens to cypher and decypher while their country was not at war with Germany'. So great was confusion that the message was sent to Hawkinge rather than to Drucat.

On 18 September the Squadron received a delightful letter from Sir Arthur Whitten-Brown, the famous World War One Squadron member and Atlantic flyer. The message read:

'I want to send you, your officers, NCOs and men, my heartfelt wishes for the success and safety of the Squadron in which I once had the honour of serving.'

S/L Geddes answered:

'All ranks join me in thanking you for your letter. Rest assured that No.II Squadron, with its present personnel and equipment will do its best to emulate the gallant example set by you and your contemporaries in the past.'.

During the following ten days inoculations and lectures continued. All mobilisation tentage contained in the Unit Transport was erected outside Nos. 1 and 2 hangars under orders of F/L Saward. The following day everything was loaded onto lorries. That same day all Squadron members received orders to remove Squadron badges from their overalls. On 27 September an arms inspection and parade took place. The following morning at 0620 hours the Squadron road party under the command of F/L Worthington-Wilmer, comprising four officers and fifty-six other ranks left Hawkinge for overseas duties. As security was considered to be of prime importance the news had been leaked that the convoy was to drive to Southampton for Cherbourg. Great excitement was shown by the men when the first vehicle with S/L Geddes in it turned left instead of right at the foot of Caesar's Camp Hill. The matter was soon ironed out when the party began embarkation at Dover. They were to be taken across to France by the Twickenham Ferry of the Southern Railway. All vehicles went aboard safely. For everyone responsible for sea transport this was a relief as it was the first time that this vessel had been used for transportation of vehicles rather than locomotives and carriages. Before carrying the

Brian Walford in front of the A-Flight locker room at Hawkinge. When the Squadron was sent to France Walford was the Squadron Adjutant.

=

HAWK

11 FIGHTER NR 7 ++++ MOST IMMEDIATE ++++

P T W R

GR 10 TO ALL ROYAL AIR FORCE UNITS AND ESTABS AT HOME

AIR OFFICERS COMMANDING MIDDLE EAST AND IRAQ

FROM AIR MINISTRY +++ TO BE ACKNOWLEDGED +++++

A34 3/9 WAR HAS BROMEXXXXX BROKEN OUT WITH GERMANY ONLY

=== 1115 +

EAF VA+ R1150 RER VA+

Received 1200 hrs at HAWKINGE
by OC 2 Sqn A Geddes.
3/9/39 Sqn Ldr

On 3rd September at 1200 hours S/L Geddes received the message that war had broken out (with Germany only). Soon the Squadron started preparations to cross the Channel and settle itself at Drucat/Abbeville aerodrome.

Squadron the Twickenham Ferry had been used to lay mines. All on board who knew this hoped and prayed that the Master knew where he had laid them. Indeed he did, for apart from seeing a single mine in mid-Channel the voyage was uneventful. At 1430 hours the ship docked at Dunkirk. Within forty minutes all the vehicles were on the quayside and ready to move south. The first leg took them to Saint Omer, where they bivouacked for the night. The following morning the convoy drove to Abbeville via Hesdin. A few miles north of the town was the village of Drucat where the party arrived on 29 September around noon. This tiny village was to become the Squadron's home for the months to come.

On 1 October the Squadron Rail Party left, with F/O Barney Benito in command. The party consisted of four officers and 232 other ranks. They travelled to Southampton via Shornecliffe. The following morning, after a very unpleasant rough crossing in an overcrowded ship they arrived in Cherbourg. It was 0730 hours, the crossing having taken 6½ hours. It was on the quay at Cherbourg that the men were to experience French hospitality for the first time — it was not until 1130 hours that they were given any food. Then they boarded a train to Abbeville, with only their kit, and some biscuits and bully beef to sustain them. Soon they knew what the provisions for the British forces in France would be: 'Buy your own food, bread and butter and pay the normal prices'. The French were quite happy to accept the help of Les Anglais as long as it was not going to cost the Republique Française a single centime. When the Rail Party finally arrived in Abbeville, Squadron lorries came to pick them up and drive them to Drucat where they were billeted in tents.

Lysanders taking off from Hawkinge.

On 6 October at 0300 hours the Air Party was ordered to prepare for departure to France. After very bad weather in the morning twelve Lysanders led by S/l Geddes took off from Hawkinge. The first leg of the flight took them to Shoreham where all the aircraft refuelled. Then they took off for the second stage across the Channel. At 1555 hours they made landfall at Le Treport. In an immaculate formation the Lizzies went on to Abbeville. Upon their arrival they first did several circuits over the town before touching down at Abbeville aerodrome. The flight had taken the Squadron one hour and twenty-five minutes.

For the first two weeks the Squadron was allowed to settle in and get familiar with the local area. On 10 October flying commenced and all pilots flew over the 3 Corps area to get familiar with the landmarks of the part of France they were now responsible for. They shared Abbeville aerodrome with another Lysander squadron, No.26. This squadron had its billets north of the airfield at La Triquerie which belonged to the Lovvencourts, an ancient and noble French family. The first operational sortie was flown on 13 October. Unfortunately bad weather made photography impossible. The same day AVM G.H.B. Blount ABE,MC, AOC RAF Air Component, Field Force, visited Abbeville. Nos.II and 26 Squadrons as well as No.51 Wing Headquarters paraded on the aerodrome. Then the AOC inspected the troops and addressed them.

As mentioned, the Squadron was billeted in the village of Drucat. The almost 400 British servicemen outnumbered the villagers and as a consequence there was not enough room for the men. The only solution at short notice was to put them into tents and at the same time modify and enlarge existing billeting facilities. They also had to build dug-outs to accommodate those working at the dispersed sites on the aerodrome. Conditions were so poor that Geddes decided to have new buildings erected for a dining hall and recreation and equipment stores to replace inadequate tentage. The airfield itself was a square grass field without any facilities. Sanitation was appalling, not at all satisfactory for S/L Geddes who considered hygiene a prime necessity in maintaining morale and ensuring full preservation of manpower. In the meantime he had to face more problems. At first the Squadron was looked upon by the villagers with rather mixed feelings. The sudden invasion of about 400 foreigners threatened to disturb the quiet farm life of the villagers. Some expected the local girls to be raped before the month was over. Others deeply resented the British, whom they considered strange and pompous. Virtually no-one among NCOs and other ranks spoke any French. Only the local teacher spoke some English, as did the ladies who lived in the castle — Comtesse le Rocquigny du Fayel and her daughter-in-law Comtesse Marie Thérèse de Mython d'Harcelines, whose husband had been called up to serve in the French Army in the Maginot Line. For one person, however, the arrival of so many foreigners opened a world of profitable possibilities. The owner of La Drucaterie, the village shop and inn rubbed his hands. He was going to get rich faster than he ever could have imagined. Within a few days he raised prices and exchanged Sterling for Francs at a ridiculous rate. S/L Geddes' first priority was to curb inflation and try to divert some of the profits from La Drucaterie towards a Squadron PSI fund. He paid a visit to La Drucaterie and told the owner that it would be quite easy to start a Crossley shuttle to Abbeville every day to enable the Squadron to buy goods at more reasonable prices. He also informed the man that it only needed three words to keep every single Briton out of his establishment: 'OUT OF BOUNDS'. This came as rather a shock. The fear of an RAF boycott made the shopkeeper very co-operative. It was agreed that a locked money box would be set up on the counter and that a percentage of each purchase would be put into it by the proprietor in the presence of the buying airman. The box was to be emptied daily by the appointed RAF officer and the money was to be put into a fund to provide amenities for sports, Christmas presents and so on. Furthermore the owner agreed to display a price list for all to see in both the inn and shop. The prices on the list would not be changed without consulting S/L Geddes. The CO knew that he played with high odds, but fortunately the shopkeeper seemed to be so amazed by Geddes' actions that he agreed to them all.

Then Geddes paid his respects to the Comtesse De Mython. The meeting was not very successful. Without any ado she had been informed by the French authorities that she was to vacate the eastern wing of the Castle which was to become

Ivor Worthington-Wilmer (left) and Brian Walford (below). Brian still wears the Squadron badge on his flying overall. Immediately after the war broke out all badges were removed. Ivor was killed on 4th July 1940 when as a Flight Lieutenant in No.18 (Burma) Squadron he was shot down in a Blenheim. He was buried at Zwartewaal cemetery southwest of Rotterdam, where his grave is the only RAF one in that area. His remains rest among those of the the villagers, a fitting memorial to a brave man.

the Officers' Mess as well as the Squadron headquarters. Geddes, who was not used to dealing with nobility, came across as very stiff and distant. In her diary she wrote:

> 'Some of the officers are very kind and somewhat shy. Their commander however seems to be a very hard man. He says very little and seems to be working 24 hours a day. When I see him he just nods at me and walks on without any conversation'.

It was not until Andrew Geddes returned to Drucat in December 1987 that things were ironed out. He explained his attitude as an effort not to bother the Comtesse any more than absolutely necessary and she said that she did not quite know what to think of him. After a lovely lunch in the 'old' dining room they parted as friends.

Drucat was and still is a beautiful little village. It consists of numerous small houses and a few farms. Today people from Saint Omer, Béthune and Abbeville own cottages for the weekends in Drucat. There is a small town hall and a picturesque church. The castle is in the centre of the village. It has an impressive gate through which a lane leads to the entrance door of the house. The present Comte, Hubert de Mython, only lives at the castle in the summer and during long weekends. A caretaker now maintains the garden which is no longer as beautiful as Squadron members remember it from their stay in 1939-40. The castle has changed its appearance dramatically: during the war German officers lived in it and when they retreated in 1944 they

Tim Wimbush.

Far right: Ivor Worthington-Wilmer.

burned the castle down. Once restoration was complete it looked an entirely different place.

Soon after Geddes' conference with the shop and inn keeper the airmen began to join the villagers in La Drucaterie and drink a glass of French beer, a red wine or a Pastis with them. They would try their very first French words on the locals and little by little understanding and friendship grew. Prices were reasonable and as Geddes kept the men on a short leash there were no problems between them and the locals. In the meantime S/L Geddes had other problems to solve. As mentioned earlier the dining hall and recreation room consisted of a number of 180lb tents joined together and raised on struts to take big stoves. They were fine for the summer, but quite useless if the winter was going to be very cold. Geddes therefore drove through the countryside to see if he could find any suitable material for better facilities. In the neighbourhood he met the owner of a saw mill. They talked and soon an almost unlimited supply of wood arrived on the Crossleys. Geddes 'won' corrugated iron from the Corps' Royal Engineers and soon weather-proof buildings appeared on the village square.

While building went on operational sorties were flown as well. Two days after the first sortie an accident happened. F/O Benito took off from Abbeville in KO-U at 1620 hours to take oblique photographs. He was accompanied by his air gunner Corporal J. Crick. As the weather deteriorated Benito was forced to fly to a nearby strip, called Labuissiere, south of Béthune. At 1700 he successfully landed there. Half an hour later he decided to try take off. All went well but while in the air the worsening weather again forced him down. He flew to Frelinghien aerodrome but unfortunately the failing light and ground mist obscured the fact that the field had become a swamp. Immediately after the Lysander touched down the wheels sunk into the mud and the Lizzie turned on its back. A bit shaken Benito got out, to see that Crick had been injured on the head. He was taken to Lille military hospital with concussion. Benito could do little else but call his CO, report the accident and ask for a crash party to have a look at the Lysander. They did not need long to see that the Lysander was damaged beyond repair.

On 28 October three French officers arrived for a three-day course on British Army Co-operation procedures. They were Lieutenants Bequart, Schill and Macheraz. All were gunners and served with the French 51st Division. They left a little wiser and probably wondering why the British took everything so seriously.

Most of the daily reports in the Squadron Operations Record Book have one thing in common: nearly every sortie being spoiled by the weather. In the north of France the constant low cloud, rain and mist made aerial reconnaissance very difficult and at times extremely dangerous. High steel towers on hill tops connected HT cables and as there were no maps available with these cables marked on, the pilots had to 'find out' for themselves. Even so, the Squadron produced thousands of photographs of the Corps area. At times while carrying out their duties the Lysanders were fired upon by Allied AA-guns. On 6 November no less than eighteen shots were fired at Grant-Govan when he flew over Merville aerodrome. By hastily firing the colours of the day he hoped to stop the gunners below. For some reason the men below decided to have another go at him, so Grant-Govan cleared the area as quickly as possible. Three days later, again over Merville, similar shots were fired at

F/O Lang. S/L Geddes had enough of this and demanded an immediate conference with HQ 51st (French) Division. He succeeded in convincing the French that they should try to do something about it.

The weather continued to interfere with daily routines. On 11 November, Armistice Day, the Squadron participated in an exercise with 3rd Division. It was a shambles. The weather was horrible and the W/T communications were constantly being jammed by interference from a French transmitter at Litte. On 14 November A-Flight was sent to Nantes for a month. The road party spent the night at Le Mans, reaching their destination the next day. Squadron R/T tenders were detached to their operational stations, being 4th Division and 16th (French) Corps. The Ops. Record Book gives little information about these exercises. It does report in detail, however, on the fact that the remaining part of the Squadron went to a concert in the Stella Palace Cinema at Abbeville on 25 November and that entertainment was also provided by the 'Expeditionary Force Institute Mobile Projector' at Abbeville. Many activities took place in December. With the weather at last improving on 2 December Air Marshal Sir Charles Burnett, KCB, CBE, DSO, visited the Squadron in his capacity as Inspector General of the Royal Air Force. The AOC, Air Component accompanied him. On 5 December S/L Geddes with twelve men departed for Seclin to participate in the rehearsal for the coming visit of HM King George VI, who would view His troops the following day. It had been agreed that a fly-past should be made to show the Sovereign the might of the RAF in France. Therefore six squadrons had been ordered to prepare one aircraft each and present it in pristine condition. The participating squadrons were:

No.II (AC) Squadron with a Lysander
No.26 (AC) Squadron with a Lysander
No.59 (AC) Squadron with a Blenheim IV
No.85 (F) Squadron with a Hurricane
No.87 (F) Squadron with a Hurricane
No.615 (F) Squadron with a Gladiator

Of course No.II (AC) Squadron did its very best to present the King with a spotless aircraft. Since due warning had been given the least dented Lysander had been prepared to showroom standard and kept under cover until the big day. Then someone found out that the hangar was upwind of the aerodrome and, for take-off, would have to be taxied over a considerable distance through mud and soft ground, due to a sudden thaw after severe frost and heavy snow. F/L Jimmy Drysdale therefore was told to taxi the aircraft to the downwind hardstanding where it would be prepared for take-off with all its Review gear. As the aircraft was spotless Drysdale was to taxi only, not to fly. The aircraft

Second day of mobilisation. Pilots of No.II Squadron prepare for departure to France from RAF Hawkinge.

Hawkinge 1939. Lysanders preparing for take-off in a formation of three. L4692 leads. Hardly visible in front of L4692's propeller is Gibraltar Cottage, a beautiful little house which was destroyed by a Stuka attack in 1940. Immediately after mobilisation dummy hedges were painted on the grass to make the airfield look like innocent farmland from the air. This was highly successful, although in a different way than expected. An RAF fighter pilot, somewhat confused by the information that a dummy airfield had been constructed near Hawkinge mistook the real aerodrome for the dummy and landed not far from it in farm land with genuine hedges. When he climbed out of what was left of his fighter he said that he had thought the real hedges to be the painted ones.

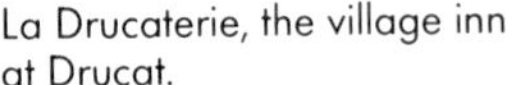

La Drucaterie, the village inn at Drucat.

The castle as many pre-war Squadron members will remember it. When the Allies returned to Abbeville in 1944 they found the castle burned by the Germans before they withdrew north.

Top right: Officers' Mess, Drucat 1939. While the Squadron was stationed at Abbeville aerodrome the Officers' Mess was in the right tower of the De Mython Castle. After the Squadron returned to England the castle was taken over by the Germans who burned it down when they were forced to leave in 1944.

left the hangar and was soon in difficulties. The wheel-spats had to be removed since they often jammed in the mud. One airman sat on the tailplane to reduce the risk of the aircraft nosing over if it got stuck in the mud again. It was a tedious business and the condition of the carefully prepared fuselage was not improved by the mud and spray being disturbed by the propeller at almost full throttle. Drysdale knew every soft patch on the grass area and at least reached a position were he knew that a sounder patch lay upwind of him for a short distance. In that wind take-off would be possible as long as no-one but the pilot was on board. Near the despatching area there was a patch where he could land again without making the aircraft any dirtier. Jimmy decided to make this short hop and gave the signal for the airmen on the ground to stand clear. Unfortunately one airman saw nothing of this: the chap sitting on the tailplane. In his position he could not see what the pilot signalled and probably paid no attention to his colleagues walking away from the Lysander. With a steel helmet on his head, a gascape tied to his chest and wearing long gumboots he patiently waited until he was told to vacate his position. Once Drysdale gave full throttle for his take-off, it was too late. The slipstream locked the poor man's legs against the leading edge of the tailplane and his upper body was pushed backwards. Laying flat on his back on the tailplane he saw the earth moving faster and faster underneath the aircraft. While taking off Drysdale noticed some tail-heaviness but otherwise the Lysander took off without further difficulty. It was not until he looked over his shoulder that he saw the fluttering cape of the airman. Immediately Drysdale made a very cautious landing. All ran to the aircraft to help the airman from his rather unpleasant position. When asked later by the CO how the flight had been the airman answered: 'Well, Sir, I cannot really say. I had never flown before. However, when I saw the hangar going past underneath me I thought "This cannot be".' The Royal Review took place the next day without any unusual occurrences. Watching the aircraft passing overhead the King had no idea what bizarre events the No.II Squadron Lysander and its pilot had experienced the day before.

Visits of dignitaries went on continuously at Abbeville. On 9 December Air Commodore. Capel, SASO Air Component, gave a talk to the officers. The next day French officers of 16th Corps entertained the CO and two other Squadron officers for lunch. On the 12th Sir Cyril Newall, the CAS arrived at Abbeville. At the same time the Squadron flew affiliation exercises with No.615 Squadron at Nantes. Leslie Henson's concert party came to play for the Squadron. From 15 December constant artillery recce sorties had to be flown. For the first time since their arrival in France members of the Squadron were allowed to go to England for a short leave. New arrivals joined the Squadron, they were P/Os Baker and Dearden. Preparations for Christmas were made. One day Comte De Mython who served on the Franco-German border as a cavalry officer came home and joined the officers for supper. On Christmas Day at 1300 hours the airmen had their dinner. At 2359 hours the Officers sat down for dinner in the Cafe Continental at Abbeville. The following day the NCOs had their Christmas dinner and in the evening a Squadron dance was held in the Stella Cinema. On 31 December Captain Balfour, the Under Secretary of State for Air, visited the Squadron while on the same day F/L Anderson left to assume command of No.613 Squadron.

The absolutely atrocious weather during the winter of 1939-40 remains in the minds of all who served on 'Shiny Two' during that period. There was an amazing frost with occasional Arctic blizzards. Yet at times S/L Geddes ordered practice alerts which were not at all popular with the members of the Squadron. F/L Bruce, the Medical Officer, remembers these alerts with great aversion:

> 'Deep snow lay on the ground for weeks and the frost was exceptionally hard. In spite of this S/L Geddes would order a practice night test on the airfield to test Squadron efficiency. I cannot remember what the actual proceedings were, but I vividly remember myself sitting in a dug-out, my teeth chattering with cold and my limbs frozen, not feeling particularly kindly towards the CO'.

On 2 January 1940 three Gloster Gladiators of No.615 Squadron landed at Abbeville for further affiliation tests. While the CO flew round in an open Tiger Moth to watch these exercises the Gladiators and Lysanders 'fought' each other. Unfortunately the weather forced the whole thing to end prematurely. As the ground at the aerodrome was covered with molehills airmen had to go onto the field every morning carrying pickaxes to destroy them. Nevertheless all three Gladiators lost their tail wheels on the almost concrete molehills and had to be declared unserviceable for some time. P/O Anderson sustained a broken wrist when he jumped from a lorry and fell on the ice-bound road. After the Gladiators had left Hurricanes from No.87 Squadron arrived. They too flew against the Lysanders. A very welcome visitor was Colonel Festing who had been the Squadron ALO before the outbreak of the war. Bernard Newman lectured on the Maginot Line and all were duly impressed by the impregnable defences the French had built on their border with Germany. On 11 January the Squadron carried out low level attacks against troops of 11th Infantry Brigade. Then, suddenly, on 14 January, all leave was cancelled. A German attack against Belgium was expected. The storm blew over and everything returned to normal. The cold in France seemed to be a bigger problem than a possible German invasion. P/Os Doidge and Chapman had to be admitted to Le Tréport hospital after they fell ill with bronchitis. A sense of boredom seemed to cause a lack of discipline in places. Therefore the AOCiC RAF Component sent a message to all his troops:

> 'Today the British Air Forces in France are united under one command. The one ideal that inspires us, one and all, is to do our utmost in helping to win this war. This ideal resolutely and unselfishly maintained will overcome all difficulties great and small, of whatever nature, whenever they arrive. In the months to come let us keep this ideal before us with our friends and Allies of the French Air Force, who have done so much for us since we have been here. We will fly wing-tip to wing-tip, doing our share with the Allied armies in the field, to bring this war to a speedy and decisive conclusion.'

There were other ways to combat boredom. S/L Geddes was offered one such solution. However, he could hardly consider it to be an 'official' one. One day a gentleman came to Drucat castle and asked the guard if he could see the Commandant. He presented his card, saying his name was Monsieur Gaby and that he was in the entertainment business. Andrew Geddes

While the Squadron was stationed at Abbeville and Drucat some of the men left their marks on the walls of the castle. Some scratched the RAF emblem in the wall, others expressed their feelings about being in France: 'A Damn Bad Show...'

remembered Monsieur Gaby as if he had entered his office yesterday. Gaby was dressed rather like an undertaker in black tails and top hat. He said that he felt very sorry for these poor English boys who were so far from home serving their Country and helping their French brothers in arms. He realised that here in Drucat apart from a very poor local wine in that small café little entertainment was available. As a proud son of France he believed it to be his duty to help Monsieur le Commandant to maintain morale and keep the men content with their work. Therefore he, Monsieur Gaby, had come to offer his assistance to the Commandant to keep his men on the path of righteousness. He happened to be the proprietor of a house where gentlemen could be received in an atmosphere of hospitality and kindness. There were ladies from the best families to chat with the men and serve them the best food and drinks at very reasonable prices. For a small fee these ladies could also give the men the feeling that they were at home with their loved ones. Geddes remembered:

> 'Slowly it came to my mind what kind of hospitality this man was talking of. Looking at him with the large pearl in his tie-pin, smelling of the perfume he used I asked him rather bluntly if he was a bully. Gaby pretended not to understand the meaning of the word. Then I asked him if by any chance his house was a brothel and if the girls were prostitutes. Gaby stressed that he did not like that expression since it gave people the wrong idea of his business. He came closer to my table and said: "And, you understand, mon Colonel, that I am a man of reputation who knows how to show his gratitude to you if we reach an agreement. I could make a donation to you or you could have the hospitality of my house for free". I got so angry that I told him to go to hell, leave my office and never show himself in Drucat again. Then I called one of the guards and told him to march Monsieur Gaby out at gun point. The man was fear-stricken and left with considerable speed'.

Of course the airmen soon heard of Monsieur Gaby and his establishment. In no time they knew the address and after a few weeks the first customers came to see the Medical Officer . . .

Quite a lot of problems had been experienced with R/T communications. There simply were not enough sets. The few available were awful and refused to work most of the time. On 20 January 1940 a first consignment of 150 new sets was distributed to the RAF Component of the BEF. A further 200 were expected through the generosity of Lord Nuffield. It was quite amazing to think that communications depended on the kindness of private people. In any case the sets worked magnificently. In January S/L Geddes went on leave for the first time, handing over command to F/L Drysdale. The Rt.Hon. W. Wedgwood Benn MP 'entertained' the Squadron by lecturing about 'Politics and Economics'. Most of the Squadron were more interested in the answer to the question 'How to keep warm in France'. Two more new pilots arrived in January. They were P/Os Dudeney and Thomas. Soon they were followed by an 'Old Boy', Captain George Everett. He had been an ALO in 1936-37. It was his third tour with the Squadron.

The Squadron continued to share Abbeville aerodrome with No.26 Squadron, with its billets around 'La Triquerie', a castle north of the field. Twice they invited No.II (AC) Squadron for a guest night. Twice it ended in disaster. In one case an airman was killed in the flames when a petrol lamp exploded. It was not the only sad incident. While at Drucat the Squadron had a suicide in its ranks. An airman shot himself in the latrines beside the village square the morning he was due to return to England for a short spell of leave. A subsequent inquiry soon gave the answer to his extraordinary behaviour. At first he had refused to go on leave, saying he was not interested in going to England. He was told, however, that he was to go anyway as it could be a long time before he was able to get a second chance. Eventually he reluctantly accepted the date allotted to him. As the day of departure approached, instead of being cheerful at the prospect of going home he grew more and more depressed, until the fatal incident happened. No-one had any idea why he had taken his life. However, it was discovered that he had a relationship with a married woman in Dover. By some coincidence the woman's husband, who worked in a local club as a bouncer and who was an amateur boxing champion, had intercepted the love letters written to his wife by the airman. Then, after some time, knowing that the airman was about to return to England, he had written the poor Casanova a letter explaining in detail what gruesome injuries he was going to inflict on the airman once he had left the boat from France. In panic the airman tried to escape leave. When this proved impossible, rather than speaking with a friend or the CO, he had gone to the toilet and killed himself. It was very sad indeed. On the practical side the airman's funeral presented problems to the Squadron. He was the first Squadron casualty in France. Besides, it would be very difficult if not impossible to bury him with military honours if top brass knew how he had died. S/L Geddes decided that it would be best for the man and his family if the suicide were ignored and declared death while on active service. The wing padre decided to take the funeral service and those who knew more about it were sworn to secrecy: everything was carefully worked out. But even the best laid plans can come adrift. The financial allowance for the expenses of an airman's funeral was checked and a local undertaker was told to produce a coffin at the approved British price. The Frenchman was very surprised when he heard how much the Squadron was allowed to spend and assured S/L Geddes that he would do a top job. Since the deceased was a 'Camerade' the CO need not worry at all. When the coffin arrived everybody was absolutely bewildered by the final product. Its size and splendour made it look rather like a scale model of Reims cathedral, with handles and Gothic ornaments all over. In the meantime the sexton of the cemetery had been given all details of the standard arrangements for an airman's funeral. The Squadron adjutant had had a pre-funeral meeting with the undertaker to make sure that everything went like clockwork. On the day of the funeral it rained as usual and the cortège, consisting of a staff car and a Crossley three-ton trailer with the enormous coffin, set off from Drucat to the nearby cemetery. There was no band, just a trumpeter. The service went off according to the book, until the actual moment of interment. The sexton had put all sorts of fancy grass imitation on the planks around the grave, so that it was hard to see exactly where the edges of the grave were. When it came to the bearers lowering the coffin it was found that it was a great deal longer than the standard British war grave and the enormous thing would not descend. The padre kept a cool head, completed the service by placing a good spadeful of earth on top of the coffin and concluded the ceremony. After the party had left, the sexton and his men enlarged the grave and workmen lowered the coffin with little ado. It showed that, however carefully things were planned, arranged and organised there were always gremlins to snarl them up.

Drucat Castle in 1939 (above) and 1989 (left). The Squadron officers were billeted in the right wing of the castle. No.II Squadron flew from the aerodrome of Abbeville, a former Imperial Airways Emergency Airfield on the London-Paris route. Unfortunately the only bathroom of the castle was on the side where the Comtesse de Mython lived. So, for baths all officers had to drive to Hotel Tête de Bœuf in Abbeville once a week. The same day the Squadron left Drucat German officers came and commandeered it. During the war pilots of JG26 lived in it. When the Allies approached in June 1944 the Germans set fire to the castle virtually destroying it. After the war the French government compensated the De Mython family and the castle was re-built.
Unfortunately the outer shape changed dramatically. The two towers disappeared, while the ground floor was reconstructed differently; less windows were built and the roof was changed.

CHAPTER 6
No.II (AC) SQUADRON AND THE BLITZKRIEG

At the beginning of the New Year the position of RAF units in France was as follows:
Headquarters and HQ-unit — Maroeuil
1st Air Formation Signals — Etrun
No.3 British Air Mission — Valenciennes
No.1 Air Stores Park — Bertangles
No.2 Air Stores Park — Ferfay
No.3 Air Stores Park — Velu
Central Maintenance Unit — Amiens-Glisy
No.81 Squadron (Communications) — Amiens
No.62 Fighter Wing Servicing Unit — Rouen-Boos

Army Co-operation Aircraft
No.50 (Recce) Wing Athies
No.4 Squadron: Mons-en-Chaussee (Lysanders)
No.13 Squadron: Mons-en-Chaussee (Lysanders)
No.51 (Recce) Wing Abbeville
No.II Squadron: Abbeville/Drucat (Lysanders)
No.26 Squadron: Abbeville/La Triquerie (Lysanders)
No.52 (Recce) Wing Poix
No.53 Squadron: Poix (Blenheims)
No.59 Squadron: Poix (Blenheims)
No.70 (Recce) Wing Rosieres
No.18 Squadron: Meharicourt (Blenheims)
No.57 Squadron: Rosieres (Blenheims)

Fighter Aircraft
No.60 (Fighter) Wing Lille-Seclin
No.85 Squadron: Lille-Seclin (Hurricanes)
No.87 Squadron: Lille-Seclin (Hurricanes)
No.61 (Fighter) Wing Vitry
No.607 Squadron: Vitry (Gladiators)
No.615 Squadron: Vitry (Gladiators)
No.67 (Fighter) Wing Bussy-le-Côte
No.1 Squadron: Vassincourt (Hurricanes)
No.73 Squadron: Rouvres (Hurricanes)

The horrible winter had been a real test for the Squadron, the restrictions on night flying and the wireless silence ordered by the French were a great nuisance. In spite of this the Squadron kept up a full programme of low flying over the area between Le Mans and the coast. It continued affiliation exercises with Gladiators around Abbeville and in the Somme valley and flew artillery observations for the British and the French, when these were firing live rounds on the ranges of Metz. The air gunners practised air to ground firing and many photo recce sorties were flown. Regular sports meetings were organised. Nos.II and 26 Squadrons played football at La Triquerie. The RAF did its very best to develop good relations with the French. Unfortunately there were mutual misunderstandings. Not only the language proved to be a barrier, different ideas about warfare caused problems too. Often S/L Geddes found the French rather suspicious and unwilling to share intelligence. The French on their side got the idea that the British felt superior and looked down on them. On one occasion Geddes was to meet French artillery officers at the French headquarters at Loos in order to explain, translate and if necessary modify, the British Army co-operation and artillery observation principles. The day started with a 'meeting session' which took from 1000 to 1200 hours. Then there was a 'joint luncheon' from 1200 till 1500. Between 1500 and 1700 hours Geddes was able to explain to the French what the British ideas were. However, at 1700 hours the meeting was concluded as all the French officers wanted to go to their quarters to prepare for the evening meal, which took from 1900 hours until midnight. When Geddes returned to Drucat it was close to sunrise and rather than going to bed he had to catch up with a lot of work which had to be done for the Squadron. Almost forty years later Geddes said:

> 'I found it very boring and hopelessly useless. The system seemed to serve the purpose of a better contact; for me it meant that I lost a lot of valuable time. Co-operation between both nationalities was not practised at the levels where everything would happen if it came to a fighting war. I learned one thing: the appreciation of *la cuisine francaise*. The French cooked wonderful meals, quite different from what we used to eat . . .'

The Squadron also had contact with the French army in nearby Saint Riquier, where initially an RAF Hospital was set up. The Monastery of Saint Riquier had been taken over by the French Medical Corps. Part of the monastery was used as an RAF Emergency Hospital, particularly for casualties who might not survive the long road journey to Dieppe. As a hospital it was a very grim place, not in any way up to RAF standards. The Squadrons at Abbeville were quite relieved when communications with Dieppe improved and the RAF General Hospital there also got facilities as a Casualty Station. The French officers at Saint Riquier were very friendly and keen on improving the Entente Cordiale. The Squadron had reciprocal guest nights alternately at Drucat Castle and the monastery. Difficulties in communications were overcome in a special way. The mixed group of officers would sit around a long table on which a lot of French-English and English-French dictionaries had been placed. Conversation was in French or English, not both languages at the same time, in ten-minute stretches, regulated by Mr. President. Anyone who got into lingual problems could freely reach for the dictionary without penalty. It all went extremely well and both groups seemed to learn bits and pieces of each other's language. The real improvement came, however, with the arrival of a French liaison officer to the Squadron. This man proved to be exceptionally kind and efficient and became the best friend the Squadron had in France. He was an NCO, called up at the outbreak of the war. Andrew Geddes remembered this NCO as if he met him yesterday:

> 'I was doing some paper work when a battered car entered the grounds of the castle. I could easily recognise it as French-driven for the sentry near the door disappeared in a cloud of dust when the car stopped. A French artillery Quartermaster Sergeant came out and asked to be taken to "Commandant Geddes". One of my officers escorted him into my office. Before I could say anything the chap drew the smartest salute I had ever seen. Then he looked at the ceiling with the look of someone who was about to announce the end of the world and shouted with a pompous voice: "AGENT DE LIAISON, MARECHAL DE LOGIS-CHEF, RAOUL JABLONGONNET, A VOS ORDRES, MON COMMANDANT!!" I was stunned. While saying all this he did not stop for a single second. The words came out of his mouth like a waterfall. Then he looked at me in anticipation. Then I was caught for a second time. Before I could welcome him a voice came from the ante room saying: In that case we had better call him Mr. Smith. Thus he became known among us as Mr. Smith. Since he was an NCO it was against regulations to give him accommodation in our Mess. Since, however, these regulations said nothing about civilians, the problem was solved easily. In peace time he was the Paris-concessionaire for the little Bambinot cars made by Peugeot. He had a great sense of humour and spoke reasonable English. He supported us more than 100% and fought the French authorities if this was to the Squadron's advantage. He saved us hundreds of pounds in protecting us from French profiteers. Since he was such a good chap we allowed him to bring Mrs. Smith to Drucat. She looked after the Officers' Mess catering and was a superb chef. She became a sort of "mum" for the men, even sewing on the odd button.'

The RAF was considered to be strong enough to be a decisive factor in the event of the outbreak of hostilities between Germany and the Allies. Holland and Belgium, both neutral, had only small air forces. Most of their aircraft were old and slow. The only reasonably modern aircraft was the Fokker G-1, a twin-engined heavy fighter of which the Dutch had about twenty-five. Both the Belgian and Dutch air forces were substantially weaker than the RAF in France. Basically each RAF Squadron had about sixteen aircraft at its disposal, meaning that the total strength of the RAF in France was a little over 200 aircraft.

Three No.II (AC) Squadron Lysanders in a vic over Abbeville aerodrome.

February 1940 was a month of snow, frost and thaw. Often flying operations had to be cancelled. This was very unfortunate, as the Squadron was to receive new aircraft directly from Brize Norton. In spite of the weather, on 4 February the first new aircraft were collected by F/L Eyres and P/Os Hallam and Rogers. The next day the airfield was declared unserviceable again after the thaw set in, changing the field into a quagmire. New arrivals that month were F/O Pimm and P/Os Mason, Wooldridge, Sherry and Watts. Wooldridge had a rather unnerving start as he had to make a forced landing near Béthune due to icing and a snowstorm the day after he arrived. F/L Eyres caught influenza and P/O Stuart had to stay in bed with laryngitis. On 25 February part of the Squadron travelled to Paris where they saw a rugby international in the Parc des Princes between the teams of the French and British armies. By the end of the month the replacement of the original Lysanders had been completed. Now all the Squadron aircraft were Mark IIs, making life for the technical ground staff much easier.

The affiliation exercises had taught the Lysander pilots a couple of valuable tricks. The Operations Record Book gave a number of conclusions which could help the pilots to survive an enemy attack:

'1. Lysanders must use to the full their manoeuvrability and low speed, principally, the steep climbing turn at high and low speeds near the ground.

2. Lysanders should make full use of natural features, such as woods and valleys, when using low-flying evasive tactics, and use could also be made of reasonably tall buildings, such as windmills, in evading an astern attack at ground level.

3. Lysanders should not dive either singly or in formation to evade fighters, unless the fighters have delivered an attack and are a considerable distance away, thus allowing the Lysanders sufficient time to reach ground level before the next attack.

4. When a Lysander becomes detached from a formation it must use evasive tactics to rejoin it.

5. Lysanders can successfully take the offensive against single Gladiators.'

Soon pilots were to learn the value of these lessons. The only problem was that they never had to encounter Gladiators. Their opponents were the rather faster Me109s and Me110s. As there was a possibility of air crews being shot down over hostile territory F/L Kaye came to lecture the Squadron on escape and evasion tactics. Soon after the Germans invaded North West Europe RAF servicemen would have to use these lessons, as Basil Embry was to find out.

At times there was friction with local farmers. Some of them were upset about the Squadron carrying out air-to-ground firing exercises. To iron out the problems the OC No.51 Wing W/C Fowler met a deputation of the local farmers in the hangar at Abbeville aerodrome.

While the pilots continued training hair-raising incidents could happen. Two lucky people were P/O Grant-Govan and his air gunner A/C Jones. One day they were en route from Abbeville to Le Mans on a low-level cross-country sortie. It was a misty morning with hoar-frost and snow patches about. Skimming the countryside Grant-Govan dived into a valley failing to see HT cables running between two tall pylons located in the wood. Lysander KO-W flew straight into the wires at about 150 knots airspeed. The deceleration before the cables broke was so sudden that the air gunner looking aft banged his head very severely against the rear interplane tubing. The cables fortunately broke and the immediate short circuit did not affect the Lysander which still had some rudder and aileron control. Grant-Govan, however, had no engine power since the propeller blades had been wrapped around the engine cowling with the wires festoned above and below the fuselage, trailing behind. In his predicament Grant-Govan had only one course of action. He landed straight ahead. The wind was virtually nil. His landing was very fast but fortunately on a frozen grass field running uphill from the bottom of the valley. Landing was a three-pointer and the aircraft went over the crest of the hill at almost flying speed. Grant-Govan then received a nasty surprise; finding a road into a wide cutting across the ridge at right angles to his track. He kept the stick back, left his feet off the brake and made the Lizzie virtually leap over the cutting in a semi-stalled condition. The cutting was wide enough to allow two lorries to pass. One way or the other the Lysander made it and with a terrible blow the aircraft hit the ground on the other side. The sturdy undercarriage survived the impact without breaking off. The aircraft got airborne again and then came to a standstill after an almost vertical fall. The entire tail wheel disappeared into the ground. Apparently it was possible to do helicopter landings with a Lysander . . .

Entertainment proved to be a difficult job. Basically there were two sorts of entertainment in the Squadron: the 'intellectual' and the 'pleasant'. It goes without saying that the CO favoured the first. The various activities organised in March and April 1940 were:

15 March: Mr A.F. Tschiffely gave a lecture on his 10,000-mile ride on horseback from Buenos Aires to Washington.

16 March: With the kind voluntary co-operation of Monsieur Santueil, a noted antiquarian who is an expert on the history of the Picardie and Major Roberts, an English resident in this district, it was possible to arrange for a descriptive excursion through

Abbeville aerodrome 1939-1940. Left to right: Alex Cox, Vivian Kelly, Bill Shearman, Bill Mason and Peter Watts.

Saint Valery-sur-Somme and the battlefields of Crecy during the afternoon.

24 March: In the afternoon a football tournament took place at Abbeville. No.II Squadron vs. Abbeville and No.26 squadron vs. The French Army.

31 March: In the afternoon there was a voluntary outing to Le Tréport for those not on duty and a football match was held there between the garrison and No.II Squadron.

01 April: ENSA Cinema show in the Stella Palace Abbeville.

04 April: No.II Squadron played No.26 Squadron at the Abbeville stadium. No.26 Squadron won 6-4.

05 April: Mr. F.S. Smythe gave a lecture in the dining hall to the Squadron entitled 'Himalayan Adventure'. Great appreciation was shown by the Commanding Officer.

06 April: Football match at the Abbeville Stadium. No.II Squadron vs. Royal Tank Regiment. The match was won by the RTC. Score 5-0.

21 April: A representative RAF soccer team played Base Aerienne 117 at the Parc des Princes, Paris. One third of the Squadron were given facilities to attend.

28 April: 570685 LAC Humphreys J.E. of No.II Squadron won the RAF Component Cross Country race from a field of approximately 150 competitors.

29 April: ENSA Concert Party attended in Béthune by four officers and eighteen other ranks from the ALG there.

Other means of entertainment were to be found privately in Abbeville. There were many cafés and restaurants and, if necessary, Monsieur Gaby was available with his 'young ladies from the best families'.

The wet weather had a serious effect on the soil of Abbeville aerodrome. On 19 March 1940 the AOCiC BAFF Air Marshal A.S. Barratt CB, CMG, MC, accompanied by AVM C.H.B. Blount CBE, MC, visited the aerodrome and met pilots and air gunners of both squadrons. The same day RAF bombers had attacked Hornum seaplane base at the southernmost tip of Sylt. The raid had been a retaliation for a German raid against Scapa Flow and had been rather massive for this stage of the war. Thirty Whitleys and twenty Hampdens had been dispatched. Spirits were high after the bombers returned. However, reconnaissances during the first week of April had revealed that everyone had been over-optimistic. Only slight damage had been caused. That night all RAF stations in France received signals to the effect that German retaliation was now expected. No raid materialised, but gun posts were manned all night and the defence system was on alert from half an hour before dawn. On 22 March S/L Geddes fell ill with German measles. When a second-in-command arrived in the person of S/L Mulliken the latter could go to work immediately as the CO was confined to his quarters for five days. Geddes had to stay in bed and therefore was unable to participate in a happy occasion at the castle. On 24 March Comtesse De Mython gave birth to a son, Hubert. The Squadron presented her with a silver mug. The inscription on it read:

> 'HUBERT, 24 MARCH 1940, FROM THE OFFICERS, ROYAL AIR FORCE AT DRUCAT'.

This gift was tremendously appreciated. When Air Commodore Geddes re-visited Drucat in 1987 it was the first thing the Comtesse showed him.

Lysander KO-O on a tactical reconnaissance sortie somewhere over Northern France, early 1940.

On 30 March F/L Saward left the Squadron and was posted to HQ No.52 Wing as Squadron Leader, Signals. April 1940, in spite of the German invasion of Denmark and Norway, was the last relatively quiet month for the Squadron. On the 10th S/L Geddes received orders to open an Operations Office at Béthune/Labuissière. The following day A-Flight left Abbeville to take up a new post at the landing ground there. On 20 April S/L Geddes was promoted to Wing Commander with effect from 1 March.

Then came May 1940. The Squadron dispersed. C-Flight left for Senon to join No.87 Squadron which had left Lille-Seclin. They formed a composite squadron. Many of the British Squadrons had also found new aerodromes elsewhere in France. By 1 May 1940 the Army Co-operation Squadrons had been moved to other bases in France:

No.4 Squadron: Monchy-Lagache, det. Clairmarais.

No.13 Squadron: Flamicourt.

No.II Squadron: Abbeville, dets. Labuissière/ Senon.

No.26 Squadron: Dieppe, det. Arras.

No.53 Squadron: Crecy.

No.59 Squadron: Poix, dets. Vitry and Rennes.

No.18 Squadron: Rozières.

No.57 Squadron: Rozières, det. Rennes.

The fighter squadrons had moved as well. As for C-Flight No.II (AC) Squadron it was not until May 6 that the first sorties were flown. Escorted by high-flying Hurricanes they were to try to lure the Germans into attacking them so that the Hurricanes could bounce the Germans. The Lysander pilots were not too happy with this job. Before being recalled to Drucat the Squadron also carried out recces of the 51st (Highland) Division area. On 9 May C-Flight received orders to prepare for the return flight to Abbeville as the international situation was rapidly deteriorating. However, the same day this order was cancelled by telephone.

In the early hours of 10 May 1940 all hell broke loose when, with unexpected ferocity and suddenness, German troops invaded The Netherlands and Belgium, carefully avoiding a frontal attack against the Maginot Line. While German paratroopers landed in Holland, Senon aerodrome, like very many in France, Belgium and Holland, was bombed by the Luftwaffe. No less than seventy-five bombs were dropped on it. Fortunately they did not inflict any damage on personnel and equipment. Immediately C-Flight was ordered to return to Abbeville. Yet at 0530 hours Abbeville was also bombed: incendiary bombs fell all round the dispersed aircraft and one HE bomb made a large crater in the ground. Sappers under Lt. Horan RE promptly filled the crater. The happy days of Drucat were over. No more thoughts of sport and leisure, no more illegal visits to Monsieur Gaby. No.II (AC) Squadron went to battle for the second time in its existence, or rather, battle came to the Squadron. At mid-day C-Flight road party left Senon aerodrome and the aircraft took off. The next morning all vehicles were back at Abbeville. In the meantime C-Flight aircraft had been refuelled and armed, the crews preparing themselves to support 3rd Corps. F/O Lang left Béthune-Labuissière by car in order to reconnoitre Ledeghem aerodrome as a possible ALG during the BEF advance into Belgium. The same day a signal came from the AOCiC:

> 'The Air Officer Commanding-in-Chief congratulates all Squadrons of the Air Component on the splendid work they are doing, on their magnificent spirit, the information they have obtained and the enemy aircraft they have destroyed'.

Apart from F/O Lang, F/L Jimmy Drysdale of C-Flight accompanied by the Medical Officer and the Senior AILO also drove to Ledeghem. On 14 May an advance party of C-Flight moved from Abbeville to Bethune en route for Ledeghem, having arranged to billet in the Belgian town of Moorsele. The following day the main road party arrived at Ledeghem to find it occupied by No.615 Squadron. It was decided that No.II Squadron would occupy Wevelghem aerodrome. When Drysdale arrived there he found the airfield deserted. The Belgians had left in a hurry. Instead of a tidy Belgian air base Wevelghem was the scene of devastation and apparent panic. Hangars had been burned down, the grass field between the railway and the main road had been perforated by bombs and Belgian aircraft had been destroyed and abandoned. There was not a single Belgian air force representative to be found. While C-Flight landed and the ground crews pushed the aircraft into the devastated hangars to give them some protection, Drysdale and Everett set out to find civil authorities to co-operate with. They soon found that they themselves would be the only authorities available. After a fruitless search they returned and began work on Wevelghem to make it suitable for aircraft operation. Telephone lines had been cut, waterpipes had been torn out of the walls and toilets and wash basins lay smashed on the grass. Yet all kinds of secret and confidential documents were found on desks and in cupboards. Some offices were cleaned out by ground staff and used to operate from. As the German air forces seemed to rule the skies it was decided to start the Lysanders in the hangars, taxi out at full throttle and take off almost between the hangar doors. Soon a Royal Engineers detachment arrived from Béthune having had considerable problems trying to get through the mass of fugitives moving south. Immediately after their arrival the Engineers began filling the bomb craters and rolling them flat. On top of these repairs they put up sheets of hessian sacking painted to resemble crater shadows. One sight made a deep impression on all. Right between the entrance gate was a large bomb crater blocking the entrance. It was obvious that the sentry outside had been hit and had disappeared in the blast. All that was left of him was an ear, pinned into the wall of the guard house by a shell splinter.

On 14 May the disposition of the Squadron was as follows:

A-Flight: Béthune-Labuissière ALG.

B-Flight: Abbeville aerodrome.

C-Flight: Wevelghem airfield.

At 0900 hours, on 15 May however, a signal came, instructing that the Squadron's main aerodrome was to move at once to Béthune-Labuissière as the Germans were moving west very fast and were expected to try to encircle both the BEF and the Belgian army. At 1430 hours the Squadron aircraft left Abbeville. A small road party, slowed down by masses of refugees left too. It would become a rather familiar sight for the Squadron. The general situation for the Allies did not look very good on 15 May. One day earlier the Belgian Prime Minister had begged King Leopold to withdraw into France. The King, thinking of his father's example in 1914, had refused to do so, although the government could no longer stay in Brussels. The Germans had crossed the Meuse and the RAF had suffered very badly over Sedan. German bombers had flattened the centre of Rotterdam on 14 May, killing about 800 civilians and forcing the Dutch to surrender the following day. On the 16th the Belgian government established itself in Ostend. The BEF began to retreat from the Dyle line. At this stage of the war all the Squadron aircraft were divided between Belgium (one Flight) and Labuissière (two Flights). At Abbeville only a small contingent of MT vehicles had stayed behind with some AA guns for airfield protection. While all this was happening No.II Squadron flew armed recce sorties for 3rd Corps. The Lysanders carried small bombs on each wing stub totalling twelve twenty-pound Cooper anti-personnel bombs with which they were supposed to attack German tanks. Then there was an alarming development; aerial reconnaissance showed that German Panzers had come as close as twenty miles east of Béthune. Their aim seemed to be to encircle the BEF in a clockwise attack towards Boulogne and Calais. It was decided that HQ 3rd Corps would move to Ronq, where it re-established itself at 1200 hours, 16 May. It had been a wise move and all believed that at least for a few days they would be safe from the German spearheads. Whilst there a very strange thing was discovered by a Lysander of No.II Squadron. Not far from the HQ building was a piece of grass-land. While flying over it the pilot noticed that someone had cut a large fig leaf shape in the grass. The fig leaf happened to be the emblem adopted by 3rd Corps . . Investigations revealed that it had been done by an elderly couple who claimed they had merely wanted to feed their rabbits. Disbelief is obvious in what the diarist wrote in the Operations Record Book of the Squadron:

> 'This explanation seemed to satisfy 3rd Corps Intelligence . . .'

When a German break-through near Laon was reported a British unit, called Macforce after its commanding officer General Mason MacFarlane, was sent in to stop the gap and guard the right flank of the BEF which was withdrawing from the line of the Escaut River. Their major task was to cover the crossings of the Scarpe River from north west of Douai to St Armand. During the following days many 'Forces' had to be dispatched to fill gaps in the defence line. They were Petreforce (Major General Petre), Frankforce (Major General Franklyn) and Polforce (Major General Curtiss), all being sent to everywhere the French seemed to have problems. Unfortunately the German advance developed at such a speed that all Forces had to turn and withdraw to prevent themselves from being cut off. No.II (AC) Squadron was to fly tactical recce sorties for Macforce and report on the progress of a German column in the Cambrai area. It was a dicey job — the Lysanders were entirely on their own in a very hostile sky. It was obvious that the Squadron would suffer losses and one of the first crews to run into serious trouble were P/O Clifford Dearden and his air gunner AC Patterson. While flying Lysander KO-N they were intercepted by no less than nine Me109s who believed them to be easy prey. Dearden ably eluded attacks by flying at ground level. Although his petrol tank was holed thirty-two times he managed to stay in the air and fly for another twenty minutes before landing at Douai aerodrome. While Patterson stayed behind with the Lizzie, Dearden returned to Béthune to see if he could gather a team to repair the aircraft and help him fly it out. Unfortunately he approached No.13 Squadron and its CO S/L 'Fatty' Gray, who was very unhelpful and made the Squadron lose a valuable aircraft. It was not until a few days later that No.II Squadron had some kind of revenge for Gray's action.

At 1600 hours, 18 May, F/L Drysdale received orders to prepare to abandon Wevelghem aerodrome and return to Béthune prior to departure for England. It was obvious that nothing could stop the German advance. Brussels had surrendered to the Germans and the general situation was getting hopeless. The Belgians were on the west side of the Scheldt River east of Gent. South of them was the BEF. Further south the French First Army held the line between the Rivers Dender and Sambre. The most worrying thing was that the Germans had broken through the French Ninth Army and were speeding west, north of Peronne and south of Cambrai. They were aiming for Abbeville and then for the Channel ports. The Squadron's Operational Staff which was at Rong with HQ 3rd Corps was ordered to leave and drive to Boulogne where they should meet the Squadron road party. They left at 2100 hours. The last road party to depart was C-Flight's, leaving Wevelghem at 2130 hours that night.

The same day, at Douai aerodrome AC Patterson, who was still with KO-N, was ordered to set fire to his aircraft. It was necessary for S/L Gray himself to order Patterson to do it. The poor air gunner was hopping mad, but being overruled

While the officers of the Squadron were living at the castle of Drucat, the wife of the proprietor, Comtesse De Mython gave birth to a son, Hubert. On the occasion the officers presented mother and child with a silver mug. Today it is a proud possession of the same Hubert, now Comte Hubert De Mython and owner of the castle.

Ivor Worthington-Wilmer in Lysander KO-H over Abbeville, April 1940.

by a CO in no uncertain terms he could do little else but reluctantly obey. However, when No.13 Squadron landed at Abbeville only a few hours before the Germans arrived, they got a nasty surprise. In spite of the seriousness of the war situation morale in No.II Squadron rose when they heard what had happened to the people who had destroyed one of the Squadron aircraft. Immediately after landing at Abbeville all No.13 Squadron aircraft had grouped around a petrol bowser to get a last bit of fuel before returning to England. Right at the moment that they were filling their tanks a group of German bombers attacked the aerodrome. As the AA guns had already left there was no protection, so the airgunners removed the .303 guns and set up some kind of perimeter defence. All the other personnel hurried to the nearby slit trench for cover. One No.13 Squadron pilot who will remain unnamed tried to outsmart all the others and rushed to a nearby trench. He dived into it head first only to discover that he had sought shelter in the remnants of one of No.II Squadron's mobile latrines. When the Squadron road party left they had put the latrines on top of their lorries and left. One can imagine what happened. With full flying kit, and parachute still on, the pilot disappeared into the soft and very smelly substance. Screaming for help the poor chap surfaced. Nobody was willing to lend a helping hand and he was ordered to stay down-wind from the others while the briefing took place in the open. His gunner was not at all pleased to have to join his pilot for the journey home. Once the story spread among the various RAF stations in the south of England the poor man was given a new name: P/O Brown-Job.

The next day, 19 May, No.II Squadron entirely abandoned Abbeville. It was obvious that the Lysanders were too vulnerable to operate over the battlefields as they had been doing for the last nine days. The Squadron was told to return to Lympne. For the road party it would be a very eventful journey. Forty years later Comtesse De Mython showed me her diary, in which she had written what happened when the Squadron was at Drucat. She had seen the Squadron leave the village and knew that bad things were about to happen. In her diary she wrote:

> 'They left when the Germans were only a few kilometres from Abbeville. I will never forget what happened two days after the last RAF car had driven off. An aeroplane circled over the castle as if the pilot was looking for something. Then it disappeared and returned flying low over the trees. It landed in the meadow behind the house. While the engine kept running the pilot jumped out and ran to the house. I was so amazed to recognise him as Lieutenant Benito with whom I had become very friendly while he stayed at the castle. He came in through the little door of the salon and said to me: "Madame, if you were my mother I would order you to come with me. Now I can only beg you". I told him I could not leave the house. Then he stepped back, stood to attention and saluted me with great solemnity. He turned and ran back to the aircraft. It took off, circled over the castle twice and disappeared. I never saw Mr. Benito again. At 5 o'clock in the afternoon a German staff car drove in. Without much ado they requisitioned the first and second floor. They stayed until 4th September 1944. When they were forced to withdraw they burned the house down.'

For the air crew it was just a short flight to the relatively safe shores of England. For the road party it was an entirely different matter. While on their way among all sorts of refugees, military and civilian, British, French, Dutch and Belgian they encountered help and high spirits as well as panic and suspicion. While the German armoured divisions were moving west, the retreating Allies were in constant fear of saboteurs and franc-tireurs. Belgians would fire upon the French, the French would shell the British and the British would defend themselves against the Belgians. Meanwhile Stukas and Messerschmitts would swoop down and machine gun the long columns trying to escape from the carnage of war. Communications were non-existent. At times the British would think that a bridge was firmly in the hands of the French who in turn would believe the bridge had already been blown up by British soldiers. Rumours said that the Germans had captured Belgian lorries and were using them to speed up their advance. Consequently Belgian MT convoys were fired upon. Other rumours said that the Germans had taken an

RAF aerodrome and seized perfectly serviceable Lysanders, as a result of this some British AA batteries fired upon any Lysander they saw. Andrew Geddes remembered a striking incident in which the ignorance and lack of information was clear:

'The Germans had come as close as forty miles from HQ 51 Wing. Shortly after we heard this a phone call came in. It was a sergeant from HQ 51 Wing. He was belly-aching us about some utterly ridiculous triviality and insisting on speaking to the OC No.II Squadron. When he got me on the phone he started lamentations about some admin. error we had made. It was not at all important but to him it seemed to be the key problem to be solved in order to win the war. I got very upset and asked him if by any chance he had heard that there was a bl..dy war on. Would he please leave the safety of his desk and have a look outside and see if anything was happening. After a few minutes he returned and said that all was perfectly quiet apart from a few French tanks coming through. I asked him if he had seen the markings on the tanks. He said he did not know and suggested that he would have a second look. Again he returned and said: "I am so sorry Sir, they are not French, they are ours for they have white crosses on their sides". He must have seen similar crosses on our tanks during exercises. I then explained that the crosses were in fact black, with white lines around, which was the usual marking for German tanks. It must have come as a shock for him for without saying anything more he put down the phone. When we tried to contact him again half an hour later we got no answer. They must have been put in the bag right after the first call. By the way, we never got to solving his admin problem'.

The RAF had lost so many aircraft that it was no longer possible to provide the Lysanders with any fighter cover. They had to do the job on their own. On the last day of the Squadron's stay on the Continent the CO ran into trouble.

On the morning of 19 May he had been told that 3rd Corps was about to withdraw across two bridges over the Scheldt River near the town of Oudenaerde in Belgium. As no-one knew who controlled the bridge a Lysander was to be despatched and sent there to reconnoitre the area. Geddes decided he was to carry out this sortie. With his air gunner LAC Clarke he took off from Béthune. Upon approaching the bridges they saw twenty Stukas preparing to dive bomb. They were circling at about 5,000 feet. Geddes decided to attack. He used two main principles of war for this attack: surprise and offence. After his safe arrival he wrote in his combat report:

'Evidently the leader of the Stuka formation had not seen us, or he might have thought that we were one of their Henschel Army Co-op aircraft. Without paying any further attention to us he led the first section of ten down to attack the bridges. One obvious way of avoiding suspicion was to join the tail of the nearest Stuka in his dive and follow him down. This I did. Pulling up from the dive it was quite a different matter with all the enemy aircraft in line astern in my gunsight with the underside of the fuselages, undercarriages and engines exposed. I gave a long series of bursts and I saw splinters flying off one aircraft. At the top of the first climb in my attack I saw that we had put the gunner in one Stuka out of action. However, my attack seemed to have alerted them all and the whole line peeled off and began attacking me. As surprise was lost I went down to ground level in defensive circles. One particular aircraft then kept on my tail and kept firing at us with its 20mm cannon. This was a rather unpleasant surprise, since according to my knowledge and information from intelligence the Stuka only carried machine guns in front. My air gunner reported on the intercom tube that his guns were jammed, so until he had cleared the stoppage, I was defenceless in the rear. We flew extremely low and at times the undercarriage brushed through the trees, fortunately without any effect on the performance of KO-T. I could beat the Stuka in flat turns without spinning due to the Lysander's automatic flaps and slots. However the German pilot almost tricked me. When I

Bill Shearman and Sergeant Spurr often flew KO-L when the Squadron was based at Abbeville aerodrome.

Captain George Everett was the AILO (Air Intelligence Liaison Officer) with No.II Squadron. He was posted to the Squadron twice. In May 1940 George flew a Belgian aircraft from Wevelghem to England, rather than destroy it or have it captured by the enemy.

managed to get on his tail at a reasonable speed and looked like closing in for the kill he flapped up his dive brakes and appeared to stop dead straight ahead of me. Without any brakes at low altitude I was forced to overshoot him and all he then had to do was to apply full throttle and pull up his nose. He caught me from behind in a very vulnerable position. The first time he did this he fired a short cannon burst at us which passed between the cockpit and the struts. I knew that he was using incendiaries because when the shells went ahead of me I could smell burning phosphorus. Luckily Clarke soon put his guns right and I was able to do a lazy turn to get the Stuka nicely lined up and fire another burst. Immediately the pilot pulled up and baled out. The Stuka crashed into a small wood near the village of Kruisbosch east of Oudenaerde. I made sure I got away as fast as I could. I landed at Wevelghem and reported my clash with the Germans to the AILO who was still there. F/O Doidge drove to the scene of the crash and confirmed the kill by telephone. Belgian soldiers captured the German pilot. He was handed over to us and locked up in a cage in Béthune. The gunner was killed during the battle'.

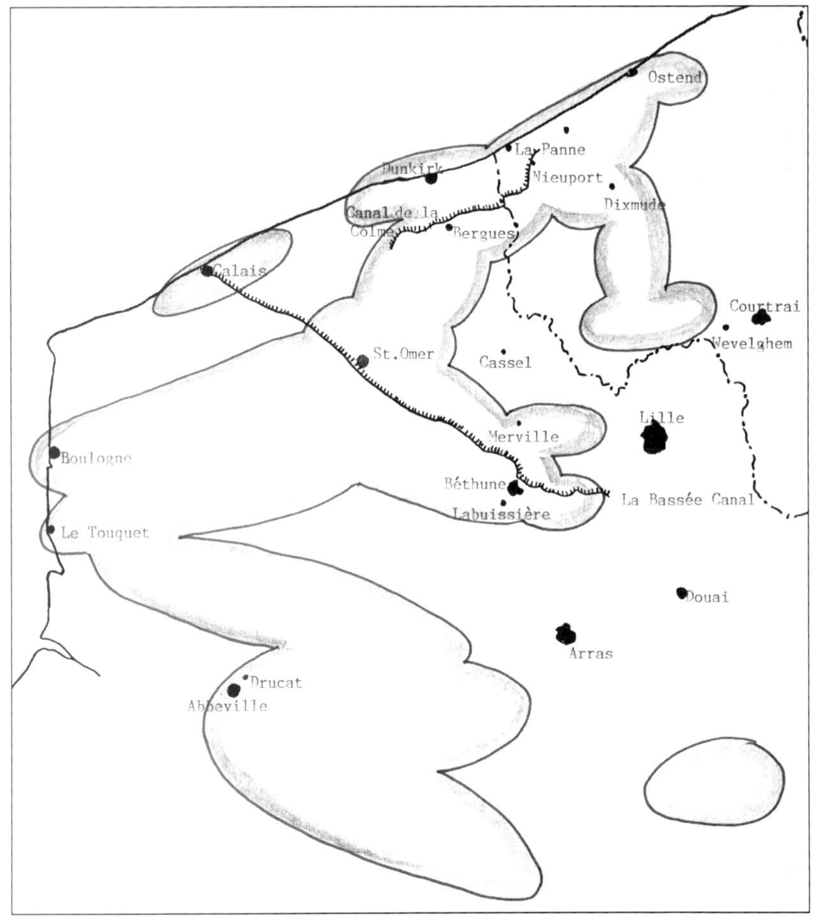

Areas reconnoitred by No.II (AC) Squadron between 10 May and 1 June 1940.

After Geddes had returned to Wevelghem he was told that the airfield was to be evacuated immediately. Soon all engines were running. George Everett had found a Belgian air force Leopard Moth. The aircraft looked alright and after the engine had proved to be running smoothly it was decided to take it back to England rather than leaving it behind or destroying it. When Tony Doidge was back all Lysanders and the Leopard Moth took off. Half an hour later C-Flight landed at Labuissière. At 2000 hours they took off again heading for home, Geddes ordering the Flights at Labuissière to depart as well after he had received written orders to do so. Due to insufficient light C-Flight landed at Berck-sur-Mer at 2105 hours. Geddes never saw his opponent. The German was soon liberated by the first German troops entering Béthune. At the same time as C-Flight road party left Wevelghem for Boulogne Squadron HQ received a note saying that all essential stores, ammunition and W/T equipment had to be taken to Boulogne as quickly as possible. F/L (now Group Captain) Brian Walford remembered:

> 'Suddenly Andrew Geddes landed at Labuissière. He leapt out of the Lysander and shouted at us to leave and get out via Boulogne. Then he rushed back to his aircraft, jumped in and took off again. This "getting out" was easier said than done and I was somewhat at a loss as to know where to begin. "Relax and let things develop around you" was the advice of S/L Mulliken, our unruffled XO. Geddes' car was in for repairs, so, rather than leaving it behind we towed it with us behind a tractor all the way to Boulogne, arriving there the next day'.

At 1100 hours, 20 May the Squadron Headquarters main party embarked, leaving P/O Amor behind in charge of the MT convoy which was to drive all the way to Cherbourg before they were able to find a ship to take them home. The main party disembarked at Dover at 1500 hours and entrained for Tidworth where they were accommodated for the night. At 2200 hours the previous evening most of the Squadron aircraft had landed at Lympne. C-Flight, however, did not leave the Continent until 0500 the following day when they took off from Berk-sur-Mer landing at Lympne at 0645 hours. Three hours later the Squadron took off again and flew to Bekesbourne. Eleven hours later orders came to fly on to Croydon where they arrived at 2100 hours. The aircraft were dispersed around the aerodrome while the aircrew were accommodated in the main building. A party of one sergeant and twenty-six men from No.110 (Canadian) Squadron arrived to carry out maintenance on the aircraft. Four Lysanders and crews were temporarily posted to No.16 Squadron for operations from Lympne.

Individual drivers forming a small road party had a long way to go before they finally returned home. One of the drivers was Charles Cross. Not an RAF serviceman but a regular soldier in the Army, he and his unit had been attached to No.II Squadron. He sat behind the wheel of his vehicle all the way to Cherbourg. He remembers how the ALO, Captain Galsworthy, had given orders to move and rendezvous with the remainder of the road party who were said to be waiting north of Abbeville. The roads were packed with refugees and driving was slow and careful. When the group arrived at the meeting point there was nobody waiting for them. They waited for hours before it was decided to have a look for themselves. First they drove to La Triquerie where No.26 Squadron had been billeted — they had already vacated the place, there was not a single person to be seen. Yet the presence of the RAF was evident. They found kitchen equipment, a destroyed lorry and bits and pieces of abandoned uniforms and equipment. Fortunately No.26 Squadron had also left some food. The bread was hard as rock but the men decided to take it with them, just in case. Then they drove to Abbeville aerodrome hoping to meet someone over there. When the party arrived the aerodrome was still a hive of activity. All the Lysanders had left but a four-engined passenger plane of Imperial Airways was still there, engines running. It was being loaded with all sorts of equipment. The members of the convoy tried to find someone able to advise them what to do. But all they got was the order to continue to Cherbourg, so they drove through Abbeville and soon joined the long column of refugees. They saw civilians, victims of German strafing attacks, lying on stretchers along the roadside. They also encountered hostility from French soldiers who waved their fists and rifles at the RAF servicemen. Halfway to Rouen the column suddenly stopped and soldiers set up machine guns while people rushed into the fields. Three twin-engined German aircraft came closer and dropped sticks of bombs which fortunately fell in the fields and not on the road where vehicles had been left behind in the panic. When the column arrived in Rouen the lorries were parked under trees in a side street. Eventually a Frenchman reluctantly gave them some water and early the next morning the convoy proceeded to Cherbourg where it arrived in the evening after an uneventful journey.

The thing that angered the British was to see many brand new crated radial aircraft engines lying along the roadside; dropped there by someone to become a prize for the Germans. At Cherbourg the convoy was directed to the quayside and the Office Van which Cross had been driving was loaded aboard the ship. RAF personnel boarded the freighter. Cross explained that he had been attached to an RAF squadron and asked if he could also go on board. All his kit was in the van. The Army Lieutenant supervising the loading said that the ship was for RAF personnel only. As Cross and his colleagues were in Army green the ship was off limits. Then the ship's siren sounded and the planks were pulled on board. Suddenly the Lieutenant turned to Cross and his friends and said that he would look the other way while they got on board. The soldiers were the last to leave Cherbourg harbour. Cross remembered:

> 'I was very upset when we sailed. It was shattering and above all humiliating to have to leave like this. For some odd reason someone had given orders that all rifles, pistols and machine guns had to be left behind. A huge pile lay there waiting to be captured by the enemy. I never saw so much valuable equipment left behind so unnecessarily'.

P/O Amor's convoy also reached the coast. They had to drive as far as Nantes before they found a ship. Amor tried to convince Jablon-Gonnet/Smith that he and his wife should go with them to England. 'Your country will be occupied. They will never occupy England', he said. Politely the Frenchman declined. He had only one request: could the British please give him a rifle and ammunition. He was given what he asked for. Then Jablon-Gonnet and his wife walked away into the town. He never looked back. It was the last the Squadron ever heard or saw of him. When the Allies liberated France in 1944 Air Commodore Geddes, then Air Cdre (Plans), Second TAF, had enquiries made on behalf of the Squadron to trace the French couple and see if they needed help. After some months Geddes got official news that Marechal de Logis-Chef Raoul Jablon-Gonnet had been killed in battle on 19 June 1940, three days before the French signed the Armistice in the Forest of Compiègne. No trace was ever found of his wife.

Peter 'Dingbat' Edinger flew with the Squadron during the battle over France and Flanders. He was killed on 8 September 1941, a twenty-five year old Wing Commander and OC No.12 Squadron, flying a Wellington bomber to Berlin. He rests at the Reichswald Cemetery in Germany, less than ten miles from the Squadron's base until December 1991.

CHAPTER 7
DUTY NOBLY DONE

The Squadron's return to England did not mean that it stood idle. On 21 May F/O Hallam was the first to spend the night back at Hawkinge in readiness for a dawn sortie. At the same time the Squadron Main Party proceeded from Tidworth to Croydon where it arrived at 1600 hours. They all were given the opportunity to take a bath and have a meal. The officers were put up in the Croydon Aerodrome Hotel. In spite of the Squadron being virtually broken up it was ordered to continue flying tactical reconnaissance sorties. On 22 May the Squadron was ready for action, the Operations Record Book entries for that day show the tremendous workload the Squadron was subjected to after their frustrating experiences in Northern France and Flanders.

> 0400: F/O Hallam took off for Tac/R in Boulogne area. Landed 0530 hours.
>
> 0620: P/O Stuart took off for Tac/R in Foret de Crecy-Champagne area. Landed 0755 hours.
>
> 1100: P/O Mason took off for Tac/R in Etaples-Fauquembergues-Theronamne-Arras area. Landed 1300 hours.
>
> P/O Shearman took off for Tac/R in Etaples-Montreuil-Hesdin-St Pol area.
>
> 1550: F/O Doidge took off for Tac/R in Merville aerodrome area. On the return flight he engaged a Ju87 aircraft which was eventually shot down by his rear gunner LAC Webborn. This crew also shot down a He126.

At first it had been quite an uneventful flight for Doidge and Webborn flying KO-U. That changed dramatically when they flew about a mile south of the French town of Cassel at about 1630 hours. Not far away from them were a group of German dive bombers, flying on a parallel course at about 1,000 feet. The Stukas paid no attention to the lonely Lysander as they were engaged in bombing the town. When the Germans pulled up after the attack one of them passed through Doidge's gunsight who gave it a burst making the Stuka turn sharply to port. This brought the German in front of Webborn who put a full pan of ammunition into the Ju87. The Stuka turned on its back and crashed. By this time a number of Hurricanes appeared and engaged the Stukas which were no match for the fighters. Three more dive bombers crashed. Doidge left the area and flew west. At about 1645 hours he spotted a Henschel He126 reconnoitring a village. Doidge turned to attack the German but when the pilot saw the Lysander coming in he turned tail and fled, diving down to ground level. Having the advantage of height and gaining speed in his dive Doidge pressed on until he was about 450 yards from the German. He attacked from astern and gave a long burst. The Henschel fell into a wood and exploded on impact. Then the Lysander itself was in trouble, for while Doidge circled over the crash site to see what had happened several German machine guns fired upon the Lysander. Doidge left the scene as quickly as possible, to be credited with two 'kills', the second and third for the Squadron since war had broken out. At the same time six Lysanders had taken off to participate in a bombing raid against German targets on roads south of Boulogne. The crews detailed for this sortie were:

> F/L Edinger and Cpl Chadwick; P/O Henderson and P/O Kelly; P/O Grant-Govan and LAC Jones; P/O Smithers and Cpl Bovington; P/O Thomas and LAC Dixon; P/O Wooldridge and LAC Jordan.

Basically, the whole attack proved that the Lysander was not at all suitable for these kinds of missions. However due to the scarcity of aircraft, the Lysander crews had to oblige. All Lysanders were armed with four twenty-pound bombs under each wing stub. The brief was to approach the targets at 5,000 feet and dive to 3,000 feet to attack. Once the bombs had been dropped the pilots had to get clear of the area as quickly as possible using ground features as cover. Between 1930 and 2000 hours all the aircraft took off. The sortie nearly ended in disaster. First of all the aircraft had taken off between five- and fifteen-minute intervals. This meant that each aircraft had to fly over enemy controlled territory without any protection, depending solely on the crew's individual skill. However, all six aircraft found their targets and dived down to attack. While passing the 3,000 feet mark they released their bombs, only to find out that a ghastly mistake had been made at Hawkinge where they had been bombed up. Instead of HE bombs, so-called 'F' bombs had been hung under the stubs. Each bomb carried a small parachute to delay its fall when used in a low-level attack. No-one had told the crews and not one of the crews had checked the bombs prior to take-off. One can imagine their horror when, failing to see their bombs explode, they suddenly found themselves surrounded by bombs floating down on parachutes. Wildly manoeuvring Lysanders now tried to evade their own bombs. One of the pilots, P/O Grant-Govan had hang-ups over the target. When he returned to Bekesbourne and landed the impact caused two bombs to release themselves. They immediately exploded underneath the Lysander killing poor Jones, injuring Grant-Govan and destroying the aircraft. P/Os Henderson and Kelly failed to return. Henderson was killed and buried at Pihen-les-Guines not far from the Channel coast. It was not until much later that news was received of Kelly having been taken POW. Henderson and Jones were the first Squadron members to be killed in action. Malcolm Lessels George Henderson was the son of Air Vice-Marshal Malcolm Henderson CB, CBE, DSO. All the other aircraft returned home, P/O Wooldridge wounded by a splinter in his hand.

In spite of this, recce sorties had to be continued. The following day P/O Mason reconnoitred the Merville area while F/O Hallam tried to find German armoured vehicles in the Calais region. During the afternoon F/L Eyres flew a Tac/R over the La Panne area. Two days later Benito and Webborn went looking for enemy tanks. P/O Baker and LAC Galloway flew over Boulogne, St. Omer and Béthune. They returned at 0830 hours with a cross strut in the rear of Lysander KO-L shot away by ack-ack. At 1045 F/O Lang and LAC Evans appeared over Béthune. When they landed at Bekesbourne Lysander KO-E had also been hit by German fire. At 1235 P/O Watts and LAC Simms were sent over the dunes of Dannes to try and find the whereabouts of a battalion of the Welsh Guards which was reported to be hiding from the Germans. Unfortunately no sign of the Guards was found. P/O Scotter, who was to become one of the best Lysander pilots in later days, flying agents into and from France for SOE, went on a Tac/R over the battlefield. They took off at 1730 hours. Upon their return Scotter wrote a Combat Report having left his Lysander at Hawkinge damaged beyond repair:

> 'We were engaged by enemy heavy AA in the vicinity of Gravelines, to avoid which I did a steep diving turn to starboard. The AA immediately ceased, and my air gunner reported "Messerschmitts port above". About 1,500 feet above me were fifteen Me109s. I executed a steep diving turn to the right and four or five Me109s attacked, using a similar method of the old type of astern attack used by the RAF. I do not know if we were hit during this first assault. As the enemy aircraft turned after delivering their attack I dived for ground level under full throttle. When we came out of the dive we were attacked by three enemy aircraft approaching from the starboard quarter. During this attack my air gunner engaged the enemy continuously and observed the enemy aircraft on the starboard quarter break away leaving a trail of black smoke. We were then attacked by relays of aircraft until crossing the coast some four miles SW of Calais, when all attacks were broken off.
> Tactics adopted:
> Attack No.1: 4 or 5 aircraft attacked, using old type of astern attack. Evasive actions: Steep turn to starboard and full throttle dive to ground level.
> Attack No.2: One aircraft on the starboard quarter, one astern and one on the port quarter, attacked with cannon in that order. My air gunner fired on the aircraft firing from the starboard quarter, causing him to break away with black smoke trailing from his fuselage. He was unable to fire at the aircraft dead astern, but engaged the aircraft on the port quarter, who attacked rather later than the other two aircraft.
> Result: Aircraft attacking from port quarter gave a steady burst of cannon fire which first passed beneath our aircraft and then hit the undercarriage and petrol tank sump. He then broke away.
> Attack No.3: We were worried by six aircraft attacking continuously from all angles. One aircraft trying to attack from below, but we were too low and he gave up before his attack developed. Another aircraft crossed our bows and I engaged him with my front guns without result. A third formated on us about 100 degrees to port. He appeared to be

KO-O on patrol, May 1940. The machine gun pointing up is clearly visible in the rear cockpit.

Malcolm Henderson was killed over Boulogne on 22 May 1940. His air gunner P/O Kelly was taken prisoner by the Germans. Malcolm was the son of AVM M. Henderson CB, CBE, DSO. P/O Henderson's body rests at Pihen-les-Guines War Cemetery near Calais.

watching us, perhaps gauging our speed or trying to draw the fire of my air gunner from the aircraft astern. By this time we were approaching the coast west of Calais and were being engaged by enemy ground forces. This had the effect of holding off the enemy aircraft. They finally broke off their attack at the coast line.

Results:

Attack No.1: Nil.

Attack No.2: Enemy aircraft on starboard quarter believed to be shot down by my rear gunner, while we received cannon shot in the undercarriage and petrol tank sump from the aircraft attacking on the port quarter.

Attack No.3: We received damage from cannon fire badly in the port main plane, in the fuselage and in the tail unit. We also received one shot through the engine cowling on the lower side, believed to have come from enemy ground defences.

During the engagement my air gunner kept a continuous and steady fire on all attackers, but was unable to observe results except for the one aircraft mentioned in Attack No.2. We flew Lysander KO-X.'

While Scotter limped home to Hawkinge two other Squadron Lysanders were active over Calais, which was surrounded by the Germans. P/Os Robinson and Kelsh in KO-T spotted a battery shelling the town. F/L Eyres and LAC Philpott at the same time hedge-hopped into the Abbeville-Bernaville area in KO-E trying to gather information for the ground forces. Upon their return they reported that contrary to what was thought the Germans seemed reluctant to use abandoned airfields. They probably expected them to be booby-trapped. Therefore German aircraft were dispersed in fields near woods.

On 25 May the situation around Calais was extremely worrying. British and French troops defending it had been cut off, while the Germans controlled the town and the last remnants of the Allied forces had withdrawn into the Citadel. The Germans pushed north after crossing the La Bassée Canal, forming a wedge between the Allied lines. There was an enormous gap between the British and Belgian troops. King Leopold of Belgium had decided to remain with his soldiers whatever happened. At the same time His troops tried desperately to build a defensive line behind the Leie River. The troops in Calais were running out of ammunition and supplies. Yet the Chief of Air Staff sent a message to the Air Component:

'Congratulations to all units of the Air Component. I have the highest admiration for the great work they have done, often in the most difficult situations and against heavy opposition. The untiring efforts of both the Ground and Flying personnel has rendered valuable aid to the Allied Forces and are worthy of the highest praise. I am confident that in the new situation the Air Component will add to the high reputation which it already has gained'.

In spite of Calais being cut off the Cabinet had decided it was right to fight to the end. Therefore No.II Squadron was ordered to participate in a joint mission with naval and other aircraft to take supplies to the defenders of Calais. The encircled garrison consisted of one battalion of the Rifle Brigade, one of the 60th Rifles, the Queen Victoria Rifles and a battalion of the Royal Tank Regiment with twenty-one light tanks and twenty-seven Crusaders. Besides this there was a French detachment of similar strength. Brigadier Nicholson, Commanding Officer of the British troops, knew that he was to stay and follow his troops into captivity or death.

The No.II Squadron crews detailed to fly to Calais were:

F/L Drysdale and LAC Clark in KO-U;
F/O Pimm and Cpl Pickles in KO-S;
P/O Shearman and Sgt Spurr in KO-F;
P/O Dearden and P/O Bostock in KO-C;
P/O Cox and LAC Sim in KO-D;
P/O Dudeney and LAC Jarvis in KO-V;
P/O Mason and Cpl Oliver in KO-P;
P/O Baker and LAC Galloway in KO-L.

P/O (now W/C) Shearman wrote an account of this sortie after he returned.

'On Sunday evening, May 26th we were all suddenly recalled to the aerodrome from Canterbury, where most of us had dispersed. On arriving at Bekesbourne we were told that there was a job on that would entail getting up at 0330 the next morning, ready to fly as soon as it was light. Machines and crews were detailed and we got to work preparing the machines for the next day's job. We were not told what the job was to be but rumour, very strong rumour had it that we were to drop supplies somewhere. Jimmy Drysdale, who was to lead us knew the details, of course, but when "Mother" Baker asked him what they were he said he did not know. "Because", said Mother, "I have never dropped any before". I took my own gunner, Sergeant Spurr in the back. Incidentally, on this show I flew a C-Flight machine with no armour plating in it and no self sealing-tank, while my own machine which was completely modified was flown by a C-Flight pilot. Having completed our work we got back to the Royal Mountain Hotel for a late supper and so to bed. Up again in the early hours of the next morning and arrived at the aerodrome in good time to find the sky completely overcast by some very low cloud. We took off independently at some thirty second intervals. I was off third, and I remember that just as I opened the throttle I caught sight of Jimmy Drysdale going round in a steep bank about fifty feet off the ground and did a couple of circuits of the aerodrome only occasionally catching sight of the other machines, which by that time were all off the ground. Sometimes they were too close for my liking in that visibility. I had just decided that it was too dangerous to go on to Hawkinge without knowing what the weather was like at that end when I saw a red Very light fired from the aerodrome recalling us. As we were landing Johnny Rogers was ringing up our destination for a weather report, and was told that the weather was clear at Hawkinge, the cloud bank finishing a mile or so to the north. Accordingly we took off again and, climbing through cloud proceeded to Hawkinge independently. On arriving there we found numerous other aircraft, Hectors and Lysanders from Nos. 26 and 613 Squadrons landing. Most of these, I understand, had already done a show that morning. We left our machines to be loaded up with containers, for we had by that time been told what we were going to do and trooped over to the Operations Room to be instructed. On our arrival there we were told that we were not wanted immediately and that we could go over to the Officers' Mess and wait until we were sent for. We sat around in the mess making a pretence of reading the papers and trying to gather details of what we were in for. I met a fellow called Webb, who had learned to fly with me on the Reserve in 1936. He was now in the Auxiliary Air Force with No.613 squadron, commanded by S/L Anderson, who had been my Flight Commander on No.II Squadron for about eight months in 1939. Webb had already been over to Calais once that morning and was standing by to go again with us, which was to be the big party. On the first occasion they had dropped water to the troops and lost one lad by AA fire from the beach as they were coming out. A lot of useful information was obtained from the lads who had already been on the first sortie. After we had been waiting for some time, we decided that it would be a good thing if we were to get some breakfast so we all trooped into the dining room and clamoured for food. Catering at Hawkinge must have been quite a problem at this time for they were always getting odd people arriving at all hours who required feeding. Some time after breakfast about eight Swordfish of the Royal Navy landed. These were to support us. As they were landing we were told to report to the Operations Room and we all breathed a sigh of relief. Things were beginning to happen at last.

'As there were so many of us we gathered in what had been the Link Trainer Room. The Wing Commander stood up on a chair with a large scale map of Calais in his hand and told us what was expected of us. Apparently there were two parties of Allied troops in the city, one actually on the beach east of the pier and another in the

On 26 May 1940 the Squadron participated in dropping supplies for the besieged garrison of Calais. Westland Aircraft Ltd. published a poster showing Lysanders over fighting British troops. Unfortunately the garrison had surrendered the day before the drops took place.

Citadel west of the pier slightly inland. The Lysanders of No.II (AC) Squadron had to drop their loads in the Citadel, and the Lysanders and Hectors of Nos.26 and 613 Squadron were to drop theirs on the party on the beach. We were warned that as the Citadel measured only about four hundred yards by two hundred we would have to go down very low in order to get our containers on the target first go, especially as there would be no time to have a second crack at it. To make things a little more difficult we had to fly across the target the short way as we had to turn right and come out west of our point of entry to avoid banging into the Lysanders and Hectors of the other party. While we were at our work the Hectors of No.613 Squadron were to bomb and machine-gun ("One machine-gun", murmured S/L Anderson) the Huns to the east, and the Swordfish were to perform a similar offensive for us to the west, the object being to make the Boche keep his head down and not worry the supply droppers with too much AA fire. The WingCo went on to tell us that it was very important that the garrison should hold out. It was therefore worth taking considerable risks in order that the supplies should be delivered. He had also asked for fighter protection for us and had been promised at least one squadron of Defiants. We were to take off and fly line astern, the eastern party first, followed by the western or Citadel party, that is to say, us. The ground strafers were to go in first in both cases.

'We climbed into our machines and tested the bomb switches, the loaded containers having been put on the racks in our absence. Our containers were filled with small arms ammunition and grenades. The first party took off, the Hectors having two 110lb bombs slung under their wings and taking quite a long run before they raised themselves into the air. Then the Swordfish of the Nautics waddled out and turned into wind, two 110lb bombs and about eight 40-pounders under their wings. One felt strangely confident in these crews and aircraft, in spite of all the struts and wires of which the aircraft seemed to be built. Coming off the ground after quite a short run they turned left and flew out to sea without anymore ado. Then it was our turn. We knew we should have no trouble with our load for you could load the Lizzie up as much as you liked and she would still come off the ground like a bird. We went out over Folkestone and headed towards France (we let the Navy do the navigation) at about 2,500 feet. About half way over we found a layer of thin cloud at about 2,000 feet. There was a certain amount of shipping in the Channel, chiefly transports and destroyers. The main evacuation from Dunkirk had not yet commenced. About seven miles from the French coast we turned left and went lower, down to about 500 feet. Ahead we could see thick brown smoke over Calais. Due north of the town we left the first party and flew south. The Swordfish went ahead and slightly to our right. After that I did not see them again until we had fulfilled our mission and were on the way home. In front of us was the town under its pall of smoke, as yet all we could see was the beach and the pier sticking out towards us. I found myself flying above but level with Bill Mason and, knowing that there would be no room for a crowd over the target I did an S-turn and dived down behind him. We were now level with the end of the pier and down to about 100 feet. Some inhospitable Huns began firing at us from the end of the pier and we started to jink to avoid the AA fire. I made out my plan of approach, deciding I would go into the town with the lighthouse on my right. This lighthouse was slightly inland and I could only get occasional glimpses of it through the smoke. Below me was an amazing picture, the like of which I had never seen before. All over the town were fires burning with the most vicious red flames and the smoke being changed by the sun from black to dirty brown at the bottom to the most beautiful shades of gold and brown at the top. The whole of Calais was obscured by the smoke which was thicker than any fog I remember. I plunged into the murk keeping a wary eye open for the top of the lighthouse which was just visible slightly above me and to my right. Turning, I went between the lighthouse and the tops of some large buildings on my left and a little below. Now I could just make out the three aeroplanes which were in front of me, and as I caught sight of them I saw the leader drop his containers, but the Citadel was still invisible. Mother Baker was now letting go his containers and soon it would be my turn but still no sign of the target. Suddenly I was through it and the whole scene lay before me, the shattered and burning houses around the fort, then the Citadel itself surrounded by moats. I saw that one of Baker's containers had fallen into the water but the other was on the right side of the ramparts. I determined not to let mine go too early, Bill was just dropping his. Jinking furiously to dodge AA fire we passed over the moats, then the other ramparts, some more walls, then I saw some smashed buildings in what appeared to be the centre of the Citadel. I pressed the switch to release both containers, being so low that it was unnecessary to allow for the parachutes to be drifted by the wind. Permitting myself a sharp right turn I looked back to see both my containers had landed amongst several other parachutes, but could see no movement in the fort. I concluded that the enemy could see into it and that all our troops were keeping their heads down. Still jinking I passed out over the beach on which I could see a lot of men and equipment which looked suspiciously like our own. I continued my evasive tactics until I was about a mile out over the sea, where I considered I was out of range of anything the Huns might try to throw at me from the shore. Off shore I discovered a glorious mix-up of Lysanders, Swordfish and Hectors. It was not possible to distinguish my own party so I tacked myself on to a Swordfish and returned to England in company with him. Approaching Dover we beat up a transport on its way home full of troops who cheered and waved at us. They must have seen us going in earlier and guessed that there was a party going on somewhere. From outside Dover I saw that the Hawkinge Hoodoo was sitting on top of the cliffs so I broke off company with my Naval friend and went round the weather proceeding directly to Bekesbourne. I was the first man back, the others arriving as I was climbing out of my aircraft. All our chaps got back safely, but I heard later that Dicky Dixon of No.26 Squadron had collided with a Swordfish in the smoke of Calais, both aircraft going down. They also told me that a Lysander had tried to fly through the Hoodoo and had flown straight against the cliffs killing both pilot and gunner.'

It had been a bold action of the crews flying outdated aeroplanes to help the Army at Calais. During the four days fighting at Calais the RAF had driven off several German bombers. Twenty British aircraft were lost. Twice the RAF dropped supplies. Pilots and gunners had shown great courage and determination. S/L Anderson when interviewed by Airey Neave whilst Neave was researching for his book *The Flames of Calais* said: 'Some of our crews came straight out of Flying Training School and had never flown a Hector before, nor dropped a bomb nor fired a gun'. Yet they went in to help the army below. It was obvious why Shearman did not see any movement in the Citadel when he flew over. Before the supplies came down Brigadier Nicholson had been forced to surrender. All supplies fell into German hands. The defenders had already been marched away into captivity. At 0756 hours a message was transmitted from Dover to Calais:

> 'To O.C. Troops Calais.
> From Secretary of State.
> Am filled with admiration for your magnificent fight which is worthy of the highest tradition of the British Army'.

Calais never acknowledged receipt. Nicholson himself became a POW and died in captivity in 1943. The day Calais surrendered the biggest operation ever to save the BEF commenced; Operation Dynamo. No.II (AC) Squadron continued its sorties over the enemy. They were to suffer heavily doing it.

On 27 May King Leopold of Belgium informed Lord Gort that the Belgian Army was exhausted and that surrender was inevitable. The next day he signed the terms of surrender and was taken prisoner with his troops. The Belgian government declared the King no longer able to rule the country and took over his prerogative powers. While in Norway British, French and Polish troops chased the Germans out of Narvik 850 vessels assembled at the British coast ready to sail for Dunkirk. The same day P/O Dearden and LAC Williams took off for a Tac/R over the St. Omer-Bourbourg-Spijcker area to find suitable targets for bombers. F/O Lang and Cpl Tomkins reconnoitred the Abbeville-Amiens region to see if the Germans had already taken over abandoned Allied aerodromes. At 1455 hours P/O Cox and LAC Sims flew over the battlefield. They returned at 1720 hours. These daily sorties revealed that the Germans seemed to be building up for a final thrust. Little did they know that Hitler had ordered his troops to stand still and leave Dunkirk to the Luftwaffe. It saved the BEF. The Operations Record Book vividly describes the tremendous effort put in by the Squadron:

29.5.40:

0400. P/O Sherry and LAC Radford carried out a Tac/R in the area Dixmuide-Ypres. Tasks in general, any movement on roads running E to W for enemy AFVs with special attention to Forest in H57. Tasks in particular, to locate enemy petrol dumps or concentrations suitable for offensive bombing action. Owing to low lying mist the pilot was unable to penetrate the area but succeeded in locating a battery which was shelling Dunkirk.

0510. P/O Chapman and Cpl Pickles carried out a Tac/R sortie in the coastal area between Dunkirk and Ostend. While flying at 3,000 feet NE of Dunkirk his starboard main plane received a direct hit on the leading edge by an AA shell which blew away three ribs, as far back as the main spar. Although the pilot had no control over his aircraft below 100 mph it was successfully landed at Hawkinge. The pilot, in order to keep an even keel found it necessary to use full bank and full left rudder.

1230. P/O Baker and LAC Galloway carried out a Tac/R in the coastal area around Dixmuide. The tasks were to locate suitable bombing targets. Several were reported including 24 heavy lorries towing what was believed to be large calibre guns.

1230. P/O Thomas and LAC Dixon carried out Tac/R in the Dunkirk area to flash-spot batteries shelling the port.

1520. F/O Benito and LAC Webborn carried out Tac/R to locate suitable bombing targets. Three targets were reported which were considered suitable for bombing action.

1600. F/L Drysdale and LAC Clark carried out a Tac/R sortie in the St Omer area to locate suitable bombing targets. The pilot returned a negative report.

30.5.40:

0730. P/O Robertson and P/O Kelsh carried out a Tac/R sortie in the Ypres area.

1445. F/L Edinger and Cpl Chadwick carried out a weather test over Dunkirk in extremely bad conditions.

1630. P/O Lambert and AC Rance carried out a Tac/R sortie in the Dunkirk area. The pilot failed to make landfall owing to the weather conditions.

1715. F/L Edinger and Cpl Chadwick carried out a second weather test over the Dunkirk area.

1855. P/O Scotter and LAC Phelps successfully carried out a Tac/R sortie in the Dunkirk-Bourboug area.

1925. F/O Lang and Cpl Tomkins carried out a successful Tac/R in the coastal area Gravelines-Bergues-Furnes-Nieuport.

31.5.40:

1120. P/O Dearden and LAC McCoy took off from Bekesbourne for a Tac/R sortie via Hawkinge.

1315. F/L Eyres and LAC Philpott, Tac/R south of Canal de La Colme (St Omer-Nieuport) 5 miles in depth. Tasks in general: Spot and pinpoint flashes of enemy batteries in area. Tasks in particular: Is there an enemy battery in the fork of the road south of Socx? Is there an enemy battery near

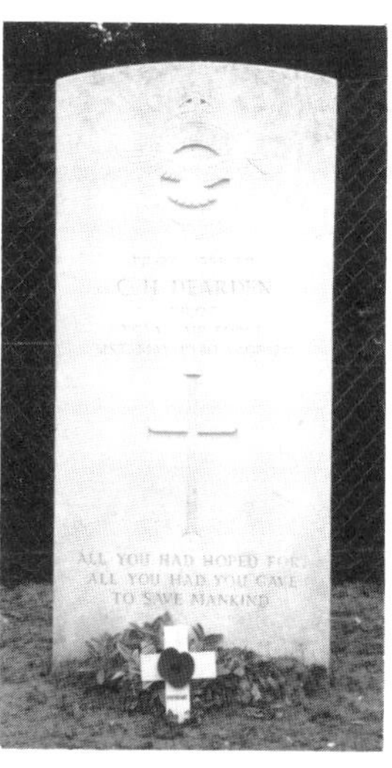

On 31 May P/O Officer Clifford Dearden and his air gunner LAC McCoy were shot down while flying a recce against German guns shelling the beaches of Dunkirk. On 1 June Clifford's body washed ashore and was subsequently buried at the Municipal Cemetery of La Panne, a seaside resort near the border between France and Belgium. McCoy's body was never found.

Steene? The pilot returned a negative report on the tasks in particular. He spotted a battery in action south of the Canal de la Colme.

1350. P/O DEARDEN HAS NOT RETURNED.

1630. P/O Shearman and Sgt Spurr. Tac/R in the area St Idesbalde-Furnes-road to Dixmuide-road to Ostend. Tasks in general: Locating bombing targets. Tasks in particular: 1) Movements on the road west of Nieuport. 2) Report on bridges over the Yser River (Bridges intact).

1800. P/O Mason and Cpl Oliver. Tac/R in the Abbeville area. The pilot was unable to complete the reconnaissance having been attacked twice. Once by a Me109 and once by two Me110s. He spent 20 minutes fighting them off. The machine was undamaged except for one bullet hole. The air gunner received an abrasion on the head.

1910. P/O Smithers. Area Dunkirk-Gravelines-Bergues-Furnes. Tac/R successfully carried out.

01.6.40:

0410. F/O Doidge and LAC Michelmore. HAVE NOT RETURNED. Area five miles in depth east of the line Nieuport-Dixmuide-Beverin-La Panne. Tasks in particular: Locate enemy batteries in the area. These batteries were strafing the Dunkirk beaches.

For the entire evening of 31 May the Squadron waited for news about Dearden and McCoy. When they failed to return it was assumed that they had been shot down by the enemy. When on 2 June nothing was heard of Doidge and Michelmore the same had to be feared for them. On 3 June W/C Geddes wrote to the men's parents. The author was able to contact the Dearden family in 1987. They kindly permitted him to continue the story of their brother:

On 31 January 1941 the Casualty Branch of the RAF informed Dearden's father that his son was now presumed dead. However, on 11 September 1941 Dearden's parents suddenly received a Red Cross letter from the Beaussart family, who lived at Labuissière where one Flight of the Squadron was stationed in 1940. The letter was in English and had passed German censors. It was addressed to Clifford Dearden personally:

> 'Hoping you are all quite well and so your people. Shall be happy to get news from you all. Often we speak and think of you all. H. Beaussart'.

The letter had been posted on 21 May to Dearden's home address. Father Dearden immediately contacted W/C Geddes, who replied that the Beaussarts ran a café at the Labuissière aerodrome and did the cooking for the Officers' Mess. Their daughter, Madeleine, ran the bar and attended VAD classes in Lens during the daytime. She spoke some English and spent the time teaching the officers a bit of French. Geddes continued:

> 'I have made certain enquiries about possibilities of some of our chaps lying up there, with a view to escaping. The advice given by experts is that we should not correspond with the Beaussarts at all. It will only attract Gestapo attention to them. I have passed the details on to the proper authorities and they have methods of checking up on the local situation there without anything going through German post. Without further news, I regret that we must assume that Clifford is no longer alive'.

Geddes was right. On 9 October 1943 Dearden's parents received definite news that their son had indeed been killed and was buried at La Panne cemetery after his body had been washed ashore on 1 June 1940. The body of LAC McCoy was never found.

CHAPTER 8
ARMY CO-OPERATION NEW STYLE

From 1 June 1940 all operational flying stopped and the Squadron was given a rest. The experience in Northern France and Flanders had shown that the Lysander was not suitable for offensive operations. Besides, the threat of a German invasion necessitated the availability of as many squadrons as possible on British soil. The Squadron established an Officers' Mess at Highland Court and Administrative Headquarters at Biffrons House, Bekesbourne. The men were accommodated under canvas once again and work started to provide essential services. On 8 June, however, the Squadron received orders to move to Hatfield, Herts. Once more tents were put up. On 10 June W/C Geddes opened a Squadron Operations Office at Headquarters 11 Corps with F/L Rogers as 'F/L Ops.' and Capt Noel East of 5 AIL Section as GIII (Air) Liaison) to the Corps Commander Lt.-Gen. H.R.S. Massey, CB, DSO, MO. F/O Benito was promoted Acting Flight Lieutenant and took over from Jimmy Drysdale who had been awarded the DSO for his excellent leadership during the supply drops over Calais. On 15 June the Squadron opened an Advanced Landing Ground near Matham's Wood. It had been used a few times before during the 1937 manoeuvres. It was called Sawbridgeworth. Very few would have imagined that in a year's time the Squadron would have built its own airfield there. F/L Edinger was put in command of the ALG and took two Flights with him. Besides the whole of 5 AIL Section, the photographic trailer and all night flying equipment departed for Sawbridgeworth. A Flight Office was established at Blount's Farm on the southern edge of the ALG. One Flight remained at Hatfield. Unfortunately there was one minor snag: during bad weather the ALG was too wet to be used even by Lysanders. Andrew Geddes believed it could not be worse than Hatfield was. This airfield was de Havilland property and the de Havilland folk were not pleased with the Squadron. For No.II (AC) Squadron it was a dead loss as well. First of all there was an intense conflict of interest between de Havilland Management and W/C Geddes: de Havilland considered 'their' airfield to be strictly civilian while Geddes was of the opinion that it was a military establishment since the Squadron's arrival. As far as de Havilland was concerned aircraft production was the prime task; Geddes intended to fight the Germans. The result was a guerilla war. Geddes accused de Havilland of 'peacetime aircraft production mentalities' while de Havilland was appalled to see how the Squadron claimed and took priority whenever something happened that looked, sounded and smelled like an 'invasion threat'. De Havilland accused No.II (AC) Squadron of 'attracting German attention by their wireless traffic' and they bluntly refused to put their private AA guns at spots where Geddes believed they would protect both the factory and the Squadron. If No.II Squadron wanted AA guns they should request them through the Air Ministry. Then some joker on the Squadron spread the rumour that de Havilland had made a deal with the Germans: If the Luftwaffe came to bomb the Squadron the de Havilland guns would remain silent. If the guns kept quiet the Luftwaffe would not bomb de Havilland and aim for No.II (AC) Squadron only. Of course someone in de Havilland heard it and took this accusation very seriously. The result was a bitter complaint directly to the Air Ministry stating that no deal whatsoever had been made between de Havilland and Hitler. An Air Ministry official had to travel to Hatfield to iron things out.

F/L D.I.C. Eyres preparing for take-off at RAF Bekesbourne. The starting-trolley has been connected.

P/O Chapman flew with the Squadron when it was temporarily based at the de Havilland Airfield, Hatfield. Colin Chapman was killed in September 1944, a twenty-five year-old Wing Commander.

During the period prior to the Battle of Britain, all Army Co-operation squadrons received orders for a new kind of warfare: Gas. Nos.II (AC), 4, 26, 225 and 614 Squadrons began to prepare for gas-spraying on the invasion beaches of the east coast. The idea was to poison all possible landing places and make life as difficult as possible for the Germans. In 1939 Lysanders, Blenheims and Battles had been planned to carry thirty- and 250-pound gas bombs and spray tanks. The possibility of German gas attacks had been considered very seriously as well. Vehicles and aircraft had been painted with special gas detection panels. Anti-gas parties had been trained and practised regularly. Limited supplies of phosgene and mustard gas bombs had been shipped to France in case the RAF needed to retaliate for an enemy attack. When the British withdrew, these supplies had to be transported home with top priority. No.II (AC) Squadron's gas-spraying duty was limited to a blister gas used with the standard SCI (Smoke Curtain Installation). The gas was kept in cylindrical metal tubes of 250 pounds with 13.25 gallons charging capacity. And, with Britain in mortal danger, the RAF had asked for a large increase of the available stocks. It was intended to use only aircraft types cleared to lay smoke to spray gas if retaliatory gas warfare was ordered.

At the same time No.II (AC) Squadron was to fly coastal reconnaissance to spot approaching invasion barges which were lined up by their hundreds in the ports of Holland, Belgium and Northern France. On 15 June the AOC No.22 Group came to Hatfield to discuss the present situation with W/C Geddes, who also had to attend regular meetings at HQ11 Corps.

In spite of being non-operational as far as duties overseas were concerned, pilots could still run into serious problems. On 18 June at 2200

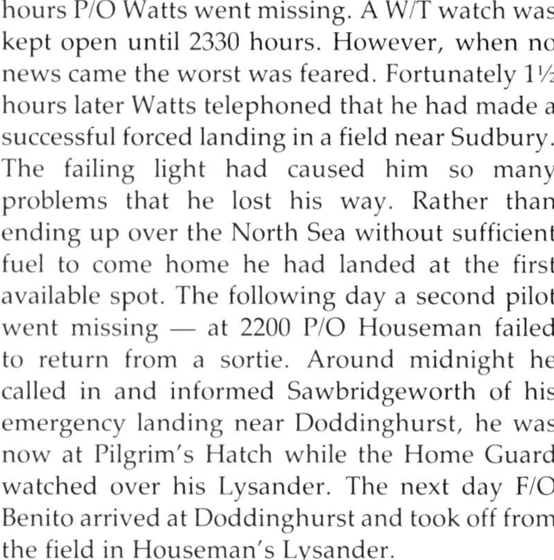

hours P/O Watts went missing. A W/T watch was kept open until 2330 hours. However, when no news came the worst was feared. Fortunately 1½ hours later Watts telephoned that he had made a successful forced landing in a field near Sudbury. The failing light had caused him so many problems that he lost his way. Rather than ending up over the North Sea without sufficient fuel to come home he had landed at the first available spot. The following day a second pilot went missing — at 2200 P/O Houseman failed to return from a sortie. Around midnight he called in and informed Sawbridgeworth of his emergency landing near Doddinghurst, he was now at Pilgrim's Hatch while the Home Guard watched over his Lysander. The next day F/O Benito arrived at Doddinghurst and took off from the field in Houseman's Lysander.

On 26 June The Rt.Hon. Winston Churchill MP visited HQ 11 Corps and Geddes was presented to the Prime Minister. Then, from 29 June gas spraying commenced with no less than 47,250lbs of charged SCIs issued to the Squadron. It looked a grim prospect with World War 1 massacres at hand . . .

Daily anti-invasion patrols had to be carried out. Even though the Squadron was not officially operational the Lysanders flew daily. Being part of No.34 Wing under Group Captain Lousada the Army Co-op squadron was rather self-contained; they were certainly self-accounting and had their own ground defence officers posted to the squadron. No.34 Wing was attached to HQ Eastern Command at Luton Hoo and was responsible for advising their GOC and his staff on all air matters affecting the Army, ie., reconnaissance, close support, photography etc. It was also to advise on the use of the RAF in support of ground forces. The Wing had certain administrative control over the stations and squadrons. Lousada often visited Sawbridgeworth which he remembered as 'a very muddy place with wooden huts under the trees'. When Army exercises took place — and then there were a lot — No. 34 Wing would set up an Operations Room with the Army Ops. Room and deal with strategic requests for the RAF to carry out, as against tactical requests to squadrons direct from their Corps or Armoured Divisions. Many lessons had been drawn from the experiences during the fighting in France and Flanders. ACM Brooke-Popham wrote a long paper for which members of the Squadron had to testify: W/C Geddes and four airgunners recently promoted to sergeants, Clark, Oliver, Webborn and Tomkins told about their experiences whilst flying against an overwhelming enemy. It was soon agreed that the fighting days of the Lysander were indeed over.

Other visitors in July 1940 were AVM Blount who came to see the CO before attending a

Pilots at Marshall's Airport. From left to right Peter Watts, 'Fifi' Eyres, Bill Shearman, 'Porky' Brown and Bill Mason of B-Flight.

conference with the GOC 11 Corps. Slowly new ideas about Army Co-operation developed. On 4 July P/Os Robinson and Kelsh escaped death when their Lysander crashed while trying to force-land near Romford after getting lost in the darkness. Robinson escaped uninjured but Kelsh had to be taken to hospital. In the meantime many new ALGs were being established and a lot of effort had to be made by some pilots to find them. For example there were Farnham Green and Ugley, being mentioned in official documents for the first time.

In July 1940 it was proudly noted in the Ops. Record Book that 'His Majesty the King has been graciously pleased to give orders for the publication of the name of Leading Aircraftman 638107 Harper H.J., cook and butcher, who had been mentioned in despatches by the AOCiC'. On 24 July Jimmy Drysdale and his air gunner Sergeant Clark both received their decorations at Buckingham Palace, a DSO and a DFM respectively. By the end of July the Squadron happily said goodbye to Hatfield. It was the end of an unhappy marriage and both parties were pleased to separate. The Hatfield Flight and its supporting staff moved to Cambridge. On 30 July the Advanced Party left and after a few days nothing remained to remind people that No.II (AC) Squadron had ever been there. On 31 July another visit by AVM Blount took place. He discussed with W/C Geddes the arrangements for the Squadron taking responsibility for the air support of both 2 and 11 Corps. Again the Squadron was split up. C-Flight was at Marshall's Airport, Cambridge, responsible for 2 Corps. They joined with 22 EFTS. A- and B-Flights remained at Sawbridgeworth, working for 11 Corps. C-Flight's Officers' Mess was at the Airport Hotel. Unfortunately different interests clashed once again. First of all the OC 22 EFTS was not at all happy with C-Flight interfering in his pupils' circuits and bumps. Secondly he was quite unwilling to accept a 'fighting' Flight over his 'practising' school. Andrew Geddes remembered how an attempt was made to solve this problem:

> 'They were building a small satellite to Marshall's Airport at Bottisham to relieve the traffic of Tiger Moths, Lysanders and other aircraft at the main aerodrome. Bottisham was just levelled clay soil about three miles due east of Marshall's. Some civil servant at the Air Ministry decided that this strip was quite suitable for Army Co-operation Lysanders. However, as it was extremely wet we could hardly use it. Besides, it tended to tangle up in the traffic of Wellingtons from Newmarket and another Lysander Squadron at Snailwell. It was obvious that we could do very little if we had to operate from this field.'

Geddes' constant complaints about the obsolescence of the Lysander finally satisfied top brass that a decision had to be made about a new aircraft. When their decision came, Geddes was utterly 'horrified, upset and disgusted'. He had hoped for cannon-armed fighters like the Hurricane, instead he got orders to start trials with Boulton Paul Defiants and Fairey Battles.

Air Gunners from left to right Sgts. Jarvis, Williams, Oliver, Spurr, Philpott and P/O Brown, also of B-Flight.

For the time being however, anti-invasion patrols in Lysanders remained one of the Squadron's main tasks. One patrol was from the River Nene to Wells-next-the-Sea, while the other was from there to Lowestoft. At about the same time C-Flight was detached from the Squadron to join up with No.26 Squadron and fly Tac/Rs for 2 Corps. As an emergency measure it was decided that non-operational aircraft should be used in the event of a German invasion. This scheme was known as the 'Banquet-Plan'. One part of this involved the Tiger Moths and Magisters of the FTS. Under 'Banquet-Light' these aircraft were to be fitted with light series bomb racks carrying eight twenty-pound fragmentation bombs. These Banquet-Light units were to come under the operational command of an Army Co-operation squadron commander. Initially No.II (AC) Squadron's Banquet-Light Flights were to be provided by 22 EFTS at Cambridge and 6 EFTS at Sywell. Later, when No.268 (AC) Squadron was formed from Nos.II and 26 Squadrons at Bury St Edmunds they took over the 22 EFTS Flights, leaving 6 EFTS with No.II (AC) Squadron. W/C Geddes regularly visited both schools and some exercises took place. One can imagine what it looked like when on 17 August Tiger Moths attacked Sawbridgeworth in a low-level bombing attack.

This glorious manor house, Great Hyde Hall, Sawbridgeworth, Herts, was the Officers' Mess for No.II (AC) Squadron. Today it is advertised as 'superb luxury apartments and houses created within a magnificent Georgian hall, set in delightful, landscaped parkland with excellent access to central London'.

The Army constantly asked for support during their exercises: in August 1940 one of these took place. The Operations Record Book said:

> 'Two tactical recces provided for scheme with 4 Corps. Cambridge aerodrome used as ALG for purpose of exercise. A combined operation was carried out between 52 Division and 1st Armoured Brigade. A- and B-Flights co-operated with 52 Div using Wattisham as their ALG. Cambridge co-operated with 1st Armd Bgde. Four sorties were allotted to the Brigade, two being carried out in the morning and two in the afternoon. Lysander R2030 piloted by F/L A.D. Bryant crashed while carrying out a dive-bombing attack on 52 Div at Stradishall. F/L Bryant was admitted to Bury St Edmunds Hospital.'

W/C Geddes personally carried out the Defiant trials. Forty-five years later he admitted to putting the aeroplane through the most rigorous tests 'hoping to find enough reasons to get rid of the crate as quickly and definitely as possible'. On 31 August a message was received at 2300 hours:

> 'Convoy of enemy ships steaming due West at 15 knots 120 miles off Norfolk coast.'

Was this the start of Banquet-Light? Immediately the entire Squadron bombed up and a dawn sortie was ordered to prepare for immediate action at 0430 hours. Fortunately the enemy convoy changed direction and headed south. The order to prepare for combat was cancelled.

September started off as a quiet month. Little was noticed at Sawbridgeworth of the Battle of Britain raging further south. Daily sorties were flown and patrols carried out. However on the 7th everything changed suddenly and dramatically. At 2045 hours the codeword 'Cromwell' was signalled to army units all over Britain. It meant that conditions were suitable for a German invasion of Britain. However it did not mean what many thought: The long expected attack by Hitler's troops. No.II (AC) Squadron also prepared for the defence of the country — Invasion Alert N.1 was brought into force and all Squadron personnel were recalled from leave. At 2130 hours the codeword 'Cromwell' was received again. All aircraft at Marshall's and Sawbridgeworth were prepared for battle. This was it. During the night the Luftwaffe carried out the first of many nightly raids on London. They were to continue for twenty-four nights causing tremendous devastation and costing thousands of lives. During the following day No.II (AC) Squadron flew continuous recce sorties over the North Sea to try to find the approaching German invasion fleet. The sea remained empty. On 10 September the situation relaxed a bit and everything returned to normal. The next day a large manor house, Great Hyde Hall, not too far from the ALG was requisitioned as a billet for No.II (AC) Squadron personnel during the coming winter. On 11 September C-Flight arrived from Cambridge and B-Flight took its place there. The fear of an invasion rose again when during a dawn sortie a young pilot accidentally fired a green Very light while off the coast. Again the alert sounded and everybody waited for the Germans. Great emphasis was given to camouflage and in order to see how well the Army camouflaged itself many sorties were flown and pictures taken of Army units digging in and hiding. In September orders came that the Squadron establishment was to be reduced from eighteen to twelve aircraft. An entire Flight was posted to Bury St Edmunds to become, with two Flights of No.26 squadron, the nucleus of No.268 (AC) Squadron.

On 19 September Adolf Hitler gave the Supreme Headquarters of the Wehrmacht the order to abandon preparations for Operation 'Sea Lion'. Britain had won the battle, now it set to winning the war. The RAF began bombing German positions along the Channel coast and on the 23rd 119 bombers attacked Berlin. An official announcement from the Air Ministry claimed 2,167 German aircraft had been shot down during the Battle of Britain. The Germans were said to have lost 5,148 valuable aircrew. The RAF finished September by attacking armament factories at Magdeburg, Hannover, Stuttgart and Bielefeld. Hitler now knew that the plutocrats in Britain had no intention whatsoever of giving up the struggle. By the end of the month Squadron Headquarters moved to Sawbridgeworth. Little by little Andrew Geddes was getting a station of his own . . .

During October 1940 the Squadron got a taste of the Luftwaffe's presence for the first time since June. On the 16th a Junkers Ju88 crashed about a mile southwest of Bishops Stortford Church, blowing up on impact. It was an aircraft of Stab II/KG30. Its crew Hauptmann Hass, the Commanding Officer of the Gruppe, and Feldwebels Suhr and Kessels were killed, as was a passenger, a German war correspondent called Penfold who had joined the crew to witness the glorious deeds of the unit. The aircraft was a Ju88A-5 with registration 4D+DM. Two days later the Germans seemed to have found Sawbridgeworth itself. Two parachute mines fell near Great Hyde Hall during the night. One mine exploded in mid-air breaking a number of window panes. Unfortunately 11 Corps 'Z' HQ was demolished. On 20 October the Germans returned, this time their bombs came down at 0800. Nine fell on the cricket field of Great Hyde Hall — the Squadron was very upset as no cricket could be played for several days. When on 30 October HM King George VI visited HQ 11 Corps W/C Geddes had the honour of being invited to be the King's guest for dinner. In the meantime German night raids against London continued in spite of the Germans' unwillingness to invade the country.

On 1 December 1940 Army Co-operation Command was formed. It consisted of two Groups, No.70 being the Training Group and No.71 the Operational Group. AOCiC was to be AM A.S. 'Ugly' Barratt, KCB, CMG, MC, Group Commanders were Air Cdre J.B. Cole-Hamilton as AOC 70 Group and AVM P.C. Maltby, DSO, DFC as AOC 71 Group.

W/C Geddes received the OBE in the 1941 New Year's Honours list. The same day he was visited by the new CiC Army Co-op Command who inspected the aerodrome and the Squadron Headquarters. A Mr. C.J. Aincey of the Hertfordshire War Agricultural Committee visited the station too; he had a misguided proposal to plough up the aerodrome and turn it into farmland. After a rather short discussion with W/C Geddes he left with mixed feelings and the certainty that this plan was ridiculous as far as the Squadron was concerned. In January Geddes got involved in a new, exciting but very secret aspect of flying. For some time Whitley bombers had been used by Special Operations Executive (SOE) for regular sorties over Occupied Territory. A No.II (AC) Squadron pilot, F/O E.N. Baker had already participated in some of these missions. Geddes received the request to pick out one or two very good pilots, tell them nothing and practise night landings and take-offs with them during the following nights. He was told that they would need to be able to fly on nights which were both moonless and overcast. Geddes picked

Above: At first conditions at Sawbridgeworth were quite primitive. 'The Farm' was the Squadron's HQ and Mess.

Below: P/Os Charles, Dudeney and Scotter. Scotter became a pilot with No.419 (SD) Flight and carried out many dangerous and secret missions to occupied France. Dudeney lost his life and Charles became a leading pilot at Biggin Hill.

Gordon Scotter. On 30 December an officer presented himself to Geddes. He produced a letter from HQ 71 Group. The letter introduced the officer as S/L Knowles who was to give Geddes details about a special job in which the assistance of No.II (AC) Squadron was considered to be vital. Two of the Squadron's most experienced pilots were needed, but no other members of the Squadron were to be told about the reasons for their training nor about the nature of their new job. Knowles pointed out that the chosen pilots had to be able to land a Lysander on the smallest possible piece of ground under all weather conditions. They should be able to find their destination without any navigational error, to land, to stay on the ground very briefly and to take off again without any help. The very first illegal landing in France had taken place during the night of 19/20 October 1940 when F/L Wally Farley, now the OC No.419 Flight and an old boy of No.II (AC) Squadron, had landed a Lysander and taken off without being noticed. It was the beginning of what were to become known as the 'Black Lysander Flights'. Geddes subjected the chosen candidates to a rigorous programme of training; they practised at the end of Sawbridgeworth airfield with the aim of achieving the shortest possible landings and take-offs. From a local shop he bought three bicycle lamps with Ever Ready batteries to mark a triangle on the ground. The pilots were to land, move and take off within its boundaries. At the Squadron many stories abounded as to what this was all in aid of. One aspect, however, could not be practised: the reality of Germans in the neighbourhood or, even worse, of Gestapo waiting in ambush for an aircraft to land.

At times former Squadron pilots visited Sawbridgeworth. One of them was 'Dingbat' Edinger, now a Squadron Leader commanding a bomber squadron. He was to be killed while flying Wellingtons over Germany and his body now rests at the Reichswald Cemetery in Germany not far from Laarbruch — the Squadron's recent home. In fact many old boys who had flown with the Squadron at the outbreak of the war were not to survive it. Ivor Worthington-Wilmer was killed on 4 July 1940 when his Blenheim of No.18 Squadron crashed near Rotterdam. He rests at the small village cemetery of Zwartewaal, a solitary RAF grave among the graves of the villagers. Derek Maccaw died on 8 August 1940.

Top right: Brian Walford in one of the Squadron Lysanders.

Lysander KO-D (T1532) flying over while the air gunner takes his photographs. The wheel covers have been removed to keep the mud from clogging the wheels while taxying, taking off or landing when the aircraft was operating from soft ground.

He was a pilot with No.238 Squadron. Jimmy Drysdale was killed in September 1941 as OC No.305 (Polish) Squadron over France. Grant-Govan's luck ran out on 24 May 1942. F/O Rogers died in a crash in Egypt on 1 September 1942. Eddy Lang was killed in action over France on 29 December 1944, a Wing Commander. Of the twenty officers serving with the Squadron at the outbreak of the war only nine were still alive when the war was over.

Though the Americans were neutral many of their officers visited British aerodromes to see for themselves how the RAF stood up against the enemy. The American government being pro-British had to reckon with the public opinion in the States where a majority, led by people like Charles Lindbergh, advocated neutrality and 'America for the Americans'. One of the visitors to Sawbridgeworth was an American Colonel called Kennedy. He worked at the US Embassy in London. His official job there was ALOAAF (Air Liaison Officer to the American Armoured Force). His visit to Sawbridgeworth was considered important and everything possible was done to make him happy. He arrived at the station on 2 February at 1100 hours. He was accompanied by S/L Edinger and officially met by W/C Geddes who invited him to inspect the guard of honour. Then Kennedy inspected the Admin Officers and the Airmen's Dining Hall where he was shown the airmen having their meal. During the afternoon Kennedy was taken around the aerodrome to see the layout, visit the Flight Offices and meet some of the officers. During the evening a guest night was organised which anyone of any importance attended. There were Lt–Gen. Massey, AVM MacEwan, Brigadier Bissett, Captain the Hon. C.S. Rodney and Captain Campbell the GIII (Air) to HQ 11 Corps. The next morning Kennedy was taken up in a Lysander and flown over the area. A planned bombing demonstration had to be postponed due to fog, but at 1400 hours the squadron demonstrated photographic reconnaissance with Kennedy attending the briefing and debriefing of the pilot. The photographs were developed and printed in nineteen minutes. Kennedy was very impressed at the speed with which the Squadron worked. After having lunch with Lt–Gen. Massey the Colonel left the station and peace returned to Sawbridgeworth.

In February 1941 the rear armament of the Lysander was changed from one Vickers gun to two .303 Browning machine guns. The first new aircraft were collected from Barnstaple. S/L Mulliken who had been the XO since early 1940 was interviewed by AVM Maltby, CB, DSO, AFC prior to his posting to command No.614 Squadron. S/L Skelton succeeded him at the Squadron. The need for a second in command was clear. Geddes spent most of his time going to and coming from meetings with Army commanders. On 19 February F/O Baker who had been posted to No.419 (Special Duties) Flight was reported missing after a sortie over Belgium for SOE. After some time it became known that they were prisoners. S/L Knowles returned to discuss further employment of No.II (AC) Squadron pilots in SOE.

Geddes got something of a shock when he received orders to prepare himself for a posting back to the Royal Artillery at the end of his secondment to the RAF. He immediately got the Old Boys' Network in motion to have this decision revoked. AVM Maltby, a personal friend and someone who appreciated that Geddes' experience of RAF matters was more valuable than his knowledge of Artillery movements, wrote a letter on behalf of the desperate CO. He suggested that Geddes should be forwarded to a Junior Officer's War Staff Course at Camberley or Milney. There was, however, a problem. Hitherto, officers who had attended such a course had been sent back to the Army. Maltby wrote to say that he was quite willing, without making any promises, to throw open further employment for Geddes as a Staff Officer in Army Co-op Command with further periods of flying duty. In his response Geddes pointed out that his position

For a while the use of Fairey Battles (top) and Boulton Paul Defiants by Army Co-op squadrons was contemplated by the Air Ministry. Trials were carried out and soon it was proved that neither of the two were in any way useful. Soon they were replaced by Mark III Lysanders and P40 Tomahawks.

Message dropping at Sawbridgeworth, 1941. With hands behind his back is F/O 'Dopey' Hall. The two Army officers are Squadron ALOs, Major Noel East and Captain Chas Grivee. Two Naval officers are interested witnesses. In the background Blount's Farm is visible.

At first living conditions at Sawbridgeworth were utterly primitive. Peter Watts, one of the Squadron pilots, does not seem to enjoy the prospect of having to live in a tent. Peter was killed in August 1941.

as a re-seconded officer on his third tour of duty in the RAF was quite unique with regard to the time served in the RAF and the Army. When he applied for a third secondment he was led to understand that he was coming in to command an Army Co-op squadron as a substantive Squadron Leader for three years, having completed an initial tour of four years as a Flying Officer, a second tour of six months as a Flying Officer and 2½ years as a Flight Lieutenant — making a total of ten years' seconded service, which was the maximum allowance under Royal Warrant for a combatant officer to serve with another service. He had taken No.II (AC) Squadron on 1 May 1939 and had hoped to remain OC until 1 May 1942. With the outbreak of war Geddes' re-secondment had been prolonged for the duration of the war. No.II (AC) Squadron was Geddes' chief interest since he had first joined the Squadron in December 1935. The Wing Commander had a simple wish: he wanted to command his Squadron until the final victory. He had no desire whatsoever to go to Camberley where they reared future GSOIIIs. Provided that he would be permitted to return to the Squadron immediately after this course Geddes would rather go to Milney, as he was already familiar with the problems of Combined Operations, although what he really wanted was to stay with the Squadron. A final decision about Geddes' career was postponed for the time being. Geddes could continue leading the Squadron and preparing pilots for Special Duties. Further, he was responsible for lectures to the Home Guard on how to build mock craters in roads, and the Squadron was to carry out gas spraying and to help the London AA belt calibrate their guns.

Geddes' tremendous zeal was not unnoticed. On 15 March Geddes and his family were invited to Buckingham Palace where he was to receive the OBE from the King. Incidentally, while the CO was safely in London, the entire Squadron set out on a rabbit hunt in Matham's Wood . . .

In the early hours of 20 April another German raid on Sawbridgeworth took place. A factory near Squadron Headquarters was set on fire. By

May 1941 the Defiant trials had still not been concluded. W/C Geddes was still involved in 'exchange of views' and was desperately trying to have the whole scheme abandoned. On 21 May a happy event took place when F/O Gordon Scotter was awarded an immediate DFC for his Special Duties flights. It was in May too that the name of a new aeroplane was recorded in the Squadron diaries: a Lysander W/T set was taken to Henlow to be built into a Curtiss P40 Tomahawk. It looked as if the replacement for the Lysander had been picked. As for the Lizzies, a new officer arrived at the Squadron. He was F/O 'Whippy' Nesbitt-Dufour who had to undergo training prior to be posted to No.1419 (SD) Flight at Stradishall. W/C Geddes collected him in a Squadron Tiger Moth and flew him to Sawbridgeworth. In his book *Black Lysander* Nesbitt-Dufour later wrote:

> 'For the rest of May I flew Lysander R2626 for all I was worth and after ten days could get airborne in under 36 yards in anything but a dead calm and could literally touch down within a couple of yards of where I wanted to. This is no credit to my flying as the type was very easy to handle and, in fact, virtually designed as a STOL aircraft. Having satisfied Wing Commander Geddes as to my ability back I went to Stradishall. . .'

Gordon Scotter made his first SD-Flight in April 1941 when he flew Lysander V9287 to a small field near Chateauroux between Levroux and Brion in Vichy-France. He received a well-deserved immediate DFC for bringing home his 'Joe' in spite of being chased by German fighters, after a very rough landing and a very suspicious looking group of cars approaching the field at high speed before he took off again.

In the meantime the Squadron continued flying for the Army and testing the Defiant. Geddes was able to convince the Army of the absolute necessity for concrete runways if they ever wanted to be supported by aircraft better than the Lysander. However, before the Army set to helping Geddes out Grant-Govan had one of his famous narrow escapes once again. He was on a calibration sortie over the London area. This was not entirely without danger as the AA people had a very simple philosophy: 'If it flies overhead it is hostile and should be shot down'. Flying over the AA belts was a very cold high altitude business and sometimes Lysanders developed serious troubles due to carburettor icing. Grant-Govan came through the clouds at dusk, aiming for Essex. Flashing his lights to be recognised as a friend he hoped that the gunners below would be so kind as to miss him. Then the airscrew suddenly stopped in the one blade up two blades down position, in fine pitch, with minimum drag below. Grant-Govan tried to get the engine started again or at least alter the

In 1941 the Squadron code was changed from KO to XV. On this photograph LAC Welburn had himself immortalised in the cockpit of a Squadron Lizzie.

Two Squadron pilots standing on the muddy ground of Sawbridgeworth. The officer with the Mae West is probably F/O Robinson, the other one is F/O Hall. The state of the field convinced Air Ministry of the need to put Sommerfeld track on the ground.

Great Hyde Hall, Sawbridgeworth, 1941. Visit of Field Marshal Sir Alan Brooke to No.II (AC) Squadron. The Chief of the Imperial General Staff (CIGS) visited the Squadron after one of its pilots, F/O Gordon Scotter had been awarded an immediate DFC for his Special Duty flights to Occupied France. The CIGS is seated in the middle. On his left hand side is the C/O, S/L Andrew Geddes who had served under Brooke when the latter was a Lieutenant Colonel in the Royal Artillery and Geddes was a mere 2nd Lieutenant RA.
Some of the gentlemen on this photograph can be identified.
Front row, left to right: F/L Rogers (F/L Ops), ?, S/L Skelton (2 I/C), AVM Maltby, FM Sir Alan Brooke, W/C Geddes (OC), Capt. Noel East (AILO), ?, ADC CIGS, ?.
Second row, ?, F/O Lights (AG officer), MO ?, RA Major, RA Captain, Senior I.O., F/L Chapman, Captain Colchester Garrisson, Gordon Scotter, F/L Houseman, Squadron Acc.Off.
Third row, RA Officer, ?, ?, Alan Brooke's son, F/O ?, P/O ?, P/O ?, RA officer.

position of the blades by steep diving, however everything remained solid. By this time he had passed Waltham Abbey and lost too much altitude to reach Sawbridgeworth. Furthermore, in coming out of his last dive he found that even with the tail fully trimmed and the stick right back he could not get the aircraft to climb nor could he get it to slow down below a speed which could give it anything but a shallow landing in the dusk. He chose the largest piece of grass which he could see in the gloom and with his famous 'GG luck-and-skill' finished up about ten feet from a grim looking stone wall. It had been another narrow escape. Unfortunately his luck ran out later when he was posted to an Air Sea Rescue Squadron and was still flying Lysanders. One day he flew along the French coast trying to find a downed pilot. A German fighter caught up with him and shot him down.

The presence of a secret agent or 'Joe' at Sawbridgeworth caused a few problems when one day a wingless Flight Lieutenant was posted to the Squadron as an 'Assistant Adjutant under Training'. Many officers were rather upset when this person was declared excused from all kinds of duties: Duty Officer, Orderly Officer etc. Unfortunately it was not possible to inform them why this man got such kind treatment. In fact, while at Sawbridgeworth his training took place under great stress. However, as no-one knew what the stranger's job really was, the officers would call him all kinds of unpleasant names, the kindest one being 'Mr. Do-Little'. Finally, he almost created a riot one day when he walked into the Officers' Mess at Great Hyde Hall. On his chest he proudly displayed a brand-new DSO ribbon. Some men immediately reported him as improperly dressed and demanded from their Squadron Commander, who was Station Commander as well, that he should stop this 'wingless wonder' from disgracing the uniform with what was probably a stolen ribbon. He never did anything but sit in the Mess reading the papers and taking long strolls on the aerodrome. Geddes tried to save the situation by saying that it was belated recognition for his heroism during the days of Dunkirk and that this man was soon to be posted to the Middle East. Geddes was not going to accept any more chitchat about the whole matter. Strangely enough, a week later the CO almost had a fit and virtually dragged the man out of the dining room when he entered for breakfast with a newspaper under his arm. Fortunately no-one had noticed that it was yesterday's issue of the *Paris Soir* magazine which the man had brought back with him from another secret trip to France . . .

Soon rumours were heard at Sawbridgeworth that the Lysander days were about to come to an end. On 7 June W/C McIntyre came to the Squadron to see what changes had to be made at Sawbridgeworth to receive a new aircraft, the Curtiss P-40 Tomahawk. The following day representatives of Army Co-op Command and 10 Works Area followed. The next step was the departure of the CO and two officers to Old

Sarum for a Tomahawk conversion course. Soon other pilots followed. July was spent training and each day the Operations Record Book entry read: 'Flying training continued'.

On 2 July Marshal of the RAF the Viscount Trenchard GCB, GCVO, DSO, DCL, LLD, accompanied by AVM Sir Arthur Barratt KCB, CMG, MC, inspected and addressed the Squadron. On 8 August S/L D.I.C. Eyres who had flown with the Squadron during the early war days returned to become second in command vice S/L Skelton. After W/C Geddes' return, the final check-out of all pilots for the P-40 was carried out by a group of instructors from the School of Army Co-operation. All pilots passed the check-out flying Harvards. Four days later the first brand new Tomahawks arrived from Messrs. Cuncliffe Owen, the manufacturers. They were Tomahawk IIs with liquid-cooled Allison engines. The aircraft were coloured dark earth, dark green and sky with medium grey codes, which by now had changed from KO to XV. Standard roundels were applied while the spinners and fuselage band were sky. No.II (AC) Squadron thought it was ready for battle again. However, the Squadron was not destined to employ this type operationally.

Many pilots found the P-40 Tomahawk a difficult aircraft. If not handled with great care the P-40 would groundloop immediately. It was a good machine, as long as the pilot knew exactly what he was doing. The photograph above shows P/O Davies on the port wing of his No.II Squadron P-40.

CHAPTER 9
BACK TO THE BATTLEFIELD

Tomahawks U, S and W in close formation.

In September 1941 all the pilots had been checked out on the Tomahawk. But things did not go at all well at first. On the ninth, P/O Larsen, one of the Norwegians who had been posted to the Squadron ground-looped AH945. The next day P/O Constant did the same with AH928. On the sixteenth F/O Scotter force-landed AH940 after the engine failed on take-off. The propeller and belly of the aircraft were damaged but Scotter escaped uninjured. Immediately after this all the Tomahawks were grounded. Investigations soon showed that a lot of improvements were necessary to make the aircraft operationally safe. One of the complaints was that the exhaust flames were so long that the pilots could not see anything when flying at night. More efficient flame dampers were installed. September was not only a sad month for flying. On the twenty-first, fifteen-year old Doris Bird was killed by a Squadron lorry towing a water trailer. Police inquiries showed that the driver, a Leading Aircraftman was not to blame. The following day Squadron representatives attended her funeral. On 16 October an AC2 was charged by Police for using obscene language on a public highway and was handed over to the military authorities to be dealt with. The next day W/C Geddes left the Squadron after having commanded it for more than two years. He was posted to Army Co-op Command and sent to North Africa to report on close air support and bombing during Operation Crusader. He considered his departure from the Squadron as 'one of the saddest moments in my life'. S/L Eyres assumed temporary command. At about the same time Lieutenant General Massey who had been such a great support for the Squadron handed over command of 11th Corps to Lieutenant General N.M.S. Irwin, CB,DSO,MC,psc. Whilst all the teething problems with the Tomahawks were being dealt with important changes took place in the higher echelons. On 14 August 1941 No.71 Group had been disbanded and in its place two Wings were formed. Nos.34 and 35 (Recce) Wing became effective on 23 August. Nos.II, 4 and 268 Squadrons became part of 34 Wing. The Wing was commanded by W/C (later Group Captain) Charles R. Lousada, an ex-Squadron pilot.

The P-40 remained a troublesome purchase. Many pilots expressed their opinion about the aircraft and said it was one of the poorer products of the American war industry. The Americans were not at all pleased with these opinions and made bitter complaints about the pilots' resentment of American aircraft. Lousada wrote a letter to all squadron commanders in his Wing informing them that the Chief of Air Staff was very concerned about the impression being created in the United States that the British were not making proper use of the equipment provided under the Lend-Lease Act. Winston Churchill had already stated that it was 'imperative that the campaign now under way in the USA to discredit the Administration by alleging that we were making inefficient or improper use of American supplies should be promptly and fully countered'. The Americans, however, had no practical experience of the difficulties of adapting Their equipment for the war purposes of the British and were therefore inclined to imagine that the weapons and aircraft turned out by their factories ought to be put into action against the enemy immediately after they were delivered to the United Kingdom. American observers had reported to Washington DC that crated aircraft were standing unpacked at some of the RAF aerodromes for at least three months. RAF officers tended to 'crab' American fighters and, according to the same observers, the maintenance of American aircraft was deliberately inefficient. Of course these statements had some truth in them; however, the problems were caused by the diversity of equipment arriving from the USA. Lousada stressed in his letter that there were shortages too in several branches of the US forces and that it naturally exasperated American officers to think that the RAF misused equipment of which their own troops were in urgent need. So all negative comments on the P-40 were to stop. The Squadron, now equipped with these aircraft, had to fulfill all requirements from the various Army units. Therefore the Lysanders were put into service again while the P-40 remained on the ground. S/L Eyres was faced with a difficult problem. At the same time all kinds of minor problems had to be solved. First he had to tell the AC who had used obscene language that he was to serve twenty-one days detention. The next day he had two men in front of him, charged with desertion. Four days later AC Lax, the Station Despatch Rider was killed when he collided with a lorry. The weather was terrible and hardly any flying was possible. In order to keep the Squadron on its toes various lectures took place. S/L Eyres accompanied thirty other ranks to the Phoenix Theatre in Bishop's Stortford to watch German propaganda films. A dance was held at Long's Cafe to raise money for the Squadron's Compassionate Fund. Since the burden of being both a Station and a Squadron Commander was very heavy S/L Eyres' job as Station Commander was taken over by F/L Horn MC. This was rather ridiculous as now the Squadron Commander was senior to the Station Commander. This could have caused serious frictions had the Station Commander been anyone other than Horn. He was a delightful man, liked by almost everybody in the Squadron. He had been a racing enthusiast and was a prominent figure at Brooklands. He still used his private Daimler, suitably camouflaged.

One of the Tomahawk pilots in those days was Jim 'Jump' Davies. He joined the Squadron on a foggy afternoon in November 1941, being posted from the Old Sarum School of Army Co-operation. He had been trained as a pilot at Hullavington. With no time to waste he was authorised to fly the P-40 the day after he arrived. It was one of these days with visibility nil. The moment Davies was airborne he was lost. He called the Squadron W/T for a fix but all he got was a lot of noise but no contact. So he flew a square search and as luck would have it about an hour later, when he was almost out of fuel, he flew over what looked like a dispersal with a P-40 standing on it. By a second stroke of luck he saw a glimpse of Sawbridgeworth's Summerfeld track runway. He landed as quickly as possible.

At Great Hyde Hall was a Link Trainer where the pilots practised the Lorenz Blind Approach System. Having been an Army officer in the Derbyshire Yeomanry Davies felt at home with No.II (AC) Squadron, as life in the Squadron incorporated a lot from both branches of the Forces. While at Sawbridgeworth Davies met a young Code and Cypher officer, Section Officer Peggy Copleston. They have been happily married since 12 August 1943.

One of the exercises in which the Squadron participated was 'Scorch' which took place between the fourth and ninth of December 1941. The Lysanders had to do the job. It was during this exercise that the news of the Japanese attack on Pearl Harbor reached England. As sorry as many may have felt for the Americans, quite a few were relieved to know that the vast American potential would now be used to the advantage of the Allied cause.

'G' was the last Lysander allotted to No.II Squadron before the arrival of the short-lived P-40 Tomahawk. Here she stands at RAF Sawbridgeworth, with two ·30 machine guns in the gunner's cockpit.

The officer Commanding No.II (AC) Squadron, W/C A.J.W. Geddes (right) with F/L G.C. Edwards (middle) and Captain C.J.S. Ashley, 1941. As an Army Co-op Squadron No.II constantly dealt with army matters. Here aerial photographs are being evaluated and discussed during one of the many exercises in which the Squadron lent a helping hand.

RAF Station Sawbridgeworth was a product of improvisation. It was built first and then reported to the Air Ministry who were wondering about vouchers of a station of that name. The original Advanced Landing Ground was situated between Matham's Wood and the NW-SE road near Blount's Farm.
1. Aircraft hardstands with tail wheel bridges hidden under the trees
2. Quadruple Lewis guns
3. Open pits in the wood for Mustard spray containers
4. Ruin and moat of an old priory
5. Flight offices and crew rooms
6. Road blocks
7. Petrol stores with four-gallon tins
8. Two runways and peritrack made of Sommerfield track
9. Road to the main billets in Sawbridgeworth
10. Guard room, ambulance, fire tender and wind indicator
11. W/T station
12. All the night flying pick-up training with Lysanders was done within the old area, usually the Lizzies would come from the north over Matham's Wood and land, assisted by three Ever Ready lamps.

At the end of the month a new CO took over from Eyres. His name was S/L Riddell, who arrived the day before Christmas. The Operations Record Book for Christmas Day reads: 'Officers and NCOs served lunches to the men'. On 3 January 1942 Sir Archibald Sinclair, the Secretary of State for Air, accompanied by Gp. Capt. Sir Louis Greig landed at Sawbridgeworth at 1555 hours. During his forty-five minute stay he inspected A-Flight, the Maintenance Flight and the Airmen's Cookhouse. It was the time when the very existence of the station was the subject of discussion. Conferences, a visit by AM Barratt, everything indicated that a final decision was at hand. Fortunately it was decided that Sawbridgeworth was to remain what it was, an RAF aerodrome. Now that the future of the station was secured the time had come to think of a replacement for the ill-conceived Tomahawk. S/L Eyres and F/L Houseman were invited to come to Duxford to see a new aircraft, the North American Mustang. It seemed to be exactly what an Army Co-operation squadron needed. It was a fast moving and extremely manoeuvrable aircraft making it less of a sitting duck when flying on low-level recce sorties. For the time being, however, the Squadron would have to make do with the P-40. Using this aircraft No.II Squadron participated in various exercises such as 'Repulse', 'Bones', 'Armour B', 'Armour C' and others. On 26 March the first Squadron pilot was sent to Duxford to have a flight in the Mustang. F/L Gates was the lucky one to be chosen. In April all Squadron pilots went to Bottisham to get to know their future aircraft. The Mustang Mark I was a marvellous aircraft.

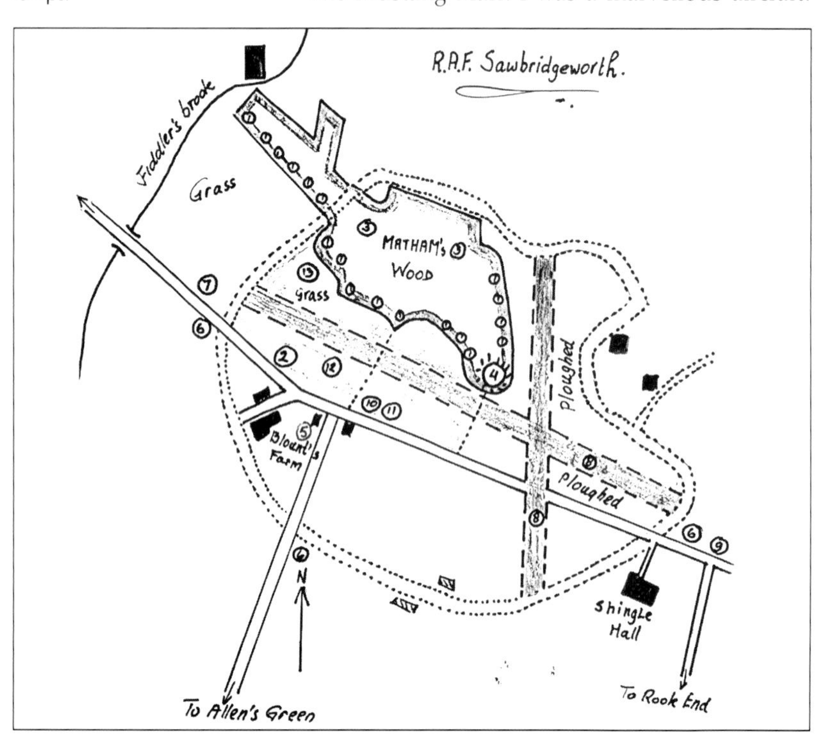

It was fitted with a 1,150 hp. Allison V-1710-39 engine and with a maximum speed of 380 mph. at 8000 feet, its ability to climb to 15,000 feet in eight minutes and its range of over 1,000 miles it was a recce pilot's dream. The Mustang carried an impressive arsenal of machine guns: with four ·50 and two ·30 guns it could destroy anything it encountered. Two ·50 guns were mounted in the engine compartment and carried 400 rounds. The other two ·50s and two ·30s had been placed in the wings. For the ·50s a variety of ammunition was available. The M2 Ball cartridge fired a 700 grain bullet at over 2,800 feet per second, and Armour Piercing M2, Tracer M10, Incendiary M1 and AP/Incendiary rounds could be used as well. The rate of fire per barrel was 800 rounds per minute. In order to carry out its Tac/R duties the aircraft carried F24 cameras mounted behind the pilot's seat pointing out to port through a clear vision panel. This camera could take a film of either 125 or 250 exposures to produce five by five inch photographs. Camera alignment was by means of a mark on the trailing edge of the port wing, and this of course required both fine judgement and a cool head when flying against defended targets to get accurate photography. Operational height for sorties was around 900 feet. Mustangs always flew in pairs; the leader took the pictures while his wingman covered him. The Mustang's sole handicap was the lack of engine power at high altitude, but this was to change dramatically when Mustangs with Rolls-Royce Merlin engines appeared.

No.II (AC) Squadron was ready for battle by April 1942. Yet Squadron pilots did not go straight into action in their Mustangs. After F/O Davies had collected the first Mustang it was found that there were no Pilot's Handling Notes. He spent about an hour inside the cockpit finding out about the aircraft. On 19 and 21 April 1941 S/L Chapman collected a Spitfire from Dyce and flew photo recce sorties to Jersey in this No.140 Squadron aircraft. By the end of the month similar missions had been flown to Dunkirk and Le Havre by F/L Houseman. While the first operational flights over enemy territory took place the Squadron Tomahawks continued to give problems at home. On 23 April F/L Hall in Tomahawk AK146 went out of control in cloud. Although Hall successfully used his parachute the aircraft crashed onto a searchlight position. On 6 May another P-40 was lost when P/O Lyons appeared to sink on the approach to RAF Sealand. His aircraft AH492 hit a stationary Boston, Lyons escaped unhurt, but a member of the Boston ground crew was killed. The Tomahawk was damaged beyond repair. The same day 'Jump' Davies had a shade of bad luck while flying Proctor Z7208. While attempting to land at Catterick the Proctor swung off the runway with a burst tyre. Nothing further happened and Davies walked away shaken. 9 May 1942 was a very memorable day for the Squadron and for P/O Peter Tonkin in particular. The Operations Record Book stated very dryly:

> '9/05. 11.10 P/O P. Tonkin whilst carrying out authorised low flying struck an overhead cable which could not be seen owing to the background of trees. Pilot uninjured.
>
> 12/05. Whilst taxying beside the runway the starboard wheel of Mustang AG401 piloted by P/O P. Tonkin struck a hole and the aircraft tilted up on its nose damaging the three blades of the propeller. Pilot uninjured.'

Sadly, worse was to happen later that day. At 1600 hours Mustang AG403 piloted by P/O Gosnell took off and after running approximately 500 yards struck Mustang AG488 piloted by P/O Wilmett which was taxying along the runway prior to take-off. After impact AG403 rose to fifty feet, stalled, flicked onto its back and crashed in flames. P/O Gosnell was killed. The next day F/O Dawson of No.26 Squadron flew the first operational sortie in Mustang AG418 over the French coast near Berck-sur-Mer. It was the first of the many 'Populars' to be flown by Army Co-op Mustangs. As for Wilmett, the month of May was to become a very tense one. Ten days after his collision with Gosnell he suffered an engine failure in AG492. Flying at only 1,800 feet Wilmett could not restart the engine but made a successful forced landing and walked away for the second time in ten days.

Sometimes Squadron members 'crossed the thin red line'. One Leading Aircraftman, a Flight Mechanic who shall remain unnamed, really got himself into serious trouble. Having been absent without leave and then having escaped from close arrest, he was court martialled on 20 May 1942.

From now on low-level operations would be part of the Squadron's daily work. All exercises were aimed at one purpose only: to fly low, fast and accurately. These future operational sorties were extremely dangerous. German defences, especially the quadruple 20mm AA guns, and the nature of low-level high-speed flying made it a very risky combination. Almost every single

No.II (AC) Squadron Mustang, Tomahawk and Battle, overflown by a flight of Mustangs.

W/C Riddell (seated) with Major Noel East (AILO) and P/Os B.E. Hawes (left) and P.J. Wilmett (right). Sadly, Hawes was killed during a cross-country flight on 28 July 1942.

day No.II Squadron Mustangs would fly low-level exercises. Every day the Squadron diarist wrote: 'Low level attacks carried out at . . .' Many former members will recall the names of exercises like 'Blitz', 'Simplex II', 'Jungle', 'Filter', 'Bullets', 'Lively' and 'Walton'.

No.II (AC) Squadron Mustang making a low pass over the runway at Sawbridgeworth.

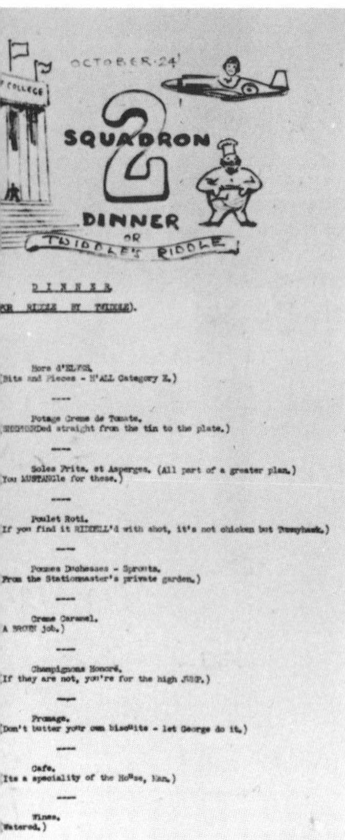

OCTOBER·24'

SQUADRON 2 DINNER OR TWIDDLE'S RIDDLE

DINNER
([illegible] RIDDLE BY TWIDDLE).

Hors d'ELVES.
(Bits and Pieces - H'ALL Category E.)

Potage Creme de Tomate.
([illegible]ed straight from the tin to the plate.)

Soles Frits, et Aspergea. (All part of a greater plan.)
(You MUSTANGle for these.)

Poulet Roti.
(If you find it RIDDELL'd with shot, it's not chicken but [illegible].)

Pommes Duchesses - Sprouts.
(From the Stationmaster's private garden.)

Creme Caramel.
(A BROWN job.)

Champignons Honoré.
(If they are not, you're for the high JUMP.)

Fromage.
(Don't butter your own biscuits - let George do it.)

Cafe.
(Its a speciality of the House, [illegible].)

Wines.
(Watered.)

Menu for the dining out of W/C Riddle, who left the Squadron for duties at the RAF Staff College. The menu was signed on the reverse by officers serving under him.

On 10 June the CiC Army Co-op Command AM Sir Arthur Barratt arrived at Sawbridgeworth at 1000 hours. The entire Squadron formed up for a parade. The next day during Exercise Lively the aerodrome was 'attacked'. On 13 June the No.1 alert suddenly sounded at 2130 hours. During the night all Air Defence Localities were occupied and the officers manned Battle Headquarters. Ten days after this exercise the famous American journalist Quentin Reynolds visited the Squadron accompanied by Group Captain Lousada and Brigadier Duncan. They saw a demonstration of Tactical Reconnaissance, Message Dropping and aerobatics. The following day F/O Sheperd had to make a forced landing while taking off in Mustang AG607. Wilmett had engine trouble with Tiger Moth N4954 a few days later while P/O Hawes successfully landed a Mustang which had caught fire in the air. Sadly, P/O G.D.P. Young was killed in a flying accident after carrying out air-to-ground firing practice and LAC Dodds drowned while swimming in the river near the aerodrome. The month of June had been a particularly sad one for the Squadron.

July was another month full of exercises. First there was 'Bury' which took four days. Then on 7 July P/O Symonds damaged his aircraft AG8456 while taxying. Captain Belchradsky and Lieutenant Brabence, two Czech officers, spent ten days with the Squadron to learn Army Co-op tactics while on 20 July S/L Chapman left the Squadron to go to RAF Staff College at Camberley. On 24 July a big day was organised at Sawbridgeworth to introduce the Mustang to the press. No less than fifty correspondents saw the Mustang being flown to its limits. One of the spectators was Sergeant Roy Thorn of the RAF Regiment who recalls having seen for the first time a demonstration of the effects of napalm. All spectators, hundreds of infantrymen, and the Duke of Cornwall were quite amazed to see what this new jelly could do. Numerous photographs were taken and all agreed that this was the aircraft the RAF had been waiting for. Unfortunately, four days later P/O Hawes, who had successfully force-landed his Mustang in May, was killed near Penzance when he crashed in AG478 during a cross country flight.

On 5 August an AC2 named Potter was apprehended in Liverpool after having been absent for no less than six months. Both he and another AC2 were court matrialled six weeks later. Very few other things but exercises hapened that month. The first American national joined 'Shiny Two' that month, P/O Sims. On the eighteenth P/O Wylie flying Tiger Moth DE358 crashed into a tree while taking off from Felstead. Both he and his passenger Captain Hansen were slightly injured. On 28 August top brass invaded the aerodrome — Colonel Sir John Turner and Members of the Air Ministry Staff came to see a demonstration of the use of camouflage nets. Also present were AVMs Bottomley, Robb, Henderson, Air Cdres Yool and Whitworth-Jones, and Group Captains Pike, Opie, Lousada and Fitch. At the same time everything was being done to ensure good relations with the Americans. That may have been the sole reason why the Squadron played a baseball match against American officers and duly lost.

While the Squadron practised on 19 August 1942 a savage battle raged on the French coast. Canadian troops and British Commandos had landed at Dieppe for what was called a 'reconnaissance in force'. Air Marshal Leigh-Mallory had been given command of forty-six Spitfire, eight Hurricane, three Typhoon, four Mustang, seven Boston and Blenheim squadrons to clear the sky over the ground forces. During Operation Jubilee the RAF had flown nearly 3,000 sorties and lost 100 aircraft. Sixteen hours later it was all over. Canadians and Commandos were marched into captivity. The Germans were sure that any attempt to penetrate their defensive lines at the Atlantic Wall was doomed to failure. The Squadron had not played a part in the battle, yet they were to go into action very soon.

The RAF Regiment played an important role on the aerodrome. The safety of Sawbridgeworth depended on the men of 2440 Squadron RAFR. Sergeant Roy Thorn was one of these men, having arrived at Sawbridgeworth in September 1940 he witnessed the gradual change from an ALG to an aerodrome. When the regiment arrived all they had were a few old Hotchkiss machine guns. Eventually the squadron received Lewis guns with which they manned the gun pits. They also manned a steel tower in the woods adjoining the aerodrome with twin Browning machine guns. During September a number of Royal Navy Fairey Fulmars operated from the aerodrome. W/C Riddell was dined out as he had been posted to RAF Staff College. His farewell dinner on 24 October was a smashing success. The menu gave several delicacies such as:

'Sôles Frits, et Asperges (All part of a greater plan)
(You MUSTANGle for these).
Poulet Roti. (If you find it Ridell'd with shot it's not chicken but Tummyhawk).
Crème Caramel (A brown job).
Wines (watered).'

Some look upon the Riddell-time with mixed feelings. Riddell was a poseur, but one who had a great deal of fun from his posting. He would sometimes give an order and finish with an imperative 'At Once', especially when it was quite impossible to comply with. He kept a board at the Squadron office with a special cage drawn on it in which was put the photograph of an officer whom he deemed guilty of 'finger trouble'. When he left, one of the Flight Commanders S/L Houseman took over temporarily but on 29 October disaster struck — three Squadron Mustangs were lost in one day. P/O Leah belly-landed 'E', P/O Crosby bailed out of 'B' over Bicester and P/O Williams fatally crashed at Ware in 'A'. During October one exercise followed the other. In November Norwegian pilots from a Spitfire squadron joined No.II Squadron to familiarise themselves with Army Co-op flying. One of them was F/O Anton Christopher Hagerup. He had served as a fighter pilot during the German invasion of Norway in April 1940. On 18 November 1942 while flying a Squadron Tomahawk Hagerup crash-landed near Cheddington. The same month P/O Gordon-Crosby crashed on landing Tomahawk AK144 at Sawbridgeworth. He was only slightly injured.

The Mustangs had a different paint scheme than the Tomahawk. They were camouflaged dark green and dark sea-grey with medium sea-grey undersides. The aircraft in Army Co-operation Command began to delete unit code letters so the individual aircraft letter was moved to a new position ahead of the roundel. November was a turning point in the Squadron's history.

On 14 November the first two Squadron Mustangs took off from Sawbridgeworth for the first operational sortie over occupied territory since 1940. At 1335 hours S/L Houseman in AL995 and F/L Kenning in AM112 headed for Holland to take oblique line overlaps of a German RDF station at Domburg on the island of Walcheren. Crossing the English coast at Clacton they flew at extremely low level until making landfall at 1415 hours near Zoutelande at the western point of the island. Due to the low cloud the pilots had to take their photographs from 350 feet rather than from 1000 feet as ordered. The returned at 1505 hours with excellent photographs. Unfortunately the photographs were useless as they had been taken from too low an altitude. Four days later both pilots returned to Domburg. They crossed Bradwell at fifty feet making landfall at Zoutelande and once again skimming the wave tops. This time their photographs were exactly what top brass needed. From November 1942 the Squadron flew 'Populars'. The first sortie of this kind was carried out by P/O Ingham and Sgt McLeod on 22 November. The took off from Sawbridgeworth at 1445 hours. Their brief was to take oblique photographs of the town of Zierikzee and of the railways in that area. The sortie was quite eventful. The pair made landfall west of Flushing in error. Ingham decided to fly on round the island of Walcheren. Switching on his camera and taking violent evasive action he flew as low as he dared, encountering heavy and light flak from four flak ships and coastal batteries west of Flushing. The aircraft was hit three times. Nursing his Mustang back to base Ingham found he had no hydraulics to operate his flaps and

Top: In July 1942 the first Mustang Mark I arrived at Sawbridgeworth. Here XV-U stands next to the last Lysander to serve with No.II (AC) Squadron. P/O Tonkin (right) explains the differences and advantages to S/L Brown, an RAF Public Relations Officer.

Mustang XV-U with engine running. Unlike later models the Mark I had two machine guns in the nose, under the propeller.

brakes — his aircraft crashed on landing. Ingham walked away unhurt, but the first Squadron Mustang was lost. McLeod arrived home safely. On 28 November Ingham wrote to his father:

'. . . I am telling you this on condition that you don't tell anyone, especially Jean or mam. I was leading my section of two on that day, and we were near where we spent our holiday on the coast, when I was seven years old. Well I got into some trouble and my plane was hit three times by cannon and one lump hit my dinghy on my back. I managed to get back OK, but the plane was damaged and I crashed on landing. I was not hurt much; just a bruise on the arm. I think I was the luckiest chap alive. It seems queer that during broad daylight, the first thing I thought of when I was hit, was you, mam and Jean. If I had dreamt it, it would not have seemed so unreal, but it was all so perfectly clear at the time, I think that it is the nearest I will ever be to finishing my career, but I didn't seem at all afraid, just annoyed. The fellow with me was the sergeant I told you about, and he wasn't even scratched. It is all over now and it certainly hasn't affected my flying at all.'

On 29 November the Squadron lost its first pilot since it had gone into action again. 'Popular' sorties were very dangerous indeed as P/O Cunningham, a New Zealander was to find out. With F/L Hall as No.1 he was detailed to take obliques of the coastline between The Hook of Holland and Westkapelle. The Operations Record Book for 29 November 1942 states:

'Both crossed out The Naze 0 feet. F/Lt. Hall climbed up to 2,000 feet on approaching the Dutch coast. P/O Cunningham flying lower on the sea side — made landfall at Terheijden — turned on to course and flew for eight minutes — F/Lt. Hall then turned to return to base — P/O Cunningham crossed underneath him. F/Lt. Hall looked back and saw him following — he called him up and gave him the course he was steering but received no reply. F/Lt. Hall then flew on for another five minutes and on looking back could not see P/O Cunningham. He continued and made landfall north of Harwich. North Weald sector station continued calling on VHF until dark but had no reply. Weather poor with rain showers. 63 exposures taken verify bad weather conditions. P/O G.M. Cunningham (NZ) reported missing.'

In December the weather was so poor that six aircraft and ground crew were posted to Hunsden to enable the Squadron to continue operations. Two new ALOs arrived, Captain O'Brien of the Inniskilling Fusiliers and Captain Abbott RA.

Below right: How low can you go?
Mustang XV-W, AG623 making a low pass over RAF Sawbridgeworth on 24.7.42. Unfortunately AG623 was lost on 26.5.43 over St Albans Head, killing the pilot F/O D. Hirst.

Bottom: Officers of No.II Squadron at Bottisham February 1943.
Back row, left to right: F/Os R.G. Gent, P.N. Leah, R.H. Andrews, M.P. Dunkerley, I.W. Harris, N.J. Miller, R.G. Epps (MO), P/O J.B. McLeod.
Centre row, F/Os P.A. Hay-Neave, D. Hirst, A. Whitten-Brown, H.F.C. Joy, J. Ingham, P. Tonkin, P.M. Gordon-Crosby, R.C. Cooper, T.B. Meek, K. Drysdale (Eng. Off.) Lt. A.C. Hagerup, F/O R.W. Hunton-Carter, Capt. R.N. Wilson (ALO).
Front row, F/Ls J.F. Fletcher (Signals), P.R. Jones (Adjutant), H. Davison (A Flight Cdr.) S/L A.E. Houseman, W/C P. Stansfeld (CO) Maj N. East (ALO), F/Ls P.B. Hall (B Flight Cdr.) G. Kenning (C Flight Cdr.), Captain J.R. Abbott (ALO).

During December the following 'Populars' were flown:

7/12. 1237-1444 hours F/L Sheperd (AM113)–P/O Tonkin (NZ) (AM254): Den Helder-Egmond.

9/12. 1138-1345 hours F/L Kenning (AL995)–P/O Miller (AM113):Bergen-IJmuiden.

16/12. 1133-1325 hours S/L Houseman (AM113)–Sgt McLeod (AL972): Noordwijk-Westkapelle.

27/12. 1226-1332 hours F/O Davies (AM113)–Sgt Smith (AM254):Goedereede-area.

27/12. 1226-1319 hours F/O Harris (AL972)–P/O Andrews (AM112):Goedereede-area.

29/12. 1103-1235 hours F/O Davies (AM113)–Sgt Smith (AM254):Goedereede-area.

29/12. 1102-1242 hours F/O Harris (AP203)–F/O Andrews (Al969):Goedereede-area.

The Squadron diarist wrote that the 29/12 sortie had been a very costly recce. After having made landfall four miles south of Noordwijk at 1147 hours a photographic run was made in a southerly direction. F/O Davies did not see Smith again after turning south. Davies joined the other two aircraft and returned to base with them. No R/T communication was received from Sgt. Smith. Davies had two S.A. bullet holes in the wing of his aircraft but had no knowledge of being fired at. The photographs covered the target area but not in sufficient detail to fulfill the requirements of the task. It was assumed that Sgt Smith went down between Oostvoorne and Havenhoofd in The Netherlands.

30/12. 1251-1431 hours F/L Kenning (AM112)–P/O Mims (AL972):Goedereede-area.

30/12. 1251-1438 hours F/L Hall (AP203)–F/O Harris (AL969):Goedereede-area.

31/12. 1126-1248 hours F/O Ingham (AP241)–P/O Tonkin (AL972):Goedereede-area.

In retrospect it is interesting to note that from December 13 pilots of No.II Squadron flew twenty sorties in seven days, being airborne for twelve hours and fifty minutes.

The aerodrome was often unserviceable due to the wet soil, so flying took place from Hunsdon from which twenty sorties were carried out. On 25 January 1943 W/C Riddell returned to the Squadron and was its CO for a short period of time. During the same month the Squadron left Sawbridgeworth and, led by an advance party on 30 January, departed for Bottisham. The Sawbridgeworth days were over for the time being. The battle against the Germans went on. During January two successful 'Populars' were flown against the island of Schouwen in the Scheldt Estuary. The pilots were Sgt McLeod and F/L Hagerup on the third and F/L Kenning and F/O Mims on the thirteenth. During the first sortie Hagerup attacked the AA gunners at Haamstede aerodrome. During the second sortie F/O Mims had to divert to Hunsdon after Flak damaged his hydraulic system.

W/C Riddell left again on 3 February to take up duties at the Air Ministry. Five days later a new CO arrived. He was W/C Peter Stansfeld, an ex-Tank Corps officer who had flown Lysanders with No.II (AC) Squadron before the war. Again the Army was in command of the Squadron.

One of the new entries in the Squadron was F/O Whitten-Brown, son of the famous Old Boy who had at one time crossed the Atlantic. In March 1943 the Squadron participated in 'Spartan', the largest Army mobility exercise ever held in Britain and one intended to iron out problems likely to be met in an invasion of Occupied Europe. They operated from Bottisham, Westcott, Newmarket, Cranfield and Duxford. During this time the Duke of Gloucester paid a visit to the Squadron. Soon after 'Spartan' the three flying Flights moved to Fowlmere leaving the Headquarters and Maintenance Flights at Bottisham. However at the end of April the flying Flights returned to Sawbridgeworth, 2½ weeks after the HQ and Maintenance Flights.

'Spartan' was an important exercise to sort out problems that might arise during the invasion of Western Europe. The Squadron took part in this exercise and were visited by top brass. Left to right: AM Sir A.S. Barratt (AOCiC Army Co-op Command), W/C Stansfeld (OC No.II (AC) Squadron), General Andrews (USAAC), S/L Houseman (Second in Command and ADC to Gen. Andrews).

Mustangs Mark I XV-U, AG550 and XV-X, AM112 over Cambridgeshire. 'U' is being flown by W/C Geddes who was CO at the outbreak of the War and who was posted to HQ Army Co-op Command afterwards.

Above: Squadron pilots being briefed before take-off. Left to right: F/O Skinner, F/L Hall, S/L Houseman, F/O Hunton Carter and F/L Kenning.

Top right: F/O John Beaton McLeod was the third pilot to be killed during the sad accident on 26 May 1943. Here he is seen standing (left) with the ALO Major Noel East and an Army Sergeant at a debriefing.

It was whilst the Squadron was flying from Fowlmere that the shipping reconnaissance sorties code-named 'Lagoon' started. All sorties took place off the Dutch coast. It was during one of these Lagoon sorties, on 19 April, that F/O Gordon-Crosby went missing. Between 1103 and 1125 hours four pairs of Mustangs took off from Coltishall and Fowlmere. The eight participating pilots were F/L Kenning (AM112) and P/O Butt (AG623), F/L Hall (AP203) and F/O Skinner (AM234), F/O Andrews (AL969) and F/O Gordon-Crosby (AG464), F/O Hirst (Al972) and F/O Miller (AG550). They had been detailed to reconnoitre a large part of The Netherlands from north to south. The first pair were to fly over the area Nordeney-Schiermonnikoog, the second pair Schiermonnikoog-Vlieland, the third pair Vlieland to Egmond while the fourth pair had orders to cover the area from Egmond to the Hook of Holland. Between 1330 and 1400 hours seven aircraft returned. Kenning and Butt landed at Coltishall after an uneventful sortie. Hall and Skinner reported ten trawlers off Ameland steaming east. Andrews came back alone. At the debriefing he reported that he had lost sight of his No.2 shortly after starting the target run and had received no reply to his radio calls. Gordon-Crosby was never seen or heard of again. Hirst and Miller returned safely. Hirst landed at Coltishall while Miller had touched down at Bungay, an American base. They had had quite a hectic flight. They reported thirty fishing vessels south of Ymuiden. Three escorting vessels had opened fire after they spotted the Mustangs. Near Noordwijk both had been fired upon by five vessels. After photographing eighteen cargo vessels they had set course for England.

During April the Squadron returned to Sawbridgeworth. 'Populars' and 'Lagoons' continued, with sixty-six and twenty-eight sorties being flown respectively. The Operations Record Book showed that during April twenty-three pilots flew no less than 125 hours and 44 minutes during these sorties.

On 24 May 1943 S/L Houseman left the Squadron and went to Staff College. He was replaced as Squadron Leader Air by S/L B.O.C. Egan-Wyer. On 26 May disaster struck No.II (AC) Squadron. After having twice postponed Operation 'Asphalt', it was to be carried out. 'Asphalt' was a Ranger sortie to carry out offensive operations on rail movements in the area Rennes-Laval-Le Mans-Chateaubriand-Blain-Redon-Rennes. At 1650 hours ten Mustangs took off from Thruxton. The aircraft and pilots were: F/L G. Kenning in Mustang XV-X; F/O N.J. Miller in Mustang XV-U; F/O J.B. McLeod in Mustang XV-Y; F/O D. Hirst in Mustang XV-W; F/L P.B. Hall in Mustang XV-J; F/O M.P. Dunkerley in Mustang XV-N; F/O D.B. Andrews in Mustang XV-K; F/O H.F.C. Joy in Mustang XV-D; F/L W. Sheperd in Mustang XV-A and F/O P.A. Hay-Neave in Mustang XV-E.

Flying in line abreast formation they encountered a wall of fog at Kimbridge St Albans Head at zero feet. Kenning gave the order to climb. Unfortunately F/Os Miller and Hirst and P/O McLeod failed to clear a hill which was hidden by fog. All three aircraft flew straight into it killing the pilots. The remaining aircraft returned to Thruxton after failing to locate the three missing aicraft. F/O Dunkerley returned late with hydraulic failure and effected a safe landing. The operation was subsequently cancelled. Nevertheless two days later operations continued as scheduled. On 31 May Hirst and Miller were buried at the RAF Cemetery Brookwood. W/C Peter Stansfeld, S/L Padre Perkins, Major East, F/L Kenning, F/L Waterfield, F/O Gent, F/O Meek and Sgt Pearce attended the ceremony. F/O Leah attended the private funeral of P/O McLeod in Glasgow.

The appearance of the radial-engined Focke-Wulf FW190 increased the risks of reconnaissance flying. Suddenly the Squadron started losing quite a few aircraft through combat with this new German aeroplane. The FW190 fighter was a great threat to the Squadron Mustangs. It was able to out-climb, out-dive and out-manoeuvre the Mustang. The Mustang was a comfortable aircraft with its armchair-type seat and its electric system, many pilots considered it the easiest aircraft to land, but all these comforts were of no use if a FW190 jumped it. Some of the Squadron pilots went to Farnborough from Odiham where the RAF had a FW190. It was a Mark A-3 model with a 1,700 horsepower BMW 801D-2 engine. The aircraft had been delivered by a German pilot, Oberleutnant Armin Faber of III./JG2 who, after getting lost, had landed by mistake at Pembrey, South Wales on 23 June 1943. The mock combat exercises were rather revealing. It took quite a time for the Mustangs to catch up with the FW190 and the exercise confirmed the Squadron's doubts. The only manoeuvre recommended by Army Co-op pilots in case of an encounter with an FW190 was to fly as low as possible and carry out steep turns as the Mustang gave plenty of warning of a stall during a steep turn, unlike the FW190 which did not seem to give any warning at all. Byron Jones, one of the Mustang pilots, remembered one No.II Squadron pilot doing just this and the FW190 chasing him suddenly flicked into a spin and crashed. The cause of this disastrous behaviour was the German pilot making excessive use of the electric tail-trimmer, an ingenious invention of the Focke-Wulf engineers in an attempt to tighten an already very tight 'g' turn, the FW190 eventually entering a high-speed stall from which there was no recovery. According to Jones, the No.II Squadron pilot took a camera-gun shot of the FW190 and was subsequently credited with a kill . . .

A good feature of the Mustang was its strength during a forced or crashlanding. One of the Squadron pilots, F/O Brickwood was shot down whilst flying very low and ploughed into a forest. After crashing into trees and thick undergrowth the aircraft came to a stop minus the engine, wings and fuselage but the cockpit was fully intact so that all he had to do was to jettison the canopy (there was no sliding facility because it was literally screwed down) and step out of the aircraft. Brickwood walked back into the mess about three months later after a long and eventful journey with the Resistance.

During June 1943 big changes took place. On the first Army Co-operation Command ceased to exist. No.34 Wing and presumably No.35 Wing also came under the control of No.12 Group. By the end of the month No.34 Wing left the operational control of the Army's Eastern Command and moved to Hartford Bridge coming directly under TAF HQ and becoming GHQ Recce Wing. No.II (AC) Squadron continued flying Lagoons and Populars. The main area of interest for the Squadron was the Dutch coast.

Two Squadron Mustangs making a very low pass over RAF Sawbridgeworth.

Mustang XV-B making a low pass over press and other officials. 24.7.42.

The Operations Record Book entries for June showed that nothing escaped the Mustangs' cameras:

1/6 Lagoon. Hook of Holland-Ymuiden-Texel.
2/6 Lagoon. Hook of Holland-Ymuiden-Texel.
3/6 Lagoon. Hook of Holland-Zandvoort-Den Helder.
6/6 Lagoon. Hook of Holland-Ymuiden.
13/6 Lagoon. Hook of Holland-Zandvoort-Texel.
14/6 Lagoon. Den Helder-Zandvoort-Hook of Holland.
15/6 Lagoon. Hook of Holland-Zandvoort.
17/6 Popular. Blankenberge-Nieuwe Sluis.
19/6 Lagoon. Hook of Holland-Zandvoort-Den Helder-Fexel.
20/6 Lagoon. Zandvoort-Hook of Holland-Zandvoort.
27/6 Lagoon. 10 miles N of Texel-Den Helder-Zandvoort-Hook of Holland.
28/6 Lagoon. Noordwijkerhout-Bergen aan Zee-Texel.
29/6 Lagoon. Den Helder-Ymuiden-Hook of Holland.

During the sortie of 3 June F/L Kenning (AM112) and F/O R.W.F. Carter flying Mustang AL972 were attacked by two FW190s; Carter's aircraft was last seen in flames and believed to be shot down off the Dutch coast. Tens of thousands of photographs were taken. On 29 June Wing Commander Peter Stansfeld was posted to GHQ Recce Wing at Hertford Bridge. S/L Egon-Wyer took over.

Below right: Six Mustangs over Sawbridgeworth. 24.7.42.
XV-A was lost over Ware on 29.10.42, killing P/O Williams (AG605);
XV-B was lost over Bicester on 29.10.42, P/O Gordon-Crosby bailing out (AG456);
XV-E was lost at RAF Sawbridgeworth on 29.10.42 with P/O Leah escaping (AG633);
XV-F (AG638?)
XV-D (AG370?)
XV-W was lost over St Albans Head on 26.5.43, killing F/O Hirst (AG623);

Bottom: P/O Peter Tonkin (RNZAF) behind the controls of XV-U (AG550). This particular aircraft was lost on 26.5.43 after a Ranger 'Asphalt', crashing near Kimmeridge in Dorset and killing its pilot, F/O N.J. Miller.

On 3 July a Squadron party was organised in the Officers' Mess at Sawbridgeworth where the Squadron had returned once again. The party was a great success and was attended by many old friends such as Group Captain Lousada, Wing Commander Stansfield and others. On 8 July Lieutenant General Templar DSO, OBE, the new 2 Corps Commander, visited the Squadron. On 12 July orders came to move again. The new Squadron base was to be RAF Gravesend. The Squadron was to share it with No.4 Squadron. On the sixteenth everybody arrived there and was moved under canvas. Gavesend's Station Commander was an old No.II Squadron pilot, W/C Anderson DSO, DFC. The same day all airmen were subjected to physical examinations for duties overseas. Anybody who was found unfit was posted away. A new experience were the trips some of the officers made on board a destroyer of the Royal Navy.

During July a new kind of operation was introduced, 'Distil'. The idea was to intercept German Junkers Ju88 bombers trying to lay mines. In spite of five mass sorties no 'Mausi', as these aircraft were called, made an appearance. These sorties called for a big effort, each time six to eight aircraft were detailed. On 4 July the Squadron had some success when it spotted a German convoy. Two German vessels were attacked and damaged. The next day F/O Butt was killed during landing, after one of the many 'Lagoons'. His aircraft struck the ground, exploded and burned out. He too was buried at Brookwood. The total number of sorties flown in July was very impressive:

Operations 'Distil'	28 sorties
Operations 'Lagoon'	24 sorties
Operations 'Popular'	6 sorties
Operations 'Escort'	4 sorties

An Escort operation was flown on 14 July to protect an Air-Sea Rescue Anson trying to locate a downed crew. Unfortunately the search was fruitless. On 7 August all personnel of No.130 Airfield left Gravesend and moved to Odiham. August was one of those months in which the Squadron paid dearly for the dangerous sorties it was flying. Twenty-eight 'Popular' sorties were flown. On 25 August F/Os Tonkin and Andrews were trying to take photographs but were attacked by Me109s. Tonkin got home but Andrews was shot down into the sea and had to be reported missing. Three days later F/O J.B. Day failed to return when he had to ditch after a Popular sortie with F/O Maitland. The next day one of the Norwegian pilots, Captain Jean-Hansen lost his life when he crashed in France. At the end of August S/L Gray was appointed OC No.II (AC) Squadron.

The tasks that were carried out by the Squadron gave an indication that the defensive war was about to end. First there were the many photographs the Squadron had to take of the French coast after many months of similar duties over Holland. In September, forty-one 'Populars' were flown, eight 'Patrols' and twenty-six 'Pontoons' (convoy escorts). During one of the 'Pontoons' one section of No.II Squadron was attacked by Spitfires. F/O Weighill's aircraft was damaged by two cannon shells and two ·303 bullets. Then there was 'Operation Starkey'. An enormous convoy left England and pretended to be sailing directly to France for an invasion of Occupied Europe. The idea was to alert the Germans and see what their reaction would be. Basically there was no reaction at all.

The final shape of the Squadron as a unit of TAF was fixed on 4 September, when Establishment WAR/SR/8B came into force. Basically it shaped the Squadron into a fighter as opposed to an Army Co-operation force. The Officer Establishment was as follows:

1 Squadron Leader (Squadron Commander)
2 Flight Lieutenants (Flight Commanders)
16 Flying Officers (Pilots)
1 Flying Officer (Adjutant, Non-Flying)

The Squadron strength at that time was thirty-four pilots. The aircraft were still Mustangs.

Byron Jones joined the Squadron in September 1943. Being very new in the Squadron, Jones and another pilot were quite amazed to hear that they were to fly Tactical Reconnaissances, low level Photo Reconnaissances, 'Rangers', 'Rhubarbs' and Shipping Recces. As they knew absolutely nothing about ships they were sent to London Docks for a few days at sea with a convoy which was to sail up the North Sea.

> 'It so happened that we were attached to an American Liberty ship which was captained by an over-generous American who kept insisting that we were doing 'a grand job' and deserved a rest at his winter residence in Florida. He kept saying that all he had to do was to certify in the ship's log that we were both unfit to be removed from his ship. We eventually managed to disembark after quite a struggle at Loch Ewe which in those days was the pre-Atlantic crossing point. We were about two days late returning to the Squadron. However the CO Mike Gray was very understanding and we suffered no reprimand. We did not learn much about warships but knew a lot about Liberty Ships and where the bar was . . .'

Chocks away for Mustang XV-B, AG456. This particular aircraft was lost over Bicester on 29 October P/O P.H. Gordon-Crosby baled out successfully.

On 20 September the Squadron left Odiham and moved to Hutton Cranswick. One week later two Squadron pilots, F/Os Weighill and Hope were attached to the Guards Armoured Division for two days to observe the soldiers during exercise 'Blackcock'. The two pilots must have been shocked . . . during the exercise the Squadron pilots flew seventy-one sorties in ten days. After only a fortnight at Sutton Cranswick the Squadron was told to move again, after the conclusion of the Guards' Exercise. An old Handley Page

In July 1943 the Squadron was temporarily based at Gravesend to form No.130 Airfield.
From left to right:
Back row: F/O Percival, F/O McPherson, F/O Reich, F/O Leah, F/O Smith, F/O Lumsden, F/O Andrews and F/O Dunkerley.
Middle row: F/L Hollingbery (Adj.), P/O Drysdale (Eng.), F/O Cooper, F/O Corrigan, F/O Meek, Capt. Tufte-Johnsen (RNAF), F/O Tonkin, F/O Shayle-George and F/O Weighill.
Front row: Capt. Abbot (ALO), F/L Fletcher (Sign.), F/L Wakefield, F/L Davison, S/L Egan-Weyer, Maj. East (ALO), F/L Sheperd, F/L Kenning DFC and F/L Redman.
Not present were F/L Hall, F/O Hay-Neave, F/O Gent, F/O Joy, F/O Skinner, F/O Leventon, F/O Hope and F/O Day.

F/O Ingham was killed on 16 October 1943 when his Mustang collided with F/O Griffith's aircraft of No.4 Squadron over Basingstoke.

F/O Dunkerley was killed in action on 9 November 1943.

Harrow provided the Squadron with air transport for the camp kits and the officers who did not fly a Mustang. The Harrow left Hutton Cranswick at 1100 hours and landed at Tangmere about two hours later. The new airfield would be Odiham again. The Operations Record Book gives a vivid description of the move.

> '3 October. 130 airfield was now at Funnington and MT was provided at Tangmere to convey gear. Main Air party left Hutton Cranswick at 2400 hours and flew direct to Funnington. The Road party consisting of three 3-ton Crossleys carried the Adjutant and seven airmen. They left Hutton Cranswick at 1330 hours and reached Grantham at 1900 hours stopping for the night at No.1 RAF Regiment Depot Grantham.
>
> 4 October. Main Party continued journey and reached Odiham at 1800 hours. The Adjutant contacted the Admin. Officer of 130 Airfield by telephone at Funnington and was instructed to await 130 Airfield's arrival at Odiham.'

For the time being the Squadron was put under canvas. This was not at all appreciated. On 15 October Squadron and Airfield moved into winter quarters at RAF Station Odiham. 'Move much appreciated as tent life becoming unpleasant', wrote the diarist. The next day F/O Ingham was killed when his Mustang collided with an aircraft of No.4 Squadron whilst practising an attack drill over Basingstoke. F/O Griffiths DFM of No.4 Squadron baled out but was burnt badly. Both aircraft fell clear of the town. This accident was particularly sad for F/O James Ingham as he was expected home on leave the following week to see his wife and five month old daughter. Ingham was buried at Burnley Cemetery on 22 October. The following day, 23 October, Air Marshal d'Albiac, the AOCiC TAF visited the Squadron. Four days later AVM Brown DSC, AFC, the newly oppointed AOC 84 Group followed.

The various sorties were now all directed at the French coast. Quite a lot of the November photo recces went to Normandy. Only very few officers in the RAF knew why pictures were taken of the beaches north of Bayeux. During Ranger sorties Mustangs attacked German convoys and trains. On 7 November Colin Maitland successfully encountered a Me109. It crashed in flames. On 9 November however another No.II Squadron pilot was killed, F/O Dunkerley. When he was in the Mess a volunteer was asked to join W/C Anderson, the 130 Airfield Commander, for a 'Ranger' sortie from Odiham against a train on a track somewhere in Normandy. They crossed the French coast between Cabourg and Dives and flew on track to the railway junction at Mezidin. They attacked three locomotives and about 20 trucks. Intense German Ack-Ack came up and over the village of Perrey en Auge Dunkerley's aircraft AP169 was hit. Dunkerley tried to bail out but his aircraft was too low and it crashed in flames. Anderson was hit as well but he managed to return to Odiham. Michael Dunkerley knew the danger of being an Army Co-operation pilot; only twenty years old, he wrote his last will in May 1943. Little was he to know that he would die on the last day of his active duty with the Squadron. In his last will he wrote:

> 'Dear Mother and Dad,
>
> Here is my will and I hope you will find it fair and reasonable. It is comprehensive and I know Dad will fix up anything for which I have not accounted. Please be generous with any small things which members of the family could put to use: I do not like to think of things being kept about the house as sentimental decorations. I suggest my uniform be sold, unless you know of any RAF officer who could get into it. Should I be posted "missing", I cannot honestly say the chances are good in Army Co-op Command, but which ever way you hear, let there be few tears or regrets. The Almighty could hardly have blessed me with a happier family and home life, and thus I am sure His grace and blessings will follow me, whether I stay or am to pass on. I can only thank Him now that I have been spared this long to help in the fight against evil and so others will follow if we drop out of the struggle, until Victory is won.
>
> May God make us worthy of Victory and Peace.
>
> Michael.'

On 11 November F/O Hay-Neave crashed fatally near Beachy Head. Anyone thinking the coming winter would mean some well-deserved rest for No.II (AC) Squadron was entirely wrong. On 14 November 1943 the Squadron moved to North Weald, and on the last day of the month the Squadron returned to RAF Sawbridgeworth, joining No.35 (Recce) Wing which had come directly from Odiham. These moves had no effect on the Squadron's operational effort.

While at the new base the Squadron did a lot of flying training. Captain Tufte-Johnsen and F/O Burt had the opportunity to do aerobatics in a FW190.

So came the last month of 1943. For many days the Squadron stood down due to the weather. Still many operational sorties were flown — the target for December was the Dutch coast which had not been visited by the Squadron for some months. On 25 December the Squadron celebrated Christmas. Peace on Earth was still a wish but not a reality. On the last day of December Captain Tufte-Johnsen left the Squadron as he had been posted to HQ RNAF.

CHAPTER 10
EYES AND MUSCLES

In January 1944 a new target was found for No.II (AC) Squadron's cameras: the V-1 launching sites. These operations got the code-name 'Noball'. The first photographs of these threatening weapons and their launching ramps were taken by F/L Colin Maitland and F/O 'Jonah' Jones on 4 January. All told, some seventy photogaphic sorties were flown that month, partly from Benson and partly from North Weald. The Squadron lost two pilots, F/Os Graham and MacPherson. The loss of these two was particularly tragic for Jones. On the twenty-eighth Jones and MacPherson were briefed to fly a 'Noball' against the V-1 site near Abbeville. As Jones was about to board his aircraft the CO Mike Gray called him back and said that Jones could not do this trip. He was to report to Aston Down immediately for conversion training onto Mosquitoes. Jones asked if he could do the job anyway and leave after returning from Abbeville. Gray insisted that Jones brief the stand-by pilot, F/O Mick Graham. Having no reason to disobey the CO, Jones told Graham what the brief was. At 1300 hours MacPherson in AM183 and Graham in AP237 took off. The subsequent report stated that neither aircraft had returned. Later Jones was told that they had been jumped by FW190s and shot down. Jones felt horrible:

> 'I often visit Mick's grave at Abbeville and feel that perhaps it should have been me buried there. Would the same thing have happened to me? This sort of thing happened time and time again during the war. However, I never got used to it'.

On the next day at 1506 hours F/L Harris and F/O Brickwood took off from Benson for a photo recce of the French coast. Shortly after the pair coasted in north of Cayeux Brickwood suddenly indicated that he would have to force land. F/L Harris then turned back and began to orbit one mile off the coast. After three minutes and having heard nothing from Brickwood he returned to base where he landed shortly after 1630 hours. Brickwood was reported missing. On 5 February F/L Miller of HQ 35 failed to return from a photo recce sortie to the Oisemont area. On 12 February 1944 a slight change in equipment took place when the Squadron received cannon-armed Mustang Mark IA aircraft from No.186 Squadron which in return received No.II Squadron's aircraft. It seems that the weather and the wet clay of Sawbridgeworth kept the Squadron from using its own base until 29 February. After the Benson detachment had moved to North Weald, the entire Squadron and No.130 Airfield moved home to Sawbridgeworth. No less than eighty-three photographic trips of various types were flown in February, during which the Squadron suffered no losses. There was a slight reduction in operational flying during March. The Squadron went to Dundonald for lectures and a short course on naval bombardment spotting. No-one really appreciated the need for these exercises but all was to become clear within ten weeks.

The Squadron's only blow against the enemy during this period occurred on 28 March when F/O Burt flew so low over Creil Plage that his wing tip cut a power cable.

In April the Squadron moved one step closer to the Continent and the Second Front when on the fourth it moved to Gatwick to form No.35 (Recce) Wing with Nos.4 and 268 Squadrons. The PR effort did not change much from March but in addition thirty-four Air-Sea Rescue sorties were flown. One of these ASR sorties was carried out to search for Group Captain Donkin. After six days and five nights in his dinghy the Group Captain was found by a light naval craft which was minesweeping off the Downs. During the afternoon of 20 April F/L Corrigan and F/O Howells flew a Tac/R mission in search of tanks thought to be entraining at Aubigny station. They followed the railway line from St Pol to Doullens, frequently being shot at but failing to see the tanks. The following day Exercise Freedom, an escape and evasion exercise, began at 0800 hours. For the sake of the exercise a simulated coastline ran along the London-Brighton railway line with the sea to the eastern side. The object of the escapists was to reach certain points on the coastline (Horley and Redhill Police Stations) by 1700 hours or as soon after as possible. They were attired in uniforms (some with modifications) and carried the following articles:

a) Form 1250 and a letter to the Police authority in a sealed envelope. Two pennies and a compass were carried in the pocket.

b) A Ration pack.

The following rules were to be observed:

a) Escapists were to speak only broken English.

b) No civilian property was to be stolen.

The escapists were dropped in various districts of Surrey and immediately after this were reported to the police. On 21 April there were twenty-three participants, eighteen being from No.II

(AC) Squadron and five from No.4 Squadron. Of these, ten escapists successfully evaded capture and arrived at Horley Police Station which was that day's destination. In his report the 35 Wing Intelligence Officer S/L Irving wrote:

> 'The exercises were undoubtedly successful and many of the escapists claim to have learned from them. In addition, considerable enjoyment was derived from those taking part. The success of the exercise was due to the whole-hearted co-operation very willingly extended to us by the Chief Constable of the Surrey Constabulary Area; in particular we are most grateful to the Superintendent of E division for his unstinted help in preliminary advice and subsequent organisation. We are also most grateful for the enthusiastic co-operation of the Police, No.2777 Squadron RAF Regiment and other services who took part.'

S/L Mike Gray checking the Mustang camera at Odiham, 1944.

Another report focuses on the efforts of S/L Gray and F/O Haselden of No.II (AC) Squadron to evade capture. In the best wild west and Keystone Cops police tradition this escape was a riot from start to finish. The fantasy could only have been enhanced if the escapees had commandeered a funeral cortège. Gray and Haselden were dropped in a side road just north of the main Guildford-London road. They got a lift from a civilian car to Esher, having decided to wait until lunch time and pinch a car from the car park at the Bear Hotel. This they were unable to do as all Service cars were either attended or immobilised. They then managed to get the 'cockpit drill' of a double-deck bus from the bus terminus outside the *Windsor Arms*. Two things prevented them from taking a bus: the chance of driving a large bus with East Acton on the front in the Dorking direction was small and the bus always filled up with people as soon as it came in. They gave up the bus idea and walked along to the fire station where they tried to start a NFS van without success. They began to walk out of the fire station when they saw a lovely big ambulance. They jumped in and it started first time so both escapees drove out on to the main road much to the surprise of a man who was repairing the back of the ambulance at the time. They reached Leatherhead without trouble and by ringing the bell managed to keep a fair speed. However, between Leatherhead and Dorking they were picked up by traffic policemen and two MPs on motor cycles. For the next four miles a first class chase ensued, including an attempt by the police to set up a road block. Fortunately for the evaders they left enough room for them to manoeuvre around it by driving up onto the pavement. At this point the ambulance's radiator was boiling madly so the two decided to get off the road. They turned up a lane which, as luck would have it, took them into the courtyard of a large house which had been taken over by the Army. They jumped out of the ambulance, Haselden pausing to throw a large lamp at the police who were hard on their heels. This allowed Gray to get through a window and into the house. Haselden was caught by an enormous MP weighing at least eighteen stone. S/L Gray ran through the house and saw a room marked 'Ante Room' and went in. He was caught by the speed cop and an Army major but got away for a few minutes by kicking the Major on the shin. Finally they were taken to the courtyard and heavily guarded by police and MPs. For Gray it was the end — he was taken to Police HQ and duly released. Jack Haselden, however, decided that though captured he was not yet a prisoner. While he was taken to MP Headquarters in a car, with four MPs on motorcycles as escort, he managed to jump out of the car when it stopped at a traffic light. Dashing up a street and into an alley and then through a door, he found himself in a butcher's shop, where he tried to persuade a rather slow-witted butcher to hide him. Unfortunately the Police arrived before this could be done. Jack made another dash and once again got through the Police, only to be captured in a nearby garden. Knowing now what kind of escapist Haselden was the Police made sure he could not move a finger until he was safely locked up. But Gray and Haselden were not amongst the most sensational escapists during 'Freedom'. One couple, who shall be nameless, made an admirable escape from an airfield in a captured Tiger Moth. Both were happily unaware that the pinching of an aircraft was against the exercise rules.

In May PR trips increased to sixty including some Noballs and a dozen Tac/Rs. One of the more interesting targets mentioned in the Ops.

Record Book for May was a German Wurzburg radar.

'23.5.44. 1441-1535 hours F/L Maitland-F/O Buckie. Pinpoints of Wurzburg by both Two wireless masts about 60 ft. joined by wire at 989639 and 991641. Intense light flak from target as aircraft approached and covered target. Intense light flak along coast from St. Valery en Caux to 2 miles W of Veules les Roses. No.II claims light post destroyed 005645 unidentified twin-engined aircraft at 5,000 ft in mid-Channel course NE-SW.

1452-1640 hours. 1 pinpint of apparatus nearest coast. Wurzburg standing apparently undamaged. Intense accurate self destroying flak from target area and beyond inland. No.2 (F/L Furneaux in FD530) was hit, reported turning inland. No.1 (F/O Burt) ordered him to turn seawards. No.2 baled out 5 miles SW of Etretat. Now reported safe.

24.5544. 1112-1209 F/L Weighil-F/L Varley. RDF Le Treport. Wurzburg appeared damaged. Intense inaccurate light flak from Bethancourt.

1110-127 F/O Percival/F/O Kay Hai Tan. Target area had been bombed. Wurzburg appeared untouched, remainder of site considerably damaged. Light Flak from Le Hamel. Intense light and medium Flak from Arromanches (. . .) No flak from target area. No enemy aircraft. Target claimed. Six trucks 40 troops by concrete mixer Mouth of La Seulles River'.

On 25th May the AOCiC 2nd TAF Air Marshal 'Maori' Coningham visited No.130 Airfield. He had a long talk with all the Squadron members about the effort the Squadron was putting in. On 28 May three pairs of Mustangs carried out photo recces. One pair, F/L Harris in FD500 and F/O Hope in FD565 took off from Gatwick at 1652 hours to take photographs of the German radar station at Fruges/Predefin. First they encountered intense light flak from Etaples. Then they saw tracer from Royon, followed by flak from Azincourt. The pilots made two passes while the cameras photographed the damage. Flak came up from the target area and along the route on the return journey to the coast. Over Neufchatel Harris' aircraft was hit. The cockpit filled with thick smoke and Harris warned F/O Hope that FD500 had been hit. Trying to gain altitude Harris' aircraft was hit again and Harris knew that his aircraft would never return home. He reached for the lever and released the hood. However, the canopy remained where it was and Harris was trapped. Desperately he used all his strength to free himself from the aircraft, suddenly, the canopy gave way and fresh air filled the cockpit. Harris released his straps, jumped overboard and immediately pulled the ripcord. The tail of the Mustang flashed by, there was a tremendous jerk and Ivor Harris was gently floating in the air. he noticed that he was no more than 100 to 150 feet from the ground. Hope, circling around to look for his leader had seen him bailing out of the aircraft but no further observations were possible; he could do little else but return to England and report what happened to Ivor Harris. News came much later that Harris had been killed and there was sadness about another pilot having lost his life. However, this was not the case. After he landed between the sand dunes Harris freed himself from his parachute, climbed on a dune and tried to find out where he had come down. Soon he found that he had landed at the worst possible spot, between long rows of barbed wire next to a wooden shield saying: 'Achtung, Minen'. He turned around, followed the line of dunes and walked straight into a German patrol. In 1991 he remembered:

Dundonald, March 1944. From left to right: O/C Dundonald, S/L Gray, Lt. Stevens FAA, Tonkin, Harris, Maitland, Howells, Corrigan, Reich and Burt.

'They took me to an emplacement where they bandaged my wrist which had been slightly burned. Then I was interrogated very briefly by a German officer. I told him nothing so they took me to a room with a bunk and locked me up for the night. The next morning I was handed over to two Germans who were to accompany me to Germany. We took the train from Boulogne to Calais. From there we travelled to Lille. The Germans were quite friendly but did not take their eyes from me. When we arrived in Lillie it was dark. The Germans apparently felt that I could make an attempt to escape. They made me walk in the middle of the road while they followed on my left and right. After half an hour we arrived at the local prison which looked about 500 years old. They locked me up with only one thin blanket. There I found out that in a cell next to me was a S/L Russell, Commanding

Officer of the Typhoon squadron which had attacked the radar station I had photographed later that day.'

The next day both Harris and the Squadron Leader were escorted back to the railway station to travel to Brussels where Harris was interrogated for the first time. The interrogator was very friendly and joked about Harris growing a beard. Five minutes later Harris was escorted back to his cell. In the corridor were other POWs; Americans, British and Canadians, all aircrew.

While Harris was a prisoner, the Squadron prepared itself for things to come. By the end of May all operational flying came to a standstill. In order to build up aircraft serviceability all Mustangs were kept on the ground and all personnel were kept within the barbed wire of their station.

On 6 June No.II (AC) Squadron went slightly mad. Amazingly only one short line in the Operations Record Book records it: 'D-Day' . . . Yet it was the beginning of over 400 sorties in one month. With twenty effective pilots out of a possible twenty-five and ten aircraft they flew thirty-six sorties during D-Day, mostly spotting for naval bombardment. Bob Weighill and F/O Shute were airborne at 0500 hours and were over the beaches when the first soldiers reached the sand. In Volume IIII of *Royal Air Force 1939-1945* Hillary St G. Saunders described what happened.

> 'As dawn broke and the summer sun began to shine uncertainly upon the coast of Normandy, F/L R.H.G. Weighill of No.II Squadron, 35 Wing, flying a Mustang to spot the fall of shot of HMS *Glasgow*, looked down upon a scene so often imagined, so earnestly longed for by millions — a scene which at that golden moment became an accomplished fact.
>
> 'The sea was littered with ships of all descriptions'', he reported afterwards, ''ploughing doggedly towards the enemy's coast, looking very grim and very determined. The bombardment was terrific and one could actually see the shells in the form of red and white lights as they left the ships and flew towards the shore . . I stayed at 1,000 feet and watched five of the naval vessels, which were about a mile from the beach, turn broadside on, proceeding to belch flame and destruction. It was a most terrifying sight, for as they fired what I now know to be rockets, a sheet of flame fifty yards long completely enveloped the ship. By this time, the first boat was almost ashore, and, as I watched it, the front came down and the men inside jumped into the water and ran towards the beach. It was a wonderful moment when I reported that the first men had actually landed.'

Bob Weighill may well have been the first eyewitness of the landings. By 1015 hours the invasion waded ashore and started the battle to build a bridgehead large enough to receive reinforcements and materials. At about that time, an ex-member of the Squadron also flew over the area. It was Air Commodore Andrew Geddes, now DSASO of 2nd TAF. He had taken his own highly polished Mustang, its cameras now fitted with 8-inch lenses, and raced along the British/Canadian beaches, to bring the first photographs of the landings to Headquarters. It was rather unusual for an Air Commodore to fly this sortie, but, as Geddes remembered many years later, 'even a platoon with machine guns would not have been able to keep me from doing this'. Geddes wanted to be there and had decided that

Gatwick, April 1944.
Left to right: Back row: F/O Cormack, F/L Davies (NZ), F/O Hope, F/L Edmunds MC, F/L Weighill, F/O Brodrick, F/L Furneaux, F/O Varley and F/L Gent.
Seated: F/O Tasker, F/L Reahil, S/L Gray, F/L Maitand, F/L Corrigan (RCAF), F/O Percival.
Front: Capt. Wilson (ALO), F/O Shute, F/O Reich.

if he was shot down over enemy territory he would kill himself. He photographed the area from 800-1,000 feet, and thus provided the Commander-in-Chief with a valuable panorama of the battlegrounds. Today these photographs have found a prominent place in the flying offices of No.II (AC) Squadron at RAF Marham, according to Geddes 'the best place for these photographs to be on display'. What did Geddes see while flying over the beaches? The village of Le Hamel was shrouded in smoke and dust from which emerged the purposeful figures of troops. At some places they were already three miles inland; at others half that distance. Vessels were ferrying troops and equipment to the beaches. Here and there fires had broken out, and damaged vessels drifted about the coastline. At some places small German convoys could be seen, some of them fleeing in panic others heading for the coast. However, as Geddes approached the Cherbourg peninsula, he saw a place where the shore seemed to be congested with vehicles, craft and men with no sign of penetration beyond the sea wall. Fires could be seen within 500 yards of the beach. It was Omaha beach where the 116th American Infantry of the 1st Division were fighting a desperate battle to reach dry land and stay there. Back again over the heads of the invaders he flew, taking note of everything: a direct hit on a house near the harbour mouth of Port en Bessin; spouts of water where shells were falling near some of the ships; one or two fires a short distance inland; a damaged landing craft, half awash, but the most majestic sight was HMS *Warspite* bombarding at anchor with her attendant small craft laying a smoke screen round her. What impressed him most of all were the figures of men, the morning light upon their bayonets, moving slowly, remorselessly, forward. The air was very bumpy, and since the cloud base was below 2,000 feet, the sky was congested with aircraft, because the top cover, the low cover and the naval spotting aircraft were all working at the same approximate height. From time to time pilots could be heard on the VHF telephone, say 'Going down to investigate'. But above all Andrew Geddes felt a great sense of satisfaction: 'They kicked us out of the Continent at Dunkirk and gave us hell for a long time. We had been on our own at first, fighting with our backs against the wall. And now we came back to cash the bill and show them that they would never get away with their vile system and their contempt for people's God-given rights. It was the happiest day in my life and I was grateful to be able to play a minor part in this proud day.'

During the evening of D-Day there were some Tac/R sorties. Although the Squadron was stationed at Gatwick the procedure for aircraft on D-Day sorties was to land at Lee-on-Solent after their first sortie, refuel, and then do another sortie before returning to Gatwick. The landings in Normandy put an end to PR for some time. All the post D-Day sorties for June were offensive Tac/Rs of road and rail communications.

1944. John Young, Bob Weighill, Jack Varley, Percy Percival and Jimmy Chun sitting on the wing of a Squadron Mustang chatting with Ron West.

While the Allies pushed the Germans away from the coast and the first French soil was liberated, Ivor Harris wondered what would happen to him. After a couple of days he was marched to the main railway station of Brussels. He and the twenty-odd other prisoners did not know where they were going until, after many hours, they saw that they had entered the railway station of Cologne. There they experienced for the first time the effect of the Allied bomber offensive. Immediately after the air-raid sirens sounded the prisoners were ushered into the cellars of the station and waited for things to come. They shared the cellars with hundreds of German civilians who were not very pleased to see the enemy airmen sheltering with them. After a few tense hours the POWs were taken back to the train. Late that night they arrived at their temporary camp, the Luftwaffe Interrogation Camp at Oberursel near Frankfurt.

> 'I was locked up in the Cooler in a small cell with a bunk, a blanket and a jar of water. There was no window, so no light from outside. The next morning a German took me away for a threatening and brusque interrogation in a nearby building. The interrogator insisted that name, rank and number would not be enough and that I needed to say quite a bit more to improve my present situation. He said that the

Gestapo would be quite interested in me as I was a reconnaissance pilot. When I refused to say anything I was put back into my cell. They left me alone for three or four days until the next interrogation took place. The tone of voice as well as the treatment remained very hostile and threatening. Then he made some reference to the invasion and it was not until then that I realised the invasion had taken place. In fact, I had lost all sense of time since I had been taken prisoner. The next German interrogator chose an entirely different approach. He introduced himself as Herr Scharff. He was very charming and apologetic about the treatment I had received. He stressed he would never behave like his predecessor. And quite frankly I had to force myself to understand that this was only done to break my resistance. He did not make any attempt to extract information from me. It seemed as if he was genuinely worried about my health and well-being as a POW. The only reference he made to the invasion was that "the German High Command of course knew that Normandy was merely a diversion and that the real thing would be at the Pas de Calais, would I not agree?" '

'The tenth day of my stay in Oberursel I was visited by a chap who spoke English with a strong German accent. He introduced himself as a representative of the German Red Cross and suggested I would give him my home address to enable him to inform my relatives. Quite frankly I told him to bugger off. The German left with an angry face. Herr Scharff too seemed to be fed up with me for after three weeks I was moved to a military hospital and then to Wetzler, from where they took me to Stalag Luft III Sagan.'

So began a year's period of captivity for Ivor Harris. When he arrived at Sagan the inmates were still recovering from the shock of the murder of the prisoners who had been part of the 'Great Escape'. Harris was taken to Hut 101, where one of the prisoners was the actor Rupert Davies. He played volleyball, softball and rugby. He listened to the secret receiver and was able to follow the progress of the war.

On 20 June the first Squadron aircraft landed in France. It was the third time No.II (AC) Squadron arrived since Becke had touched down near Amiens in 1914 and Geddes had taken the Squadron to Abbeville in 1939. F/Os Burt and Kemp landed at an advance strip, probably B2 or B3, due to bad weather. After that one in three sorties landed in France for various reasons before returning to Gatwick. By now the Squadron flew the new Mustang Mark II which was faster than the ones they had previously.

The next step towards the Continent was made on 27 June when No.35 (Recce) Wing and No.130 Airfield moved to Odiham. The casualty rate for June had been high. On the fifteenth the Squadron lost F/O Reich, who became a prisoner of war. He was seen by Ivor Harris one day at Oberursel when Harris stood in front of the window of Hanns Scharff's office during another interrogation.

Two days later, on 17 June, F/O Tasker was killed. On the twenty-seventh F/O Wilson died and two days later the Chinese pilot, F/L Kay Hai Tan went down. It had been a very costly month for the Squadron.

The programme for July was much the same as June, Tac/Rs of roads and railways, but only 300 sorties were flown. Apart from some engagements with the Luftwaffe the Squadron got involved in occasional brushes with USAAF P-47 Thunderbolts, overzealous in protecting their bombers from anything that came close. The Yanks still had a lot to learn.

Then, on 29 July came the moment the Squadron had been waiting for: back to France, this time as part of No.35 Wing and accompanied by No.0002 Servicing Echelon. The Squadron ground crew, the Servicing Echelon, 35 Wing HQ and some spare Squadron pilots were flown in to B10, Plumetot, and joined up with the Sea Party who were already there. Aircraft and pilots, twenty in all, arrived at 1740 hours and two sections were available for action shortly after arrival. Plumetot was only eight miles behind the front and gun fire could be heard clearly. Life at Plumetot was not without risk, especially after a determined group of German soldiers broke through the Allied lines. They established themselves in a tower fairly close to the strip and proceeded to carry out sniping operations. One of their shots even went through S/L Gray's tent. As a result of this tents became rather unpopular and the pilots were soon digging dug-outs, a most unusual sight. Operational flying commenced the day after the Squadron arrived. On the thirtieth eight Tac/Rs were flown, the next day fourteen.

In August the Squadron broke all records and carried out 624 sorties for the loss of one pilot missing, and one missing believed killed. They were F/O Shute on 10 August and F/L Haselden on the twelth. Haselden's No.2 had later reported how Jack's aircraft had been hit in the wing, and exploded before it crashed. The death of Jack Haselden was especially sad for S/L Mike Gray, who lost his closest friend and a valued section leader. Haselden had recently been awarded the DFC. His father was W.K. Haselden, who for years had been the dramatic cartoonist for *Punch* magazine.

Early in August, in an attempt to soften up Caen, the strategic bomber force was called in and from their airstrip the Squadron had a grandstand view of the raid. They felt the ground vibrating as Caen was reduced to rubble. At the beginning of August the Squadron had been the only 35 (Recce) Wing Squadron in France. On the tenth No.268 Squadron arrived just in time to move with No.II to a new strip, B4 at Beny-sur-Mer. On 16 August No.4 Squadron arrived, re-uniting the Wing. Most of the sorties were Tac/Rs but photography crept back in and there were a few Arty/R trips, just like the Squadron had done in its earliest days. There was a slight reduction of flying effort in September, but to make up for it the Wing had four moves. First to B27 Boisney on 3 September where the ground party had to contend with wind and rain while pitching the tents. On the sixth the Squadron moved to B31 Fresnoy Folny. During the moves S/L Gray left the Squadron and returned to England. His successor was S/L Maitland who assumed command on 7 September. It was his second tour with the Squadron, having previously been with 'Shiny Two' from April 1943 till June 1944. On the eleventh the 35 Wing moved to B43 Fort Rouge/ Saint Omer where the civil population turned out in strength on their Sunday walk, to watch the squadrons landing. Finally on the twenty-seventh of September the Squadron arrived at St Denis/Westrem in Belgium. It was a former Luftwaffe airfield and everyone was pleased to say goodbye to their tents for a while and find quarters in some nearby buildings which had to be checked for booby-traps first, however. On the day of the Squadron's arrival at Saint Denis/ Westrem two Mustang pilots ran into trouble during two separate sorties. F/O Bremner was shot down by flak shortly after crossing enemy lines. Luckily he managed to force land his aircraft in friendly territory and was safely returned to base. A second pair took off at 0645 hours. F/L Gerald Percival led the formation with F/L West as his No.2. Their flight was to be a routine tactical reconnaissance of the area Utrecht-Arnhem-Nijmegen-Hertogenbosch. The Allied armies had pushed the Germans as far north as the River Waal. Two days earlier the British troops at Arnhem had failed to carry out their task of securing the Rhine bridge. It had indeed been 'A Bridge Too Far'. To punish the Dutch for the railway strikes ordered by the Dutch government in London, Reichskommissar Arthur Seyss-Inquart gave orders to stop food deliveries from the east of the Netherlands to the densely populated west of the country. Percival and West knew nothing of the catastrophe which awaited the Dutch in the months to come. Their concern was a slow-moving train travelling from Culembourg to Geldermalsen on the German occupied island of the Betuwe between the Lek and Waal Rivers. It had to be a German train. Ordering

Gerald Percival was shot down over Holland while attacking a German train. He successfully force landed and stayed out of the hands of the Germans for three weeks, helped by Dutch patriots. After having been in occupied Holland from 25 September until 15 October 1944 he was handed over to an Allied armoured car and returned to his own troops.

West to stay up, Percival went down to take a closer look at the train, the length of which was much greater than usual, while the cargo was amazing. Approximately sixty flat trucks were loaded with tanks and armoured vehicles. The train had engines at the front and rear, and was well-protected by anti-aircraft guns, to the front, centre and rear. Percival radioed HQ, giving a description and told West that he was going down to attack it. He realised the train had to be stopped before it reached the shelter of a railway station and the cover of heavy German anti-aircraft guns. He circled around and made a broadside attack, at treetop height, aiming for the leading engines. After seeing many of his bullets strike home he saw a satisfying release of high pressure steam rise from the first engine. However, the intense fire from the train caught his plane and Percival knew his Mustang was mortally wounded. Part of the rudder and about two feet of a wing tip had been blown off, the aircraft had also been hit in the radiator, fuselage and engine. At a height of 200 feet Percival had

Ann van Koeverden risked her life by escorting Percy Percival through occupied territory to the Waal River. Together they crossed the river and reached the Allied lines.

little alternative but to fly straight ahead and land immediately. The aircraft came to a halt not far from the little village of Asch. Gerald Percival's sortie came to an end in a meadow along the Heunisdike near the farm of the Van Koeverden family. He had miraculously escaped any personal injury, but was a bit shaken. He destroyed the aircraft instruments before running from his Mustang as fast as he could. Percival was well aware that he could expect little mercy from the Germans, being only a little over a mile from the train he had just attacked. Percival ran in a southerly direction until, exhausted and seeing a shed on stilts, he crawled gratefully underneath. Unfortunately the shed was a hen house. The hens objected noisily to Percivial's presence, attracting the attention of a woman who emerged from the nearby farmhouse. She shouted something to Percival. When he tried to make her understand that he was an RAF officer she got very excited and indicated that Percival should leave immediately by waving her arms away from the house. Percival left, but without regrets — during his very brief rest under the stilted hut the hens had shared their fleas with him. He walked for some time, keeping himself well hidden by the hedges surrounding the small fields. Like any downed airman, Percival had his fair share of luck during the first part of what was to become a successful evasion. On hearing heavy vehicles on a nearby road Percival dived into a deep ditch to hide. Fortunately it was full of tall rushes, growing thickly in dark water. He waded in and crouched as low as possible, becoming almost totally submerged. While hiding he could hear the voices of German soldiers who seemed to be searching the area. They passed without seeing Percival and after some time he crawled out, very wet and very cold. Following the Germans from a safe distance Percival continued walking. After what seemed like hours he suddenly stood in front of a farmer who immediately understood Percival's predicament. Percival had made contact with farmer van Koeverden. The farmer pointed at a large hay barn across the field. Climbing into the hay, inside the barn Percival was able to take off his clothes and bury himself in the well stacked hay warm and comfortable. Tired as he was, the pilot immediately fell asleep, not to wake up until the farmer came and beckoned him down. After scrambling back into his damp clothes Percival followed the man into the farmhouse where he was given some bread, a piece of cheese and a large bowl of milk. After this welcome meal Percival was taken back into the barn, the farmer indicated by pointing at his watch that the pilot was to stay there till midnight. A little after midnight the farmer returned and took Percival into his house. In the large kitchen was a man in a black uniform, a Dutch policeman. At first Percival thought that the farmer had given him away but it soon turned out that the policeman had come to help. He spoke a little English and explained that he had two bicycles with him. Percival was told to follow him but keep a distance of 20-30 yards behind the policeman. If they should meet any vehicles the pilot was to jump off his bike and hide until all was safe again. They rode for some time and eventually arrived at a very large house. They entered the house through the back door into the kitchen. It was clear that the owner was a wealthy man. Though Percival did not know it at the time, the name of this gentleman was Anthony Beijnen. He was a somewhat eccentric entrepreneur and a great sportsman in his younger days. During the Paris Olympics of 1924 he had won a gold medal as one of the Dutch rowing team. Married to a Yugoslav opera singer he lived a quiet and very prosperous life in the village of Beusichem on the southern bank of the River Lek. Anthony Beijnen was a member of the local Resistance group. His large house 'De Engelenburg' (The Angels' Castle) had been partially commandeered by the Germans as Percival was to find out to his horror. Little did he know that under the circumstances it was the safest place to be. Beuischem was crawling with Gemans. 'De Engelenburg' had a German Colonel and his staff as unwelcome tenants, in a house only five hundred yards away, the Commander in Chief of the German Forces, Colonel-General Blaskowitz, had his Headquarters. Across the Molenweg road at 'Johanna's Hof' (Joanna's Court) a German telephone exchange had been billeted. It was not Percival's idea of a safe hiding place, but for the time being he had to accept it. The housewife who greeted Percival and the policeman gave the pilot a glass of hot milk and had him taken upstairs to the attic, which was entered through a door at the rear end of a cupboard. In the attic he found a mattress and some blankets. He stayed at the house for 4-5 days. His hosts were extremely kind but one evening during his stay he had a terrible fright. Several German vehicles swung up the drive, and peering through a crack in the tiles Percival saw a number of German officers being welcomed by Beijnen. After some hours the Germans left again with great hilarity; they were obviously quite drunk. Afterwards the pilot discovered that these social evenings were a cover used by Beijnen to prevent the Germans becoming suspicious about his real activities. After a few days Percival was moved from the house and taken to a farmhouse on the bank of the River Lek. In this house, called 'De Oven' as it stood at a place where a brick mill had once been, lived a widow, Mrs Wammes, with her two young daughters Griet and Riek and her two sons Hans and Godert. The farm consisted of three sections. The cow-byre was at one end, then there was the central part where the family kept food and wood and at the other end were the living quarters of the family.

During the first evening that Percival was there the faggots which were piled up at one end of the room were removed. A concealed trapdoor in the floor was opened and out climbed a well dressed man. His name was Terlouw and he was a Veterinary Surgeon. Being a prominent local citizen he had been put on a Geman black list and was likely to be executed if the local Resistance did anything against the Germans. Warned by someone who knew of his fate Terlouw was now in hiding. Percival and Terlouw were to become partners in hiding — they played endless games of cards and if the coast was clear they would walk along the river. In spite of the danger and the necessity for absolute secrecy, photographs were taken of the family and their two guests. Godert would sit between Percival and Terlouw in the living room. The two Wammes brothers had themselves photographed with the British pilot between them on a bench in front of the house and the entire family with 'Underdivers' and the horse had themselves photographed on top of the dike with their backs to the river.

Percival spent two weeks with the Wammes family. He helped them on the farm and was able to observe the comings and goings of German soldiers, who came to the farm twice while he was hiding. Percival became anxious to move on as the number of German troops in the area was increasing. He was concerned about the danger he represented to the family. The Germans organised razzias all over the country in an effort to round up every available man for work on the German defences. One afternoon in October just after Percival had heard that the Allies were advancing all over Brabant a young girl on a bicycle arrived at 'De Oven'. She had come to take the Englishman through the German lines. Her name was Ann van Koeverden, the daughter of the farmer and a courier for the Dutch Resistance. Her husband had been a Reserve officer in the Dutch Army in 1940. Rather than surrender to the Germans he had withdrawn with a Dutch unit into Belgium and France. Via Dunkirk and Abbeville he had reached Brest and crossed to England to continue the battle against the Germans. Since her husband's departure Ann had rarely heard from him. While he fought from London she risked her life at home; her task was to ensure Percival's safe return to his comrades. A second bicycle was found for Percival and off they went. Percival's bike had long since lost its tyres, but was ingeniously equipped with rope wrapped and tied onto the bare rims. This made cycling hard work and most uncomfortable. The girl took Percival back to her parents' house where he was introduced to her mother. She was a remarkably brave lady, hiding at one time three airmen, as wall as coping with two German officers who had been billeted with her. After a short rest Percival and his guide continued the bumpy journey to Tiel in the hope of finding a boatman to take the pilot across the River Waal into liberated territory. Near the end of the journey disaster almost struck. On turning into one of the main streets of Tiel they ran into a German checkpoint. Ann's quick thinking saved a dangerous situation. They immediately left their bicycles against a shop wall, and taking Percival's arm led him across the road chatting away in Dutch, which of course Percival did not understand, in front of the Germans. They they joined people who were going into a church where a wedding was in progress. The girl's quick reaction saved Percival from imprisonment, and probably her own life. After the ceremony they left the church and walked back through the side streets to a baker's shop. The building they entered adjoined an enemy barracks and they were able to watch the Germans from an upstairs window. At dusk just before curfew they were led down to the riverside to a fisherman's hut. Percival and Ann remained inside the hut for two days before someone was found who had a licence to fish at night and who was willing to take the risk of taking the pilot across the river. The fisherman led them to his boat and made them lie down in the bottom covered with nets and fishing gear. Then the man gently rowed to the middle of the stream and began to fish, at the same time making sure that he was gradually difting towards the other bank. When he was as close as he felt was safe Percival and his guide climbed over the side and dropped silently into the water. They swam to the bank where they were met and taken to a house about five miles south from the river. They were welcomed with blankets and warm food. Here Percival said goodbye to Ann. Still being in territory where both German and Allied scouts roamed he was picked up by a British armoured car. It had dashed some ten miles through this part of the country to rescue five airborne troops who had escaped from Arnhem. Percival's fateful sortie over Holland had been his eighty-fourth operational flight — on 13 October he visited his Squadron on the way home to England.

While Percival was spending an unwilling holiday in occupied Holland the Squadron returned to coastal Tac/R with an occasional line overlap photo trip to Holland at the end of the month, and one Arty/R trip. The following month brought a renewed flying effort, over 400 sorties being flown, eight percent of them being Tac/R and then yet another move. This time the Squadron went to B70 Antwerp/Deurne. The only casualty that month was F/L Ridley-Martin

DFC who was shot down by Flak near Gorinchem in Holland on 11 October. He made one of the fastest evasions in the history of the Squadron: Ridley-Martin was found by the Resistance and hidden before there were any Germans in sight. The leader of the LO-group, a Resistance organisation that mainly dealt with people who had a reason to hide, kept the pilot in a safe house. There he stayed with a small group of Allied aircrew: Lt. Col. Frebe, Major Cannon and 1st Lt. Otto Smek of the USAAF. Without much problem Ridley-Martin stayed in the small village of Wernhout until it was liberated on 27 October. He returned to the Squadron one day later. The number of sorties flown was down to 300 in November, with about the same proportion of Tac/R, but Arty/R jumped to eighteen sorties. Sorties, however, were not the main item of interest that month. On 1 November, RM805 arrived, the very first of the Vickers Armstrong Spitfire XIV aircraft. These Spits were powered with a Rolls-Royce Griffon 65 engine, armed with two 20mm cannons and two ·50 machine guns. In addition they were fitted with a F24 camera in the rear fuselage. They were destined to remain part of the Squadron's equipment for a little over six years, second only in length to the eleven years of the 'Brisfits' in 1920. On 7 November F/L Morai lost his life while flying a sortie. Four days later F/L Swanson was killed when his Mustang was shot down and crashed near the hamlet of Rijkerswoerd not far from Elst between Rhine and Waal.

Back in Sagan Ivor Harris, the unfortunate pilot who had landed in the middle of the Atlantic Wall prior to D-Day, got involved in his first attempt to escape. One day he and three other PoWs were taken to the stage of the Camp Theatre. To his utter amazement his companion pulled on the back of a seat and revealed the entrance of a hatch to a tunnel. They climbed down and entered a small room with an air pump, from where they crawled into another tunnel. It was one of the most sophisticated constructions Harris had ever seen in his life. Lamps lit the tunnel which ran a long way in the direction of the fence. Unfortunately the tunnel was never finished.

By 18 November nine Spitfires had arrived, when Squadron Leader Maitland and Flight Lieutenant R.G. West made their first operational sortie with them, a Tac/R in the Rotterdam area. Five days later the Squadron left Belgium and moved to a new country when the first aircraft landed at B77 Gilze-Rijen in Noord Brabant. The move did not halt the flow of Spitfires. There were fourteen on strength by 27 November and then the faithful Mustangs started to go. Ten left on 29 November, but the remainder saw the year out. On 6 December F/O Hynes was killed near Bergen op Soom in Holland. On the twenty-second F/O Buckie died when his Mustang crashed in the garden of a house at Noorderweg 35 at Oosterbeek. It was the same area where two months earlier British airborne troops had fought so desperately to seize the Arnhem bridge.

With the beginning of the last year of the war the future looked bright for the Allies. The aircraft of Air Marshal Coningham's 2nd Tactical Air Force constantly covered the advance of the Expeditionary Forces while the Germans had to use all their remaining aircraft to defend the Reich against the fleets of bombers hammering their cities to rubble. Yet the Germans planned a last offensive to try to change the odds. At first light on 1 January 1945 over 800 German aircraft took off from all over Germany. Their brief was to attack 2TAF's airfields and destroy as many aircraft as possible. On 15 December 1944 Major General Dietrich Peltz, the mastermind behind the plan, called Operation Bodenplatte, had assembled his commanders in a small inn near Bonn to explain his plans. He intended to attack sixteen Allied airfields in Belgium and Holland. With ten Jagdgeschwader at his disposal he reckoned he would be able to wipe out 2nd TAF and thus allow the German ground troops to reach Antwerp and cut off the British and Canadian troops north of the German Army's planned thrust, ready to cross the Rhine. Three code words would be vital for the success of Bodenplatte. 'Varus' followed by a number would inform the Luftwaffe commanders that the operation was to go ahead on the date mentioned by the number. This signal was to be confirmed by the code 'Teutonicus', which would allow the commanders to assemble their pilots and brief them. Then a last code, 'Hermann', would give the exact time of the attack. As the

No.II (AC)Squadron losses in Central Netherlands.
1) F/L Gerald Percival 27 Sept 44 Evaded.
2) F/L Swanson 10 Nov 44 Killed.
3) F/O Buckie 22 Dec 44 Killed.
4) S/L Colin Maitland 18 Mar 45 Killed.
5) F/O Blundell-Hill 01 Apr 45 Killed.

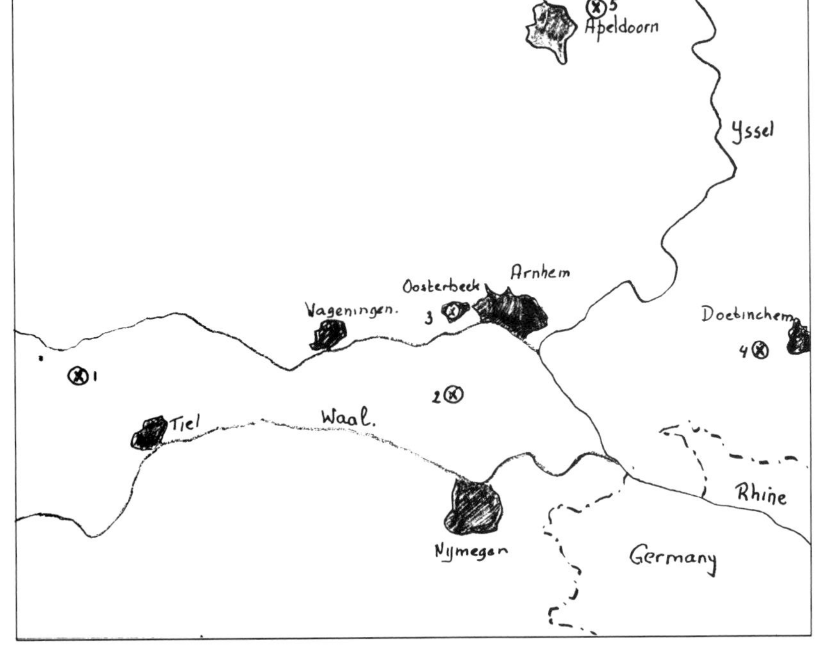

Luftwaffe had lost over 500 pilots in December Peltz would have to attack with less men than planned. Nevertheless on the afternoon of 31 December 'Varus 1.1.45' was transmitted and this was soon followed by 'Teutonicus'. At 0920 hours 'Hermann' was transmitted and all Luftwaffe personnel involved prepared the aircraft. It was hoped that the Allies would be too busy celebrating the New Year to expect a German assault of this magnitude. Peltz was right. In his Report on 2nd TAF AM Coningham would write:

> 'During the winter period I was forced by the weather and the difficulty of transporting the heavy tonnages of all-weather material, to concentrate the 2nd TAF on a small number of airfields, from which they could operate continuously. This led to congestion on most of the airfields available. The enemy, appreciating his increasing danger from the air, took advantage of this and carried out a well timed, simultaneous attack on a maximum number of British and a few American airfields, by means of his fighting force which, owing to careful husbanding of his resources throughout the winter, had reached considerable proportions.'

The Luftwaffe units involved in Bodenplatte were considerable indeed. They consisted of 14 Geschwader: Jagdgeschwader 1(Oesau), 2(Richthofen), 3(Udet), 4, 6, 11, 26(Schlageter), 27, 53, 54, and 77, Schlachtgeschwader 4, Kampfgeschwader 51 and a special Staffel of JG104. The aircraft used for this surprise attack were mainly Fw190A-8s and D-9s, 109G-10s and K-14s and the new Me262s. Shortly before 0830 hours this armada took off from thirty-five airfields between Stuttgart in the south and Delmenhorst in the north. Jagdgeschwader 27, after taking off from Hesepe, Achmer, Hopsten and Rheine was to come from the north and attack Gilze-Rijen where No.II Squadron was now based. They were to be supported by elements of Jagdgeschwader 3 who, after taking off from Gutersloh, Paderborn and Lippspringe, were to attack Gilze-Rijen from the east. JG27 was also to carry out attacks against Brussels-Melsbroek. At Gilze-Rijen personnel of three RAF squadrons, Nos.II, 4 and 268 were recovering from a very pleasant party. Their aircraft, Mustangs IA and II, and Spitfires IX and XIV were dispersed all over the airfield, mostly in hardstands once built by the Germans themselves. At 0829 hours two Spitfires XIV of No.II Squadron flown by F/L J.M. Young (RM805) and F/L E.J. Packwood (RM708) took off for a Tac/R in the triangle formed by the towns of Leeuwen, Hilversum and Arnhem. Little were Young and Packwood to know that they were about to become the first to run into Peltz's air fleet. At 0905 hours they were flying at 5,000 feet, west of Amersfoort. Packwood suddenly spotted two Ju88s, escorted by more than thirty Bf109s and FW190s. They were flying west. Young and Packwood immediately turned up-sun of the enemy formation and then dived down to attack the rear section by surprise. Packwood attacked a Me109 from dead astern and slightly above. With the German pilot making no attempt to evade Packwood closed to 150 yards and emptied a five-second burst of cannon and machine gun fire into the 109. First the 109's right wing broke off, then the aircraft turned on its back and crashed in a mushroom of flames. At the same time John Young warned base by radio to tell them that something looking like a small bomber force with fighter escort was entering Allied air space. At approximately 0910 hours the first German fighters swept down over Gilze-Rijen. The attack took about forty minutes and involved Bf109s, Fw190s and Me262s. The AA guns of the RAF Regiment responded very quickly and the eighteen guns of 2736 and 2845 Squadrons fired over 800 rounds at the intruders. When the attack was over the RAF Regiments claimed to have destroyed three German aircraft with five damaged. When a search went out to investigate the area they found two Bf109s on the south and south-west sides of Gilze-Rijen, as well as the remains of a Me262. No.4 Squadron's Form 540 recorded seeing a Bf109 hit in the cockpit while roaring over the airfield and then belching smoke as it flew away. One German pilot bailed out and was locked up in the guardroom. The RAF Regiment suffered three wounded and some of the lorries in the MT park were damaged. Anti-personnel bombs landed dangerously close to the control tower and seven men of the No.123 Wing holding party, still at the airfield after the mainparty had left for Chièvres, were wounded. One of the Wing's Typhoons was damaged and an Anson of No.82 Group Communication Squadron had been peppered by Ack-Ack shell fragments. However, when the attackers had disappeared investigations showed that relatively little damage had been caused. Unfortunately No.II Squadron lost one pilot that afternoon. He was F/L P.J. Garland in Spitfire XIV RM803 who with two other pilots had been on a Tac/R. On their return at about 1500 hours, Garland bounced badly on landing, stalled, crashed, the aircraft landing on its back and Garland was killed in the ensuing fire. His death was particularly sad as this meant that all four sons of Patrick and Winifred Garland had died flying against the Germans. Their eldest son, Donald Edward; had been awarded the Victoria Cross. The final result of Operation Bodenplatte was twofold. The RAF had lost about 200 aircraft which could be replaced very easily while the Luftwaffe lost somewhere near 300 aircraft and, what was worse, 214 pilots.

In *The Battle of the Airfields* author Norman Frank says:

While the Squadron was based at Deurne airfield near Antwerp HM King George VI accompained by Field Marshal Montgomery, AM 'Maori' Coningham and G/C Anderson visited the men of 'Shiny Two'. F/L Trevor Mitchell introduced some of the pilots to His Majesty.

> 'Operation Bodenplatte was planned as a lightning blow to smash the British and American forces in north-west Europe. In fact it turned out to be the Luftwaffe's final act of self-destruction.'

General Adolf Galland, the German fighter ace who had been ordered to husband his fighters for Bodenplatte, said it best when he called it 'The final dagger thrust into the Luftwaffe's back!'

Freezing fog impaired operations in January. The last Mustang sortie was flown on 17 January 1945 when F/Ls McElwain and Woodbridge did a Tac/R of the Arnhem area. The last two aircraft left the Squadron on the eighteenth. The weather over Western Holland was horrible. It was very cold and hundreds of thousands of Dutch people who still lived in occupied Holland suffered tremendously from cold and lack of food. The weather improved in February, there were only two days when flying was impossible. 288 sorties were flown. Included in the total were forty-five Arty/R trips. Most of the sorties were flown over the Reichswald Forest. Lack of visible targets and low cloud prevented shooting however. Two days earlier the Squadron lost F/L Malcomson. On 10 February F/L McElwain shot down a Me109 in the Arnhem-Apeldoorn-Borculo triangle, while his No.II, F/O Jeffries damaged a second one.

In the middle of February 1945 the Russians advanced in the direction of Sagan. The POWs expected to be liberated at short notice. Unfortunately the Germans decided to move the prisoners to the west. Within four hours the prisoners were ready to leave on foot in sub-zero temperatures, carrying as much food as they could. Ten thousand men, escorted by Germans moved slowly to the West. They walked two hours at a time with ten-minute breaks. During this march Harris had a very close call. He ate something that had gone foul and started vomiting after a few minutes. The last thing he remembered was vomiting blood. He fainted and became unconscious. Later he was told that he lost so much blood that his heart actually stopped. A German Medical Orderly who was with the prisoners successfully revived Harris by injecting him with adrenaline straight into his heart. The Germans produced a horse-drawn cart and put Harris on it with other wounded and sick prisoners. The small group ran into trouble when an SS-unit caught up with them. The commander of the SS-men wanted the prisoners to clear some rubble, but the German escorting the POWs explained that the men were too sick to work. The SS-officer walked to the cart and said something in German whilst pointing at his machine gun. Like a flash the men jumped off the cart and did what the SS-officer wanted. After twelve hours Harris's group caught up with the main column. At a railway station the prisoners were put into cattle trucks. After a few days the group arrived at another railway station from where they were marched to Stalag 3A Luckenwalde, about thirty miles from Berlin. It was there that Harris was struck by dysentry. There was no medical attention available and the situation looked desperate. Yet, after a few days, the Germans decided to take about 800 prisoners and move them again. With their sick, the men marched to Luckenwalde railway station, determined to stay together at all costs. The end of the war was near, now everything had to be done to make sure that the prisoners survived. The train that would carry them further west never arrived. American fighter bombers attacked it and left it in a total shambles. The prisoners were delighted. Everybody was marched back to Luckenwalde.

In the meantime the squadron received orders to leave their base in Brabant. The comfort of Gilze-Rijen had been too good to last and on 9 March No.35 Wing moved to B89 Mill with its sand, Nissen huts and a landing strip that never seemed to be into wind. The Spitfires were particularly affected by the Mill crosswind and on occasions No.268 Squadron had to take over. To support the great Rhine crossing the Squadron began to attack river traffic such as barges and tugs. Tactical and artillery reconnaissance continued to be flown. The Squadron also became very expert in ground-strafing while F/O Anderson on a Tac/R from Mill destroyed a V1. On 18 March 1945 the Squadron lost its Commanding Officer Colin Maitland while he was flying a Tac/R in the Emmerich-Elten area in his Spitfire RM812. A young Dutchman, H. Arfman witnessed the last moments of the Officer Commanding No.II (AC) Squadron:

> 'Sunday 18th March 1945 was a beautiful sunny and clear day. During the morning

there had been some fog. In the afternoon at about 1500 hours the German Flak detachment of 3.7 AA guns started firing from their positions at the Stokhorstweg and the Weerdje near the railway. They were aiming at a lonely Spitfire which had come low from the east. The aircraft was soon hit. It fell away to port and the pilot abandoned the aircraft using his parachute. Unfortunately both aircraft and the pilot hit the ground at the edge of a meadow close to the Dichteren viaduct where I was standing. I ran to the site and was soon joined by a few Germans from the battery. Later the pilot, whom I now know as the Officer Commanding No.II (AC) Squadron, was buried at the Municipal Cemetery of Doetinchem.'

That evening the Squadron had a 'wake' in his memory. The party became so riotous that in their exuberance they wrecked the Mess at Mill. It was a prefabricated building which remained intact, however none of the furniture or glassware remained in one piece. The next day Group Captain Anderson ordered the Flight that was on stand-down to depart in a three-ton lorry and not to return until the pilots had been able to refurnish the Mess. Fortunately for them the Rhine had just been crossed and by joining a convoy they were able to cross over a Bailey bridge into a small town on the other side. Some say it was Emmerich, others claim it was Wesel. The town had been bombed and shelled for several days prior to the crossing and was consequently in a shambles and deserted by the civilians who had lived there. With their existing feeling towards the Germans the pilots found it no problem whatsoever to enter the house and take whatever they needed for the Mess. Triumphantly they returned to Mill with chairs, tables and plenty of glassware. Group Captain Anderson's orders had been followed to the letter. Maitland's place was taken by S/L Mitchell. The Squadron carried out Tac/Rs of the crossing of the Rhine on 24 March. On 1 April the Squadron lost F/L Blundell-Hill. Four Spitfires had taken off from Mill at noon to reconnoitre the area north of the Rhine. At about 1400 hours two aircraft were heard flying above the clouds near the town of Apeldoorn in the central part of the Netherlands. An eyewitness report says:

'Suddenly one aircraft came down through the clouds and turned into the direction of Apeldoorn railway station. The anti-aircraft guns on railway lorries near the Vossenweg opened fire immediately. The aircraft was hit and crashed in a meadow behind the house of the Boevenbrink family at the Egelweg. The pilot was killed instantly. The Germans could not care less about his body. They put an armed guard around the wreckage and refused to have the body taken away. The next morning Mr. and Mrs. Boevenbrink went to a German officer and explained that it was inhuman to leave a man's body between the wreckage like that. Shortly afterwards German soldiers removed Blundell-Hill's remains.'

In the archives of Apeldoorn a German document of 10 April 1945 addressed to the Burgomaster of Apeldoorn reads:

'Funeral of enemy casualties.
At the Heidehof Cemetery the following enemy casualties were buried:
Grave nr.14 Blundell-Hill, F/L Englishman, born 12.1.1923, killed 1.4.1945
Grave nr.15 Venne Dennis, Private. American, born 23.4.1910, killed 5.4.1945'

F/L Blundell-Hill was the last No.II Squadron pilot to be lost during the Second World War.

On 12 April some new Spitfires fitted with a 'tear drop' canopy arrived and six days later, much to everyone's relief, No.35 Wing moved to B106 Twenthe. It was another ex-Luftwaffe airfield, with brick buildings, but it meant dispersal again. However that was willingly tolerated, for this place offered many advantages. April also saw the sortie total cross the 300 mark for the first time in 1945. Eighteen Tac/R sorties were flown between 1 and 4 May. On that day at 1830 hours Germany surrendered.

One day earlier, on 3 May Ivor Harris heard a lot of banging and crashing outside the POW Camp. When he got out of his bunk and looked out of the window he saw Soviet tanks covered in infantry drive straight through the barbed wire. The Germans had apparently fled during the night. Unfortunately, little changed for the prisoners. Now they had Russian guards instead of Germans. They were not allowed to leave Stalag 3A. It looked rather grim. Fortunately the group

No.II (AC) Squadron pilots at Deurne airfield, Belgium. Seated on propeller F/O Davis. On the wing from left to right: Peter, Critchley-Salmonson, Ron Kemp, Doug Buchie, -??-, Bremner, Jimmy Chun, Holbech, -??-, John Young. Standing from left to right: -??-, Chris Blundell-Hill, -??-, Tony Krakowski, Jim Swanson, Woody Woodford, Ron West, -??-.
Seated: Trevor Mitchel, Colin Maitland (CO) and Clifton Mogg. On the ground are Tug Wilson and the Squadron Adjutant.

of prisoners consisted of various nationalities and one chap who spoke some Russian convinced the Soviets that they had liberated a POW camp rather than an ordinary prison. The Russian attitude changed completely. They allowed the prisoners to send parties outside the camp in order to retrieve food from nearby farms. Cows were slaughtered and soon former prisoners could be seen swimming in a nearby lake. However, it was extremely dangerous to leave the camp. Some prisoners tried to make it to the Allied lines. Several were never heard of again. Great commotion was caused inside the camp when the Soviets began to single out prisoners with an Irish name. They explained to the British officers that the Irish were anti-British; their country had been neutral and consequently all men with Irish names were considered pro-German. It took a while before the Russians understood that they were doing the wrong thing and that a name did not mean everything. Ivor Harris had recovered so well that he was put in charge of a group of British NCOs who had been prisoners in a nearby compound. Every morning Harris discovered that five or six of them had escaped the camp and were trying to travel west under their own steam.

Squadron Leader Colin Maitland DFC was killed in Holland shortly before the end of the war when his aircraft was hit by Flak while he attacked German positions.

On 8 May 1945 — whilst at Twenthe — the Squadron celebrated VE-day when there was a sudden call from Operations that a pair was needed for a recce. Unfortunately F/L (now AVM) 'Flossie' Moss happened to be standing next to the Commanding Officer S/L Dick Mitchell in the bar. He was immediately detailed, along with F/L Reg Hodge, to report for briefing. They were to undertake a recce as far as Flensburg as it had been reported that the Germans were, despite the signing of the surrender, pulling out to Norway to continue a lost battle. Moss and Hodge were to establish the veracity of this claim. As it was quite a long sortie it necessitated refuelling at Lubeck — which had been captured only a few days previously. In order to obviate the need to refill the drop tank they flew to Lubeck on their main tanks and landed at Lubeck with a full drop tank. As this was not the norm, and as Moss had failed to relieve a full bladder before take-off his concentration was not what it should have been. The result was a rather heavy landing which all but caused Moss an embarassing accident. On instructions both pilots simply pulled off the runway and did not taxi around to the dispersal. Moss was grateful for that for he was now able to stand on the trailing edge and relieve himself on the grass below. Imagine his consternation, whilst in full flow, he saw a Junkers Ju88 diving towards him at full throttle. Before Moss took a headlong dive for what he hoped would be a safe, but wet, cover, he realised that the Junkers' undercarriage was down and it in fact landed alongside Moss to surrender. What the German crew thought of RAF aircrew behaviour will remain a mystery for while Moss was still performing the aircraft was surrounded by armed personnel. Not because the Germans were dangerous but to prevent Allied servicemen from taking the German's Lugers and watches as souvenirs. Hodge and Moss subsequently took off for Flensburg and established that whilst there was a fair amount of shipping there was no evidence of a German withdrawal. Hundreds of German aircraft had been lined up, some of them straight from the factories, to be surrendered to the Allies. It was the last operational sortie flown by the Squadron.

For Harris it looked like a brighter future. By 21 May a large convoy of American trucks driven by Russian soldiers arrived at the camp where Harris and his colleagues waited to be evacuated. They were taken to the River Elbe. The number of ex-POWs was down to a mere 500 now. After a hair-raising ride the trucks, with most of the drivers drunk, and the liberated prisoners arrived at the demarcation line. They were welcomed by Americans with Studebaker trucks. The next stop was Halle airfield. Here Harris had his first encounter in a year with white sheets, clean blankets and real bread. By courtesy of an American, Sergeant Harris also tasted his first alcohol in a year. It was a shocking experience. Two days later Dakotas landed. Harris and his friends were flown to Brussels. A very well-organised reception followed with hotels, new clothing, money and cigarettes. On 28 May 1945, exactly one year after he had bailed out of his Mustang, Harris boarded a Lancaster bomber and started the last lap of his long journey. After less than an hour the Lancaster landed at Dunsfold in Surrey, where a young lady gave Harris his first cup of English tea. Then Harris and others took the train to Uxbridge for the final administrative details. He was issued with a ration book and given the opportunity to make a few phone calls. At Uxbridge a wonderful reunion took place, on the staff of the unit there were S/L Mike Gray, Harris' CO at the time he was shot down, and F/L Dougie Reich, who Harris had last seen in the yard at Oberursel.

CHAPTER 11
B.A.F.O.

As soon as the shooting war was over the Squadron turned its hand to formation flying to gain the skills necessary for the various fly-pasts organised by No.84 Group. The first took place on 15 May and the route covered The Hague and Amsterdam. The following day the Hanover area was visited and the final flypast was on 27 May when the Squadron flew over Groningen. At the end of the month the Wing moved to B118 Celle in Germany. After the move to Celle things were pretty slack. There was a fair amount of flying but the post-war photo demands had not yet started and the emphasis was on formation flying. The runway at Celle started to show signs of wear and tear, and on 18 June the Squadron went to B150 Hustedt, a few miles to the North. Celle was still the Squadron's main base and aircraft were flown there for inspections. The pilots lived there, being taken by road to Hustedt each morning and brought back in the evening. During July, the Squadron returned to England for a fortnight's Armament Practice Camp at Warmwell to practise both air to air and air to ground firing. Whilst the Squadron was enjoying the delights of Warmwell, 2 TAF was disbanded on 17 July 1945 and the air force in Germany became the British Air Force of Occupation (BAFO).

After the Squadron's return to Husted flying training continued. In August the first steps in the breaking up of No.35 (Recce) Wing began. On the twenty-sixth the Squadron lost its first pilot in peace time, F/L Arrakowski who was killed in a road accident. Two days later No.4 Squadron left to become a light bomber squadron formed from the pilots and aircraft of No.605 Squadron. The departure of No.4 Squadron would have left the Wing without its High Level Photo Reconnaissance (HLPR) element, but six pilots and six Spitfires PRXI were posted from No.4 to No.II (AC) Squadron and became C-Flight on 14 September. Whilst all this was happening A- and B-Flights were involved in yet another flypast. This took place on 15 September over The Hague, in honour of Queen Wilhelmina of The Netherlands and to commemorate the Battle of Britain. For the flypast the Squadron operated from its old wartime base of Gilze-Rijen and according to the official write-up, the flypast 'subsequentially enhanced the reputation of the Royal Air Force in Holland'. On 16 September the Squadron returned to Husted and finally back to Celle the following day after the runway resurfacing was complete.

There was another big change, if only an administrative one, in the composition of the Wing. On 17 September, No.268 Squadron was disbanded and renumbered No.16. As the year drew to its close, flying training began to give way to operational flying as the Squadron began to receive various photo tasks, but the number of pilots continued to drop because of demobilisation. The Squadron's strength was down to ten pilots by the end of the year and for a time there was only three aircraft available. The Wing CO, Group Captain A.F. Anderson DSO, DFC, once a Flight Commander on the Squadron, left in December to take a post at the Air Ministry. The shortage of pilots was the reason for the Squadron reverting to two Flights. A-Flight was to do the Tac/R work with the Spitfire XIV. B-Flight was to fly the PR work equipped with the Spitfire XIX. During February and March 1946 more Spitfire XIXs arrived. Weather permitting, B-Flight was now fairly well occupied with several photographic tasks. A-Flight, however, left the snow and sandstorms of Celle behind it and headed north with six aircraft and pilots for the Armament Camp at Sylt from 13 February until 5 March 1946. At the end of March, No.16 Squadron were warned of their impending disbandment and on 1 April three officers were posted to No.II Squadron. Their aircraft were returned to England soon afterwards. On the sixteenth a further two officers were posted across, and that just about wound up No.35 (Recce) Wing. It was officially disbanded on 22 June and became RAF Station Celle with No.II Squadron being the sole recce squadron in the BAFO. On 24 April 1946 S/L D.W. Barlow DFC took over command from S/L Mitchell. By the end of May most of the photo demands had been met and the accent was back on training, with the station Harvard being regularly used for Instrument Flying. A-Flight went air to ground firing, at Fassberg ranges, nearly every week. In the course of all this training F/Ls Collinson and Woodhouse took a couple of Spitfire XIXs up to an indicated height of 44,000 feet which, if the air temperature of $-30°$ given by the Met Office was accurate, represented a true height of 50,000 feet. On 19 August, A-Flight with six Spitfire XIVs departed for their APC at Sylt and with generally fair weather got in plenty of flying. However, towards the end of the detachment the intensity of the flying began to tell on the serviceability of the aircraft and the return to Celle on 16 September came just in time. Back at base the

August 1954; 'The boys on the bussing bowser' at RAF Wahn. F/Os Boyer, Mackervoy, Meadley, Webb, Bailey, Winterford, Fielder, Winship, Fisher, Price, Newman, Woodhams, Trowern, Colston, Lown and Macgregor surrounding S/L Weighill.

photo tasks had begun to flow in again and both flights were kept very busy. On 26 September one of the B-Flight pilots took a XIX up to an indicated height of 45,000 feet. November started badly with an order that all Griffon 65 and 66 engines were to be grounded after 100 hours to await the arrival of a Rolls-Royce modification team. This severely reduced the Squadron's available aircraft, leaving three in A- and two in B-Flight. However, poor weather limited the PR effort, although A-Flight, with its few aircraft, managed to participate in quite a few Group interception exercises.

In the middle of November Task 966 was received. This covered a large area of the British Zone of Germany and was to keep the Squadron occupied for years. On 14 December A-Flight moved to Gatow/Berlin for a tour of duty. The intention was to send five aircraft but due to a case of unserviceability only four aircraft actually made the trip. There was a change of Squadron Commanders in December when G. Collinson took over on the fifteenth. There is an entry in the Operations Record Book saying that he was promoted to acting Squadron Leader with effect from 4 January 1947, so presumably he was commanding the Squadron for three weeks as a Flight Lieutenant.

The weather at the start of 1947 was very poor. A-Flight returned from Gatow on 4 January and as the temperature continued to drop, experiments were made with blanking off part of the radiators to keep the engines from freezing up. A-Flight returned to Gatow on 4 March with five aircraft, eight pilots and fifteen other ranks. The weather was still bad both at Celle and Gatow and when the snow eventually started to melt there were floods to cope with. A special recce sortie was flown along the River Weser to check on the ice flow down it and where there was a danger of it bursting its banks. A-Flight moved to Gatow for a third time on 10 April and then on the fifteenth the whole Squadron moved to Wunstorf, which was to become its new base. Only fourteen aircraft made the initial move. Three were left at Celle for servicing reasons. At that time A-Flight was commanded by F/L Woodhouse and B-Flight by F/L Mowbray. On 18 April both Flight Commanders were flying at 4,000 feet near Heligoland to record the blowing-up of the fortifications there. F/L Allen-Rowlandson caused a certain amount of anxiety at the end of the month when he had an aircraft up for two hours and fifteen minutes, without a drop tank. The Ops. Record Book read: 'The fuel remaining could be measured in pints . . .'

With better weather the PR Flight ranged far and wide, from Denmark to Holland. At the same time B-Flight was kept busy with exercises and oblique photography. Everybody seemed to take photographs of the Minden Gap. To quote from the Form 540: 'It must be the most photographed area in Europe'. Normally the aircraft carrying out the PR over Denmark had been landing at Sylt to refuel but on 27 June a very high-level flap developed when two aircraft landed at Kastrup for fuel. The pilots were F/L Woodhouse and F/O Linford. The Danish authorities were most intrigued by the whole affair and for a time refused the aircraft permission to return to Wunstorf. Reading between the lines it would appear that they did not approve of British aircraft taking photographs of Denmark.

The descent of the 'Iron Curtain' meant extra work for the Squadron as the pilots were ordered to patrol the border between the Western and Russian zones. Yet very little is in the Operations Record Book about this new task, which must have continued for at least four to five years.

At the beginning of July the Harvard returned from Fassberg and Instrument Flying training continued. B-Flight went down to Wahn on 17 July to fill gaps in the Basic Cover task, returning to Wunstorf on 16 August. Due to the age of the aircraft, serviceability was never particularly good and during this period the main snag seemed to be from the constant speed units (CSU). The CO had a rather close shave when his CSU stuck in the fully coarse position. He made a successful emergency landing nevertheless. It is interesting to note that, at this time, the servicing tail was definitely wagging the flying dog and five or six days before the end of each month flying came to an abrupt halt because there were no more flying hours available . . .

Although Wunstorf was technically the Squadron's home, it was unusual for both Flights to be there together for any length of time. In November 1947 it was A-Flight's turn to wander. They went up to Lubeck on the twenty-third for a gunnery attachment which, in spite of the time of year, turned out to be a very good one. They returned to Wunstorf on 15 December. The weather at the end of 1947 precluded Photo Reconnaissance. There was little improvement in the weather in the first months of 1948 as the usual snowy and icy conditions returned.

P/O Alan Bavin joined the Squadron at Wunsdorf on 9 February 1948. The Squadron still had a dual role and had a total of eight aircraft per Flight. Bavin was posted to A-Flight though occasionally pilots flew both aircraft. At this time the Squadron was part of No.123 Wing led by W/C Prosser Hanks, the other two squadrons being No.3, commanded by S/L Colin McFie and No.80 with S/L Newbury as CO. The former had Tempests and the latter Spitfire 24s. OC No.II (AC) Squadron was S/L Geof Collinson, Flight Commanders were F/L Roy Turner (A) and F/L Bob Woodhouse (B). In April, A-Flight returned to Gatow. After a Russian fighter had collided with a BEA-Viking in the corridor they were ordered to stand by for escort duty, fortunately nothing further came of this incident. It seems that the Squadron was not really involved in the Berlin Blockade and the subsequent supply operations. On the thirtieth the Squadron moved to RAF Wahn near Cologne as Wunsdorf was being used for the Airlift. Wahn had four Mosquito squadrons and a short runway made up of PSP strips, part of which was overgrown with grass making it rather difficult to see exactly where the runway started and ended. It was obvious that something had to be done to enable the pilots to see if they were still on the runway or not. Eventually a 2,000 yards runway was built making landings somewhat more comfortable.

Towards the end of 1948 Tomlinson left and a New Zealander, S/L Bill Newenham assumed command. He was a typical Kiwi: although he stuck up for his pilots whenever they were in trouble because a party had got out of hand, it was usually because he was leading from the front. A major servicing crisis occurred at the end of the year. There had been only three aircraft serviceable at the end of November and in the following months only essential flying was carried out. The weather was very bad and the few available aircraft were used for instrument flying and formation practice. In December 1948 Roy Turner died after a forced landing and, regrettably, the wrong diagnosis in Wuppertal military hospital. F/L Derek Maddox took over A-Flight. In January 1949 a Harvard was allotted to the Squadron to give the pilots a chance to do a little more flying.

One of the most popular aircraft in the postwar months at Celle was this Spitfire XIV 'Fochinell'. John West stands beside this aircraft, which belonged to Lefty Packwood.

The Station Commander at Wahn was Group Captian D.J. Eayrs, CBE, DFC who had been a Squadron pilot in 1928 when Shiny Two was based at Manston. In addition to No.II (AC) Squadron there were four Mosquito squadrons at Wahn; Nos. 14 and 98 with Mk 35 day bombers and Nos. 4 and 11 with Mk 6 Night Interceptors. January 18 is noted as a big day in Form 540; eight Spitfires were airborne at the same time, the largest number for no less that six months and a total of twenty-two hours flying were flown. The weather improved a little in February and both HLPR and low level oblique sorties were possible. The Squadron was now established for sixteen aircraft, eight Mark XIV and eight Mark XIX. In addition there was a manpower shortage necessitating that technical jobs were done by the pilots. There was one electrician, ten fitters, ten riggers and only three armourers. April was a bad month for Photo Reconnaissance and by the end of the month most of the XIXs were grounded for lack of spares, but it was possible to detach three aircraft to Utersen in May to undertake photographic commitments in that area and in the same month

A-Flight went up to Gutersloh for an exercise. At the end of May the Squadron was visited by the Chief of Staff of the Royal Australian Air Force. After their return from Gutersloh A-Flight went up to Sylt for a routine gunnery detachment from 27 June to 28 July. The scores for this detachment were very low. The stoppage rate was 1,025 rounds per stoppage. Wahn must have been the Squadron base merely in name because B-Flight were still involved in the PR commitment from Utersen. It was not until the end of August that they were brought back to complete the part of Task 966 that could best be performed from Wahn before the Squadron returned to Wunstorf. At long last some more ground crew and spares arrived in August and by the end of the month all but two of the Squadron's aircraft were serviceable. Flying was restricted in early September to keep the aircraft in good condition for the return to Wunstorf.

On 15 September 1949 the Squadron returned to Wunstorf. The formation of eight Spitfire XIVs was led by S/L Newenham and the eight Spitfire XIXs by F/L Maddox. With the departure of No.II (AC) Squadron and the Mosquito squadrons, Wahn ceased to be an RAF station on 1 October 1949.

Although the Squadron took sixteen serviceable aircraft back to Wunstorf, the serviceability rate soon began to drop as all minor inspections and second line servicing had to be done at Celle. It would not have been so bad had Celle been established for the task. As it was they were more interested in keeping their own aircraft flying. The situation continued to deteriorate until December when the Squadron started to do its own minor servicing, after which aircraft serviceability began to improve. The year ended fairly quietly with, apart from Exercise 'Agility' One and Two in October in co-operation with the Fleet Air Arm, routine flying.

A-Flight started its New Year's wandering by departing for Sylt on 23 January, staying there until 17 February. It was a very poor detachment and the stoppage rate was appalling. The scores for academic air to ground gunnery was 18% for operational 5% and air to air 4.7%. Whilst they were up there S/L Newenham left and S/L Red Bartlett DSO took command on 6 February 1950. He was a much liked CO having had wartime experience. Bad weather in March cut down the PR work and a shortage of spares reduced the amount of flying generally. Things livened up a bit when a runaway ·50 machine gun poured a stream of bullets into Wunstorf village, luckily without causing any casualties and an interesting situation arose early in April when both the BAFO IREs were away on courses and no new instrument ratings could be issued. At the end of April A-Flight departed for Sylt again. Now the scores were: academic air-to-ground gunnery 15%, operational 11% and air-to-air 6.5%. B-

A vertical camera is being loaded into a Spitfire PR XIX of No.II (AC) Squadron.

Flight back at Wunstorf was in a very sorry state because of the age of the aircraft and the lack of spares. On average they only had two aircraft serviceable per day.

In May 1950 No.4 MFPS which had been responsible for the Squadron's photographic processing amalgamated with the Squadron; the CO having disciplinary powers over its personnel. In June came the culmination of all the recent formation flying practice when four Spitfire XIVs and four Spitfire XIXs took part in a flypast as part of the BAFO Air Display. The formation was quoted as having been 'superbly led by F/L Maddox whose training and navigation was remarkable'. The flypast made a fitting end to his four-year tour; he left at the end of the month. The end of June brought a change of scene for the Squadron when it moved to Buckeburg on 29 June. It was ready to operate again on 1 July, but although the serviceability of A-Flight's aircraft was still good B-Flight could only muster three or four aircraft each day. When the Squadron moved to Buckeburg the MFPS moved to Bad Eilsen and became independent from the Squadron again.

Sadly, one of the Squadron pilots, F/O Bernard-Smith, lost his life when he collided with an Anson in the Buckeburg circuit. While at Buckeburg the Squadron entered the jet age. During Exercise Cupola, held in August the Squadron's Spitfires were often intercepted by Meteors but thanks to their manoeuvrability and relatively low speed had very little trouble in evading them. The annual autumn Exercise, Broadside, which started on 3 September kept the Squadron busy, but they were still able to fit in their regular air to ground sorties and the average score for the month was 24%.

In October 1950 a Meteor 7 trainer arrived with an instructor, F/O Farley who had been seconded to the Squadron. Later in the same month S/L Bob Pugh, who had some jet aircraft flying experience and had just completed a tour in Training Command, took over command of the Squadron. On posting to BAFO, of which No.II (AC) Squadron was a part, Pugh reported to the AOC 2 Group for an interview. He had been told that he was to assume command of a Vampire FGA squadron. However, as he had experience of two types of Meteors — the Marks 3 and 4 — was a QFI, and an IRE, the AOC 2 Group decided that he was to take command of 'Shiny Two'. At Buckeburg there was no 'Wing' structure, and hence no operational supporting staff: there was no Squadron Adjutant, this job was done by a pilot as a secondary duty; there was no squadron technical officer, the senior technical staff were the SNCOs i/c A- and B-Flights and there was an acute shortage of riggers. The fact that some of the pilots were SNCOs meant that they could not serve as Operations Officers.

It was during the conversion to the Meteor that a new feature of the Buckeburg runway was discovered — when wet its surface began to resemble a skating rink. One morning in November two pilots went off the far end of the runway in quick succession and F/O Farley, the QFI, only just avoided a third accident. S/L W.A. Crawford DPMO(F), from HQ BAFO spent a week with the Squadron lecturing and discussing the medical aspects of high speed/high altitude flying. A few weeks later, on 30 November the first Meteor FR9 arrived. More Mark 9s arrived in December and as Bavin was the longest serving member at that time he was given the job of evaluating the aircraft in the tactical reconnaissance role. The Meteors were initially finished silver overall with black serials and codes. Later they were camouflaged glossy dark green and dark sea grey with PRU blue undersides. The Meteor was a great advance and with its battery of nose-mounted cameras and four 20mm cannons proved a worthy successor to the Spitfire. On 16 December Pugh flew the acceptance flight of the first Meteor fitted with an ejection seat. The Squadron now had its full complement of pilots. Usually pilots were sent solo after only thirty minutes' instruction. Nevertheless A-Flight managed to get airborne in their new mounts and were suitably impressed by the Meteor, but it was not until 10 January 1951 that they were used on a task, achieving good results. On 18 January 1951 the Spitfires were flown back to England via Eindhoven in Holland. When the aircraft landed at Eindhoven there was a forty-knot cross wind to welcome the Squadron's arrival. It resulted in three aircraft staying behind at the Dutch air force base. One had a broken propeller and two had coolant problems. The next day the others flew on to Tangmere, from where it was only a short hop to the respective M.U.s.

On 26 January Mr. Anthony Eden, accompanied by the CiC BAFO visited the Squadron. The shortage of riggers was still acute, but the conversion of B-Flight to the Meteor PR10 was to begin in February. F/L Cole FDC, who had taken over A-Flight, took the last Spitfire XIV back to the UK on 6 February and later in the month successfully carried out the first trip in a Meteor FR9 fitted with full wing tanks. One of the big problems in the whole conversion programme was the bad weather and the lack, at first, of a trustworthy let-down aid. The air traffic controllers were not yet skilled enough to work with the much faster aircraft. Things had improved by February and to iron out the final few problems a tape recorder was installed in ATC so that both pilots and controllers could evaluate what they had said and done.

On 21 March 1951, two days after his wedding to round-the-world flier Richarda Morrow-Tate,

Michael Townsend arrived at Buckeburg. Though claiming to remember only a few little bits and pieces his recollections are worthy of mention:

> 'The joys of Pimms at 4d, Service parties, wild boar hunts and the riding school under Herr Homringhausen at Gutersloh were one side of the personal coin. The other was the appalling Married Quarters position. The machinations of keeping one's family somehow in BAF once having got them over on holiday were terrific. At one time I was stationed at Buckeburg and my wife was four hours driving away in a surplus Married Quarter at Luneburg . . .
>
> My outstanding memory is of the CO Bob Pugh personally converting the Squadron from Spitfires to Meteors without a single accident or failure. I can still remember my feelings as the airfield dwindled after the first take-off and climb in a Meteor 7 and I wondered how I would ever keep it within sight of the runway close enough to do circuits and rollers. I need not have worried. Bob nailed us down to a firm drill and it worked.'

As the Meteor 9s were grounded for Townsend's first month on the Squadron, he was one of the pilots detailed to ferry the last Spitfires to England. The four aircraft were flown by S/L Townsend, F/O Wooldridge, F/S Durys and Sgt. Power. For Mike Townsend it would be a memorable last Spitfire sortie. Having recently married and with his wife living near Cambridge, Townsend arranged for himself to fly PS915 home to Britain. After more than forty years he still maintains that he was not sure whether PS915 had to be taken to Oakington or Cosford. So that day he flew first to Oakington. Then, after finding his way through the thick industrial haze over the Birmingham area he finally found Cosford. It appeared to have been closed down for a Bank Holiday. There was not a single soul there except for a friendly Air Ministry constable whom Townsend persuaded to help him push the Spitfire into a hangar. For PS915 began a long series of different tasks, including service in the Far East with No.81 Squadron and 'THUM-Flight' (Temperature and HUMidity) from Woodvale, until it was retired on 12 June 1957. A month later three Spitfires, including PS915, landed at Biggin Hill. PS915 would become a Static Display Aircraft at West Malling and Leuchars. It played a static role in the film *Battle of Britain* in 1968 and then returned to Leuchars were it remained until 1975. On 21 February that year it was transported to RAF Brawdy to see if it would be suitable as a back-up for the Battle of Britain Memorial Flight. A long story of movements began, first to RAF Coningsby, then to St. Athan, and then back to Brawdy, where it became a gate-guardian again. On 13 June 1984 the aircraft was taken to British Aerospace where a long and intensive reconstruction started. On 16 December 1986 her engine roared to life again when S/L Paul Day took her out of the hangar and flew PS915 for the first time since 1957. Now PS915 is a proud member of the Battle of Britain Memorial Flight and at the same time the oldest No.II (AC) Squadron aircraft still in service with the RAF.

The change from propeller to jet was not easy. The Meteor's handling was rather touchy at times. On 15 February 1951 Mike Cole had to land his Meteor in a bit of a hurry after the aircraft compass failed and left him puzzled as to his whereabouts. On 7 March 1951 the first Meteor PR10 arrived. During this period a major nuisance was that the PR Flight at Fighter OTU was still equipped with Spitfires. Therefore replacement pilots had to do their conversion on the Squadron, causing more work and reducing the Squadron's operational efficiency. Another delay was caused when all Meteors were grounded for modification to the aileron controls on 20 March.

Once the aileron problem had been solved a PR10 was used on a task for the first time by B-Flight on 5 April. A-Flight, now quite at home with their FR9s, were using them on their twice-weekly air-to-ground firing programme with steadily improving results. The strength of the Squadron was now twelve officers, nine NCO pilots, eight SNCOs, fourteen corporals and forty-two airmen. On 13 April the Squadron was visited by the Secretary of State for Air, the Right Honorable Arthur Henderson MP. The last of the Spitfire XIXs had left for the UK on 11 April and a week or so later B-Flight was told that they would soon be exchanging their PR10s for FR9s. This was because a complete PR squadron would shortly be coming to Germany, thus allowing the whole of No.II (AC) Squadron to be employed in the FR role. The PR squadron was No.541 and they arrived at Buckeburg on 7 June. In order to build up their numbers of experienced pilots, four pilots of B-Flight were posted to them. The remainder of B-Flight now started on a conversion programme to FR work and from their PR10s to FR9s. All this was happening in the absence of A-Flight who had taken their six FR9s and one T7 on the 4 June to Sylt for the first time.

Maybe this is the place and time to explore the reasons why this tiny peninsula in Northern Germany was so tremendously popular with the Squadron. There is no Squadron member of those days who does not remember 'Abbysinia Beach' in the summer, or the wildfowling during the winter detachment. Families could stay with the Squadron at the Viking Hotel and for the more adventurous Squadron pilots there was the opportunity to fly Tempests with the Towing Flight. With the new jet the pilots were required to perform one trip up to 35,000 feet, just to hear and feel what it was like to fire their weapons at that height. The Flight returned home on 28 June. Although the Squadron had been jet-equipped for 7 months, replacement pilots from the OCU at Stradishall were still not jet-trained and it was not until 27 August that the first jet-trained replacement arrived, one Sergeant Paddy Blackwell-Smyth.

With the return of A-Flight from Sylt the Squadron plunged into four months of exercises. 'Thunder-Flash', a joint RAF/RN exercise, 'Nickel Coin', 'Stopgap, I and II', and 'Clean Up' were all fairly short but they did show that the shortage of fast-filling bowsers could easily lead to the cancellation of sorties. In the midst of all these short exercises normal flying training continued; B-Flight flew their first air to ground firing sorties and the Squadron had its first ejection when Sergeant Tickner while finishing off a training sortie got into difficulties in an embedded CuNim. He found himself at 11,000 feet heading vertically downwards with 400-plus on the Air Speed Indicator. He decided that the time had come to abandon the aircraft. He ejected successfully and suffered only slight facial wind-burns and a twisted knee.

On 1 September 1951 2ATAF was formed out of BAFO. One of the tasks of 'Shiny Two' was the spotting and directing of army artillery fire from the air. It had been a Squadron job since World War I and the Squadron was tremendously skilled at it. The Royal Artillery ran a refresher course each year for Army Co-op pilots at Munsterlager in procedures and R/T phraseology. This was followed by live shoots controlled by the pilots initially from a ground observation bunker on the range and then from the air. The 1951 course was noteworthy for two reasons. One was that in one of the ground-controlled shoots a Flight Commander managed to land a twenty-five pound shell about fifteen yards from the bunker and secondly, because this was the first time that artillery was controlled from jet aircraft. However, it was the last year in which such training was done.

Longer exercises started with 'Counter-Thrust' during which the Squadron operated from Buckeburg. Immediately after this exercise was over B-Flight went to Wahn for exercise 'Cirrus' and

RAF Wahn in 1949. Spitfires XIVs and XIXs, ground staff and pilots. Standing left to right: F/O A.C. Bavin, F/O J.C. Darjan, F/O C.S. McDonald F/O J.L. Towler, F/O P.J. Aubrey, F/L J.L. Bayley, F/L D.A. Maddox, F/L R. Woodhouse, Captain D.L. Rowlands (GLO), F/L P.O. Palmer, F/O B.C. Bernard-Smith, C.R. Blackwell and W/O F. Devrell. In the background are Mosquitoes.

on 26 September A-Flight went to Luxemburg for 'Jupiter', a USAF exercise, being joined two days later by B-Flight from Wahn. It took the Flight, aided by an airlift of USAF C119s, just over twelve hours from the time they were told to move to being settled and in bed in Luxemburg. As No.II (AC) Squadron had its own fleet of lorries one of the first tasks for the pilots was to learn to drive the Thorneycroft three-tonners. A convoy of twenty-five lorries would drive to Luxemburg for Exercise Jupiter, consisting of refuellers, water bowsers, enormous photographic processing vehicles and many more. Miraculously most of the Squadron reached its destination on time and in one piece. During the exercise, the Squadron was visited by General Eisenhower. After 'Jupiter' A-Flight returned to Buckeburg on 1 October for a week, while B-Flight went back to Wahn for Exercise Combine. The Squadron was re-united at Thorney Island from 10 to 16 October for Exercise Surprise Packet, where they exercised in both the ground attack and recce roles. Finally, everyone was back at Buckeburg by the twenty-first. In September 1951 the Squadron was awarded the Duncan Trophy for its achievements in all-weather flying and training. The CO, Bob Pugh had every reason to be proud of the Squadron when the Trophy was handed over to him by the CiC 2ATAF Sir Robert M. Foster on 24 October during a ceremony which included a parade at Buckeburg. The Duncan Trophy was, at that time, awarded annually to the squadron with the best all-weather flying record. In No.II Squadron's case it covered the period 1 February 1950 to 31 January 1951, so most of the flying had been done with the good old Spitfires. A few days later the Squadron prepared to move to Sylt for a month. This would be the first time that the Squadron had been to an Armament Practice School since July 1945. John West who joined the Squadron in September 1951 vividly remembers the APS at Sylt. While he was waiting to take off one day, a Tempest touched down and almost immediately flipped over. The pilot, F/L Jock Weir, was hanging upside down by his straps with petrol dripping into the cockpit canopy below his head. Fortunately he was quickly extracted. While at Sylt the Squadron worked a system whereby one Flight flew in the morning and the other in the afternoon. The next day the Flight from the afternoon would fly in the morning (perhaps four trips, as they were only fifteen to twenty minutes long) would not be flying again until the afternoon of the following day. This tended to produce a continual party atmosphere, and Sylt was notorious for high jinks as the three or four squadrons present there tried to outdrink and outsing the rest. The more cynical said that in those days 'AC' stood for Alcohol Consumption rather than for Army Co-operation. During those days Danish pilots would be attached to the Squadron while on APC. They mastered 'AC' best . . . After the Sylt detachment, which suffered from bad weather, the Squadron returned to Buckeburg hoping that they had seen the last of Sylt for the year. However, this was not to be. On Christmas Day, 1951, three Meteor PR9s accompanied by three Meteor PR10s of No.451 Squadron and two Ansons of the Communications Squadron with the Squadron ground crew flew up to Sylt on a hush-hush job. They returned on 2 January. The Form 540 unfortunately gives no details whatsoever. It was from Buckeburg that one of the Squadron pilots, Jock Wardhaugh was killed while flying a low-level recce sortie on 4 December 1951. The weather at the beginning of 1952 was much the same as usual, snow, sleet, ice and fog, though flying took place whenever possible. There was an escape and evasion exercise held in the winter of 1951-1952, named 'Pluto Paddle'. Squadron pilots were dropped from a blacked-out bus late one evening in snow-covered mountainous country near Scharfoldendorf before the moon was out. Their job was to find their way back to the Hannover-Bielefeld Autobahn without getting caught by the Army, who were acting as the hunter force. F/O Peter Wooldridge and F/L Townsend opted to walk flat out on the main roads and get behind the hunter force before the start of the search. They succeeded and were first home covering the distance in seventeen hours. No-one had told them they should not start their evasion run before the Exercise had begun. The Squadron pilots also attended a course at the Winter Survival School at Ehrwald in the Austrian Tyrol.

One of the flying tasks carried out was tests with a wire-recorder fitted to one of the Squadron aircraft by the RAE at Farnborough. The initial test in February 1952, showed that the voice reproduction was good. Consequently it was used on one of the small exercises in April. At the beginning of March B-Flight went north and operated from Schleswig during Exercise Skandia II. The weather was fairly reasonable and there was plenty to be seen on the ground. No.541 squadron left Buckeburg for Gutersloh on 3 April and when No.II Squadron's first six aircraft airborne that morning returned to land they found the circuit 'Fully occupied by nineteen aircraft of 541 Squadron who were saying farewell to Buckeburg in the traditional manner, aided by four pilots of the Squadron'. Four No.II Squadron aircraft had to be diverted to Wunstorf because of the congestion. On 16 April it was the Squadron's turn to say farewell to Buckeburg, but although Gutersloh was their ultimate objective they spent a month at Sylt first. The weather deteriorated towards the end of the month and great problems were experienced due to the

Pilots of No.II (AC) Squadron, June 1951.
Standing left to right: Sgt. J. Take, F/L R.A. Turnbull, P/O R. Smith, P/O A.C. Bavin, Sgt Clarke and Sgt. R.J. Rhodes.
Seated left to right: F/L J.R. Palmer, F/L M.J.B. Cole DFC S/L R.M. Pugh AFC, (OC) F/L C.A. Wade, and F/L M.E. Townsend.

unserviceability of the target-towing Tempests and with the towed target once it was airborne. The 2ATAF recce build-up was completed with the formation of No.79 squadron at Gutersloh. Following the departure of the FGA Vampires from Gutersloh to one of the newly built airfields on the North German Plain, Gutersloh had become the Recce Wing with a Wing Commander Flying, Wing Headquarters and Operations Room Staff. The Wing now came under control of No.2 Group. When in April the Squadron left for the Annual Sylt APC they were not to return to Buckeburg but moved to Gutersloh in May. It was a happy station under the command of Group Captain Dudley Lewis, a firm but fair disciplinarian. On 15 May the Squadron finally arrived in Gutersloh, thus forming, in company with No.79FR and No.541PR squadrons and No.4 MFPS, the complete recce wing for 2ATAF, after a lapse of seven years. On 28 May the wing was visited by the Secretary of State for Air, Lord De L'Isle and Dudley VC, accompanied by the CiC 2ATAF.

After the return from Sylt the emphasis was on TAC/R and low level photographic training in preparation for the Exercise season. In addition to day flying, the first night flying in Meteors was carried out on 17 June.

The Squadron had a permanently attached Army Ground Liaison Officer who used to do the debriefing and was responsible for passing on the information to Brigade. Visits to the Army were a revealing and enjoyable experience; one of the more fashionable regiments near Celle even had its own pack of foxhounds. In order that FR pilots had a better understanding of the Army operational combat procedures in the field, observed camouflage techniques and got a close look at Army vehicles, Squadron pilots joined the Army during its exercises. One of the Tank Regiments allowed the pilots to drive the Centurion tanks. A third, some think it was a Hussar Regiment, regaled the Squadron with a sit-down lunch with caviar eaten with silver cutlery on a snowy white table cloth. On the other hand the Squadron pilots sometimes upset older Army officers by not taking the Army's work seriously enough. On one occasion during a TEWT (Tactical Exercise Without Troops) a discussion developed about what the Squadron could see of the troops when overflying them. The Squadron emphasised the give away nature of SSV or tank tracks leading into laager areas; that white faced soldiers should look down, not up and that most of all, it was movement that attracted the eye — they should stay absolutely still. An Army major said: 'We overcome that by doing most of our movements in the dark'. Chris Wade answered without a blink of his eyes: 'Oh, really major, we in the RAF do most of our movements just after breakfast'. It was not really appreciated.

For the Exercises June Primer and Spearhead II in June and August respectively, the Squadron moved out from its hangars and operated from the dispersal at the western end of the airfield. On 13 July the NATO air display was held at Melsbroek in Belgium. The Squadron supplied two formations of four aircraft, led by the CO and F/O Smith, for the flypast. The No.II Group contribution was a formation of seventy-six aircraft, sixty-four Vampires and twelve Meteors. There was a change of Station Commander in July, with Group Captain J.H. Chaplin DSO, DFC, going to HQ 83 Group as Group Captain Operations and being replaced at Gutersloh by Group Captain Lewis DFC. The first parade of the new Station Commander is likely to be remembered by all concerned, if only for its length, more than three hours. There was also a change of Wing Commander Flying. W/C Larsen DFC taking over from W/C Kelly DFC. The Squadron did some more night flying in July and also quite a few trips using the wire recorder. In addition there was a steady flow of aircraft to and from Lyneham for modification. For the autumn Exercise, Holdfast, the Squadron operated from Wahn between 14 and 22 September. High ranking visitors came to see how the Squadron coped with 'war'. On 20 September Field Marshal the Viscount Montgomery visited the Squadron. Other visitors were the Minister of Defence Lord Alexander and the CiC NATO, General Norstadt USAF.

With the return to Gutersloh preparations were made for another attachment to Sylt from 13 October to 13 November. The Squadron average for the detachment was 5.1% and the stoppage rate 558. During the stay at Sylt F/L Cole DFC left the Squadron at the end of his tour. F/L Palmer took over A-Flight, only to be killed six weeks later during a low-level exercise. While smashing through two farm buildings his aircraft lost both wings and disintegrated. For a while F/L Townsend took over A-Flight while F/L G.P. Young took over B-Flight on the completion of the tour of F/L Mersham, who had been in charge of the Flight. Very soon however Mike Townsend was pulled out of the Squadron as a temporary adjutant to Group Captain Lewis, the Station Commander. The weather at the turn of the year 1952/1953 did not allow intensive flying. The Winter Survival Course at Ehrwald started again and was attended by several members including the CO S/L Pugh.

Fred Trowern joined the Squadron in February 1953. Having completed the Operational Conversion Unit course at RAF Stradishall on Meteor Mk8s he and another student were selected to attempt the Flight Recce (Tac/R) course, also at Stradishall, on Meteor 9s. The posting system in those days was a little primitive so when Trowern and his fellow-trainee were called in to see the Wing Commander Flying they were told that one pilot was to be posted to Egypt while the other would to go Germany. The question was, who wanted to go where? Both young Pilot Officers hesitated for a moment. Being a man of few words and a short fuse the Wingco Flying tossed a coin. Trowern left stamped Germany while the second pilot left a bit dazed wondering where on earth Abu Suier (No.208 Squadron) was. Trowern

Buckeburg, 24 October 1951. S/L Pugh receives the Duncan Trophy from AM Sir Robert Foster. The Trophy was awarded to the RAF squadron achieving the best all-weather flying record. No.II (AC) Squadron completed the greatest amount of actual and simulated instrument flying calculated as a percentage of the total flying effort during the competition year between 1 March 1950 and 20 February 1951.

was told to report to Bad Eilsen. There he was informed that he was to go to No.II (AC) Squadron at Gutersloh. Initiation into Squadron life was fairly fierce at the time as only the Boss (Bob Pugh), one Flight Commander (Mike Townsend) and two other officers (Don Winterford and Ron Turnhill) were married and accompanied. Hence the Squadron was in the Cellar Bar en masse most evenings and new pilots were expected to leave feet first on their first night. The Occupational Forces Club in Gutersloh and sundry shady establishments in Bielefeld also did remarkably good business thanks to 'Shiny Two'.

Trowern's earliest flying shock on the Squadron was night flying. Having gone through the Meteor Advanced Flying School at RAF Driffield at the time of the so-called 'Blood Bath' and 'Phantom Dive' era, night flying on Meteor 4s and 7s had been abandoned. At RAF Stradishall was the day fighter OCU and the Fighter Recce course, night flying being strictly for night fighters and bombers. Hence Trowern's total night flying was ten hours fifteen minutes dual and fourteen hours twenty-five minutes solo on the Harvard. His surprise was probably all too evident when as a twenty year-old Pilot Officer he found himself on the night flying programme to do two sorties on 7 April 1953. The sorties comprised local flying QCH's and roller landings and a practice diversion to Wunstorf. Fortunately all went well although Trowern did have the traumatic moment at night a month or so later. Somehow, a wartime bomber pilot had fixed up a searchlight trial. Trowern and another pilot were told to fly over the airfield at about 2000 feet straight and level while some peculiar Army types attempted to blind them with their wretched searchlight.

On 13 March, following incidents that had occurred on or near the Russian Zonal Border, all aircraft were loaded with operational ammunition, belt feed mechanisms were tensioned and guns cocked. Three days later the operational ammunition was replaced by ball ammunition but the guns remained cocked for all sorties except cine ones. These sorties also showed the difficulties some pilots had navigating at a safe distance from the border of the Soviet Zone, Peter Young vividly remembered one of these incidents: 'One of the pilots called for a fix and was told to "Steer 270". He then said: "I don't want a Steer, I want a Fix", but all the Fixer Service would say was "Steer 270". The pilot without knowing must have been many miles inside the Soviet Zone . . .'

On 20 March, 1953, HRH The Duke of Edinburgh visited Gutersloh. During the afternoon he visited the Squadron hangar and met the pilots. Unfortunately the weather made the proposed flying display impossible. The next visitor to Gutersloh was the Chief of the Air Staff, ACM Sir William Dickson, who visited the Squadron on 9 April. This time the weather was better and the flying display went off as planned. In the flypast that ended the display, the sixteen Meteor 9s, eight from No.II Squadron and eight from No.79 Squadron, received a favourable comment from the AOC No.2 Group.

Detachments to Fassberg for Artillery Reconnaissance was fun. The idea was to fly a racetrack pattern at low level. Then a single twenty-five pounder gun would fire a shell over the Meteor. As the shell landed the pilot would pull up, look for the target and proximity of the shell burst, call an initial correction such as 'Add 500, go left 50' and dive down to low level again waiting for the next shell to be fired. When the pilot reckoned the shell was on target he would call 'Fire for effect'. The whole battery would then open up.

Huge Balbos (formation flights) were also very much the thing in the early fifties. Quite often on Saturday mornings Nos.II, 79 and 451 Squadrons (the Gutersloh Wing) would put up a box of boxes each (forty-eight aircraft), or if a bit short a vic of boxes each (thirty-six aircraft). Generally led by the excellent Wingco Flying John Blount this formation would make a trip round the local area with a flypast at the base followed by a hectic wing run-in-and-break. The CO liked to see at least sixteen aircraft on the landing run at once, even though the main runway at Gutersloh was only about 1,800 yards or so. Naturally the squadron rivalry and general line-shooting in the bar afterwards was pretty awful. Occasionally, for various Royal Birthdays and other celebrations such as the opening of new Headquarters at Rheindahlen, the Gutersloh Wing would meet up with wings from Wunsdorf, Fassberg, Celle and other airfields for a real monster flypast. Before or after the flypast took place aircraft would meet over the Dummer See or the Steinhuder Meer west of Hannover. Then a huge dogfight would take place, just as during the Battle of Britain. Fred Trowern remembered these dogfights: 'One minute you were in the midst of dozens of aircraft, then the next minute you were on your own, not another aircraft in sight and wondering where the hell you were. Thank God for the Weser, the Autobahns and the Minden Gap . . .'

When the F24 camera first came into service in the 1930s it was a very good camera. It was still a good camera in 1953, but with the increase in aircraft speed a new camera was required if these speeds were to be exploited. A new camera, designated FX95, was designed by Messrs. Vintens. The new camera was a lot smaller than the F24 and three of them, each with a magazine of film for 400 exposures, could be fitted in the Meteor's nose. Eight aircraft from the Wing, four from No.II and four from No.79 Squadron were modified to take the new cameras. A certain amount of manual work with hammers and files was necessary before the new cameras would fit into the mountings but finally, on 7 February 1953, the first trip of a long trials programme was flown. That it had the makings of a good camera nobody denied, it would produce sharp pictures from an aircraft flying at 150 feet at 400 knots, but there were many snags to be ironed out, especially on the processing side. A Tac/R mission could now require 1,200 exposures to be processed instead of the previous maximum of 100 from an F24. This made it impossible for the Squadron 'J' type trailer to cope using hand processing, and the only answer was an MFPS. The trials were incomplete when the Squadron left for Wahn. At the same time the regular training programme for the pilots had to continue. To cut a long story short, the MFPS remained at Gutersloh so No.79 squadron had to complete the trials by themselves when No.II Squadron was posted to Wahn in May 1953. The four specially modified No.II Squadron aircraft were given to No.79 in exchange for four unmodified ones. In March 1953 an escape and evasion exercise, Exercise Pluto Pantomime, was held. Only half of the pilots successfully evaded capture.

In addition to the camera trials the Squadron also carried out Winterisation trials on four aircraft. They were permanently parked outside for about four months, for all servicing including Minor Inspections. RAF Wahn was also Koln/Bonn Airport. Therefore the air traffic was very mixed. There were three resident squadrons: No.II, 68 and 87. In addition there was No.83 Group Communication Flight with a couple of Ansons, the French High Commissioner's Flying Fortress, the daily Sabena Dakota en route to and from Berlin and the daily BEA Ambassador to and from London. Visitors included Field Marshal Montgomery, Anthony Eden, the Canadian Prime Minister Saint Laurent, John Foster Dulles and of course Dr. Adenauer the German Chancellor. Least appreciated of all was the French B-17. The aircraft had been presented to the French High Commissioner by General Eisenhower and although totally unsuitable for its present job, the High Commissioner did not want to give it up. Until the Squadron arrived it had been kept in what was to become the Squadron's hangar. The French wanted the Fortress to stay there but when Chiefy Wilcox, the Flight Sergeant, saw it being prepared for flight by French ground crew smoking cigarettes in the aircraft in the hangar, he said 'That's enough, get it outside'. A second problem occurred when it was airborne, as the pilot only spoke French. Messages from Air Traffic Control went to the navigator who translated them for the pilot. Some of the Squadron pilots had the opportunity to experience what flying a World War Two bomber was like. Reggie Lown, who had earned a DFC while flying bombers, was allowed to fly the Fortress. He flew over Cologne pointing out various car parks that he reckoned he and his chums were probably responsible for. Then, to the consternation of all on board, he proceeded to demonstrate his corkscrew evasive manoeuvre. No-one was really pleased . . .

After that it was back to cine sorties again in preparation for a visit to Sylt from 20 April to 15 May. Although the weather was good firing was poor, the Squadron average dropped to 4.1%. Back at Gütersloh the Squadron was involved in two minor exercises and then in rehearsals for

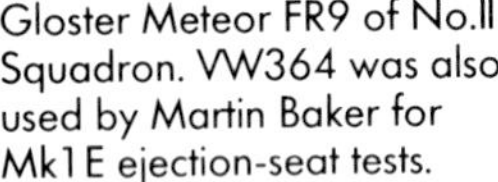

Gloster Meteor FR9 of No.II Squadron. VW364 was also used by Martin Baker for Mk1E ejection-seat tests.

the Coronation Flypast. For the Flypast the Meteor element, led by S/L Chinnery, OC No.79 Squadron, and consisting of twenty Meteor 9s and four Meteor 10s from Gutersloh and twenty-four Meteor 11s from Wahn, all operated from Wahn, joining up with the Vampire and Venom elements which operated from Wildenrath before the final run over Dusseldlorf. The rear of the procession was made up by Belgian Thunderjets.

In April 1953 Bob Pugh left the Squadron and was replaced by Bob Weighill on 29 May. The new CO had served with the Squadron before. He had flown Spitfires and Mustangs between May 1943 and September 1944. The main event during June of course was the Coronation Flypast over Bonn on 2 June. Every flight in BAFO produced four aircraft and in spite of rendezvous problems in the dress rehearsal, all went well. The Station Commander who had taken part in a 79 Squadron Meteor bought all the champagne for the celebrations in the crewrooms afterwards. The Coronation Ball at RAF Wahn where the Squadron moved at the end of June was, of course, a memorable event and incredibly lavish to those of the pilots who were only used to wartime and post-war England. Even this was marred for some by a tragedy when the Commanding Officer of one of the stations was killed in a Vampire on his final approach to Wahn, whilst his wife was on her way to the ball by car.

Immediately after the Coronation Flypast the Squadron participated in a static display of aircraft at the RAF Review at Odiham on 19 July. The 2ATAF detachment consisted of four Meteor 9s (No.II (AC) Squadron), four Sabres (No.71 Squadron) and four Venoms (No.266 Squadron). S/L Weighill commanded the whole detachment, the other No.II Squadron pilots being F/L Winterford, F/O West and F/O Moxam. Whilst the Odiham detachment were polishing their aircraft and lining them up for the great day, the rest of the Squadron was busy settling in at Wahn where they had arrived on 1 July 1953. They were to provide No.83 Group with its own recce squadron. The idea was that the No.83 Group Recce Wing should be an Anglo-Belgian affair, in keeping with the integrated nature of the Group. With this idea in mind four Belgian pilots, their F-84s and ground crew under the command of Capitaine J. Hubert arrived in August. They were to learn about recce and flying from the Squadron before forming the nucleus of a Belgian recce squadron. The Belgians, who formed C-Flight, No.II (AC) Squadron, came with the Squadron to Geilenkirchen for Exercise Coronet from 21 to 31 July and carried out the longer range sorties. Unfortunately the Belgian jets were not equipped with cameras and they had to carry out all their sorties visually. There were some problems as the Squadron Meteors could easily out-manoeuvre the Belgian F-84F Thunderjets if the Meteors were not careful. At the same time the Belgians could run the Meteors out of fuel if the Thunderjets were leading. With the move to Wahn, the air to ground range at Nordhorn became too far away and instead the range at Monschau on the Belgian-German border was used. The first sorties on 10 August produced fairly low scores, partly due to the difficulty of the targets, but as the pilots got used to the range the scores began to improve. Unfortunately the Squadron lost two pilots that month. On 31 August 1953 Arnold Smith and Ian Hinde were killed while flying together in a Meteor T7 at very low level when they hit a high-tension cable stretchd across the Rhine near Koblenz. Daily routine continued, however, with the autumn Exercise called 'Monte Carlo' which took place from 10 to 13 September. The Squadron was overjoyed to be able to operate from the comfort of its own hangar at Wahn.

F/O Fred Trowern.

Squadron Mk9s with camouflage and Squadron markings (May 1953).

As mentioned previously, only a few Squadron pilots were married and living in married quarters. Fred Trowern married in October 1953. With no quarters available for him and his wife it looked as if the marriage would begin with a long separation. It was then that Don Winterford and his wife came to Trowern's help. Winterford lived in a comfortable house at Troisdorf, some 7 miles south of Wahn. He invited the Trowerns to stay at his house, at least for Christmas. In those days pilots were not really expected to marry until they were twenty-five years old. Trowern being twenty-one and his wife one year younger realised that hiring a house or any accommodation was out of the question. To cut a long story short, they were invited to live with the Winterfords until the end of Trowern's tour with the Squadron. However, every month the young wife had to ask for official permission from the CO and the Control Commission to stay in the British Zone for another month.

Much was possible in the RAF of the fifties. However, not everything was appreciated by top brass. After a particularly fine party in the Mess, Don Winterford, Geoff Marlow and Fred Trowern decided that it would be a good idea if all the staff officers at 83 Group Headquarters had to eat their breakfast next morning with their fingers. So they got into the Mess and 'borrowed' all the cutlery. There was an awful lot and, plus the other odd items, it completely filled two large damasc table cloths. The lighter of the two they managed to sit on the chimney of a rather tall building by climbing onto the roof via an attic window. The second bundle was much too heavy so the three thought it should be hoisted up the AOC's flag pole. Unfortunately it was also too heavy to be hoisted aloft by manpower. The rope was therefore attached to the Squadron Landrover which drove off with quite disastrous consequences. The next day the three culprits were given particularly passionate, and one-sided interviews by the Squadron Commander, the Station Commander and eventually by the AOC himself. The rest of the Station was delighted by the whole prank, especially as the Duty Officer and Orderly Officer roster was taken care of by the three Musketeers for a considerable number of weeks.

The Officer Commanding, Bob Weighill, was a disciplinarian but a fine officer and a dedicated sportsman, having captained the RAF and England at rugby. Hence the Squadron fielded rugby, football and cricket teams at all levels. Weighill was very keen on aircrew vs groundcrew matches which certainly cemented morale. Furthermore he hated seeing pilots in crew rooms on bad weather days, so at the drop of a hat it was off to the squash courts, skeet shooting or, if the Boss was in a foul mood, a cross-country run, led by him of course, so there was no room for discussion. He also encouraged all pilots to participate in pistol shooting at Bisley, coached by Corporal Creasey, a shot of national standard. All in all the Squadron was a happy and cheerful unit.

On 8 April 1954 F/O Charlie Scarratt was killed. Rumour had it that he was killed while flying at five or six feet at 360 knots. Another version said that he was ploughing a furrow across a cornfield with his ventral tank when he struck a pile of potatoes or sugar beets left by a

No.II Squadron APC, Sylt April-May 1953.
Standing left to right: F/O Brian Meadley, P/O Arnold Smith, Sgt Paddy Blackwell-Smyth, Sgt Dusty Rhodes, Sgt Jimmy Tate, F/O Roy Moxam, F/S Joe Talbot, Sgt Bert Tickner, P/O Mac Mackervoy, P/O Fred Trowern and P/O Jack Colston.
Seated left to right: F/O Martin Newman, F/O Ian Hinde, F/L Don Winterford, F/L Mike Townsend, S/L Bob Pugh (CO), F/L Pete Young, F/L Ron Turnbull, F/O John West and F/O Mike Mollan.
Sleeping in front is Brutus, the Squadron Mascot.

telephone pole which knocked a wing off and caused the aircraft to plunge into a group of trees. In his recollections Fred Trowern remembered having seen the swathe several hundred yards long showing how Scarratt desperately tried to pick the aircraft up before he finally crashed. The Squadron's method of recovering mentally from such incidents was simple. The pilots would return to the Mess at Wahn by coach in their best blues and black armbands, drink Carlsberg in the rotunda until the crates reached the ceiling and then go home. That was known as 'The Wake'. The next day they continued as if nothing had happened.

Exercise Battle Royal was something different. It was the main exercise for 1954 and the Squadron operated from Gutersloh. 'C' Flight — the Belgian Thunderjets under Joe Hubert & Co — came with the Squadron, their F-84Fs still without cameras. It was a major Public Relations exercise and the press descended en masse. There was a good write-up in *Flight* and there was an excellent 'co-operation' photograph: Joe Hubert leading in his F-84F, Jock Young from No.541 Squadron in a Meteor 10 as No.2 and Peter Young of No.II Squadron in a Mk 9 as No.3. *Flight* Magazine wrote two large articles on 1 and 8 October about 'Battle Royal', 'A Combined Exercise with an Atomic Accent'. The Squadron received a lot of attention from the press:

> 'S/L Weighill, Officer Commanding No.II Squadron (Meteor FR9s), told us that, as soon as one of his aircraft landed, the film magazine was whipped out and dried prints made available within 30 minutes. Generally these were used to confirm a pilot's verbal report, though photography was sometimes the primary object of a sortie.
>
> One of the squadron's Meteors had, in fact, photographed the 'clutch' of vehicles where we ourselves were talking and the CO showed us on the print that the camouflage and cover was well-nigh perfect, though faces were gazing up at the aircraft and giving the show away, as, we were assured, they often do under field conditions.
>
> S/L Weighill reminded us that the Meteor 9 carries no vertical — only oblique — cameras, and declared himself in favour of single aircraft instead of the pairs which had hitherto been normal in the Tac/R business. As a one-time pilot of Army Co-op Mustangs he recalled that, with Me109 opposition, doubling up was definitely a good thing, with the second man watching the tail of the first: but at present-day speeds an enemy pilot would be lucky even to spot a FR9 at low level, and to make a pass could be a chancy undertaking.
>
> Operating as one flight of No.II Squadron was a detachment of Belgian F-84Gs, commanded by Captain Hubert; but as good as these are, one gathered that they do not equal the Meteor's reputation in the Tac/R role.

John Colston took Brian Johnston of the BBC on a simulated Tac/R sortie. Remembering the sortie John wrote in 1990:

> 'Brian arrived mustard keen to see what we were up to during the big summer exercise. Reggie Lown, the "A" Flight Commander had carelessly left his flying suit lying around whilst he went off to have lunch. Brian was quickly dressed in this — the only one available — and we took off. As one can imagine after a few tight turns at low level even the indomitable Brian Johnston was sick. Reggie was an eloquent man and after returning from lunch his eloquence reached new heights. Fortunately I was in B Flight . . .'

In his broadcast that evening Brian had the courage to admit that he had been very ill. Brian Meadley took the correspondent of the *Manchester* Guardian for a trip while Peter Young flew with an elderly MP. Young had been instructed by the Boss to fly Very, Very gently . . . On 28 September 1954 the *Manchester Guardian* reporter wrote:

> '. . .First they make you sign a certificate freeing them from any responsibility for anything, known as the 'blood chit', then they incarcerate you in a parachute harness and an oxygen mask and tell you what to do if the pilot passes out . . .'

He finished an admiring article with:

> 'We landed gently, the pilot ready for his lunch, and I, pale but unashamed, for something quite stiff'.

With the autumn exercise out of the way, an ever increasing amount of the Squadron's energies was directed towards the ceremonies attendant upon the presentation of the Standard, the first to be presented to a squadron in 2ATAF and one of the first, if not the first, to any squadron in the Royal Air Force. The Battle Honours, WESTERN FRONT 1914-1918, NEUVE CHAPELLE, YPRES 1915, SOMME 1916, FRANCE AND LOW COUNTRIES 1939-1940, DUNKIRK, NORMANDY 1944 AND ARNHEM 1944, had been chosen by Air Vice-Marshal Sir Thomas I. Webb-Bowen (CO in 1915) and S/L Pugh over a year previously, and now the preparations for the parade began.

The Standard party consisted of the following Squadron members:

Standard Bearer: F/O S.J. West

Standard Escort: Sgts. G.W. Knaggs and H.A. Tickner

Standard Warrant Officer: Sgt. R.J. Rhodes

The Standard Party spent two to three weeks training at RAF Uxbridge with the RAF Drill Unit. On 31 October the big ceremony took place at the Squadron's new base Geilenkirchen. The

No.II Squadron APC, Sylt, Nov-Dec 1953. Back row, left to right: P/O Dick Fisher, Sgt Paddy Blackwell-Smyth, Sgt Bert Tickner, F/Os Mac Mackervoy, Geoff Marlow, Ken Bailey, John Milner, Tony Winship, Wee Macgregor. Standing, left to right: F/O Dave King, F/O Jack Colston, F/L Don Winterford, F/L Reggie Lown, S/L Bob Weighill (CO), F/L Pete Young, F/O Fred Trowern, F/O Brian Meadley, F/O Malcolm Woodhams, F/O Martin Newman. Kneeling, left to right: F/Os Charley Scott, Roy Moxam, John West, Dave Fielder.

Standard was blessed by the Reverend E.W.L. May and presented by ACM Sir Robert Foster KCB, CBE, DFC, the CiC2ATAF, in the presence of a large and distinguished gathering. A feature of the parade was that the Squadron song of those days — Green grow the rushes oh — had been set to music as a march by the Director of No.3 Regional Band F/O Davies. The Squadron did the quick march past to the tune. It was one of the many highlights of the history of 'Shiny Two'. It is very sad indeed that 1954 ended with the death of another Squadron pilot. On 3 December P/O Dave Vickers was carrying out cine quarter attacks below cloud with Mike Webb. Both were in Mk9s. The drill was that when a pilot had taken cine film in a curve of pursuit he straightened up and broke down under the leader, then pulled up and respositioned on the other side ready for the next quarter attack. Unfortunately — probably due to inexperience — young Vickers broke above his leader, entered cloud, became disorientated and crashed.

Rivalry between squadrons was a major issue in those days. Very few squadrons, however, had a greater rivalry between them as Nos.II and 3. Both claimed to be the senior heavier-than-air squadrons and No.3 Squadron tried to make a point by having the motto 'Tertius primus Erit'. No.3 Squadron's move to Geilenkirchen gave 'Shiny Two' an excellent opportunity to teach them a lesson. For tactical reasons the master move was made while No.3 was detached to Sylt for an APC. When they returned they found that on every available chalk board and perspex surface in hangars and operations room was written 'Tertius SECUNDUS Erit'.

CHAPTER 12
SWIFT AND HUNTER

Whilst based at Geilenkirchen No.II Squadron, now commanded by S/L Mortley, gained another 'first' when it re-equipped with the first RAF jet aircraft to be fitted with an afterburner, the Vickers Supermarine Swift RF5. In preparation for the changeover from Meteor to Swift, a Vickers Supermarine test pilot, Lieutenant Commander Steele was attached to the Squadron. In February 1956, the Squadron received the replacement for the faithful Meteor with the arrival of the first Vickers Supermarine Swift at RAF Geilenkirchen. It would be too much to suggest that the Swift was a great success while serving in the Squadron though certain members seem to disagree with this statement. The first prototype of the aircraft had flown in 1951. The Swift was to be introduced as rapidly as possible, as the Air Ministry wanted an alternative aircraft in service in case the development of the Hawker Hunter was a failure. Initially the Swift was to be an interceptor, but the only Squadron using this aircraft as such was No.56. The Swift did some remarkable things. In July 1953 a Swift F4 flew from London to Paris in less than twenty minutes at a speed of nearly 700 mph. In September the same year another Swift raised the world speed record to 737.7 mph. However it soon became obvious that the Swift was unsuitable in the fighter/interceptor role and it was decided to use it as a replacement for the Meteor FR9 in the tactical reconnaissance role. The aircraft differed from the earlier Marks in that it had a lengthened nose to accommodate three cameras. One was mounted in the extreme nose cone while the other two were placed ahead of the jet intakes to make room for the oblique cameras. The first production Swift FR5 flew on 25 May 1955. Compared to earlier types the wings were different, giving it a 'saw-tooth' leading edge. Other new features included power-operated ailerons, a clear-view canopy and a 220 gallon ventral drop-tank increasing its radius of action. Its power plant was a 7,175 pound thrust Rolls-Royce Avon 114 turbojet which gave 9,450 lb. of thrust when using re-heat. The maximum speed at sea level was 685 mph and it had a range of 480 miles. It was armed with two 30mm Aden guns and was able to carry bombs and rockets underneath the wings. The Swift was not to become a very popular aircraft but in spite of this the Squadron successfully flew it in its demanding role. Swift FR5s provided both the winner and runner-up in the 1957 reconnaissance competitions held by NATO and gained first place again in the 1959 events. Besides No.II (AC) Squadron the FR5 was only used by No.79 Squadron at Gutersloh. The Swifts had standard camouflage with silver undersides and had white serials and codes.

The departure of the Meteor was to be remembered by flying a last and immaculate '2' formation over the airfield. It was considered an easy job as it had been done many times. However, the Gremlins decided to involve themselves. Flight Lieutenant A.C. East remembered what happened:

> 'As the Squadron approached the airfield and tightened the formation, the middle two of the back four hit the jet-wash of the aircraft in front. Their wings overlapped until No.2's wing tip hit No.3's engine nacelle, turning off his main fuel cock and jamming No.2's aileron The result was that both quickly fell away from the formation so that just as it came overhead, much to the amusement of members of other squadrons watching on the ground, their proud figure became a question mark! The two damaged aircraft landed safely, but the atmosphere in the Mess bars that evening was not quite what No.II Squadron had had in mind.'

The first Swift incident on No.II (AC) Squadron happened on 30 January 1957. F/O Whittam was airborne at 23,000 feet when there was suddenly a loud explosion and the engine flamed out. The reheat doll's eye had gone white indicating that the eyelids had opened. Homing to overhead two relights were attempted and even a third attempt was made, all to no avail. The aircraft now entered cloud and Whittam concentrated on his flame out circuit. He broke cloud at 2,500 feet having just passed over Geilenkirchen and travelling away from it. He decided to land downwind. To do so he turned starboard but in trying to keep his speed up he lost a lot of height. Whittam ended up thirty degrees off the runway and about 2-3 miles out. As he was low over a village he made the decision not to jettison his canopy or the ventral tank. Flying at 170-180 knots he realised he was going to land short. On the controller's advice, he decided to land on the perimeter track, which had been hidden by trees until then. He selected undercarriage down but the gear failed to lower. He then tried the emergency undercarriage but found it very difficult to select as the button was very stiff. The

On 23 February 1956 Squadron Leader Hunter arrived in the first Swift FR5 allotted to the Squadron at RAF Geilenkirchen.

wheels were locked down on the second attempt just as the Swift stalled on. No flaps were used and no further damage was caused to the aircraft. The pilot was awarded a green endorsement.

On 20 May 1957 F/L Lou Cockerill joined the Squadron from No.79. Little did he know that the following day would be such an exciting one. On an area familiarisation trip he passed close to Wildenrath airfield at about 2,000 feet. A minute later the engine died on him. While converting his odd 350 knots into a little more height, a relight attempt proved unsuccessful. He therefore turned back to Wildenrath. He put out a quick mayday on his own approach channel, which was acknowledged, but as time, height and speed were all running out, he could do little else but make a forced landing on the very end of a fortunately clear runway, with neither flaps nor undercarriage down. The aircraft came to rest on the grass, after a rather rough ride with only category 3 damage. Cockerill made a very neat job of a very nasty situation, which called for both rapid action and fine judgement. He too was awarded a green endorsement.

While Cockerill made his belly landing the rest of the Squadron participated in 'Royal Flush II'. Other participants included Dutch and Belgian Thunderflashes and RAF PR Canberras. It was a recce competition between 4ATAF (Americans and French) and 2ATAF (Britons, Belgians and Dutch). The exercise was divided into a low level and a high level competition. In the high level competition RAF Camberras competed against RB57s, which were Martin-built American Canberras. The low level competition was between Swifts and RF84Fs. Each squadron sent its best two pilots to compete in the exercise. One was to fly while the other was a reserve. Marks were awarded for shortest time from briefing to the end of the debrief, visual reports and photo pinpoint target. The Swifts were by far the fastest round the route. F/L Lawrence of No.79 Squadron came first and F/L Winship of No.II (AC) Squadron second.

On 8 July another flame out occurred but we do not know who was flying XD912 that day. The story read that the pilot was at 3,000 feet doing 360 knots a few miles from Geilenkirchen. The aircraft fuel gauges showed that the fuel tanks contained 500 pounds of fuel and all the tank doll's eyes were black, however, the low pressure fuel warning was now white. The fuel balance doll's eyes had indicated tail heavy for several minutes and the pilot had set the switch down to cure the imbalance. The aircraft was now about two miles form the airfield at a height of 2,500 feet and about 270 knots so the pilot decided to do a straight in flame out landing which was skilfully executed. The Swift flame out landing speed was very high and in this case the aircraft touched down at approximately 200 knots. It bounced a little and when properly down the pilot applied about 800 pounds of brake which was held on until the aircraft had slowed down sufficiently to be turned off onto the ORP. The runway was 2,700 yards long but even so it did show that good servicing of the maxaret unit and intelligent use of the brakes could save an aircraft from piling up in the overshoot area.

This incident brought to light a disturbing fact: if a Swift transfer pump failed there was no indication to the pilot as the doll's eye worked off the inner tank unit. This could mean that if both transfer pumps failed at once, the pilot would be denied the use of over 1,000 pounds of fuel with no indication other than out of balance trim which would only be noticed three or four minutes before flame out. As an immediate measure all pilots were instructed to return with a minimum of 800 pounds indicated as it was expected to be unlikely that both transfer pumps would fail at once. Nevertheless urgent modifications were ordered.

In August 1957 part of the Squadron was sent to Tangmere to participate in Exercise Fair Lady. In the same month other aircraft of No.II went to Norway and Denmark. Then, of course, there was the annual trip to Sylt. Under command of F/O Hugill the Squadron road party set off for the long drive to the north. Sylt was still very popular, former members all know why . . .

In October that year the Squadron said farewell to Geilenkirchen and was moved to RAF Jever, 200 miles north. Once settled there Wing Commander Mortley handed over command to S/L Wade. The Squadron was to spend almost four years flying the Swift from this base. On 16 April 1958 F/L Kelly took a beautiful photograph of a Russian Tupolev TU104 which is proudly displayed in the Squadron photo album.

On Sunday 4 May 1958, the forty-sixth Anniversary of the Squadron was celebrated, with a Drumhead Service and Parade at RAF Jever. On this occasion the salute was taken by Air Vice Marshal W.A. 'Bill' Opie, who had been OC No.II (AC) Squadron in 1938-39. Hereward, the St Bernhard mascot, marched with the party. Only a few weeks earlier he had gone AWOL and was not returned until after his being 'Missing in Action' had been reported in the local press: 'BERNHARDINER-HUND ENTLAUFEN WIEDERBRINGER ENTHAELT BELOHNUNG F/S KELLY, OFFICERS MESS RAF JEVER'.

On 22 May F/O Dick Lavender, the youngest Squadron pilot, ran into trouble while flying Swift XD929. One minute after take-off Lavender was informed by his No.1 that a small amount of fuel seemed to be venting from the aircraft. The air-to-air firing they were due to practise was cancelled due to GCI being unavailable, so fuel was burnt off for a landing. To assist this, reheat and airbrakes were to be used but on selection of airbrakes only twenty degrees was obtainable and the hydraulic audio warner sounded. A check of the hydraulic accumulater gauges showed 2,150 pounds and so the pilot cancelled reheat, throttled back, checked his trims and selected manual at the same time informing his leader of his predicament. With 2,800 pounds of fuel remaining, Lavender selected undercarriage down on the emergency system, successfully getting three greens and with the two hydraulic accumulator gauges now reading 1,000 pounds. Two minutes later they showed 200 pounds apiece so he immediately selected full flap on the emergency system. However, no more than 20 degrees of flap was obtained. While all this was happening, stratus had unexpectedly formed over Sylt from the sea, and the cloud base had dropped rapidly from 700 to 300 feet. Consequently his leader advised him to do a GCA. Contact was established with GCA after homing to overhead and normal approach pattern set-up. At nine miles finals on a step-down approach, contact was lost and Lavender returned to approach frequency where, after some delay he was given instructions via approach control. He broke cloud at 200 feet and saw the airfield at half a mile.

A quick S-turn to starboard to line up and Dick was down with 300 pounds of fuel remaining. To assist breaking he flamed out the engine on touch down. Lavender also got a Green Endorsement in his logbook. The cause of all this trouble had been a chafed pipe in the starboard wheel-well caused by a rotating wheel. The maintenance schedule was amended and now included a check of the wheel-well pipes, and all pilots were instructed to ensure that their wheels were stationary on retraction.

Not all pilots disliked the Swift. Philip Holden-Rushworth found the FR5 a pleasure to fly. At low level it was very stable and fairly manoeuvrable. At high level it was not very good being under-powered in non-reheat flight and its manoeuvrability being poor. However, only the Squadron test pilot flew the aircraft above 10,000 feet except for transit flights. Holden-Rushworth noted that the original Swift had been converted to the low reconaissance role which involved adding:

> 'a ventral tank, saw-tooth leading edges, a strake above the fuselage to improve directional stability, a reheated engine and three F95 cameras in the nose.'

Holden-Rushworth adds:

> 'I believe that one of the prerequisites for a pilot being posted to fly the Swift FR5 in the recce role was that he should have had at least two previous fast jet fighter courses. I cannot be absolutely certain about this caveat on postings but certainly everyone else on the Squadron when I arrived (with 2,200 total flying hours at the time) was at least as experienced as I was on fast jets. Having previously been an NCO pilot and QFI I was posted to No.II Squadron as a Pilot Officer six months after commissioning. The boss at the time, Chris Wade, when he received my posting notice was reputed to have assumed that I was a first tourist and to have said to his pilots that "this youngster will sort out all you old fogies . . ."
>
> The main problem with the FR5 in the low level recce role was range. From Jever we could just manage to make the Harz mountains and back at low level. If we wanted to operate any further south, i.e., in 4 ATAF, we were forced into a high-low-high flight profile. Yet I shall always be proud of my tour with the Squadron on Swifts. Even today people who know aircraft look at one with respect when they learn

that one once flew Swifts, but this was only because of their early bad reputation as a day fighter. The Swift we flew was, in my opinion, a stable old lady at low level, and I much preferred my Swift tour on No.II Squadron as a Pilot Officer to my later tour on Jaguars as a Squadron Leader. That Jaguar recce pod on the centreline station was . . .

But that is another story!'

In August 1958 'Royal Flush' took place. The prize was the Gruenther Trophy. The Battle for this trophy was hard and the umpires were ever vigilant to ensure the fairest of play. The Squadron competitiors were F/Ls Green and Bergh but the strangest accident ever to happen to a Squadron pilot was F/L Rimmington's. On 27 August 1959 he had to abandon his Swift near the town of Minden and his parachute harness was accidentally released at the wrong moment. Fortunately he was held by one leg when the strap tightened. Unfortunately he was falling head first. Again luckily for him, he came down in the middle of the River Weser. He attributed his good luck to the fact that it all happened on his birthday.

During the year many more problems occurred with the Swifts. F/L Ibbett's aircraft made a belly-landing when the undercarriage refused to come down. F/L Rimmington's plane came to grief after bursting a tyre on landing at Gutersloh during Exercise 'Topweight'. F/L Martin belly-landed 'D' after he burst a tyre while landing. F/L St Aubyn had to eject over the North Sea and landed in the water off the Sylt coast. During the major air shows in Germany in the summer of 1960 all Swift displays were flown by Rimmington, who was considered an authority on Swift matters after his adventurous experiences with the aircraft. The final Swift was delivered to the Squadron in August 1960. On 16 September 1960 S/L MacDonald took command of No.II (AC) Squadron from S/L Wade. The Swift became increasingly difficult to maintain, and finally left Squadron service in April 1961 to be replaced by one of the best aircraft of those days, the Hawker Hunter. The last Swift was unceremoniously broken up by airmen swinging axes at it with sardonic pleasure. However troublesome the time with the Swift had been for the Squadron, only one pilot lost his life flying it, F/L Greenhaugh on 22 August 1957. Nevertheless it cannot be denied that more than one pilot was quite pleased to see ground crew breaking up the last Swift.

The Squadron had carried out evaluation flights of the Hawker Hunter as early as 1956. Though the aircraft did not enter Squadron service until January 1961, when five Hunter Mark 6 jets arrived as a stepping stone to the FR10 which arrived in February 1961 while the Swifts were still flying. The Hawker Hunter FR10 was a beautiful aircraft carrying three cameras in the nose, it had a Rolls-Royce Avon 207 power plant providing 10,150 pounds of thrust. It could fly at Mach 0.95 at 36,000 feet and over 700 mph at sea level. If necessary it could climb up to 51,500 feet. Armed with four Aden 30mm guns

The Squadron's relationship with the Swift was not altogether a happy one. Often the aircraft caused problems. The landing gear had a mind of its own as can been seen on the photographs showing 'X' and 'U' in an unworthy position.

and a wide variety of underwing loads including 1,000 bombs, 2-inch rockets or a 100 gallon napalm bomb, it was an adversary to be reckoned with. Though at first camouflaged similar to the Swift the Hunter later received light grey undersides while the aircraft's fin letter was placed in a white triangle.

On the occasion of the Squadron's fifty-year association with Rolls-Royce it was visited by Lord Hives, whose son David 'Benjy' was a Squadron pilot. While his father presented the Squadron with a silver cigar box, Benjy roared over at almost nought feet taking a few quick pictures of Daddy, who of course was delighted to have a look at the photographs a few minutes after his son had landed. The Hunter had an amazing effect on squadron morale, in July 1961, No.II (AC) Squadron was involved in its first Tactical Evaluation (TACEVAL), and easily proved its ability to meet SACEUR's requirements. July was also the last opportunity for the Squadron to complete the Sylt-APC. It was the end of an era in many respects. Then, in September 1961 the Squadron moved back to Gutersloh.

In February 1962 S/L Thornton assumed command vice S/L MacDonald. Five months later the Squadron celebrated its fiftieth Anniversary — the first RAF Squadron to reach its half-century. After the Station Commander had welcomed the Burgermeister of Gutersloh, the Germans presented the Squadron with a wooden plaque bearing the coat of arms of the town. The Rt. Hon. J.P. Taylor, CBE, DL, JP, MP, Parliamentary Under Secretary of State for Air arrived with Air Marshal Sir John Grandy, CiC RAFG. While the Under Secretary took the salute a Bristol Fighter especially flown out for the occasion by Air Commodore Wheeler, an old boy of the Squadron roared overhead. Then Hunters taxied out, to fly an impressive twelve-ship '2' formation — the fact that No.4 Squadron aircraft were used in the formation is hardly worth a mention. At the Guest Night everyone turned out in mess kit and dinner jackets. Prominent guests were Air Commodore 'Daddy' Probyn, who commanded the Squadron in 1928-29, and Air Cdre Wheeler. The *Gutersloher Morgenblatt* wrote a long article about the event. One could have believed that No.II (AC) Squadron was part of the Luftwaffe.

> 'The engines of the fighters are roaring, and one after the other rolls to the start-place. And then a precise programme begins, which is seldom seen nowadays. In deep flight aircraft thunder across the airfield from the left and before anybody can turn they return from the other side. F/L Brooks flies stunts with a fighter, rolls, loops, and a manoeuvre taking the aircraft straight into heaven, then turns around and disappears into the atmosphere.'

In March 1961 the last Swift was flown out by Peter Adair. Happy faces seem to show the delight of its departure. Left to right: Danny Brooks, Pete Adair, Bob Barcilan, Dennis Fahey, Philip Holden-Rushworth and Ben Gun. In front is S/L MacDonald.

Later in the year many more important guests visited the Squadron. In September the Marshal of the RAF Sir John Slessor arrived, followed by Lieutenant General Allard of the Canadian 4th Division. In October a Hunter T7 landed with Colonel Stone on board, who had been in the Squadron long before the Second World War.

Then the Norwegians arrived with their F-86 Sabre fighters. In October 1962, the Squadron detached to RAF Chivenor for its first APC there. There was an exchange with the Americans at Laon in March 1963 which was the result of a new inter-NATO exchange scheme, started during that year. Laon was the base of the 18th Tactical Reconnaissance Squadron. The Americans and their F-101 Voodoos visited Gutersloh in July. The Labour Minister of Defence, Peter Thorneycroft also visited the Squadron and was photographed watching a briefing.

In October 1963, during Exercise 'Triplex West' four Hunters of the Squadron flew as far south as El Adem in the Libyan Desert. The men lived in tents and flew sorties with No.23 Squadron which was equipped with Gloster Javelins and with No.54 Squadron, who flew Hunter FGAs. El Adem was an enormous airfield in the middle of the bare desert. Little seemed to have changed since the time when the Allies fought the Italians and the Afrika Korps in that area, given that much of the wartime debris and many of the wrecks still littered the aerodrome's immediate vicinity. It was the first time since the Shanghai detachment of 1927 that the Squadron had left Europe. S/L Sam Toyne has particular memories of this exercise:

> 'We flew from dawn to dusk hunting for camouflaged enemy tank concentrations. Since we soon discovered that tanks when camouflaged looked like large peas we went hunting for peas. At the beginning of each

Hawker Hunter FR10 over Southern Germany on 1 October 1962. The pilot is Flight Lieutenant Coulcher.

day the fruits of our labours were studied by the joint commanders. The senior army commander steadfastly refused to acknowledge that any of our pictures had been taken during the exercise until the last day when he noticed a soldier having a wee against his tank (we did fly rather low). Enraged, since this equated to urinating upon your horse, he demanded the culprit be found and punished.

We frequently flew down to El Adem on a continuing reinforcement exercise call "Southern Ranger" and invariably delivered large quantities of milk in cartons which was in short supply. On one occasion I filled all the bulges on the lower fuselage beneath the cockpit which were normally used for empty rounds. In fact all four Hunters had a large amount of cartons stored there. At Luqa, where we refuelled, our boss, David Thornton made a particularly heavy landing. When he climbed out of the cockpit he saw the ground crew gazing at an ever expanding pond of milk underneath the Hunter caused by virtually all cartons bursting upon impact with the concrete runway. David was not at all amused . . .

I had a splended three years in the Squadron, the best flying of my 4,000-hour fast jet career'.

The detachment returned in November to continue training for 'Royal Flush' in which the Squadron did not participate due to a lack of experienced pilots.

One of the saddest developments in post-war RAF history was the near demise of the RAF Volunteer Reserve. In the years leading up to the war the RAFVR flourished and provided a healthy source of trained pilots and other aircrew, whose services were to prove invaluable in the conflict with the Axis powers. In the same way, although on a larger scale, that the Territorial Army supported the regular Army. After the war, flying with the RAFVR continued and it came to an end in 1954. Those who had continued to fly were offered ground appointments in the RAFVR and these were chiefly in Photo Interpretation. And so was formed a flight of RAFVR officers which came to be known as 7010 Reserve Flight. Not all its members were ex-aircrew, some had performed Photo Interpretation during the war and others were recruited from other ground duties. However, the fact was that a large number of people were assembled, ranging from civil servants to civil engineers, from university lecturers to school masters, and a scheme for training them as Photo Interpreters had to be evolved. Evolution is probably the right word because at their first base, RAF Culham, accommodation, equipment and training were sparse and extremely basic. However, within two years they had moved to Nuneham Park, Oxford, where their facilities were much improved and which, incidentally, had been used during the war for initial PI training courses. Instruction here began to assume a more coherent pattern. More subjects, each with its own specialist lecturer, were added as time went by covering all fields of intelligence from the three Services — Army, Navy and Air Force — including a permanent lecturer from the US forces in later years.

It has to be remembered that the RAFVR minimum training requirement was fifteen days, plus two weekends each year. While a great keenness and interest was manifest both on the part of the pupils and the instructors there was, nevertheless, always a pervading feeling of uncertainty regarding the future and whether they would survive as a flight within the RAFVR. This uncertainty was not diminished when they found themselves moved around from station to station to find an established home. The flight came uder the direct control of JSPI (Joint School of Photo Interpretation) which itself was controlled by JARIC (Joint Air Reconnaissance Intelligence Centre).

All this time the prevailing political policy was directed towards cuts, particularly in the armed forces and, hence, a solitary RAFVR flight comprising some 150 members was particularly vulnerable. Not surprisingly therefore, they suffered severe cut backs when, following a comprehensive examination which seemed to extend beyond a mere test of ability to cope with PI complexities, their number was cut to 57, and has been further reduced since. From this point in time, although the uncertainty regarding the PI's future persisted the flight settled down to a routine of fifteen days annual training plus a quota of weekends. As already mentioned membership comprised a very representative cross-section of civilian occupations which, with its background of varied wartime experiences, made for an articulate, intelligent and, as time wore on, highly trained body of Photo Interpreters.

However, it seemed that the PIs were doomed to be held only as a back-up to the regular RAF PIU at JARIC against an emergency and to carry on with normal annual training with JSPI in the United Kingdom. That was until they had the great good fortune to meet Squadron Leader John Wood, Commanding Officer of JSPI, Group Captain Raike, SASO, and Air Commodore Brian Young, OC at CRE (Central Reconnaissance Establishment) in the nerve centre of JARIC. It was this meeting which decided that the RAFVR should be launched upon the unsuspecting operational PR squadrons in Gemany. It has to be remembered that 7010 Reserve Flight was largely unknown in the RAF outside JARIC and the decision to use RAFVR officers in highly competitive NATO PR Exercise Royal Flush caused no little consternation among the Squadrons when it was first announced. This attitude was understandable because the Royal Flush exercise embraced the PR squadrons of all NATO countries and the distinction of being the winning Squadron was indeed prestigious. All personnel became involved, from pilots to armourers, photographers and PIs. Naturally no Squadron wanted to take any weak link on board and hence some resistance was encountered when the decision to use 7010 RF was made. All that needs to be said here is that those members of the PR flight who were picked to blaze the trail, such as Fred Piper, both with the Hunter and Canberra Squadrons, acquitted themselves so well that requests came back that flight personnel should be made available for future exercises. 7010 RF had arrived. It was at this point that the story of 7010 RF began to run parallel with the history of No.II (AC) Squadron which at that time was operating from Gutersloh. The impact of part-timers upon a dedicated and professional Squadron was not without some problems and tensions, yet on the whole, they were very few and quickly ironed out. This was important for both parties because, with the run-up to this major exercise, it was imperative that the whole team should be pulling together and functioning smoothly without any personal clashes. This was not to say that individual eruptions did not take place. There was the time when, in the middle of the exercise, the PIs were visited by a delegation of the top brass, one member of which was the inimitable AVM Gus Walker. In the middle of the exercise the AVM was told to shut up by one 7010 officer who, completely absorbed in his duties, failed to recognise and pay the proper respect to the visitor's high rank. It speaks volumes for the character and understanding of the AVM that he passed this gaff off with an understanding smile.

Fred Piper best sums up the general feeling of all the reservists who at one time or another worked with the Squadron:

> 'It is not easy to describe the overall air of tension which infected the Squadron at the time of the exercise. It did, however, extend from tarmac to kitchen as, inevitably, wives and families were caught up in the fever of the competition. Easier to understand were the many parties which followed the end of the exercise — happy and liberated'.

In November 1964 S/L Nigel Walpole took over command of the Squadron from S/L Thornton. What he remembers most of his 2½ years in command was that the only battle the Squadron got involved in at the time was against the weather.

> 'In that context it might all have been different had my flying arrival from RAF Chivenor, where I had been commanding No.234 Squadron, not come right at the end. It had been one of those trips in a Hunter T7 which went badly wrong when winds and weather turned against us. The first approach to Gutersloh failed and the entire Station was out there to watch the second — and certainly the last chance for a conventional landing. We struggled in — but should have known that there could be no other conclusion with Group Captain David Evans (now ACM Sir David Evans GCB, CBE, RAF Retf) firmly in control of his Station and — I suspected — the elements'.

In 1963 Peter Thornycroft MP, Secretary of State for Defence visited the Squadron. Here he can be seen chatting with F/Ls Webb, Coleman, Rayner and MacDonald.

May 1965 was a very busy month with parades, flypasts, 'Royal Flush' and last but not least a Royal Visit. At the beginning of the month Bob Hillman, Alex Weiss and John McGarvey went on Exercise Blue Diamond to Rygge in Norway and Aalborg, in Denmark. They had, as the Squadron diarist reported 'a tremendous week-end and returned with lots of "nasty" places to visit in the future for the rest of us. I gather John took up ornithology and tried to capture one of the local birds, but was beaten-off by one of the male natives'.

On the sixth of June the Squadron was visited by a team from British Aircraft Corporation as part of a station visit to evaluate the Hunter's weapon and recce abilities with a view to developing some anti-missile procedures. It was a lively discussion but it turned out to be impossible to get all the equipment the pilots wanted in, on or under the Hunters.

The weather was not very good during the month but the rehearsal flypast for the Queen's visit managed to get airborne. The CO S/L Wapole was chosen to lead the mass formation of Hunters, Javelins and Canberras. On the first rehearsal Bill Armstrong, as spare, made up a section of No.4 Squadron and after the flypast found himself in what looked like an aerobatic outfit, alarming but entertaining. The Queen arrived on the twenty-sixth and both the flypast and timing were precise; unfortunately it was Her Majesty who was a shade late. The unique event of No.II Squadron leading the whole Command was ultimately spoiled by the enthusiasm of the Germans in Gutersloh who delayed Her arrival at the airfield until someway through the flypast. Walpole remembers: 'As leader, I am still waiting for the planner to tell me what I should have done when, with six minutes to go and twelve miles of formation behind me, in bad weather, I was told simply that "the Queen is late" (not how late!). However, it was so well done that the Squadron got a new flower-bed out of it.'

In July 1966 the Chief of Defence Staff Sir Richard Hull visited the Squadron. W/C Barrett was his host.

Other than that one occasion, the weather rarely scored against No.II Squadron directly, but they did have a frightening brush with the elements during one of their 'Northern Lights' exercises. There was an unwritten rule that these routine weekends in Norway should be committed to flying or socialising — but not both! In this case the two Squadron worthies chose the former, but only after Stavanger had failed to provide the latter. No need to go through another saga of fjords, weather, cables and electrical power cuts; suffice to say that one of the Hunters staggered back to Sola very much on a wing and a prayer — and a large part of Norway had to go to bed early. Walpole was on the spot within hours, to find two very subdued pilots sporting puffs of cotton wool from their ears — from whence evidence had been drawn to prove that they had not violated the unwritten rule . . .

'Royal Flush' began on 18 June and was to take three days; it was the culmination of a long training programme, and as usual diarist Bill Armstrong recorded the moans and groans about the operational unrealities of the competition. In spite of all other commitments during the month the Squadron managed to do a few training sorties and Royal Flush went reasonably well. The only real excitement was that one of the pilots had an hydraulic leak — which led to a total failure immediately after he landed — and was stuck at the end of the runway. But in the true British and Squadron tradition it did not keep him from bringing in his valuable photographs. He hastily abandoned the aircraft, unloaded the cameras and ran, walked and even hitch-hiked back to the Squadron to complete the mission. It was the true Royal Flush spirit and it made no difference whatsoever if the men were regular Squadron members of temporary reinforcements from the RAFVR. Again Fred Piper explains what was happening:

> 'It is difficult to express in words the miracle which seemed to happen to us each year when we shook off civilian stresses and, within the fortnight allowed, did our best to adjust to the sterner disciplines of the RAF and to justify the privilege of being allowed to serve with an operational Squadron. For most of us, previous RAF service simply meant war years. It was a rather different

RAF we knew then, yet the hand of companionship extended to us by the Squadron had no less warmth than in the war years'.

July 1965 started in style. No.II (AC) Squadron had been invited to Leeuwarden AFB in the Netherlands to help celebrate its anniversary with a dinner in the Officers Mess. As it was a formal occasion Mess dress was to be worn. However, as usual with the Dutch, within the hour everything turned extremely informal. Food was good and wine plentiful and if one could stand talking about F-104 Starfighters all evening it was a delightful event. The next day everyone went back to work. The Squadron Hunters were to fly attacks over the range north of the Waddenzee. Unfortunately S/L Walpole's aircraft had a problem which caused the CO a few difficult moments and gave the local press an excuse for an entire column in the paper. The *Leeuwarder Courant* wrote in capitals: 'BRITON MAKES BELLY-LANDING IN A FOAM PATH'.

'Squadron Leader Walpole of the English Hunter team which is at the moment stationed at Leeuwarden made a successful emergency landing with his aircraft yesterday. The aircraft, whose nosewheel did not come out made a good landing on a 700 meters long and 3 meters wide foam path made on the runway by the station fire brigade. Relief was great when the pilot carried out a successful belly landing. The aircraft however was hardly damaged'.

The remainder of the detachment which finished on 9 July was fairly quiet. The weather was not too kind and the gunnery scores averaged only 22%, similar to those of a year earlier. The Squadron threw a beer call for the Dutch which was a straight swop, whisky for beer. Then they had dinner in Hotel Amicitia which ended with a determined British attack on the monument in the middle of Leeuwarden town square. The statue was duly wrapped in a large sheet properly painted with the Wake knot. After take-off from Leeuwarden the Squadron flew to laarburch while No.4 Squadron came to Leeuwarden. Nigel Walpole has a particular soft spot for Leeuwarden. However, indirectly the weather struck again on 22 November 1965, when ice prevented No.4 Squadron from overflying (with special dispensation) the celebration of Walpole's marriage to Margreet Koops, at the Town Hall of Leeuwarden. Fortunately all went well on the ground, with the whole of No.II Squadron in attendance for the three-day session. This did not mean that a CO would always have things his own way. Nigel Walpole recollects:

'I do not think we ever tempted providence too far, indeed we always kept the vicissitudes of the weather very much in mind. Paradoxically, it was our proper caution which led to the unseemly arraignment of myself, as Squadron Commander, on a base which was hosting us while the Gutersloh runway was being re-surfaced. I had taken off as a weather guard on a deceivingly clear evening, and in its beauty and my exuberance, I had carried out a gentle upwards roll (safer than my landings) through what to us was middle airspace. Locals, allegedly appointed for the purpose, had reported this great crime (aerobatics below 7000 feet) and I was confined to the base while the rest of the Squadron went on the morrow to Laon, in France, to do their worst without the discipline of their master. Fortunately the hierarchy at Gutersloh and Rheindahlen took a more pragmatic view of the incident — and we were all soon back together again'.

The Squadron always likes good fun and traditions. During a dining out night at RAF Gutersloh this Goggomobil was duly 'parked' on two tables in the ante room . . .

When Group Captain Nigel Walpole looks back on these years he describes the 1964-67 years as 'unconventional, dynamic, highly capable and erratically social, with a prominent Irish influence. With extraordinary good engineers and always enough serviceable aircraft to fly, we flew realistic sorties, well in excess of our allocated hours. We may not have covered ourselves with glory — but we did not go unnoticed!'

Another former Squadron pilot with strong feelings about his No.II Squadron past is Air Marshal Sir John Thomson, at present AOCiC RAF Support Command, RAF Brampton:

'I joined No.II Squadron when it was commanded by S/L N.J.R. Walpole, an excellent CO of strong leadership quality who had much fighter recce experience on Swifts, RF-101s and Hunters. In 1965 Walpole was working actively to bring a younger blood to the pilot strength and as a result a number of second tour pilots such as myself were posted to the Squadron. Others were Riley, Mitchell, Penny, Wilson and Hall. Younger Flight Commanders like Cracroft and Holmes succeeded older predecessors. Walpole brought in public daily debriefs of our efforts, an excellent discipline. Morale rose and No.II Squadron became one of the best Hunter squadrons in what was then a force of nine squadrons worldwide. We enjoyed the recce role and the opportunity for weapons work, overseas training to the Mediterranean and some air-to-air combat training. Walpole also revitalised the Mobile Field Photographic Unit, and as new PIs like F/L David Oxlee and OC MFPUs such as F/L Felix Leathers and his Warrant Officer Mr. Geddes appeared, this part of the Squadron also improved to a very high standard. To my dismay, I was recommended for ADC duties after only four months on my new Squadron, and appointed to the CinC RAF Germany. He kindly agreed, however, that in the circumstances he would allow me to return to No.II Squadron after a year and that if I performed well I could fly with the Squadron during his leave periods. I did so and flew some forty hours, mostly solo, in the next year. I returned to the Squadron on posting in August 1967 and assumed the duty of Flight Commander Operations from F/L Cracroft, on his posting in December. By this time the Squadron was commanded by S/L Tim Barrett, and my fellow Flight Commander was F/L Roy Holmes, an expert pilot and weapons instructor. Two and a half happy years of fine flying and excellent fellowship followed, including for me a year as the RAF Germany Hunter display pilot for the 1968 season. Low-level displays were given at Woensdrecht, Hamm, Bergodroff, Ziegenhain, Seppe, Wildenrath, Laarbruch, Hunsborn, Regensburg, Auf den Dumpel, Werdohl and Aachen, between May and September. In 1969 the Squadron competed in 'Royal Flush', this being coordinated by F/L (now AM) Sandy Wilson who had taken over at Rheindahlen from me in 1967 and returned later as F/L Training. Unfortunately we did not do very well. The other major innovation of 1969 was an 'operational phase' including simulated war profiles, fighter defended areas, gun tight gates, unexpected diversions to other bases for turnround and retasking. I am glad to say that this general idea was widely taken up by the RAF from the 1970s onwards, and our operational standards improved under this spur, and that of NATO TACEVAL. The Squadron underwent TACEVAL in 1969 and did well, achieving a 'satisfactory' rather than an 'excellent' result only because of physical limitations in the Wing Command Cell (Wing Ops.). I left the Squadron in December 1969 for the United States, posted to Texas to fly RF-4Cs with the 75th TRW, Bergstrom AFB'.

AM Sandy Wilson also has strong feelings about his Hunter days which he shared with his old friend from Cranwell, John Thomson. About this period he adds:

> 'The Hunter Wing at Gutersloh, comprising No.II (AC) and No.4 Squadron, was remarkable not only for the excellence of its Hunter FR10s in the fighter-reconnaissance role but also for the tremendous experience of its pilots. When F/L Geoff Hall and I arrived at the Squadron in May 1967 we were the only two who were not Qualified Weapons Instructors and there were no First Tourists on the Wing. I was fortunate to complete two tours on the Squadron whilst it was at Gutersloh, the first as a junior pilot and the second, following a short ADC tour to the CinC, as a Flight Commander with John Thomson. Armed with a stopwatch and a 1:50,000 map there was virtually no target, even down to small culverts hidden in trees that Gutersloh FR pilots could not find. It was an amazing wing to operate with'.

One particular exercise will always be remembered as one of No.II (AC) Squadron's greatest victories in the Hunter era: 'Big Click', when the Squadron won every single prize available for the best reconnaissance squadron in Northern Europe. One of the competitiors was F/L (now Air/Cdre) 'Tiger Tim' Thorn. He had entered the Squadron, together with three other pilots of No.4 Squadron in June 1970 when No.4 was changing to the new Harrier VTOL aircraft. For No.II (AC) Squadron the arrival of Thorn, Neale, Shepperd and Mathie was a happy occasion as, during 'Royal Flush XIV' this quartet had helped No.4 Squadron to beat 'Shiny Two'. Now they were to represent No.II Squadron during 'Big Click'. It was a competition that made great demands on the individual pilot, placing emphasis in particular on, precise navigation, timing and excellent recall of target descriptions. The six participating squadrons were No.II (AC) Squadron (RAF), No.729 Squadron (RDAF), No.411 Squadron (GAF), No.717 Squadron (RNoAF), NAW 2/1 Squadron (German Navy) and No.522 Squadron (GAF). For No.II (AC) Squadron five pilots took part, F/Lts Bagshaw, Thorn, Norton, Mathie and Bridge, who was the team reserve. The CO S/L 'Big Moose' David acted as team leader. Further

Long before the Americans had ever heard of *Top Gun*, No.II (AC) Squadron showed what Top Gun was all about. Exercise 'Big Click', June 1970. Of six participating Squadrons No.II (RAF), No.729 (RDAF), No.411 (GAF), No.717 (RNoAF), NAW 2/1 (German Navy) and No.522 (GAF), 'Shiny Two' was the best overall. The victors had themselves photographed with their trophies.
From left to right: F/L D. Bagshaw (Best overall pilot); S/L R.J. David (Team Captain); F/L W. Norton; F/L T.G. Thorn (2nd Best overall pilot) and F/L A. Mathie.

officers were the Engineering Officer F/L Hill and the PI F/L Oxlee and his team. The whole team, including the MPU detached to Aalborg airfield, the base from which the competition was mounted. The entire exercise took four days. Each pilot was tasked to fly against three targets, consisting of combinations of either pin-point targets, line-search targets, or strip searches. In common with most NATO competitions 'Big Click' was scheduled over a period of three days flying. The results for No.II (AC) Squadron were absolutely incredible, the final standings being:

Squadrons: 1. No.II (AC) Squadron.

Pilots: 1. F/L D.R. Bagshaw 74.9%
2. F/L T.G. Thorn 71.9%
9. F/L A.R.C. Mathie 61.4%
23. F/L W.L. Norton 40.6%

Photo Interpretation Teams: 1. No.II (AC) Squadron.

Photo Laboratories: 1. No.II (AC) Squadron.

One can imagine the euphoria of No.II (AC) Squadron when the trophies were presented and the speeches made. On 6 September the Hunters flew back to Gutersloh, after what had been a highly memorable event in the history of 'Shiny Two'. It was the Squadron's last victory with the Hunter FR10 before it was replaced in March 1971 by an American aircraft, the McDonnell-Douglas Phantom. As for Tiger Tim his first posting with the Squadron led to another victory: He met a WRAF Officer by the name of Rosemary Meredith, who worked as an Air Traffic Controller at Wildenrath, where the Squadron was detached for three months whilst the runway at Gutersloh was being re-surfaced. She seemed to like The Tiger and married him.

CHAPTER 13
THE RECCES FROM LAARBRUCH

If one speaks with former No.II Squadron Hawker Hunter pilots about their memories of this aircraft their eyes start to glitter and they begin to speak poetically. Fine though the Hunter was, by the late sixties it was somewhat dated for the European Theatre. It became necessary to find a more powerful replacement.

In December 1960 a twin-engined two-seater jet aircraft, the McDonnell Douglas Phantom entered service in the United States Navy. In mid-1964, after the P1154 project had been cancelled the Royal Navy ordered the aircraft, to be used on aircraft carriers. One year later the Phantom was also ordered for the RAF. On 17 February 1976, XT852 made its first flight at St. Louis, Missouri. However, it was not until May 1969 that No.6 Squadron was formed as the first all-Phantom squadron in the RAF. In December 1970 No.II Squadron obtained its first Phantom FGR2. It was a very powerful aircraft, quite different from the Hunter. Its two 12,250 pound thrust (20,515 pounds with reheat) Rolls-Royce RB 168-25R Spey 220 axial-flow by-pass turbojets gave it a maximum speed of Mach 2.1 at 40,000 feet. At 1000 feet it could reach a speed of Mach 1.15. With a service ceiling of 60,000 feet and a maximum range of 1750 miles its two crew members could inflict heavy blows at potential enemies using the armament of eleven 1,000 pounds, 126 SNEB 68mm armour-piercing rockets and the 20mm Vulcan SUU 23 rotary cannon.

The Phantoms destined to fly with the Squadron were equipped with an EMI-built reconnaissance pod fitted with a battery of F95 and F135 cameras, infra-red linescan equipment and sideways-looking reconnaissance radar. Though 'Shiny Two's' primary task was still reconnaissance it got a secondary ground-attack role as well.

The first crews for Shiny Two started their Phantom conversion at RAF Coningsby in July 1970. Led by Squadron Commander W/C Brian Stead the course included six other pilots (S/L Wilson, F/L Ireland, F/L Schuster, F/L Holme, F/L Jellicoe, and F/O Cornwall, and seven navigators (S/L Webb, S/L Essai, F/L McAuley, F/L Dunnachie, F/L Andrews, F/L Harrison and F/O Bruce). Apart from learning to operate the aircraft's sophisticated radar and inertial navigation equipment the crews were initially restricted to visual reconnaissance. However, the first set of reconnaissance equipment was delivered during the course and was first flown by F/L Nick Ireland and F/O Mike (now Gp Capt) Bruce. The sortie was not a great success as they were bounced by a staff crew which rather put off their attempts to use the pod properly – and pictures of the first target came out as a very large field with the base of a 150 feet high radio mast just showing at the top of the frame . . .

No.II (AC) Squadron formed at RAF Bruggen in December 1970 as its facilities at Laarbruch were not then complete. In fact there was not much for the Squadron at Bruggen either, apart from an empty hangar and a telephone. The Squadron received its first reconnaissance Phantom, XV485, the same month. Much thought

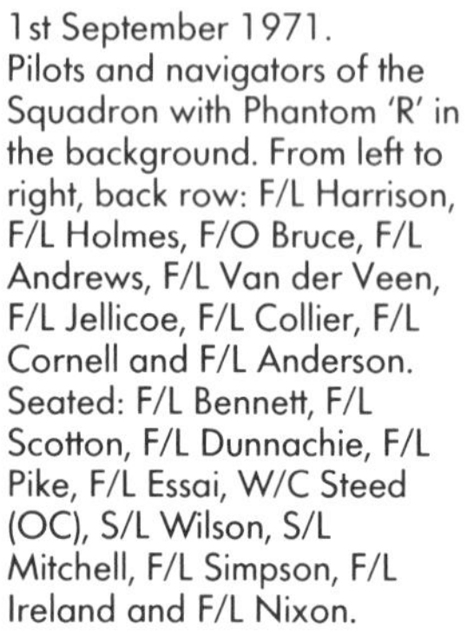

1st September 1971. Pilots and navigators of the Squadron with Phantom 'R' in the background. From left to right, back row: F/L Harrison, F/L Holmes, F/O Bruce, F/L Andrews, F/L Van der Veen, F/L Jellicoe, F/L Collier, F/L Cornell and F/L Anderson. Seated: F/L Bennett, F/L Scotton, F/L Dunnachie, F/L Pike, F/L Essai, W/C Steed (OC), S/L Wilson, S/L Mitchell, F/L Simpson, F/L Ireland and F/L Nixon.

had been given to the question of Squadron markings as Sandy Wilson recalls:

'During the Hunter era the squadron markings, comprising two black triangles, had been placed either side of the aircraft's roundel on the rear fuselage. This was not possible with the Phantom and so we came up with a solution which kept the traditional two black triangles but replaced the roundel with a white circle enclosing the Hereward knot. The traditional fin triangle was retained but we streamlined the standard aircraft tricolour to balance the triangle and this was subsequently adapted by all the other Phantom squadrons. In the Hunter days the aircraft's tail letters had conveniently spelt SHINY TWO. But with the greater number of Phantoms we expanded this to SHINYER TWO. The boss took the "S" for his aircraft, which was very appropriate since his surname was Stead. I had "W" for obvious reasons and I recall the two-seat trainer being given the "T" '.

The Squadron started flying in January 1971 and the first reconnaissance trip was flown by S/L Sandy Wilson and F/L Derek Andrews in XV485 on the eighth. F/L Brian Jellicoe and F/L Chunky Harrison flew it on its second trip the same day and not without incident. As they taxied out for their first flight on the Squadron, Harrison realised that he had only one initiator pin from the ejection seats in the holder. Brian Jellicoe was not at all pleased when his navigator asked him to taxi back. He was even less pleased when the missing pin was found in his seat . . .

A second mishap occurred when Jellicoe and Harrison were ordered to Aldergrove to collect XV486; while they went to Aldergrove their flying kit went to Heathrow. However, after a few threats British Airways got it back to Aldergrove.

The work-up of the Squadron to operational status continued with a lot of recce sorties, low level radar navigation training and weapons work on the Nordhorn range. Some of the crews had not flown low level in Germany before and this, combined with the typical German winter weather, made the first few months quite challenging. On Ireland's ninth trip in Germany his aircraft suffered a Boundary Layer Duct failure – a very serious emergency in which very hot air leaked into parts of the wing where it should not be. These were often indicated faults rather than actual ones but they always had to be treated as real. The Phantom was very heavy, just after take-off, and in the course of dealing with the emergency Ireland got very low over the Bracht ammunition dump. He was very relieved to get back on the ground after a maximum weight arrested landing.

While converting from the Hunter to the Phantom the Squadron grew to have the largest number of aircraft since the days when it flew both Hectors and Lysanders in the later thirties. For a while No.II (AC) Phantom Squadron ran concurrently with No.II (AC) Hunter Squadron. A decade of Hunter flying came to an end at 0001 hours on 1 March 1971 when the Squadron ceased operations from Gütersloh. On 1 May 1971 the the Squadron moved to Laarbruch. The Squadron consisted of one Wing Commander, four Squadron Leaders and nineteen Flight Lieutenants and Flying Officers, a total of twenty-four aircrew. All the aircrew were experienced: of twelve navigators, eight were senior to Harrison, who was on his third tour. Some, mostly good humoured, friction was caused by the eager Squadron Leaders, keen to make a good impression on the Boss. This usually involved a number of the junior officers in extra work. As a result, there was some measure of revolt amongst the workers, who formed 'The Junta'. The crewroom was renamed the 'Junta Room' and a suitable sign placed on the door. Attempts were made to make Squadron Leaders knock before entry and one or two successes were recorded. In addition the odd Junta outing was organised to which Squadron Leaders were pointedly not invited. The outings were of a cultural nature – such as to The Golden Anchor in Duisburg. The message was soon received and cordial relationships re-established between senior and junior ranks. Around this time Chunky Harrison was flying with Davy Holme over The Netherlands. As they were approaching the German border, they heard Sandy Wilson and Derek Andrews contacting Nieuw Millingen on entry to The Netherlands.

No.II (AC) Squadron, 1974. Left to right, back row: F/Ls Bond, Lishman, Dell, Burkby, Everrit and Henley. Middle row: F/Ls Hill, Wrighton, Bing, Smith, Hudson and S/L Widdowson. Front row: W/C Warren, S/L Waite, F/L Smith, S/L Jackson, S/L Simmons, F/Ls Boulder and White, S/L Morgan and F/L Threadgould, who, as Officer Commanding, would take the Squadron to Saudi Arabia during the Gulf War in 1990-91.

'Sandy was very keen on bouncing members of the Squadron and telling them that ex-Canberra operators should keep their eyes open as he had done while flying Hunters. I was quickly able to pick up Sandy on the radar and suggested to Davy that we could have a little innocent fun. He agreed and we were able to follow Sandy on the radar and sneak up behind him. A quick flash by with the cameras running was followed by a return to a co-operative RIC at Laarbruch. About 50 prints of the bounce, titled "Sandy and Derek Bounced Again" were produced before they landed . . .'

Another humorous event is recalled by Doug Todd who served as a Reserve Officer in the Squadron PI section for five weeks each year between 1971 and 1982:

'A new navigator (Al Reynolds) arrived on the base fairly late in the evening. About half a dozen of us took him into the bar, at the same time informing him of a certain game

The Jaguar.
In April 1976 W/C Sandy Wilson brought the first Squadron Jaguar to Laarbruch.

In 1979 a Squadron Jaguar took off from the Autobahn near Bremen during trials to find out if motorways would be suitable for aircraft to land on.

we played to initiate all new members. If he won each round he was given a drink to celebrate his success. Naturally it was our intention to make sure that he won each round of the game, so that by the time we finished he had had so much to drink that he just collapsed under the table. On this occasion, having got our new member to this state we decided to call in the MO and get him to put his leg in plaster. When he woke up next morning we told him that he had fallen over the night before on going to his room in the quarters and had broken his leg. The poor chap was in a terrible state as No.II was his first Squadron after OCU and he was very bothered what the CO would think of him. Little did he know that one of the six with whom he had been drinking was the CO. We played him along for three days before we relented and led him into the hoax. It showed the great spirit that existed in the Squadron.'

In September the Squadron was declared fully operational again, a great achievement by all members of 'Shiny Two'. On 25 May 1972 Nick Ireland was in a four-aircraft fly-past for a Royal Visit. It was a great honour to participate and the Squadron performed immaculately as usual. During the same month the Squadron celebrated its Diamond Jubilee. A special commemorative stamp cover was issued and flown supersonically in a Phantom.

In August a team of four crews from the Squadron took part in Northern European Command's prestigious Reconnaissance competition 'Big Click' at Sola Air Base in Norway. Led by the non-flying CO W/C Brian Stead, the team comprised four Phantoms and three crews; S/L Sandy Wilson and F/L Derek Andrews, F/L Brian Jellicoe and F/L Chunky Harrison, S/L Frank Mitchell and F/L George McAuley with F/L Nick Ireland as the reserve pilot. In addition to the groundcrew there was also a team from the RIC. As Nick Ireland recalls it was their first experience of the degree of 'gamesmanship' which developed in these competitions and turned them, over the years, from friendly get-togethers into win-at-all-costs events. There was always rivalry between the Air Forces of the various NATO countries and the Squadron played its part in this friendly war. Some of the crews took off on shipping recce sorties with photocopies from Jane's *All The World Ships* so that when they spotted a warship and its bow number they could decode it from their information and put it in an in-flight report and Misrep giving the dimensions of the vessel to the nearest inch, the make of the boilers etc – all the sort of things you could *not* from a low level pass at 450 knots!

Since No.II (AC) Squadron had swept the board with prizes at Aalborg in 1970 the pressure was on to do the same again and beat teams from the German, Danish, Norwegian and United States Air Forces. For four days each crew flew missions involving pin points, line and strip searches for well camouflaged military equipment. The competition was extremely fierce. Although Sandy Wilson and Derek Andrews led

Decimomannu 1979.
Left to right: F/L Brown, F/O Lilley, S/L Dawes, F/O Smith, S/L Norriss, F/L Robertson (ATC Liaison), F/O Southam, W/C Fowler (OC), F/L Bridge, Major Ablett, RCT (GLO), S/L Elder, F/L Sturley, F/L Bremner, F/L Collins, F/L Hopkins, F/L Gruner, F/L Daymon, Capt van de Velde, F/L Sheen, F/L Drake.

the individual competition throughout, all the other competitions were in doubt until after the final missions had been flown. On the last night all went to bed not knowing who had won. Early the next morning at 0600 hours Wing Commander Brian Stead, the Squadron Commander and Team Manager woke Dawson up and said: 'Let's go and see if there is a result yet.' Whlst driving up the parking apron they discovered that early though they were, the ground crew had been up before them and found out that the Squadron had won. This fact was self evident because, in front of the parked American aircraft, painted on the tarmac in white letters were the words: WE WON AND DON'T EVER FORGET IT. So again 'Shiny Two' swept the board, winning the Best Squadron, Best RIC, Best Groundcrew and the Best Crew Trophy, which was won by Sandy Wilson and Derek Andrews. Sandy Wilson led the team back from Sola on Sunday 27 August to a tremendous welcome from Laarbruch.

During exercises some pilots found it very difficult to accept that war exercises had to be played according to certain rules to ensure a realistic training. Sometimes the weather would be so bad that flying was impossible. Therefore the crews would actually plan a sortie and then go and sit in a small office to simulate being airborne and away from the Squadron. Then there would be some gas or chemical alert and the crews in their hut would be told to put on their respirators. They pointed out, not unreasonably they thought, that they should not have to put them on as they were 'airborne' and not affected by gas attacks. This was reluctantly agreed by the Flight Commanders who got their own back when the hot lunches arrived from the Officers' Mess. All pilots rushed out to collect their food and tuck in. However they were told that there were no lunches for them as they were all 'airborne' and away from the station. One hour later, when the crews were declared back on the base, they were allowed their lunches which of course were very cold . . .

On 2 December 1972 Wing Commander D.H. Warren assumed command of the Squadron succeeding Wing Commander Stead. In June 1973 some of the pilots and navigators went on a 'Lone Ranger' to Akrotiri. There were two aircraft involved and they staged through Luqa in Malta. However, only one aircraft was allowed to go on to Akrotiri. Ireland was fortunate enough to continue south-east. The pilot of the other aircraft was Dick Shuster who was well known for his practical jokes and sense of humour. Ireland was the formation leader from Laarbruch to Luqa and had been warned that he might have problems contacting Rome Control on the leg down the west coast to Italy and sure enough he was handed over from Milan to Rome, but no contact was made. Ireland went back to Milan control, checked the frequency and tried Rome again several times, but to no avail. Suddenly a voice came through loud and clear, speaking English with an outrageous Italian accent. Ireland was asked for the ETA at various reporting points down the coast. He began to enjoy this well-guided part of the sortie, flying a distance of over 200 miles with Rome still loud and clear. In the end Ireland's navigator S/L Essai suggested that it was about time to contact Malta. When Ireland did so he got a great telling off for reporting so very late. After the two aircraft had landed at Luqa Ireland commented to Shuster how odd it was that Rome had come through so clearly and for so long. Shuster fell

Top: The Jaguar proved to be a safe aircraft. Relatively few accidents happened. F/L Des 'Shadow' Sheen landed wheels-up by accident at De Peel Air Base on 31 August in Holland. At the same time he proved that it was possible to survive a landing on the recce pod without rolling over.

F/L Bill Langworthy landed wheels-up by accident at Laarbruch while flying a T2. Bill and the SEngO ejected successfully when the aircraft left the runway.

about laughing and explained that Ireland had sounded so worried about not being able to contact Rome Control that Shuster himself had come on the radio pretending to be Rome. In fact they had flown the full length of Italy without actually speaking to the Italian ATC organisation at all.

At times the Squadron had exchanges with other NATO units. One such an exchange was with a German Phantom squadron from Leck. The normal welcoming party was held to which the wives of the crews that had gone to Leck were invited. After a while, Mary, wife of Squadron Leader Frank Mitchell came to one of the pilots and said that one of the Germans was causing her a problem. This message was passed on to Franco, the barman. A few seconds later Franco passed a drink to give to the troublesome German officer with the message to Mary that it would take about six minutes. The mission was carried out. A little while later Mary came up again and said: 'Tell Franco it took seven minutes'. The German was out cold on the floor. Some German officers then picked up the offender and threw him under the first bush outside the Mess where he remained until the next morning. The rest of the German squadron demanded to know the recipe of the drink as this particular fellow was always a nuisance and they wanted to be able to feed him this in the future. Franco however never divulged the secret of his concoction.

Flying the Phantom the Squadron participated in exercises, competitions and air meets as well as deploying to NATO ranges such as Decimomannu, Sardinia, for weapons training. All through its service with the Squadron the Phantom remained a very popular and highly potent aircraft. During the 1973 'Royal Flush' competition, No.II (AC) Squadron won the Rosier Trophy, for the best day and night reconnaissance squadron. Wing Commander Chas Wrighton, who flew with No.II (AC) Squadron in the mid-seventies recalled:

> 'The Phantom was a great aircraft to fly in 2ATAF. At the time it could outperform anything in the theatre. You set off with a recce pod and two drill Sparrows, but for exercises you would carry four Sparrows and four Sidewinder missiles. Consequently you would start off in a "bomber" mode at 420 knots/250 feet, but if you should happen to come across a stray Lightning or fighter-type aircraft the game was on. The only problem was to save enough fuel to get round the tasked recce targets to bring the film home. We used to fly a trip of the day against three or four Squadron tasked targets and they would be fully IFREPed, VISREPed and marked. Competition amongst crews was always high to get the best results, and get picked for the next "Royal Flush" or "Big Click" team.'

The Phantom Recce Pod was a comprehensive piece of kit, although at over 2,000 pounds weight and drag penalty, crews were not always over enthusiastic about carrying it. There was some crewroom debate as to whether one could jettison it or not. Fortunately this point never had to be proved: during its time with the Squadron no Phantom was ever lost or seriously damaged. At the time the aircrew did not think much of SLAR (Sideways Looking Airborne Radar) as it meant standing off at height and flying straight and level. Subsequently they realised what a good bit of equipment it was for war and peacetime tasks; AWACs might be able to pick up cars on Autobahns, but so could No.II (AC) Squadron in the mid-seventies. The IRLS was the first on RAF aircraft and worked very well. The only drawback was that when on night operations one had to get low to get good results. For optical cameras at night the Squadron had a flash pod which consisted of a large flashing bulb at the end of a fuel tank synchronised with the cameras. The wisdom of putting many thousands of kilovolts at the end of a fuel tank never failed to impress the aircrew. The problem was that the flash was not very bright, so crews had to go down to 200 feet to get a half decent picture; nevertheless, with the flash-pod and the IRLS they got some good night results, particularly on competitions.

To practise night flying on a blacked out range the pilots and navigators used to fly radar-nav's during the day. The poor navigator would fly totally blacked out under a hood whilst the pilot would do what he was told in broad daylight. The results were surprisingly good and some navigators would become experts at massaging the INAS and map reading on the radar. This was just as well, because after thirty minutes careful navigation the pilot would see a Lightning and to the cry 'I will put you back in the same place' the aircraft would adopt fighter mode for five minutes. Needless to say that – as far as the navigators were concerned – they never got back at the same place, the pilot leaving the Nav to sort things out.

The Squadron would send aircraft to Valley in Wales to fire Sidewinder missiles against Jindivik targets and often the crews flew to Denmark and Southern Germany for landaways. There was one particularly good exercise where a pair of Phantoms would fly low level to Malta for the weekend. Routeing was through Bremgarten, low level over the Alps for a night stop at Villafranca in Italy, then low level through Italy to Sigonella and Luqa. It always helped to have an athletic navigator because he would have to bolt up a starter door after the engine was running and then strap in. No baggage pod was fitted to the aircraft, so they lived in what they could get into the cockpit. No.II (AC) Squadron crews were not always the best dressed detachment. By 1973 the Squadron Phantoms acquired new red and blue roundels and, for a short time, red and blue replaced white in the squadron markings.

A very important and integral part of the Squadron was the RIC, the Reconnaissance Intelligence Centre. Its purpose was to provide a photographic processing and interpretation facility. The RIC began life as an MFPU (Mobile Field Photographic Unit) in the early fifties and it was equipped with a mixture of specialist and 'acquired' vehicles which enabled it to support recce squadrons wherever they were deployed within Western Europe. By the late sixties No.II MFPU was based at Laarbruch supporting No.31 Squadron which was equipped with Canberra PR7 aircraft. No.4 MFPU was at Bruggen helping No.II (AC) Squadron reform with the Phantom aircraft. In 1971, when No.II (AC) Squadron moved to Laarbruch, No.31 Squadron disbanded and Nos.3 and 4 MFPU were amalgamated to form the newly named RIC. The RIC received a complete new set of equipment which was truck-mounted and housed in air portable containers (ATRELs) and also a new semi-permanent base facility (MAREL). Because at this stage the RIC was still an independent unit it was based on the edge of the No.II (AC) Squadron area so that it could serve station and squadron equally.

In 1974 the RIC was 'taken over' by No.II (AC) Squadron and formally came under the command of OCII and so when the Squadron changed from Phantom to Jaguar in 1976 the RIC remained in place to support the new aircraft. The RIC was sub-divided into two flights: Reconnaissance Processing Flight and Photo Interpretation Flight. The PI Flight viewed all the film from both the Squadron's own and the many other NATO aircraft which used Laarbruch. Photographic

Decimomannu 1982. Left to right: F/L Rae, F/L White, F/L Dalton, F/O Williams, F/L Gordon, F/L Dalgliesh, F/L Evans, S/L Sturley, W/C Thorn (OC), S/L Smith, S/L Bagshaw, F/L Osborne, F/L Gallagher, F/L Warnock.

The end of an era – late 1988.
Standing: F/L Whitehead, F/L Marchbank, Capt Steenbergen, F/L Graeme-Cook, F/L Froggatt, F/O Hill, F/L Plummer, F/L Rands, F/O Fuller, F/O Garvey, F/L Haley, F/L Stewart, F/L Holland, F/L Ferranti, F/L Noble, F/L Judson.
Sitting: F/L MacLean, F/L Knight, Major Chapman (GLO), S/L Williams, S/L Nickols, W/C Sturley (OC), S/L Hetherington, S/L Bevan, Capt Baron, F/L Livesey, F/L Turner.

Interpretation being a very specialised skill it demanded a detailed knowledge of military equipment and installations and their operating procedures; in addition, many other subjects including industries, power production and lines of communication had to be studied carefully. This knowledge combined with the intense concentration and the ability to view photography in stereo (3D) enabled the PI to produce a very quick but detailed intelligence report for the military commanders who requested the information so that they could plan further operations.

The Processing Flight consisted mainly of photographic tradesmen who were responsible for the processing and printing of selected target imagery negatives. Unlike the commercial processing and printing establishments the RIC had an extremely tight time-schedule to maintain. In order to keep production time to a minimum and allow the maximum time for imagery evaluation, the films were processed at a speed of no less than 120 feet per minute on the 70mm high speed/high temperature continuous film processing machines.

Film processing time obviously depended on the amount of film exposed; however, typical processing times using two processing machines were in the order of five to eight minutes per sortie. Printing was achieved in a similar time schedule using electronic contact or projection printers which had the capability to correct for areas of varying density within each negative automatically. Using Ilfoprint photographic paper, a touch dry print could be obtained after a processing time of only nine seconds, with sufficient permanence to satisfy all military requirements. Other tasks for which the Flight was responsible were fault investigation and defect reporting carried out by advanced photographic tradesmen and of course the all-important task of maintaining and servicing the RIC equipment, carried out by a small team of GSE tradesmen assisted by the photographers. The role played by photographic tradesmen in support of photographic reconnaissance was vital to the Squadron and the NATO units using the Squadron. Photographic reconnaissance being a team-effort of aircrew, aircraft engineers, GLO's, PI's, photographic and GSE tradesmen was the best test of the efficiency of No.II (AC) Squadron.

Knowing the value of good Public Relations, the Squadron took part in the BBC production 'Skywatch' in the summer of 1974. W/C Warren and F/L Dunnachie flew a sortie from Laarbruch to Wittering. Their mission consisted of photographing Weeze church, Cologne Cathedral, and then transitting to the United Kingdom to photograph the BBC studios at Pebble Mill Birmingham before landing at RAF Wittering, where the CO W/C Warren was interviewed for the film. It was his last job with the Squadron as he officially left the Squadron on 8 May 1975, the new CO being W/C D.C. Ferguson.

Another event was the exchange with No.717 Squadron of the Norwegian Air Force. Between 18 and 27 June 'Shiny Two' operated from NAF Rygge. During one of the sorties F/L Boulter and S/L Laite sighted and photographed the Konda-class Soviet fleet oiler *Orsk*. This was the first sighting of this vessel since it had left Soviet waters. On 20 June the Squadron aircrew enjoyed a very pleasant day on board KNM *Sauda*, a Norwegian minesweeper. During the trip a

Phantom roared over and photographed ship, crew and visitors. Soon after the Squadron returned it took part in the ceremonies at Weeze on 13 July, when RAF Laarbruch was granted the freedom of that town. The Squadron standard was paraded and a Phantom led two Buccaneers and a Hunter in a fly-past over Weeze.

In the final 'Royal Flush' of 1975, the judges noted that some crews, notably the French, had prior knowledge of some targets in the competition. It was then decided that 'Royal Flush', as it was then, should end to make way for some other recce competition. However, the Squadron won the prize for best the navigation. Also that year the Squadron participated in the Salmond Trophy for the very first time, coming second to No.14 Squadron. A major change was the beginning of operations from Hardened Aircraft Shelters (HAS), and a hardened Pilot Briefing Facility (PBF), which heralded the introduction of yet another new steed for the Squadron.

As with the Phantom, the members of the new Jaguar Squadron had formed at Lossiemouth to undertake conversion in October 1975 and included W/C Sandy Wilson (starting his fourth tour on No.II (AC) Squadron!), S/L Horace Farquhar-Smith and F/L Phil Flint. The first aircraft XZ102, was delivered from the factory at Warton on 26 February 1976 and the first sortie with the new recce pod was flown by the CO as a special commemorative mission to mark the handover between Phantom and Jaguar on 1 April 1976. Apart from testing the pod on a typical low level sortie, taking in training areas and barracks, the flight included air-to-air photography with a No.II (AC) Squadron Phantom (flown by W/C Fergie Ferguson and S/L Ben Laite) and a flypast at Laarbruch.

Interestingly both aircraft bore the tail letter 'S', both being the respective CO's aircraft, in line with Squadron tradition. The markings on the Jaguar were a direct follow-on from the Phantom with the two black triangles either side of the Hereward knot, but placed on the intake as opposed to the nose, and with the traditional white triangle on the tail fin. Also in line with Squadron tradition the tail letters were a variation on the SHINY TWO of the Hunter era and the SHINYER TWO of the Phantom era. They now spelt SHINYER TWO JAG.

From April the Phantom Squadron started to run down as the Jaguar Squadron built up. During its service in the Squadron the Phantoms flew 13,950 hours without major accidents apart from birdstrikes, a remarkable proof of the excellent quality of the aircraft, the aircrews and the ground staff.

With the departure of the Phantoms, the only postwar two-seater aircraft in the Squadron since the Westland Lysander, the pilots would go single-seat again.

The Sepecat Jaguar was the result of a joint venture between British Aircraft Corporation and Dassault/Breguet, who built 400 Jaguars to be shared equally by the Royal Air Force and the Armée de l'Air. The first French-built Jaguar flew in September 1968, followed by the first British aircraft, a little over a year later. It was powered by two 7,140 pound static thrust Rolls-Royce/Turbomeca RT172 Adour 102 turbofans, and armed with two 30mm Aden guns, with provision for up to 10,000 pounds of external ordnance and air-to-air missiles. The aircraft was originally fitted with the Marconi-Elliott navigation and weapons aiming system (NAVWASS). However, later modifications including the installation of the Ferranti FIN1064 inertial navigation and attack system gave the Jaguar a considerably more accurate and reliable system than the original Marconi NAVWASS. In conjunction with the Squadron's recce task a pod was developed for use on the centre line station. This contained a selection of cameras, which gave complete horizon to horizon cover and included an IRLS system.

During the first period of Jaguar operations the Squadron received many visitors including the new CAS, ACM Sir Neil Cameron. In August 1976 BBC TV's 'Tomorrow's World' featured the Squadron and the presenter, Raymond Baxter, was taken up by F/L (now Air Cdre) Pegnall in one of the T2s. The programme, which was broadcast in September, described a Jaguar sortie and also the full processing and interpretation of film from the recce pod.

Fortunately there were a number of very experienced FR pilots on the Squadron, including F/L Philip Holden-Rushworth, who had been on the Squadron in the days of the Supermarine Swift. The Squadron work-up included many station exercises and the development of new procedures for the operation of both aircraft and the RIC from Hardened Aircraft Shelters. Despite teething problems with the new pod the Squadron was declared operational in both the reconnaissance and attack roles on 30 November 1976.

Two months later the first Jaguar accident occurred. Shortly after F/L Langworthy took off from Laarbruch in XZ102 the aircraft rolled rapidly to port and only with use of full right rudder and spoiler did the pilot manage to recover the Jaguar to a near level attitude. The aircraft subsequently climbed to 800 feet in a gentle port turn and then rolled out of control again. As it was impossible to recover, Langworthy waited for the white sky to come round for the second time and pulled the handle. He ejected safely and landed fifty yards from his aircraft, which narrowly missed a mental home about ten miles NE of Laarbruch.

Less than two months later the Squadron lost its first pilot in a Jaguar crash. F/L Doug Stein

During the celebration of the Squadron's seventy-fifth anniversary nine Jaguar GR1 jets flew over Laarbruch forming a '2'. The following took part: W/C Sturley (Lead), S/L Nickols, S/L Hetherington, F/L Plummer (T2), F/L Noble, F/L MacLean, Capt Steenbergen, F/L Graeme-Cook, F/L Froggatt, F/L de Ferranti, F/L Judson.

was killed south of Nordhorn Range. As a member of a four-ship formation he is thought to have lost visual contact with his element leader in cloud, and about six miles SE of the range his aircraft crashed, killing Stein instantly. It was the first fatality the Squadron had suffered in fifteen years. On 2 March, after a service in the church at Laarbruch, Stein was buried at Rheindahlen cemetery.

The first Squadron deployment was to IAF Decimomannu in Sardinia in March 1977. 'Deci' was well-known to all front line squadrons and was destined to be visited regularly throughout the Jaguar years for both APCs and latterly Air Combat Training. One of the main differences compared with Sylt, where the old-time APCs took place, was the far more comfortable climate. On 1 May 1978 W/C Fowler took over from Sandy Wilson, who was to continue a brilliant career in the Royal Air Force.

In July 1977 two Squadron Jaguars participated in the flypast to celebrate Her Majesty Queen Elizabeth II's Silver Jubilee. During the same time Captain Van der Velde of the Royal Netherlands Air Force arrived to become the first Dutch exchange pilot to join the Squadron. During later years many others were to follow; Captains Arns, Stoop, Steenbergen and Den Drijver. A noteworthy individual achievement was that of F/L Langworthy who became the first pilot to achieve 1,000 hours on the Jaguar. Not only did he receive the embroidered 1,000 hours patch, he was also presented with a silver Jaguar model during the Reunion Dinner in October. Two weeks later, however, he was in trouble for a second time when he flew Jaguar T2 XX843 with the SEngO, S/L Knight as a passenger. They crash-landed at RAF Laarbruch and both ejected safely. The SEngO suffered from an ankle injury. During the Jaguar era the Squadron's deployment to various parts of Europe continued. The first Jaguar Squadron exchange was with 717 Squadron at Royal Norwegian Air Force Rygge near Oslo in Southern Norway. Other exchanges included Karup (Denmark), Strasbourg (France), Florennes (Belgium), Beauvechain (Belgium), Monte Real (Portugal), and Villafranca in Northern Italy where the Squadron flew with and against the recce Starfighters. These exchanges always proved a success in many ways, both operational and social, and have borne friendships that have survived to this day. Normally these exchanges included the participation of the Reconnaissance Intelligence Centre. The RIC had to deploy by road with their convoy of four-ton trucks, which contained the processing and viewing equipment required to interpret the film. The road move was considered an enjoyable part of the detachment by RIC-members, especially on occasions such as the drive to Villafranca, which took four days and routed through the Alps.

As the premier recce outfit in NATO the Squadron was often requested to participate in major exercises which gave valuable insight into how other nations operated their air forces. The Squadron attended 'Red Flag' in the USA on three occasions. On 1 May 1980 a new CO arrived and took over from W/C Fowler. W/C 'Tiger' Tim Thorn was to become one of the best known Commanding Officers of the postwar years. He proved to be a superb flyer, a man with a great sense of humour and a very strong emotional tie with the Squadron. In 1980 the attack capability of the Jaguar was well demonstrated during that year's 'Red Flag' when the Squadron gave an impressive demonstration of its ability. Exercise 'Treaty', Tactical Air Meets, Ample Gain Meets and many other exercises gave the Squadron very high marks in operational capability. The operational experience so drawn undoubtedly contributed to the consistently outstanding TACEVAL results achieved through the Squadron's Jaguar years.

In 1982 the Squadron celebrated its 70th anniversary. As there had not been a major reunion in five years W/C Thorn decided that this was to become a memorable one. S/L Bush, ninety-three years old, was invited to be the guest of honour. Unfortunately he had to decline due to his age and poor health. Another famous old boy was asked, Air Cdre 'Daddy' Probyn. He was ninety years old and lived in Kenya. But the long voyage would have been too much and he regretfully cancelled. However, other high-ranking 'veterans' did manage to come. There were Air Vice-Marshal 'Bull' Cannon and Air Cdres Lousada and Geddes. Many other former members were very keen to attend as well. One of them was Doug Todd, who with a coachload of old boys and their wives went across from England to Laarbruch. They all arrived in Calais to be met by the then Squadron Adjutant F/O Farrar-Hockley. He said that he had got plenty of refreshments aboard the coach to keep the group going until they arrived at Laarbruch. Everyone was hoping for some food as they had been rather short of that commodity so far that day. The refreshments however turned out to be crates of wine which the group had to remove from the aisle of the coach before they could get aboard. Within twenty minutes of leaving Calais there was an enormous 'bang' and two tyres had burst which in turn had ripped off a panel from the side of the coach. Instead of arriving at Laarbruch at 1700 hours in plenty of time for the dining-in night at 2000 hours, the unfortunate group finally arrived at 2100 hours. They were met by members of the Squadron who rushed them to their respective rooms and assisted with great gusto to help them get from ordinary clothes into dinner jackets. Todd finally entered the Mess and went into dinner with one black and one suede shoe. In candlelight and with all the drink consumed who noticed a little thing like that? The dinner was superb and Air Cdre Geddes, replying on behalf of the guests told some incredible stories about his flying career between 1928 and the mid-fifties. The next day saw a beautiful flying display including S/L Smith's four-aircraft formation, a singleton display by S/L Bagshaw, a fly-past of twelve Squadron Jaguars in diamond formation and an immaculate performance by the Red Arrows. The most touching moment occurred when John Young, a wartime pilot now badly disabled by Multiple Sclerosis, said an emotional farewell while F/L Grant Taylor flew a magnificent display over the Mess in a Battle of Britain Memorial Flight Spitfire.

For Photographic Interpreters, flying did not come into the duties of the reserve officers. However, the CO W/C Thorn felt that they should have this experience which would give them an insight as to how difficult it could be to get photography at low level, and if sometimes the pilot returned having missed the target the PIs could then appreciate the difficulties. Another reason may have been to see if they could take being thrown around at low level in a Jaguar T2. One rule was that one bought the CO and the pilot a drink if one came back having been sick during the sortie. When this was decided Todd mentioned to W/C Thorn that it would be fair for the CO and the pilot to buy the passenger a drink if he did not get sick. Todd was booked by the CO to go on a low level sortie with a Belgian pilot who had a reputation for being a complete and utter madman. Todd survived and proudly accompanied the Belgian to the bar that evening. As one can imagine, with a name like 'Todd', his nickname was 'Sweeney', but when he tried that evening in the bar to get the Belgian to say it after a few pints, the nearest that he could get was 'Speeney'. On 14 January 1983 W/C Thorn handed over command to W/C Hoare. In recognition for his work 'Tiger' Tim was awarded the AFC in the New Year's Honours list.

Since flying at ultra low level was difficult in the German Federal Republic the Squadron moved 'elsewhere' from time to time. In June 1983 No.II (AC) Squadron had deployed to Goose Bay, Canada for this purpose. On the afternoon of 16 June three Jaguars took off for a tactical formation sortie which was to conclude with an overflight of Goose Bay in Vic formation followed by a change to echelon starboard for a left hand break. Everything went wrong very quickly. No.3 aircraft collided with No.2 and there was a loud explosion. Both pilots, Steve Dalton and Brian Robinson, managed to eject safely while their aircraft crashed into the water to the west and east of Goose Bay. One pilot

During the seventy-fifth anniversary of the Squadron in 1987 Air Commodore Andrew Geddes, CBE, DSO, LoM, who had been the Commanding Officer when the Squadron flew to France in 1939 and stayed with it up to 1941, inspected the Squadron accompanied by Squadron Leader Steve Dalton.

landed near a road where he was met by a Royal Canadian Mounted Police patrol. The other pilot landed in a river and was rescued by a German Air Force helicopter. It was one of the very few accidents involving No.II Squadron Jaguars.

In 1984 the Squadron took part in trials to establish the viability of operating from Autobahns as emergency landing strips in times of conflict. The trials were a tremendous success and gave the pilots the opportunity to operate from a non-standard runway – with bridges on both ends. Other important occasions were the presentation of the new standard in May and the visit of HRH Prince Charles in July. On 28 October Squadron representatives travelled to

In 1988 No.II (AC) Squadron tested the night-vision sights for pilots. One of the guinea pigs was S/L Nickols. In recognition of their work the Squadron was awarded the Wilkinson Battle of Britain Memorial Sword.

Courteenhall, Northampton, where Major Sir Hereward Wake lived, the Wake family being the patron of 'Shiny Two'. The old standard was to be laid up in the family church. It turned out to be a wonderful weekend. In the presence of their host the Squadron met the Lord Lieutenant and his Deputy, the Chief Constable and the Archdeacon of Northampton.

On 15 January 1985 the Squadron took nine aircraft to Nellis AFB, Nevada, USA and participated in 'Red Flag'. On 31 May that year W/C Stirrup assumed command from W/C Hoare. In 1985 the Squadron embarked on trials for Night Vision Goggles (NVG) These allowed the pilot to operate at night and at low level using goggles attached to the flying helmet. The trials progressed well and the Squadron was cleared to fly night sorties on a routine to test the viability of night recces.

June proved to be one of the wettest and coldest months on record. Nevertheless the Squadron was able to exceed its task, flying 385 hours. Sadly enough two Squadron members ran into trouble in July. On 9 July F/O Baston, flying Jaguar XZ365 crashed on the hill of Bastenburg, NE of the Mohne See. He had commenced a low level abort due to poor weather when his aircraft hit the trees at the top of the hill. As it ploughed through the trees it burst into flames and disintegrated. Baston successfully ejected, although he needed stitches to gashes in his legs and treatment for superficial burns. A month later he left the Squadron to be posted to Lossiemouth. The Squadron diarist recorded:

> 'The generally poor calibre of Buccaneer crews in today's forces will allow Baston the opportunity to shine in this environment.'

A very sad accident happened ten days later. SAC Stuart 'Spike' Edwards was killed whilst abseiling on Mont Blanc. He was a very keen and able mountaineer and a member of the RIC.

As the Squadron often worked for the Army it enjoyed visiting Army units. One such visit took place in March 1986. As usual the Squadron's high speed driving techniques brought pained looks to the faces of those soldiers detailed to instruct the pilots in the finer points of AFV manoeuvring. It goes without saying that they had an entirely different view on 'speed' from that of the pilots. On one of two occasions the Commanding Officer of the Army unit even 'evacuated' valuable vehicles to unknown destinations until the Squadron departed. The pilots' attempts to show that in their 'capable' hands Army vehicles could do much more than the manual said duly alarmed their hosts.

On 14 April the Squadron was saddened by the sudden death of the OC RIC, S/L Dickinson, who had been with the Squadron since March 1983. A week later the Squadron went to Canada. Ten pilots and ten groundcrew left from RAF Coltishall in a VC10 for CFB Cold Lake. They shared this detachment in Exercise 'Maple Flag' with crews of No.54 Squadron. After four days of acclimatisation, flying started and gave the participating pilots valuable experience of operating with other air forces.

On 13 March 1987 W/C Stirrup formally handed over command to W/C Philip Sturley, who was returning for his third tour on the Squadron. By this time No.II (AC) Squadron was the only Jaguar squadron operating in RAF Germany, the strike/attack Wings at both Laarbruch and Brüggen having completed their conversion to the Tornado. The new CO was faced with a number of challenges, the first of which was to operate the Squadron from Bruggen for six months while the Laarbruch runway was being resurfaced. As this meant travelling daily from Laarbruch and working from temporary 'Bolthole' accommodation at Bruggen, every effort was made to arrange detachments to cover this period. The first such detachment was to Lossiemouth to brush up the pilots' 100-foot flying skills in preparation for the Squadron's next participation in Exercise 'Maple Flag' in Canada which followed immediately after.

The second challenge was the organisation of the Squadron's 75th Anniversary Celebrations, which were to be held in July due to the

Squadron's other commitments. However, to mark the actual anniversary, on 13 May 1987 W/C Sturley led a formation of four Jaguars over Farnborough, before landing there to an enthusiastic reception from the locals and the press.

The main Anniversary Celebrations were held at Laarbruch over the weekend of 10–12 July 1987, and guests of honour were ACM Sir Alasdair Steedman, Air Cdre C.B.E. Burt-Andrews and Air Cdre A.J.W. Geddes. The weekend started with a reception and flypast by the Squadron in a large figure two formation. This was followed by a Ladies' Guest Night at which Air Cdre Burt-Andrews presented the Squadron with a hand-engraved Squadron crest and Air Cdre Geddes presented a beautiful silver Indian rose bowl, which was to be presented annually to the best recce pilot on the Squadron. The next morning the Squadron was paraded before the Reviewing Officer, Air Cdre Geddes, who proudly took the salute watched by many old boys and distinguished guests. The parade was admirably supported by the Peninsular Band of the Royal Green Jackets. During the afternoon there was an Open Day with aircraft from many RAF and other NATO squadrons and the Open Day was signed off with a spectacular Beating the Retreat by the Royal Green Jackets. More than 700 people enjoyed a relaxed HAS-party that evening. On the Sunday morning, there was a service of remembrance in St Peter's Church followed by an informal barbeque in the gardens of the Officers' Mess. All in all, it was a marvellous weekend which convinced the Old Boys that although the flying might have changed over the years, the spirit of the squadron was alive and well.

For the rest of the summer the Squadron escaped from the Bolthole by undertaking detachments to Decimomannu and completing a very successful squadron exchange with the recce wing of F-104s at Villafranca. The Squadron moved back to operations at Laarbruch that autumn, bringing to an end a very difficult period in which 'Shiny Two' maintained its extremely high flying rate without major incident.

However, you never know when an aircraft will bite. On 16 December 1987 F/O Andy Rands, one of the first tour pilots, was flying Jaguar XZ362 on an instrument flying and general handling sortie when he faced a major emergency during a heavy weight approach to Hopsten airbase. Unfortunately he could not land at Hopsten due to the rapidly deteriorating weather, nor was he able to land at Gütersloh due to the conditions there. Eventually he put the aircraft down safely at Koln-Bonn. His coolness and skill in handling this situation saved the aircraft, and earned F/O Rands a Green Endorsement in his flying log book.

On 31 December 1988 No.II (AC) Squadron said goodbye to the Jaguar GR1. A last commemorative flight was made with a specially painted Jaguar bearing on the tail the Squadron crest and the dates 1912 and 1988, flown by the Commanding Officer, W/C Sturley.

In January 1988 F/O Sarah-Jane Fuller WRAF arrived as the Squadron Intelligence Officer, becoming the first lady officer to serve in 'Shiny Two'. Another milestone at that time was the achievement of Combat Ready status of F/L Marcus de Ferranti, which made the Squadron the only fully Combat Ready squadron in RAF Germany. Of interest, the Squadron was also at that time on average the youngest front-line squadron in the RAF.

On 26 March Ruth Seering, a well-known German journalist, who had flown with the Squadron ten years previously, visited the Squadron to celebrate her sixty-fifth birthday and to fly what was to be her last fast jet sortie, with S/L Hetherington. Needless to say, the event attracted widespread press and TV interest in Germany.

The Squadron completed the by now usual cycle of detachments to Decimomannu and war training exercises at Laarbruch. This culminated in Exercise Taceval in July 1988, which proved to be the last Jaguar Taceval in Germany in which the Squadron again justified its reputation as the premier recce squadron in the Central Region.

For some time there had been a pressing need for a night reconnaissance capability in 2ATAF, particularly to support the night all-weather operations of the large Tornado force. To meet this requirement, the Squadron developed tactics and techniques for night reconnaissance operations with the Jaguar at low level using Night Vision Goggles. This work was rewarded with the award to the Squadron of the 1988 Wilkinson Battle of Britain Memorial Sword. This prize was received by W/C Sturley, on behalf of the whole Squadron present on parade, from the Chief of the Air Staff, ACM Sir Peter Harding on 2 December. At the same ceremony, S/L Nickols received the Queen's Commendation for Valuable Service in the Air, and W/O Brown and F/S Ashton received the MSM from CAS.

To provide a full night-all weather capability, a recce version of the Tornado was being developed for the RAF, which would carry electronic sensors and employ video recording of the imagery rather than the traditional wet film photographic processing. No.II (AC) Squdron was to be the first squadron to be equipped with this new Tornado variant (the GR1A) and the changeover was planned to take place at the end of 1988. The third challenge facing the Squadron at this time was therefore the preparation required to ensure a smooth transition from the Jaguar to the Tornado. The aim was to ensure that the core of the Squadron saw through the changeover to preserve continuity of operational expertise. Some of the pilots therefore returned early to the UK to convert to the new steed. The first Tornado arrived to train the groundcrews on 13 September, and the substantial training programme was overseen by the tireless Squadron Engineering Officer, S/L Williams, who also continued to maintain the Jaguar serviceability rate at its usual high standard.

On 14 December the Squadron received the sad news that Air Cdre Andrew Geddes had passed away. F/L de Ferranti represented the Squadron nine days later then Geddes was cremated.

The last operational Jaguar sortie was flown on 19 December 1988 and the next day the Squadron Standard was handed over from a Jaguar pilot to a Tornado navigator at a parade with AM Sir Anthony Skingsley, who had previously been a Station Commander at Laarbruch, acting as Reviewing Officer.

The arrival of the first Tornado ZA394 on 13 September 1988. Left to right: F/S Galsworthy, S/L McCallum, F/L White, S/L Hill, W/C Sturley, S/L Williams, F/L Poole, F/L Haley.

CHAPTER 14
INTO THE FUTURE

At the stroke of midnight of Hogmanay of 1988. No.II (AC) Squadron closed the hangar as the last operational Jaguar Squadron in RAF Germany when the outgoing CO Wing Commander Phil Sturley handed over the 'Hereward Knot' to the new boss, Wing Commander Al Threadgould, who had previously been on the Squadron between 1970 and 1973 during the Phantom era. In February F/Ls Bruce Graeme-Cook, Karl Plummer, and Bob Judson ferried the last Jaguars back to the UK, bringing to an end a very successful period of over twelve years of Jaguar operations, the longest period of operation by the Squadron of a single aircraft type. Thanks to the careful preparations for the changeover, the new team got off to the best possible start. Most important, the core of the Squadron remained to see through the transition. This included several pilots and a good proportion of the engineers and RIC personnel. The new aircrew came from various backgrounds. The pilots were ex-Jaguar drivers. The navigators being two ex-Phantom chaps, one former Canberra recce navigator and three Tornado-backseaters. The change to a new aircraft meant a massive training programme for the whole Squadron. With the days of wet film gone and the introduction of video the size of the RIC changed too. They were now able to move into the hangar from their deteriorating MAREL accommodation.

Bringing the Squadron to operational status was an immense task for W/C Alan Threadgould and his team. Many problems had to be solved and much was asked from technicians and crews. With only three aircraft and six crews, good weather and aircraft serviceability, there was plenty of flying. By the end of March the Squadron had grown to six aircraft and eight crews. Two months later there were fourteen out of fifteen crews and the Squadron prepared to fly to Canada to explore the low-flying facilities at Goose Bay. In December 1989, 20 Armoured Brigade wrote a challenging article in *Flight* Magazine claiming that the RAF was quite unable to find the Army in the field if the Army did not want to be seen. This was too much for the Squadron GLO, Captain Berendt. After conferring with the CO, the pilots and the navigators the Squadron duly informed 20 Armoured Brigade that the Aces of No.II (AC) Squadron, were ready to meet the challenge. But before 'Shiny Two' could make its point, a first accident with a Tornado happened when on 12 January 1990 F/Ls Ian MacLean and Neil Johnson, flying ZA394, collided with a Jaguar east of Hexham in Northumberland. The Tornado crew had taken-off from RAF Wattisham to fly a reconnaissance sortie before returning to Laarbruch. Near Newcastle they collided with a Jaguar and

Above: F/L Marcus de Ferranti and F/O Craig Hill of No.II (AC) Squadron were clearly unimpressed by the idea of their Squadron re-roling to fly Tornado. They made their feelings very clear on the occasion of the last Squadron flight in the Jaguar Simulator at RAF Bruggen, by crafting a symbolic representation of their view of the whole business. This was displayed when their Squadron Commander, W/C Phil Sturley, flew the final simulator sortie.

It was out with the 'old' and in with the 'new' at midnight, December 31 1988, when the outgoing boss of Jaguar II (AC) Squadron, W/C Phil Sturley, officially handed over the Squadron to W/C Alan Threadgould who was put in charge of the new Tornado Recce Squadron at Laarbruch.

although the pilot tried everything possible, the Tornado went out of control. Both crew members ejected and the aircraft crashed. The pilot of the Jaguar was able to nurse his aircraft to Leeming and land. Both members of No.II (AC) Squadron landed heavily, with the pilot breaking one leg and the navigator both legs. They had been very lucky and fortunately no lives were lost.

Panavia Tornado of No.II Squadron.

On 11 July the Squadron took part in the competition against 20 Brigade. A Brigade column was duly located within 18 minutes of the start time and subsequently attacked. Not unreasonably the Squadron presumed to have won. It transpired, however, that the Brigade had actually hidden seven 6-inch models sitting around on a small piece of paper. To save face for the Brigade a draw was declared, but no-one had any doubt who had won.

The growing tensions in the Persian Gulf caused extra pressure on the Squadron. Everyone knew that the occupation of Kuwait by Saddam Hussain could not go unanswered and that the RAF could very well be sent to the area. The taking of Western hostages as human shields resulted in a massive build-up in Saudi Arabia and the smaller Gulf States.

On 10 August, forty-eight hours after the government had decided to deploy military forces in the Gulf, a Tornado F3 squadron was sent to Dhahran. The day before, a former Commanding Officer of No.II (AC) Squadron, AVM R.A.F. 'Sandy' Wilson, was appointed Commander British Forces Arabian Peninsula. He set up his Headquarters at Riyadh. Less than three weeks later he became both Commander British Forces Middle East (CBFME) and Air Commander (ACBFME). On 1 October Lt Gen Sir Peter de la Billiere took over as CBFME with AVM Wilson as his deputy. On 17 November 'Sandy' Wilson left and AVM Bill Wratten replaced him.

After some confusion, following a series of rumours and counter rumours, the first RAFG Tornados went to the Gulf area. F/O Spencer and F/L Seddon flew directly from Laarbruch to deliver an aircraft. Before 'Operation Desert Shield', the defensive coalition deployment, was over, members of No.II (AC) Squadron prepared for the coming events. The first Squadron members to leave Laarbruch for Saudi Arabia were personnel of the RIC, followed by the GLO, Captain Berendt. In October 1990 all Squadron aircraft were sprayed desert-pink and unusually 'visible' Tornados could be seen exercising over Germany and Belgium at low level.

On 23 November Her Majesty the Queen visited Laarbruch and met members of the Squadron. Three weeks later F/L Haigh and F/L Poole were the first Squadron aircrew to leave for the Gulf, for Tabuk where they were to join No.16 Squadron. Tabuk was a fairly large desert city, with a population of 120,000 people, situated about sixty miles from the Red Sea, and the same distance from Jordan where King Hussain was desperately trying to remain 'neutral'.

On 14 January 1991 five crews left Laarbruch as No.II (Composite) Squadron. They were W/C Threadgould, Commanding Officer, S/Ls Garwood and Hill, F/Lts Robinson, Knight, MacLeod, Hogg, Seddon and Haley, and F/O Spencer. Their task in the Gulf was to be an important one.

Having recently entered service, the recce equipment was suffering problems with the quality of its imagery. Now the video-taped information had to prove to be better than the previously used traditional film. The horizon-to-horizon infra-red Vinten 4000 linescan and the sidefacing infra-red sensors were to prove their value in the coming conflict. For the RIC it would be the first time in many years that its proficiency would mean the 'real' difference.

Three crews (Threadgould/Robinson, Gardwood/Hill and Knight/MacLeod) flew the Tornados to the deployment base while the other crews 'enjoyed the comfort' of a C-130 for the long journey. The Squadron diarist wrote:

> 'CinCRAFG saw them off and was concerned about the Boss being a little preoccupied! Perhaps it was the thought of leading a team on an eight-hour trail into a war. Actually it was the worry of the C-in-C finding out that Squadron Leader Garwood had never seen a Tristar before . . .'

After eight hours and four air-to-air refuelling brackets, they arrived at their new destination. Now the RAF had forty-two Tornado GR1/GR1As in the Gulf. The next day a C-130 arrived with two weary crews and a RIC team with their associated equipment. The other Tornado crew had arrived on a previous Sunday evening C-130, and were reunited later in the day with the 13 squadron colleagues who eventually flew in from Bruggen, bringing with them one further GR1A and two GR1s. During the day two

Squadron crews were able to fly a training sortie around the area.

The following day was mainly taken up by briefings, sorting out personal equipment, and, for some, recovering from the previous days' journey. In the meantime the remaining GR1As, 'O' and 'T' were ferried by crews from Bruggen. The Squadron aircraft now at Dhahran were: 'A', 'C', 'E', 'H', 'O' and 'T', the letters very appropriately chosen.

The Recce crews were organised into three shifts of three crews. Their work pattern was a rotation of nights off, 'early' evenings and 'late' evenings. Those on 'lates' usually finished with a hearty breakfast on the compound and, if Dave Knight was there, a couple of hands of cards in a smoke-filled room.

Late that same evening of 16 January Wing Commander Threadgould was summoned by the Force Commander to be shown the signal which would change the lives of the members of the Squadron. The crews were woken up to the news that the war had started. The initial wake-up call came in the form of an air-raid warning at 0400 hours and was followed by a second one at 0600 hours. These were, however, not the first alerts they had experienced and were thankfully only precautionary, as indeed all the others had been. At least everyone getting quite good at NBC-drills . . .

Four GR1s were launched from Dhahran to join a further eight from Bahrain on war missions. All but one returned safely. The following morning two air-raid warnings came. This time the second one was genuine and for the first time the Squadron heard the explosion when one of Saddam's Scuds was successfully intercepted by a Patriot. The Squadron diarist gave a vivid report of the attitude of both OC No.II and 13 Squadrons when it all happened:

> 'The Boss and OC13 had just got back into bed following the "RED, RED, RED", when a loud whoosh-bang was heard nearby. On looking out of his bedroom window the Boss could clearly see a small but intense fire burning only 150 metres away. Gazzys and shreddies were donned as the two COs decided what to do next. Clearly it was a bit of Scud debris but as the smoke was drifting in the other direction they got back into bed. The Boss learnt that you cannot sleep in a gazzy laying on your left side as the bed blocks up the hole . . . Nevertheless we all managed to don our respirators and suits in record time, even though it was 0430 hours.'

Eight GR1s were launched that evening, four making it to the target and all eventually returning safely, one of the number having been forced to divert with a double generator failure. The State of Israel was also attacked for the first time that morning. The Squadron diarist wrote: 'Op.Granby/Desert Storm continues . . .'

During the night of 18/19 January a GR1A of No.II (Composite) Squadron took off from Dhahran to look for a mobile Scud launcher in Western Iraq which was aimed at Israel. The task was a very important one. Basically W/C Threadgould and his navigator F/L Tim Robinson in ZA397 had to prove that there was no need for Israel to join the coalition as an 'unwanted' ally. It was the first mission by a recce-equipped Tornado GR1A. The aircraft had two 2,250 litre drop tanks under the wings and two 1,500 litre tanks under the fuselage, giving the aircraft a double fuel capacity. Wing Commander Threadgould had a bit of excitement over the 'other side' when just before the target, it became clear that as the 1,500 litre tanks were jettisoned the 2,250s stopped feeding. A quick dash for the border and jettisoning of the big tanks followed, and with help from AWACs they diverted to King Khaled Military Strip. A second pair took off, this time a No.II (AC) Squadron Tornado, ZA400, flown by S/L Dick Garwood and with S/L Jon Hill as navigator, and a No.13 Squadron crew, F/Ls Brian Robinson and Gordon Walker.

'A' in desert camouflage, air-to-air refuelling on its way to Saudi Arabia.

Above: 'Scud-Hunters' at Dhahran Air Base during Operation Granby. From left to right: F/Ls Tim Robinson, Harry Seddon, F/Os Jerry Spencer, S/L Jon Hill, W/C Al Threadgould (OC), S/L Dick Garwood DFC, F/Ls Dave Knight, Sam Macleod, Rick Haley, Angus Hogg and Rusmat Ahmed.

Burning oil wells.

When they returned they carried images of a mobile Scud launcher. The success of this sortie meant that the British Defence Secretary Tom King could show the world the image of a Scud launcher, found by Garwood and Hill. It helped to earn Garwood a well-deserved DFC. The first Vinten Linescan operation had been successful. The aircraft suffered only minor damage: a single Triple A-hole in the rudder. Sadly the weather prevented the post-recce attack by Allied aircraft but all were delighted that the recce equipment had been involved and had worked so very well. Dick Garwood remembered the sortie:

> 'It was a very, very black night, probably one of the darkest I have flown on. Once you get out over the desert, especially over Iraq, there are no lights on the ground. You fly very low. We saw the odd Bedouin encampment flash by on the left-hand side of the wing.'

As the Tornados operated at 200 feet with 'hard' ride selected on the TFR (Terrain Following Radar), at speeds around 560 knots, it a dicy job. Mostly the aircraft would stay over enemy territory between twenty and sixty minutes, so it was marvellous that the Squadron crews had returned safely.

Subsequently everyone was pleased to read in the *Sunday Mirror* of the success fo the 'Scud-busters' as they had apparently become known. The accompanying report was mainly composed of typical media hype, but it was nevertheless very pleasing to have received such flattering publicity. The following night two crews were detailed for another Scud hunt. They were to fly strip searches in an area near to the one covered by the previous crews in an attempt to locate mobile launchers. Tanker support was available and despite a last-minute jet change for all but one of the crews the mission was executed successfully. Sadly, the night's action was far from over and having just escaped one Scud attack which occurred five minutes after take-off, the two crews arrived back in the middle of a second one, which had by all accounts been quite spectacular. Once again the Patriot system proved its worth by neutralising all of the threatening missiles, and was to be called upon again in the early hours of the morning.

By Day 6 the RAF had lost several aircraft and crews due to enemy action. Two men, F/Lts Nicoll and Peters of 15 Squadron, were taken prisoner after their aircraft had been hit by a Roland SAM. They were well-known members of the Laarbruch Officers' Mess.

On 24 January AVM Wratten visited the Squadron. F/Ls Haley and Hogg flying ZA371 went on a 4.25-hour Scudhunt encountering AAA and chaff clouds. It was the longest recce sortie the Squadron carried out. Four war missions were flown the next day, two being scudhunts and two being line searches. Scuds came and were mostly destroyed by Patriots before they could cause any harm.

On 25 January Tim Robinson wrote:

'We had flown a few training missions on the fifteenth and sixteenth January before things kicked off on the evening of the sixteenth. The Squadron flew its first operational sorties on the evening of the eighteenth, looking for Scuds led by yours truly and the Boss. The one thing you notice is it is very dark in the desert, no lights for miles on end, but it does not stop you being shot at.'

During the night of 26/27 January RAF GR1As launched a short-notice reconnaissance sortie to assess the damage to bridges caused by the bombers. In the first week the Squadron had flown a total of six missions, all responsive tasking. Most of the work was done at night using terrain following systems at very low level and high speed, covering a lot of ground very quickly. Most of the sorties were flown to support the United States XVIII Airborne Corps, which comprised the elite 82nd and 101st Airborne Divisions. Thanks to the RIC and the excellent quality of the videos, the Americans could be presented with a very timely view of Iraqi positions. The video tapes of the XVIII Corps' targets, which played to full houses of US commanders and pilots, led to the Americans sending a signal in typical American English: 'GR1As ARE AWESOME, WE LOVE YOU! ! !'

After the initial phase the RAF Tornados moved to medium level operations except for No.II (Composite) Squadron which continued to fly its reconnaissance missions at low level throughout Operation Desert Storm, relying mostly on surprise and speed for survival.

The home front sent letters to the Squadron and the Squadron sent letters back. One of the regular 'reporters' was Flight Lieutenant Rusmat Ahmed, a first tourist. Some of the letters were full of jokes and good humour which gave the people at home a good idea of living conditions and morale:

'With Patriots here everyone feels very secure. Sgt Knight from the RIC put a computer printed banner on the side of one of the RIC wagons. "WE ARE THE SCUD HUNTERS", it says. The GLO is here as you know. He looks a bit like John Wayne, with that fancy black leather holster he wears, housing the 9mm. My gun is at the bottom of my locker somewhere, the best place. He was so tired last night that he slept through a Scud alert. One Scud fell short of here. It is actually the first time one has been fired during the day. I reluctantly did the SOP Scud drill – respirator, NBC kit, kevlar hat on, get under the bed. Angus Hogg's Scud drill is to stand outside with the gazzy on and watch, camera in hand. You'd be surprised how little room there is for your head and a couple of pillows under the bed when your helmet is on.'

Destroyed Iraqi airfields.

On 15 February the Squadron diarist summed up what had to be done according to the Iraqi dictator when he announced that the Revolutionary Command Council would accept UN Resolution 660 and thus victoriously end the war:

'1. There was to be an immediate cease-fire.
2. All Allied forces leave the Gulf within a month.
3. All Patriots to be removed from Israel.
4. Israel was to leave the Golan, and
5. The Allies were to pay for the rebuilding of Iraq.'

As the war in the air progressed it became obvious that Saddam Hussain would not give in. Iraq continued to suffer tremendous losses. A total of 129 Iraqi aircraft had fled to Iran while many had been destroyed by the Coalition Forces. On 17 February ACM Sir Patrick Hine, the Joint British Forces Commander, visited the Squadron. At the same time everybody anxiously awaited the outcome of the peace plan which President Gorbachov of the Soviet Union proposed to Iraq. He wanted an answer within three days. Still Saddam Hussain did not realize that he could never win this 'Mother of all Wars'. He rejected the Soviet peace plan. President Bush, speaking for the coalition gave Saddam until the following day at 2000 hours local time to start withdrawing. Meanwhile Saddam claimed that the glorious Iraqi forces, in close co-operation with Allah, were about to crush the Americans and their heretic partners. Very few outside Iraq believed his words.

Small successes by the Iraqis were all Saddam could offer his people. Scuds on Israelis cities made it extremely difficult to convince the Israelis that patience and endurance were their best hope. American and Dutch Patriots were in Israel to keep the Coalition from splitting up, as

The complete annihilation of the Iraqi Army on the road from Kuwait City to Baghdad.

28 June 1991. W/C Alan Threadgould, wearing the latest RAF hat hands over the Wake Knot and thus command of No.II (AC) Squadron to the new boss, W/C Barry Holding.

Saddam and Yasser Arafat hoped. Unfortunately one Scud got through in Saudi Arabia on 25 February and destroyed an American accommodation building killing twenty-nine people and injuring many more. The images on millions of TV screens showed how much the Coalition had to suffer in human lives. Two Squadron members passed by the scene of horror only minutes later and returned deeply impressed.

Like most participants in the war, the No.II Squadron personnel had bitter-sweet memories of the whole affair. Pre-flight the crews were quiet, checking and double-checking everything. Off-duty they tried to relax by writing to wives, girlfriends and colleagues back home. But there was no getting away from the war, thanks to TV. On the eve of the ground war the whole detachment was listening to a speech by Marlin Fitzwater, President Bush's spokesman.

F/L Rusmat Ahmed's letter to the Squadron Adjutant back at Laarbruch told exactly how these men thought about war:

> '. . . I've never been in a room with guys so intent on the news before. It was the same at work, everyone gazing at the television analysis unceasingly tossing the issue into debate. Tonight it was a non-alcoholic beer in Dick Garwood's room with the Boss and Jon Hill. Jerry Spencer came in after the speech, which we listened to on the radio. He was looking very concerned for his young years. With their life on the line you understand their vested interest. These guys want peace badly, for everyone's sake. Yet every day they do their missions with great, great credit to themselves and the Service.'

As widely reported, the weather proved a major influence on the Allied air campaign as bad weather made it exceptionally difficult to find the tanker aircraft. On 19 February a Victor tanker rolled out of an orbit, with second-perfect timing, suddenly coming out of a thunderstorm directly above F/Ls Knight and Macleod. If their aircraft had been a second late or early the visual contact required would never have been achieved in those dreadful conditions. Things got worse for them as soon afterwards they were enveloped by lightning at the most northerly point of their route deep into Iraq. Climbing out of low level the aircraft lost all its electronic counter measures due to the lightning, and was locked up by Iraqi SAMs. Fortunately an American AWACS aircraft helped the crew to escape from the 'Badlands'. Navigator Sam Macleod duly wrote in his log-book: 'A very good AWACS'.

On 28 February the Allied offensive stopped, two days after Saddam Hussain's troops had begun the withdrawal from a devastated Kuwait. On 3 March the Iraqi leadership agreed to the Allied cease fire conditions. There was little else Saddam could do. His country's infrastructure in ruins. His subjects were in turmoil and it seemed that he would soon be one of those long-forgotten dictators.

HM the Queen wrote in a message to Tom King:

> 'I am delighted by the successful completion of the military campaign in the Gulf. The Armed Forces have done us proud.
>
> I should be grateful if you would pass my

> congratulations to all those here at home, who like you, have worked unremittingly to ensure this success. At the same time my deep sympathy goes to the families of those who died or are missing, and to their wounded comrades.'

Statements followed from the Prime Minister and from many others. On 1 March the CAS, ACM Sir Peter Harding, spoke of 'relief and gratitude' and mentioned the achievements of the RAF and saluted the air force for its courage, perseverance and dedication. General John Galvin, the Supreme Commander in Europe, congratulated the British troops and said that their courage and professionalism reminded him of the finest traditions of the British Armed Forces. General Von Sandrart, the German CINCENT also mentioned the outstanding work the RAF had done, he added: 'I was struck by the high morale of the young professional RAF personnel who appeared on television, many of whom were facing combat for the first time'. No-one disagreed with what the CinCRAFG wrote in a signal to all RAF Germany units in the Gulf: '. . . Godspeed for your return home . . .'

By mid-March, nearly eighty operational missions later, No.II (AC) Squadron returned home. Kuwait was free, with its oil wells ablaze, its essential services destroyed and its freedom fighters roaming the country in their hunt for Iraqis and Palestinian collaborators. F/Ls Haigh and Poole were the first back, returning with No.16 Squadron. Most of the others returned to Laarbruch on Friday 15 March. The only pilot having trouble on the way home was the CO, W/C Threadgould. On the home journey he lost an engine and had to put in at Crete. Captain Den Drijver, the Dutch exchange pilot, who had been so terribly disappointed when the Dutch government 'grounded' him for Gulf duties, was dispatched to Crete with a jet so that the Boss and his navigator, Angus Hogg, could take it

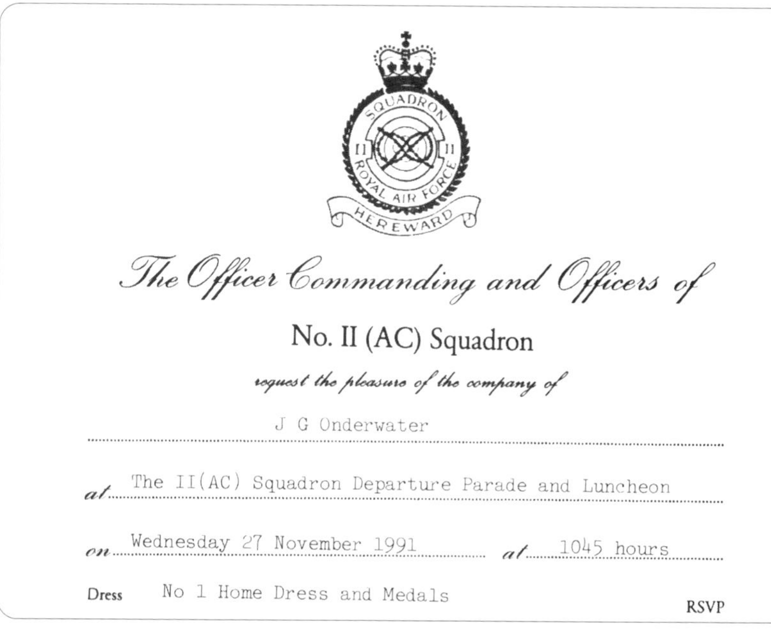
SQUADRON II II ROYAL AIR FORCE HEREWARD

The Officer Commanding and Officers of

No. II (AC) Squadron

request the pleasure of the company of

J G Onderwater

at The II(AC) Squadron Departure Parade and Luncheon

on Wednesday 27 November 1991 *at* 1045 hours

Dress No 1 Home Dress and Medals

RSVP

On 26 November 1991 'Shiny Two' said goodbye to Laarbruch. CinC RAFG Air Marshal Sir 'Sandy' Wilson and OC No.II (AC) Squadron W/C Barry Holding flew the last sortie. Fittingly this took place in the aircraft of the Dutch exchange pilot Capt Anton Den Drijver.

home. However, the jet that Den Drijver took out subsequently went sick too, and the Boss and Angus did not land at Laarbruch until Monday afternoon, three days after everyone else. A month's leave was their welcome reward.

During its deployment in Saudi Arabia the Squadron had flown more than 300 hours during night operations and almost eleven hours by day . . .

In April 1991 rumours said that the Squadron would leave Laarbruch after twenty years and return to Britain due to defence cuts decided by the government in the wake of the collapse of the Warsaw Pact. A month later it was definite: 'Shiny Two' would be based at RAF Marham from 1 December. Soon fact-sheets appeared, informing the Squadron of what they could expect in North-West Norfolk. In the fact-sheet it said:

> 'East Anglia is often considered to be remote from the rest of England and many of you will have heard of the saying "El Adem with grass" (which was supposed to have described RAF Marham in the '50s and '60s but unfortunately, the quotation has injustifiably stuck). You may have had, or still have, the feeling of being sent out "into the wilds" when you were told that II (AC) Sqn was coming to Norfolk and, especially, Marham. Particularly as the station is some distance from any large town . . .'

In June F/Ls Dave Knight and Tim Robinson participated in the flypast over London to commemorate the victory over Iraq, watched by the Monarch, the Royal Family and hundreds of thousands of proud Britons. On the twenty-ninth of the month Wing Commander Threadgould handed the Wake Knot to his successor, Wing Commander Barry Holding AFC. As for 'Shiny Two' it was business as usual . . . With the definite news that the end of forty-seven years of service outside the United Kingdom was near, the Squadron prepared for its departure. On Tuesday 26 November the Commander in Chief RAF Germany Air Marshal Sir 'Sandy' Wilson and the Commanding Officer No.II (AC) Squadron Wing Commander Barry Holding flew the last operational sortie from Laarbruch. The next day an immaculate parade marked the handover of the Squadron from RAF Germany to RAF Strike Command. The parade composition was:

Parade Commander	Wing Commander B.C. Holding AFC.
Parade Adjutant	F/L P.A. Dunkley
A-Flight Commander	S/L B.R. Collins
B-Flight Commander	S/L J.A. Hill BSc
Standard Bearer	F/O M.E. Lawrence
Standard Party W/O	W/O A. Ayton
Standard Party Escorts	Sgt D. Rooney Sgt N. H. Edwards
Supernumary Officers	
A-Flight	F/L J.W. Clarke F/L R.D. Presland B Eng
B-Flight	F/L M.I. Tomlinson F/O A.J. Davy
Parade W/O	W/O R.D. McLaughlin
A-Flight Personnel	F/S B.A. Cordell and 28 ORs
B-Flight Personnel	C/T J. McAllister and 28 ORs.

While the General Salute occurred, a Squadron Tornado roared over. The pilot and navigator were not a second early or late . . . In his address after the Inspection and the March Past Sir Andrew commended the tremendous record of service of 'Shiny Two'.

On Friday 29 November W/C Holding led the Squadron over Laarbruch for the last time. In the usual immaculate '2' formation the Tornados flew West to the North Sea and on to Marham.

In his farewell message for the Handover Parade Wing Commander Holding said:

> 'Our return to England draws to a close a long and meritorious chapter in the history of the Squadron. During this time the Squadron has performed with great distinction in the highly specialised and demanding tactical reconnaissance role. In so doing, it has played an important part in the defence of Western Europe whose solidarity has helped to secure the collapse of the Soviet Communist regime and brought us victory in the Cold War. Inevitably, these historic events are bringing about fundamental changes in the structure and organisation of the NATO alliance and in the size and disposition of the miltiary forces of its member states. Our relocation is one such change, but thankfully we will continue to operate in and contribute to the defence of NATO's Central Region, albeit from the United Kingdom Homeland.
>
> . . . You may rest assured, however, that No.II (Army Co-operation) Squadron will continue to meet the demands placed upon it and will rise to the challenges of the coming years . . .'

On the occasion of the last Tornado flight by the Squadron in RAF Germany, the CO, W/C Holding, presents an aircraft portrait to the CinC RAF Germany, AM Sir Andrew Wilson.

ROLL OF HONOUR

Members of No.II (AC) Squadron who died while serving with the Squadron

WE WILL REMEMBER THEM

Name	Rank	Role	Date
Empson, J.	Lt.	pilot	0614
Cudmore,	AM2	Airmech	0614
Waldron, F.F.	Lt.	pilot	011014
Rhodes-Moorhouse, W.B., VC	2Lt.	pilot	270415
Wilson,	Lt.	pilot	140417
Coupland, J.C.G.	Lt.	pilot	060517
Medlicott, H.W.	2Lt.	pilot	210518
Fean-Smith, W.R.	2Lt.	pilot	180118
Cornforth, N.L.	Lt.	obs.	180118
Broadbent, S.	Capt.	obs.	180218
Homersham, A.L.	Lt.	pilot	180218
Heney, C.B.L.	Lt.	obs.	090318
Collins, R.S.	2Lt.	pilot	090318
Barford, P.	Lt.	pilot	270318
Mitchell, S.J., AFM	Sgt	pilot	070718
Walton, J.L.	2Lt.	pilot	150418
Allen, R.	2Lt.	pilot	230418
Spence, L.C.	Lt.	obs.	240518
Johnson, C.M.	2Lt.	pilot	060618
Mumford-Mathews, H.J.J.	P/O	pilot	140328
Hadden, J.	F/O	pilot	020428
Wintringham, C.R.F.	P/O	pilot	270331
Ellard,	AC1	a/g	270331
Ashton, P.W.	P/O	pilot	230536
Simpson,	LAC	a/g	230536
Petrie, R.A.G.	P/O	pilot	280439
Sankey, W.	AC2	g/s	071139
Henderson, M.L.G.	P/O	pilot	220540
Jones, H.G.	LAC	a/g	220540
Dearden, C.H.	P/O	pilot	310540
McCoy, A.O'N.	LAC	a/g	310540
Doidge, A.F.	P/O	pilot	010640
Michelmore, I.R.W.	Sgt	a/g	010640
Baker, E.N.	P/O	pilot	180241
Whitaker, R.J.	LAC	g/s	040341
Burrage, K.	AC1	g/s	300541
Lax, L.E.K.	AC1	g/s	221041
Cordell, H.H.	AC1	g/s	060542
Gosnell, G.L.	P/O	pilot	090542
Parkes, C.K.	P/O	pilot	020642
Young, G.P.D.	F/O	pilot	300642
Dodds, J.	LAC	g/s	300642
Hawes, B.E.	P/O	pilot	280742
Williams, D.B.	P/O	pilot	291042
Cunningham, G.M.	P/O	pilot	291142
Smith, J.J.	Sgt	pilot	291242
Gordon-Crosby, P.M.	F/O	pilot	190443
Jump, W.H.	Sgt	g/s	230443
Miller, N.J.	F/O	pilot	260543
Hirst, D.	F/O	pilot	260543
McLeod, J.B.	F/O	pilot	260543
Carter, R.W.F.	F/O	pilot	030643
Hagerup, A.C. (RNAF)	Lt.	pilot	230643
Butt, W.R.	F/O	pilot	050743
Earl, P.J.	LAC	g/s	150843
Andrews, R.H.	F/O	pilot	250843
Day, J.B.	F/O	pilot	280843
Jean-Hansen, C.F. (RNAF)	Capt	pilot	290843
Dunkerley, M.P.	F/O	pilot	091143
Ingham, J.	F/O	pilot	161043
Williams, D.B.	P/O	pilot	290143
Hay-Neave, P.	P/O	pilot	111143
McPherson, G.I.H.	F/O	pilot	280144
Graham, M.D.L.	F/O	pilot	280144
Miller, I.S. (HQ 35 Wing)	F/L	pilot	050244
Brooks, J.C.	AC2	g/s	110244
Tasker, B.C.	F/O	pilot	170644
Wilson, P.G.	F/O	pilot	220644
Terken, P.J.L.	F/S	g/s	080744
Black, W.A., AFC	F/O	pilot	270744
Tan, Kay Tai	F/L	pilot	270944
Shute, H.J.	F/O	pilot	100844
Haselden, J.K.	F/L	pilot	120844
Morai, J.E.J.	F/L	pilot	071144
Swanson, J.A.	F/L	pilot	101144
Hines, A.C.D.	F/O	pilot	061244
Buckie, D.S.	F/O	pilot	221244
Bremner, A.	F/L	pilot	261244
Garland, P.J.	F/L	pilot	010145
Malcolmson, G.K.	F/L	pilot	080245
Maitland, C.E., DFC	S/L	pilot	180345
Blundell-Hill, C.J.	F/O	pilot	010445
Arrakowski, A.	F/L	pilot	260845
Pykett, F.	AC2	g/s	170945
Horne, A.S.	LAC	g/s	020246
Barnard, D.G.	F/L	pilot	310447
Butcher, L.F.	F/L	pilot	310147
Turner, R.	F/L	pilot	101248
Bernard-Smith, B.C.	F/O	pilot	060750
Wardhaugh, F.	F/O	pilot	041251
Palmer, J.R.	F/L	pilot	181252
Smith, A.K.	P/O	pilot	310853
Hinde, I.R.	P/O	pilot	310853
Scarratt, C.T.	F/O	pilot	080454
Vickers, D.	P/O	pilot	031254
Barnes, S.	F/L	pilot	290162
Stein, D.	F/L	pilot	220277
Edwards, S.	SAC	RIC	190785
Dickinson, J.	S/L	RIC	140486

Squadron members who successfully evaded capture after having been forced down over Occupied Territory.

Name	Rank	Role	
Brickwood, G.C.	F/O	pilot	shot down 290144
Percival, G.A.	F/O	pilot	shot down 270944
Ridley-Martin, M.	F/O	pilot	shot down 121044

a/g : air gunner
g/s : ground staff
RIC : Reconnaissance Intelligence Centre

Between April 1943 and July 1944 the Squadron lost no less than twenty-two pilots due to flying accidents and hazardous sorties over enemy territory. Fourteen of these pilots can be seen here. Some are in uniform, others are in suits. 'Civilian' photographs were to be used if a downed airman needed ID-papers in Occupied Europe. Particularly sad was the flying accident in which three men were killed on 26 May 1943 in dense fog.

First row (left to right): F/O P.M. Gordon Crosby (MIA 190443), F/O N.J. Miller (KIFA 260543), F/O D. Hirst (KIFA 260543) and F/O J.B. McLeod (KIFA 260543).

Second row (left to right): F/O R. W. H. Carter (MIA 030643), F/O W. R. Butt (KIA 050743), F/O R.H. Andrews (KIA 250843) and F/O J.B. Day (MIA 280843).

Third row (left to right): F/O M.P. Dunkerley (KIA 091143), F/O J. Ingham (KIFA 161043), F/O G.I.H. MacPherson (KIA 280144).

Fourth row (left to right): F/O B.C. Tasker (KIA 160644), F/O P.G. Wilson (KIA 220644) and F/O W. A. Black (KIA 270644).

KIA : Killed in Action
MIA : Missing in Action
KIFA : Killed in Flying Accident

No.II (AC) SQUADRON AND ROLLS-ROYCE: A LIFETIME CONNECTION

Rolls-Royce built many of the engines used by No.II (AC) Squadron aircraft. During eighty years the following aircraft were equipped with Rolls-Royce powerplants:

1920 Bristol Fighter	Rolls-Royce Falcon III	280 hp 12-cylinder liquid-cooled V-engine
1933 Hawker Audax	Rolls-Royce Kestrel 1B	530 hp 12-cylinder liquid-cooled V-engine
1940 Boulton Paul Defiant (trials)	Rolls-Royce Merlin III	1030 hp 12-cylinder liquid-cooled V-engine
1940 Fairey Battle (trials)	Rolls-Royce Merlin III	1030 hp 12-cylinder liquid-cooled V-engine
1944 Vickers Supermarine Spitfire FRXIV	Rolls-Royce Griffon 65	2050 hp 12-cylinder liquid-cooled V-engine
1945 Vickers Supermarine Spitfire PRXI	Rolls-Royce Merlin 63	1760 hp 12-cylinder liquid-cooled V-engine
1946 Vickers Supermarine Spitfire PR19	Rolls-Royce Griffon 61	2050 hp 12-cylinder liquid-cooled V-engine
1950 Gloster Meteor FR9	Rolls-Royce Derwent 8	3,500 lb thrust (2)
1951 Gloster Meteor PR10	Rolls-Royce Derwent 8	3,500 lb thrust (2)
1956 Supermarine Swift FR5	Rolls-Royce Avon 114	7,175 lb thrust turbojet 9,450 lb thrust with re-heat
1961 Hawker Hunter FR10	Rolls-Royce Avon 207	10,150 lb thrust
1970 McDonnell Douglas Phantom FGR2	Rolls-Royce RB 168-25R Spey 202 axial-flow by-pass turbojet 12,250 lb thrust (20,515 lb thrust with re-heat) (2)	
1976 Sepecat Jaguar GR1A	Rolls-Royce/Turbomeca RT172 Adour 102 turbofans 7,140 lb static thrust (2)	
1989 Panavia Tornado GR1A	Rolls-Royce/Turbo Union RB199-34R (2) 15,000 lb thrust	

SQUADRON COMMANDERS

Burke, Major C.J.	130512
Dawes, Major C.W.P.	101114
Webb Bowen, Major T.I.	080315
Becke, Major J.H.W.	020615
Murphy, Major C.F. de S.	031115
Cooper, Major R.A.	090416
Snow, Major W.R.	160817
Ross Hume, Major P.G.	280818
More, Squadron Leader B.F.	121119
Stent, Squadron Leader F.W.	180620
Butler, Squadron Leader A.J., MC	160820
Forbes, Squadron Leader L.F.	150522
Saul, Squadron Leader, R.E.	150425
Sowrey, Squadron Leader W., DFC, AFC	090127
Probyn, Squadron Leader H.M.,	010428
Toomer, Squadron Leader S.E., DFC, MC	290930
Fullard, Squadron Leader P.F., DSO, MC, AFC	120133
Green, Squadron Leader J.H.	011233
Desper, Squadron Leader N.L.	200735
Opie, Squadron Leader W.A.	210138
Geddes, Squadron Leader A.J.W.	290439
Geddes, Wing Commander A.J.W.	010340
Riddell, Wing Commander P.J.A.	241241
Stansfeld, Wing Commander P.W.	080243
Egan-Wyer, Squadron Leader, B.O.C.	290643
Gray, Squadron Leader, M.J. DFC	250843
Maitland, Squadron Leader C.A., DFC	070944
Mitchell, Squadron Leader R.J.F., DFC	250345
Barlow, Squadron Leader D.W., DFC	240446
Collinson, Squadron Leader G.	151246
Newenham, Squadron Leader W.A., DFC	281048
Bartlett, Squadron Leader, L.H., DSO	060250
Pugh, Squadron Leader R.M., AFC	011150
Weighill, Squadron Leader R.H.G., DFC	290553
Newman, Flight Lieutenant M.C.	310855
Mortley, Squadron Leader R.S., AFC	151155
Wade, Squadron Leader C.A.	120558
MacDonald, Squadron Leader C.S.	160960
Thornton, Squadron Leader D.L.F.	150262
Walpole, Squadron Leader N.J.R.	131264
Barrett, Squadron Leader T.	160667
David, Squadron Leader R.J.M.	111169
Stead, Wing Commander B.A.	071271
Warren, Wing Commander D.H.	021272
Ferguson, Wing Commander D.C.	080575
Wilson, Wing Commander R.A.F.	010476
Fowler, Wing Commander R.	060178
Thorn, Wing Commander T.G., AFC	040580
Hoare, Wing Commander F.J., AFC	180183
Stirrup, Wing Commander G.E., AFC	310585
Sturley, Wing Commander P.O., MBE	130387
Threadgould, Wing Commander A.	010189
Holding, Wing Commander B.C., AFC	010791

SQUADRON AIRCRAFT

May 1912	Bristol Boxkite
May 1912	Breguet Biplane
May 1912	B.E. – prototype
May 1912	Farman S.7 Longhorn
Jul 1912	B.E.2
Jul 1912	Henry Farman Biplane
Feb 1913	B.E.2A
Apr 1913	B.E.2b
Apr 1914	Farman S.11 Shorthorn
Aug 1914	R.E.1
Sep 1914	B.E.2
Sep 1914	R.E.5
Feb 1915	Vickers FB5
Feb 1915	B.E.2B
Feb 1915	B.E.2C
Jul 1915	Bristol Scout
Jul 1916	B.E.2D
Jan 1917	B.E.2E
Apr 1917	Armstrong Whitworth FK.8
Feb 1920	Bristol F.2B Fighter
Dec 1929	Armstrong Whitworth Atlas I
May 1933	Hawker Audax I
Nov 1937	Hawker Hector I
Jul 1938	Westland Lysander I
Feb 1940	Westland Lysander II
Sep 1940	Westland Lysander III
	Boulton Paul Defiant I (trials only)
	Fairey Battle (trials only)
Aug 1941	Curtiss Tomahawk I
Aug 1941	Curtiss Tomahawk IIA
Aug 1941	Curtiss Tomahawk IIB
Apr 1942	North American Mustang I
Feb 1944	North American Mustang IA
Jun 1944	North American Mustang II
Nov 1944	Vickers Supermarine Spitfire FRXIV
Sep 1945	Vickers Supermarine Spitfire PRXI
Jan 1946	Vickers Supermarine Spitfire PR19
Dec 1950	Gloster Meteor FR9
Mar 1951	Gloster Meteor PR10
Feb 1956	Supermarine Swift FR5
Mar 1961	Hawker Hunter FR10
Dec 1970	McDonnell-Douglas Phantom FGR2
Apr 1976	Sepecat Jaguar GR1A
Jan 1989	Panavia Tornado GR1A

SQUADRON LOCATIONS

130512 – 260213	Farnborough
260213 – 300614	Montrose (det. Limerick)
300614 – 050814	Netheravon
050814 – 120814	Farnborough
120814 – 130814	Swingate Down
130814 – 160814	Amiens
160814 – 240814	Maubeuge
240814 – 250814	Berlaimont
250814 – 250814	Le Cateau
250814 – 260814	Saint Quentin
260814 – 280814	La Fere
280814 – 300814	Compiegne
300814 – 310814	Senlis
310814 – 020914	Juilly
020914 – 030914	Serris
030914 – 040914	Touqin-Pezarches
040914 – 070914	Melun
070914 – 090914	Touquin-Pezarches
090914 – 120914	Coulommiers
120914 – 171014	Fere en Tardenois
171014 – 271114	Saint Omer
271114 – 300615	Merville (det. Saint Omer)
300615 – 090618	Hesdigneul
090618 – 201018	Floringhem
201018 – 261018	Mazingarbe
261018 – 140219	Genech
140219 – 191019	Bicester (as a cadre)
191019 – 200120	Weston-on-the-Green
200120	disbanded Weston-on-on-the-Green
010220	reformed at Oranmore
010220 – 200722	Oranmore (det. Castlebar, Fermoy)
200722 – 130222	Fermoy (det. Oranmore)
130222 – 020622	Digby
020622 – 270922	Aldergrove
270922 – 170923	Farnborough (det. Aldergrove)
170923 – 310324	Andover
310324 – 200427	Manston
200427 – 300527	HMS *Hermes*
300527 – 130927	Shanghai Racecourse
130927 – 271027	HMS *Hermes*
271027 – 301135	Manston
031235 – 290939	Hawkinge
290939 – 100540	Abbeville (det. Labuissier, Senon)
100540 – 190540	Labuissiere (det. Wevelghem)
190540 – 200540	Boulogne
200540 – 200540	Lympne
200540 – 080640	Bakesbourne
080640 – 010840	Hatfield
080640 – 241040	Cambridge (det. Sawbridgeworth)
241040 – 190741	Sawbridgeworth
190741 – 230741	Firbeck
230741 – 040841	Sawbridgeworth
040841 – 100841	Weston Zoyland
100841 – 051241	Sawbridgeworth
051451 – 071241	Martlesham Heath
071241 – 310143	Sawbridgeworth (det. Gatwick)
310143 – 190343	Bottisham (det. Westcott, Newmarket, Cranfield, Duxford)
190343 – 270443	Fowlmere
270443 – 160743	Sawbridgeworth
160743 – 070843	Gravesend
070843 – 220943	Odiham
220943 – 061043	Hutton Cranswick
061043 – 141143	Odiham
141143 – 301143	North Weald
301143 – 220144	Sawbridgeworth
220144 – 290244	North Weald (det. Benson)
290244 – 110344	Sawbridgeworth
110344 – 240344	Dundonald
240344 – 040444	Sawbridgeworth
040444 – 270644	Gatwick
270644 – 290744	Odiham
290744 – 140844	Plumetot (B10)
140844 – 010944	Beny-sur-Mer (B4)
010944 – 060944	Boisney (B27)
060944 – 110944	Fresnoy (B31)
110944 – 270944	Fort Rouge (B43)
270944 – 101044	St. Denis-Westrem (B61)
101044 – 231144	Deurne (B70)
231144 – 090345	Gilze-Rijen (B77)
090345 – 180445	Mill (B89)
180445 – 300545	Twenthe (B106)
300545 – 170645	Celle (B118)
170645 – 060745	Hustedt (B150)
060745 – 200745	Warmwell
200745 – 190945	Hustedt (B150)
190945 – 100246	Celle (B118)
100246 – 050346	Sylt
050346 – 190846	Celle
190846 – 160946	Sylt
160946 – 150447	Celle
150447 – 221147	Wunstorf
221147 – 111247	Lubeck
111247 – 280648	Wunstorf
280648 – 150949	Wahn
150949 – 290650	Wunstorf
290650 – 150552	Bueckeburg
150552 – 010753	Gütersloh
010753 – 281055	Wahn
281055 – 101057	Geilenkirchen
101057 – 090961	Jever
090961 – 011270	Gütersloh
011270 – 030571	Brüggen
030571 – 140191	Laarbruch
140191 – 150391	Dhahran (det. Tabuk)
160391 – 301191	Laarbruch
011291	Marham

D-DAY: RAF FORM 540

No.II (AC) Squadron from 0500 – 1200 hours

Date	Aircraft Type & No. Mustang 1A	Crew	Duty	Time Up	Time Dn	Details of Sorties or Flight
6.6.44	FD566 FD529	F/L R.H.G. Weighill F/O H.J. Shute	N.B.S.	0500	0735	First US landing grounded at St Homerune. Meagre light flak at St Homerune area. No enemy aircraft target engaged successfully.
	FD474 FD501	F/L G.A. Percival F/O A.R. Broderick	N.B.S.	0502	0752	Light flak from Le Havre and target. No enemy a/c. Targets neutralised.
	FR935 FR908	F/O J.R. MacElwain F/L R.G. Gent	N.B.S.	0610	0635	Targets neutralised. F/L Gent did not take off. A/c u/s.
	FD567 FD477	S/L M. J. Gray DFC F/O B.C. Tasker	N.B.S.	0610	0635	No.2 aircraft u/s. No.1 wireless u/s. Proceeded to ALG.
	FD502 FD565	F/O J.K. Haselden F/O H.H.O. Varley	N.B.S.	0556	0756	Targets engaged. Fire for effect not observed.
	FR919 FR924	F/O L.W. Burt F/O A.P. Crane	N.B.S.	0558	0843	Flak intense from La Havre and Target area. No.2 hit in main plane and returned. No.1 carried on. Wireless failure. Target engaged successfully.
	FR900 FR902	F/L G.H. Corrigan F/L W.A. Black AFC	N.B.S.	0555	0805	Targets engaged successfully.
	FD567 FD484	S/L M.J. Gray DFC F/L J. D. Furneaux	N.B.S.	0910	1208	No flak. Pre-arranged target not engaged. 100 Mot destroyed or damaged in SW corner Bois de Calette.
	FD502 FD565	F/O J.K. Haselden F/O J.H.O. Varley	N.B.S.	0912	1208	Targets engaged successfully.
	FD935 FR908	F/L R. G. Gent F/O J.R. MacElwain	F.S.	1000	1210	No.II returned. Engine trouble. No.1 completed shoots. Two dummy postions reported.
	FR902 FR900	F/O L.W. Burt F/O F.J. Hope	N.B.S.	0915	1135	Pre-arranged targets not engaged. Impromptu target neutralised. 1 Cruiser, 3 escorts steaming East from 50'5'N.Long, 2'20'W.Lat. at 1110 hours.
	FR919 FR906	F/L G.H. Corrigan F/L W.A. Black AFC	F.S.	0925	1145	No.1 wireless failure. No.2 carried out impromptu shoot successfully.

N.B.S. : Naval Bombardment Spotting
F.S. : Fleet Spotting.

ACKNOWLEDGEMENTS

The following people and institutes kindly assisted in the writing of this book by answering requests for help, writing their memories and supplying photographs. Without them this book could not have been written.

Ablett, Major R.N., UK
Aeroplane Monthly, UK
Aircraft Aviation Magazine, AUS
Aircraft Illustrated, UK
Air Crew Association
Air Forces Monthly, UK
Air Mail, UK
Aldershot Mail, UK
Allfree, D.N., UK
Amy, W/C D.J., UK
Anderson, F/L B.M., UK
Andrews, G/C D.C., MBE, UK
Archibald, Mrs. M., UK
Archives No.II (AC) Squadron GFR
Arfman H., NL
Ashmore, SI, F., UK
Atkins, W/C P.B., UK
Aviation News, UK

Barrett, W/C T., UK
Bartlett, W/C T.H.
Barton, R.J.W., UK
Baston, F/L I.J., UK
Bavin, A., UK
Bayley, W/C J.L., UK
Beijnen, J., NL
Bennett, H.B., UK
Brandsrud, A., N
Brown, H.G.W., UK
Brown, T., UK
Bruce (Jnr), W/C R.D., UK
Bruce (Snr), W/C R.D., UK
Burnley Express, UK
Buchanan, Mrs. M.J., UK
Busfield *nee* Ingham, Mrs. B.J., UK

Catt, D.G. UK
Chalmers, F/L R.D, UK
Christchurch Police, NZ
Clark, Insp G., UK
Collier, G/C J.M., UK
Collins, S/L B.R. UK
Colston, J.F.A., UK
Colwill, R.S., UK
Coulcher, W/C C.P.J., UK
Commonwealth War Graves Commission B
Commonwealth War Graves Commission UK
Connery-Ketels, C., B
Cross, Major J.R., UK
Cunningham, W.M., Det. NZ

Dalgiesh, D.C., UK
David, Gp/Capt R.J.M., UK
Davies, J.J., UK
Davies *nee* Code, Mrs. P., UK
Daw, W/C A.R., UK
Dawes, Superintendent D.B., UK
Dawson, S/L A.N., MBE, UK
Dawson, F/L K., WRAF, FRG
Day, W/C, P.W., UK
Daymon, C.P.F., Hong Kong
Dearden, Miss B., UK
Devey, H., UK
Dietrichson-Jean Hansen, Mrs T., N
Dowman, Miss T., NZ
Drijver, Capt A den, NL
Dunnachie, S/L D.J., Cyprus

Ealing Police, UK
Elder, Air Cdre R.D., UK
Evans, S/L W.G., UK

Farquhar-Smith, G/C H.W., Spain
Fathergill, Supertindent C.A., UK
Feij, Drs. J.M. Burgomaster of Breda, NL
Ferranti, F/L M. de, UK
Fife Constabulary, UK
Finbow, Chief Supt. T.P., UK
Finch, M., Zimbabwe
Fletcher, F/L R.N., UK
Flight International, UK
Flint, S/L P.A., UK
Fly Past, UK
Forces Weekly Echo, FRG
Fossey, K.R., UK
Foster, Det Sgt J.T., NZ
Fray, S/L F.G., DFC, UK
Freeston, G., UK
Fulham Police, UK

Geddes, Air Cdre, A.J.W., CBE, DSO, LoM, UK
Gelderblom, Miss S., UK
Goodsell, B.H., UK
Gordon, S/L, M.A., DFC, UK
Gowans, Superintendent R., UK
Graham, Major J.S., UK
Graeme-Cook, F/L B., UK
Greater Manchester Police, UK
Greathurst, G.A.A., UK

Hall, S/L W.B., UK
Ham, W.A, van, NL
Hamilton, S/L D.B., UK
Harris, Det Sgt A.E., NZ
Harris, S/L J.W., DFC, UK
Harrison, F/L A.J., UK
Hartley-Woolley, S/L A., UK
Harvey, W/C B.D., UK
Hellyar-Brook, Capt H., CdG, MdR, UK
Henderson, I.C., UK
Hewitt, PC A.R., UK
Hey, J.A., NL
Hives, Gp/Capt D.B., UK
Hoare, Gp/Capt F.J., FRG
Holden-Rushworth, S/L P., UK

Imperial War Museum, UK
Intercom, UK
Ireland, N.C.V., UK
Izard, S/L A.E., UK
Jeffries, Gp/Capt R.K., UK
Johns, J., UK
Johns, R.S., UK
Jones, B.T.S., UK
Jordan, A/M Sir R.B., UK
Jordan, S.J., DFC, UK

Kelsh, E.J., UK
Knight, T., UK

Laarbruch Listener, FRG
Lambert, Insp R., UK
Lancashire Constabulary, UK
Laskey, N., UK
Linford, W/C P.J., OBE, UK
Liverpool Record Office, UK
Lloyd, S/L P.V., UK
Lothian and Borders Police, UK
Lousada, Air Cdre Sir Charles R., UK
Luchtoorloog Documentatiegroep, NL

Maassen, G.H. (Renkum Archives), NL
Maddox, Gp/Capt D.J., UK
Marlow, S., UK
Mason, F/L S., UK
Matthews, G., UK
McLeod, Mrs. S., UK
McMurtrie, Gp/Capt R.A., DSO, DFC, UK
Meek, T., UK
Metropolitan Police, Chiswick, UK
Metropolitan Police, Ealing, UK
Metropolitan Police, Fulham, UK
Metropolitan Police, Golders Green, UK
Metropolitan Police, Kensington, UK
Meynell, C., UK
MoD, AHB5, UK
MoD, PM(AR)1B(RAF), UK
Morgan, J.R., UK
Moss, AVM J.P., SA
Munday, E.A., UK
Municipal Archives, Apeldoorn, NL
Municipal Archives, Bergen op Zoom, NL
Murphy, Air Cdre C.J., OBE, IRL
Museum of Army Aviation, UK

Narborough, PC M., UK
Norfolk Constabulary, UK
Nottingham Archives Office, UK
Nottinghamshire Constabulary, UK

Onze, Luchtmacht, NL
Osborne, S/L N.G., UK

Paricer, F/L J.R., UK
Parsons, M., UK

Pas, van der Col. G., E
Peaty, Det Chief Insp, UK
Pedley, Gp/Capt M.G.F., OBE, DSO, DFC, UK
Pennington, S/L A.J., UK
Percival, G.A., UK
Pinder, K., UK
Piper, S/L F.R., AE, RAFVR, UK
Plumb, S/L A.A., UK
Pooley, S/L A.F.V., UK
Porter, AM Sir Kenneth, KCB, CBE, UK
Pridige, CI K., UK
Probert, Air Cdr A.H., MBE, MA, UK
Public Record Office, UK
Pugh, S/L B.M., AFC, UK
Putten-van Koeverden, A. van, NL

RAF Inspectorate of Flight Safety, UK
RAF News, UK
Raftree, Mrs. S.C., UK
Rayner, P.R., AFC, UK
Redman, F/L D., UK
Retief, S/L P.J.T., UK
Revell, S.J., UK
Reynolds, S/L A., UK
Riley, W/C P.M., UK
RNZAF Museum, NZ
Roberts, W.H., UK
Rouse, W., UK
Rowe, Mrs. J., UK
Royal Air Force Museum, UK
Royal Air Forces Association, UK
Sharp, E., UK
Shaw, Gp/Capt M.J.F., UK
Shearman, W/C W., AFC, UK
Shuster, F/L R.C., UK
Simpson, K.C.H., GFR
Skingley, E.J., UK
Smith, J. Miss, UK
Smith, S/L R., UK
Sommerfield, F/L P.J., UK
South Wales Constabulary, UK
Soviham, S/L T.H., UK
Stansfield, Gp/Capt P., UK
Steedman, ACM Sir Alasdair, UK
Stirrup, Gp/Capt J.E., AFC, UK
Stuff, M.A., OBE, U K
Sturley, Gp/Capt P.O., MBE, BSc, UK
Sussex Police, UK
Sweeney, D., UK

Tasker, Mrs P., NZ
Tasker, S.G., NZ
Temple, S/L C., UK
Terry, Gp/Capt C.G., UK
Thames Valley Police, UK
Thomson, AM Sir John, UK
Thorheim, Lt Col (R) E., N
Thorn, R., UK
Thorn, Air Cdre T.G., AFC, MRAeS, FRG
Thorpe, S/L P.N., GFR
Threadgould, G/C, A., AFC, USA
Todd, F/L T.J., UK
Tolmie, F/S S.W., UK
Towler, Air Cdr J.L.W., UK
Townsend, S/L M.E., UK
Toyne, S/L S., UK
Trowern, W/C F.A., OBE, AFC, UK
Trudgian, Gp/Capt T.P.F., UK
Veen, Air Cdre M. van der, UK
Veldhorst, G.W., NL

Walford, Gp/Capt B., OBE, UK
Walker, Revd D., UK
Walker, AM Sir John, UK
Walpole, Gp/Capt N.J.R., OBE, UK
Wammes, J., NL
Wanganui Police, NZ
Warner *nee* Cordell, Mrs. W.M., UK
Watts, CI S., UK
Weighill, Air Cdre R.H.B., CBE, DFC, UK
West, S/L J.D., AE, RAFVR, UK
West Mercia Constabulary, UK
West, S.J., UK
Whitaker, R., UK
Whitaker, W., UK
White, C.S., UK
Wilkins, R.J., UK
Wilkinson, N., UK
Wilson, AM Sir Andrew, KCB, AFC, FRG
Willemsen, W., NL
Wings Magazine, UK
Winterford, S/L D.A., UK
Woude, J. van der, NL
Wright, Inspector M., UK
Wrighton, W/C C., UK
Wyper, S/L D.J., Hong Kong

Young, G.P., UK

The names of Squadron members and other helpers have been noted at the rank they had when the author contacted them.

BIBLIOGRAPHY

Books and articles:

D. Bell — US Air Force Colours 1926–1942
D. Bell — US Air Force Colours 1942–1945
C. Bowyer — RAF: The Aircraft in Service Since 1918
M.J.F. Bowyer — Action Stations: Wartime Military Airfields of East Anglia 1939–1945
L. Bridgman — Jane's All The World's Aircraft 1945/1946
ACM Sir Robert Brooke-Popham — Operations in France: September 1939–June 1940
A.J. Brooks — Photo Reconnaissance
P.E. Butcher — Skill and Devotion
J. Christy and J. Ethell — P-40 Hawks at War
P.R. Foster — No.II Squadron – RAF Germany's Recce Equipment (in *Aviation World*)
N. Franks — The Greatest Air Battle
N. Franks — The Battle of the Airfields
F/L A.S. Gallacher — A Short History of No.II (AC) Squadron 1981 back to 1951
W.N. Grant — P-51 Mustang
W. Green and G. Swanborough — US Army Air Force Fighters I
W. Green and G. Swanborough — US Army Air Force Fighters II
W. Green and G. Swanborough — RAF Fighters I
W. Green and G. Swanborough — RAF Fighters II
C.G. Grey and L. Bridgman — Jane's All The World's Aircraft 1939
B. Gunston — A Century of Flight
R.S. Humphreys — Hawkinge 1912–1961
L. Irving — Great Interruption
W/C C.G. Jefford, MBE, RAF — RAF Squadrons
M. Jerram — Wesland Lysander (in *Wings*)
A.G. Leguen de Lacroix — Diary of an Observer RFC from March to August 1917
P. Lewis — The British Fighter Since 1912
P. Lewis — Squadron Histories, RFC, RNAS and RAF Since 1912
Norman Longmate — How We Lived Then
Laddie Lucas — Wings of War
Airey Neave — The Flames of Calais
R. C. Nesbit — An Illustrated History of the RAF
J. Nesbitt-Dufort — Black Lysander
Northern Daily Mail, 140514 — Army Airmen's Flight
B. Philpott — RAF Fighter Units Europe 1939–1942
B. Philpott — RAF Fighter Units Europe 1942–1945
A. Price — Spitfire: A Documentary History
A. Price — Spitfire at War
J.D.R. Rawlings — 1939: The RAF goes to War (in *RAF Yearbook 1989*)
J.D.R. Rawlings — Coastal, Support and Special Squadrons of the RAF and their aircraft)
D. Richards and H.St.G. Saunders — Royal Air Force 1939–1945 (3 volumes)
B. Robertson — British Military Aircraft Serials, 1911–1971
B. Robertson — Gas Warfare and the Air (in *Air Pictorial*)
B. Robertson — Spitfire, the Story of a Famous Fighter
B. Robertson — The Factory at Farnborough (in *Wings*)
W. Rouse — Born Again: Spitfire PS915
P. Shepard — No.II (AC) Squadron returns to Farnborough (in *Air Clues*)
C. Shores — 2nd Tactical Air Force
J.R. Smith and A. Kay — German Aircraft of the 2nd World War
S/L P.A. Sneddon — The Jaguar Era in RAF Germany (in *Flight Comment*)
Jack Spence — There I Was at 20,000 Feet
W/C P.O. Sturley — Low Flying at Night – The NVG Experience (in *RAF '89*)
J.W.R. Taylor and P.J.R. Moyes — Pictorial History of the RAF I
J.W.R. Taylor and P.J.R. Moyes — Pictorial History of the RAF II
John Terraine — A Time of Courage
O. Thetford — Aircraft of the RAF Since 1918
A. Thomas — No.II (AC) Squadron Royal Air Force Camouflage and Markings
J.F. Turner — British Aircraft of World War II
Michael Turner — RAF: The Aircraft in Service Since 1918
Unknown author — A Spartan Demonstration (in *The Aeroplane*)
J. Vader — Spitfires
AVM R.A.F. Wilson, CB, AFC, RAF — Operation Granby (*RAF Yearbook 1991*)
G.P. Young — History of No.II (AC) Squadron 1912–1953
John Yoxall — No.II Squadron (in *Flight*)

Magazines:
Aeroplane Monthly
Air Mail: The Journal of the RAFA
Intercom: The ACA magazine
Royal Air Force Yearbooks 1987–1991
The Laarbruch Listener
The Royal Air Force News
Wings: The Encyclopaedia of Aviation

Other sources:
RAF Form 540: Operations Record Book No.II (AC) Squadron from 1927 (from PRO, Kew, Surrey)
RAF Form 414: Pilot's Flying Log Books of former aircrew members of No.II (AC) Squadron RAF
Air Cdre A.J.W. Geddes CBE, DSO, LoM(US), RAF (Retd) – diaries July 1939–February 1946
Archives and Squadron diaries, No.II (AC) Squadron

No.II (Army Co-operation) Squadron aircraft 1917-today

Armstrong-Whitworth FK.8 B-246/13 during 1917–18. Overall PC.10 chocolate and clear dope. V.114 with all identity markings in white. Engine cowling is mid-grey. Note that code '13' is also painted on upper rear fuselage.

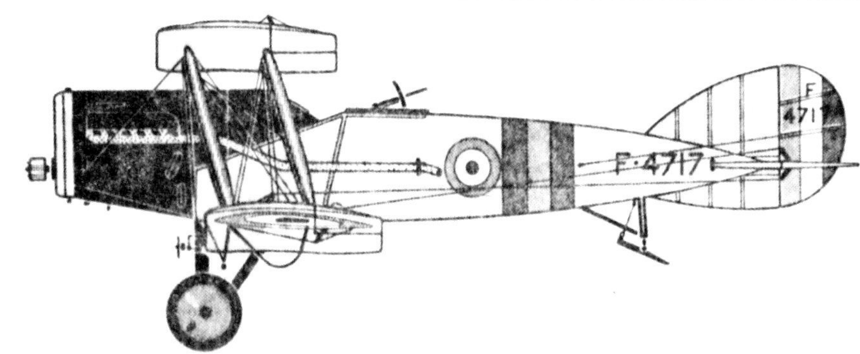

Bristol F.2B Fighter F4717 of 'C' Flight during 1924. Finish is black and aluminium dope with red, blue and red fuselage band. Serial numbers are black, wheel covers are blue.

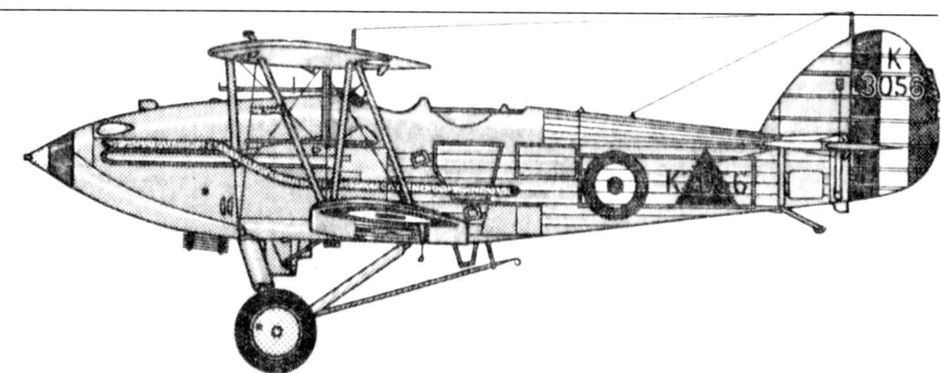

Hawker Audax K3056 of 'B' Flight during 1933. Doped aluminium and polished metal finish with yellow wheel covers and spinner. Fuselage triangle and all serial numbers are black, those on the rudder being outlined in white and on the fuselage with aluminium dope.

Westland Lysander II L6852/KO-H during 1939. Dark green and dark earth finish with aluminium dope below wings and tailplane. Codes are light grey, serial numbers are black. Type 'B' roundels on upper wings. Spinner is yellow.

Curtiss Tomahawk IIA AH934/XV-W during 1941. Dark green, dark earth and sky finish with spinner, codes and fuselage band also in sky. Spinner tip is red, serial numbers are black. Type 'B' upper wing roundels.

North American Mustang I AG633/XV-E during 1942. Dark green and ocean grey camouflage with medium sea grey lower surfaces. Spinner, name 'Eileen' forward of windscreen, codes and fuselage band are sky. Serial number is black. Type 'B' roundel on upper wings.

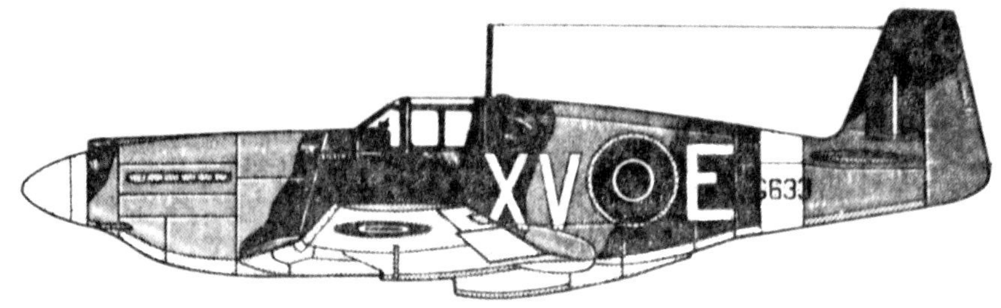

Supermarine Spitfire PR.XIX PM660/OI-X during 1947. Overall PRU Blue finish with red code letters. Serials are white on fuselage and black under wings.

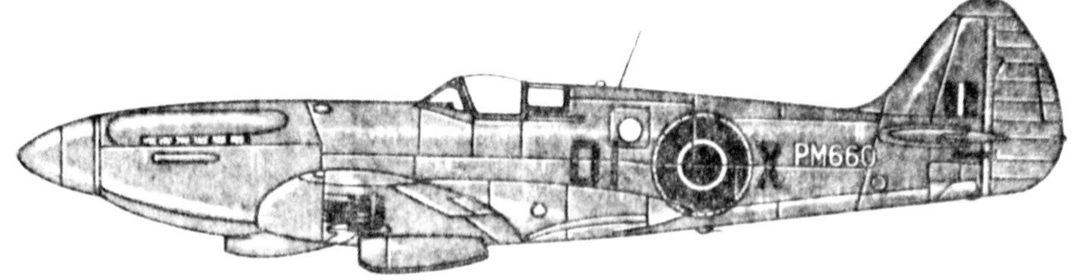

Gloster Meteor RF.9 WB116/G of 'A' Flight during 1956. Dark green and dark sea grey camouflage with PRU blue lower surfaces. Squadron rope emblem on engine nacelles and black and white unit markings on fuselage. Red fin bullet tip. Serials and code are black.

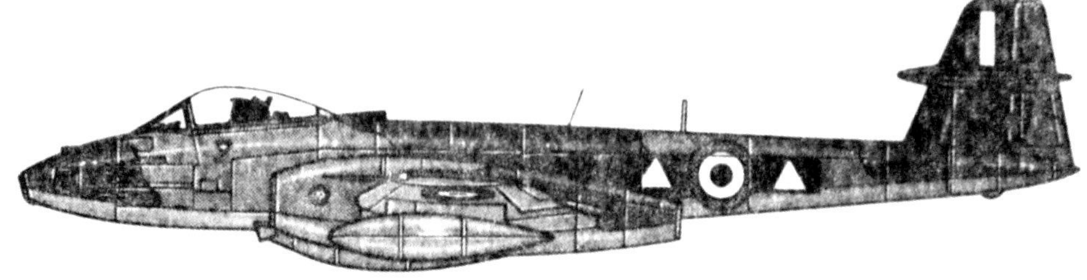

Supermarine Swift FR.5 XD916/E. Dark green, dark sea grey and aluminium finish with black and white squadron insignia, white code letter and black serials.

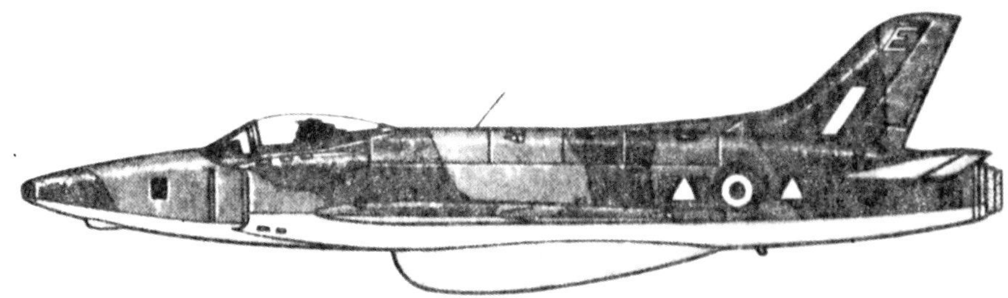

Hawker Hunter FR.10 XE556/W. Dark green and dark sea grey upper surfaces with light aircraft grey below. Squadron bars, serials and code 'W' are black whilst fuselage and fin triangles are white.

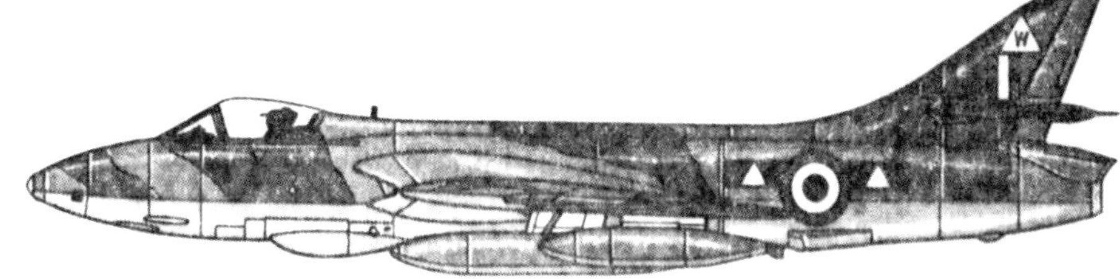

McDonnell Douglas Phantom FGR.2 XV413/E during 1974. Dark green, dark sea grey and light aircraft grey finish with all squadron markings in black and white. Serial numbers are black. National markings in red and blue only.

No.II Squadron Phantom and Jaguar insignia is black and white.

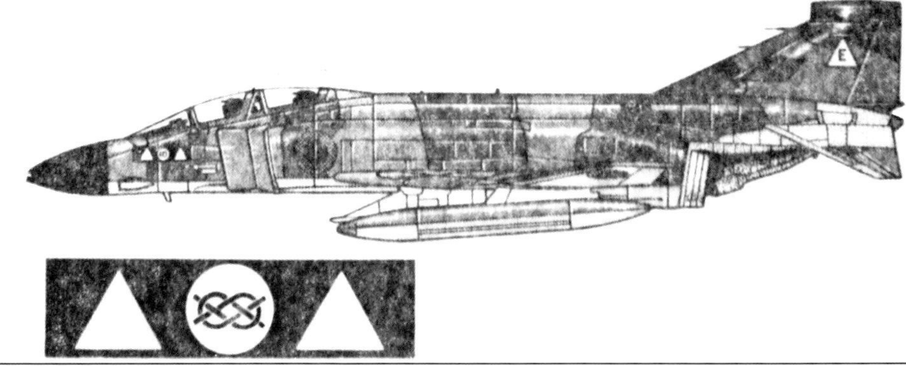

Sepecat Jaguar GR.1 XZ104/24 during 1983. Overall dark green and dark sea grey camouflage with black serial numbers and codes. Squadron trim is black and white.

INDEX